Masculinities *explores the "glorious galaxy of masculinity" through 40 loving, meticulously researched portrayals of masculine presenting women, bois, butches, studs, tomboys, MOC (masculine of center), and transmasc people. The anthology includes several famous masculine presenting women, including Brittney Griner and Del Martin, but the real gems in* Masculinities *are the moving, passionate life histories of regular bulldaggers and butches who are boldly carving out gender expansive spaces.* –Dr. Sarah Rainey-Smithback, Dir. of Women's, Gender, and Sexuality Studies at Bowling Green State University.

This is going to make herstory in such a special way for our community. I'm so glad to have been asked to participate, and congratulations on this piece of brilliance. This is really a gem. Everyone that's seen it has loved it, and friends and lovers teared up." –Koja Ray

Avery Cassell has assembled a glorious diversity of butches, bulldaggers, and bois who create a rainbow of beautiful masculinity. It's refreshing to see such a variety of expression and a celebration of women's and non-binary masculinity in a world that tells us that the masculine is a closed domain. The illustrations by all the artists sing on the page and bring each subject to life. A wonderful mix of butch icons past and those leading the charge, Masculinities *will introduce you to a whole cast of queer heroes.*
–Leigh Pfeffer, "History is Gay" podcast

MASCULINITIES

boi • bulldagger • butch • masc • MOC • soft butch • stud • tomboy • transmasc

READER'S EDITION

Volume One

Avery Cassell

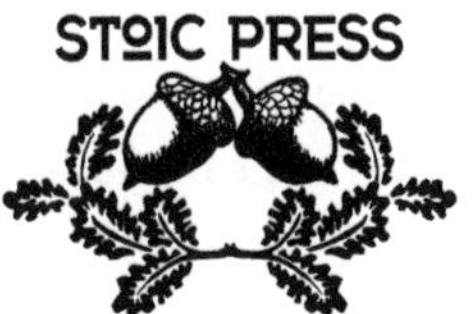

Greenfield, Massachusetts

2023

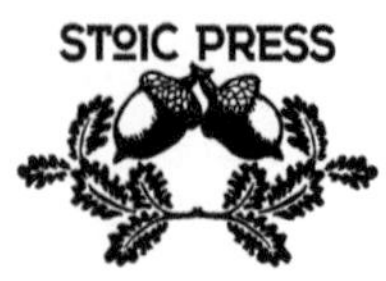

Masculinities: boi • bulldagger • butch • masc • MOC • soft butch • stud • tomboy • transmasc

Stoic Press
PO Box 766, Greenfield, MA 01301 USA
stoicpress@gmail.com

stoicpress.bigcartel.com

Publisher's Cataloging-in-Publication Data

Cassell, Avery.

Masculinities: boi · bulldagger · butch · masc · MOC · soft butch · stud · tomboy · transmasc / Avery Cassell.

Includes bibliographical references, additional resources, and selected works.

ISBN 979-8-9887469-1-1

LCCN 2023913164

1. Lesbians--Biography. 2. Lesbians--Pictorial works. 3. Lesbians Identity.
4. Biographies. 5. Illustrated works.

Illustrations by Ajuan Mance, Avery Cassell, Burton Clarke, Cheela "Rome" Smith, Diane Kanzler, Diego Gómez, Dorian Katz, Janet W. Hardy, Jennifier Camper, Jessica Bogac-Moore, Justin Hall, Leslie Ewing, Miriam Klein Stahl, M Rocket, Pat Tong, Phoebe Kobabe, Rachael House, Soizick Jaffre, and Tyler Cohen.

Front cover art by Miriam Stahl, colored by Avery Cassell

Back cover art by Phoebe Kobabe, colored by Avery Cassell

Copy editor and book designer: Diane Kanzler

Stoic Press logo designed by Diane Kanzler

Fonts used: Franklin Gothic font family by American Type Founders Collection, Mandrel font family by Insigne Design, Poster Cut Neue by Adam Ladd.

First Reader's Edition, first printing, October 2023

Printed in the United States

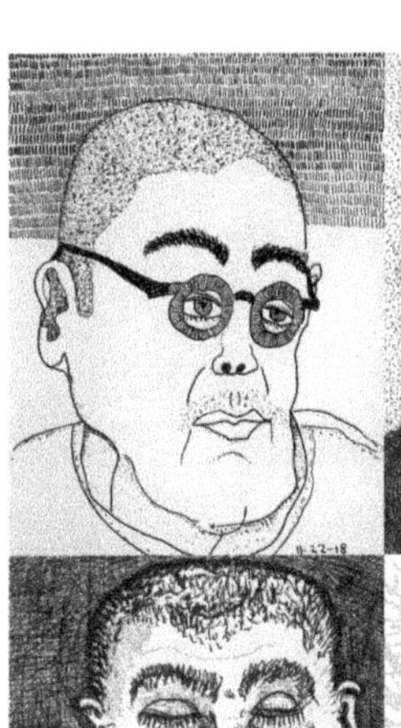
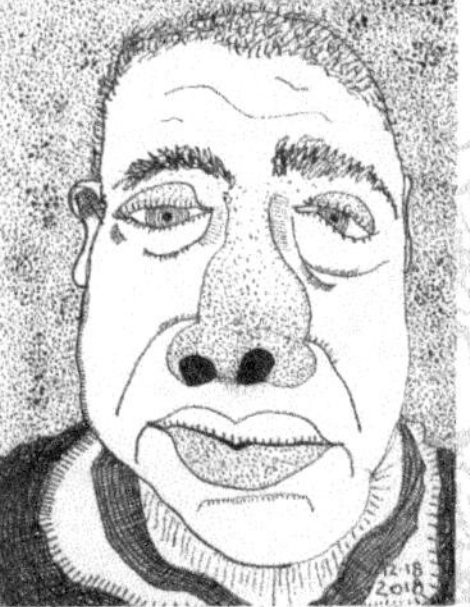
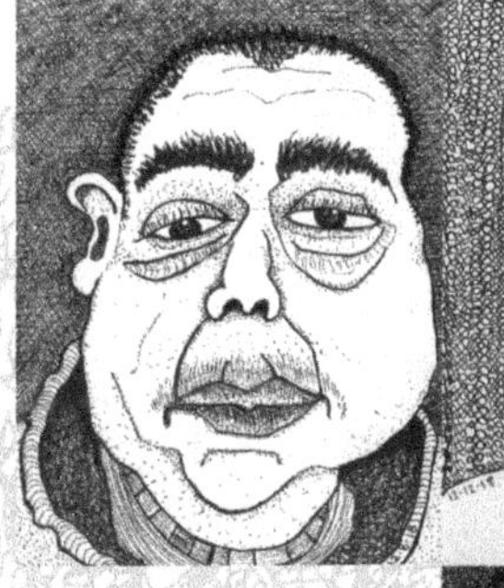
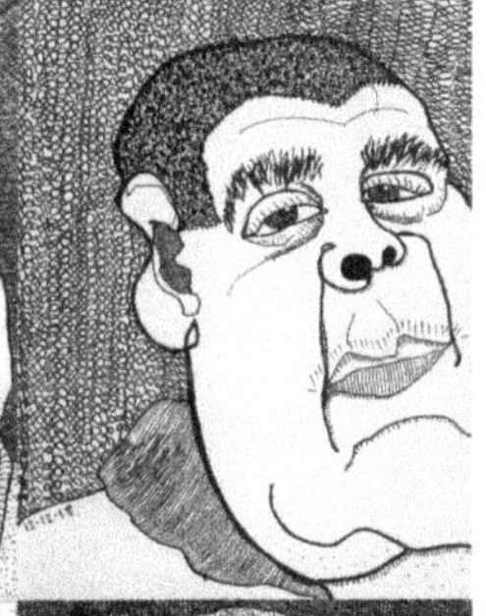
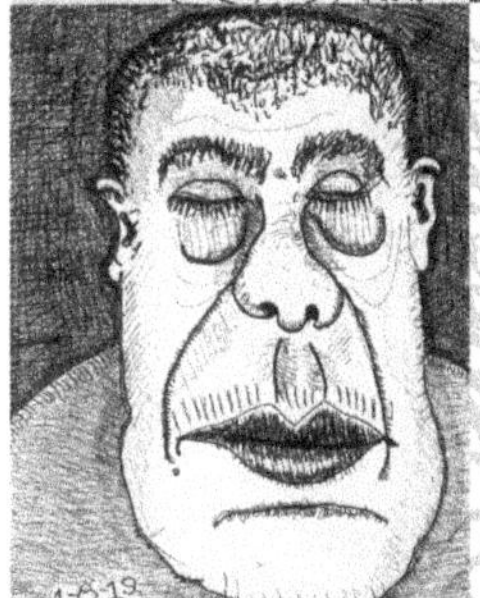

Dedication

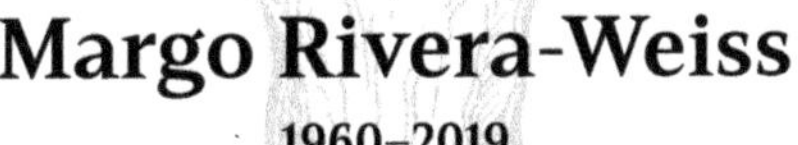

Margo Rivera-Weiss

1960–2019

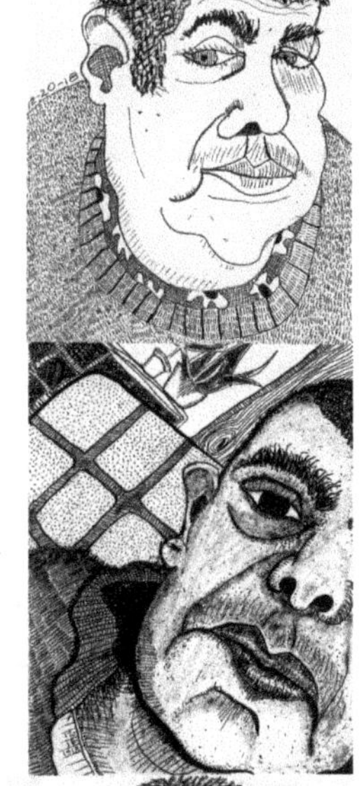

***Masculinities* is dedicated to fellow artist and butch, Margo Rivera-Weiss, whose kindness, generosity, brilliance, and creativity was unparalleled.**

At the end of 2018, in a quest to prolong their life, Margo decided to try a costly (and ultimately ineffective) protocol of extremely high doses of THC touted to retard cancer progression. Though it rendered them unable to perform basic life functions, Margo took this herb, in the form of sticky oil, for 50 days and documented each dose with a self-portrait. These are a selection of those self-portraits.

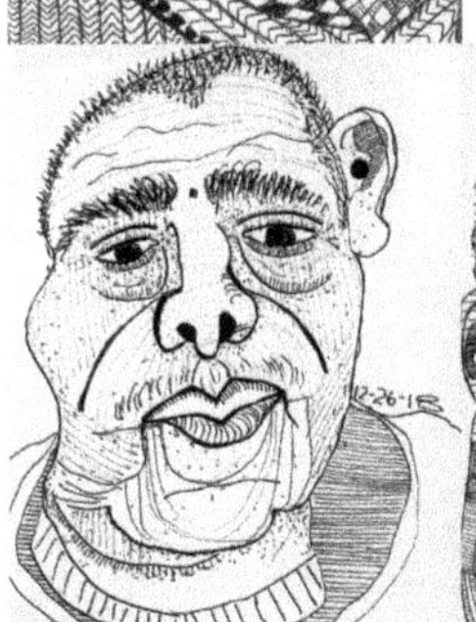
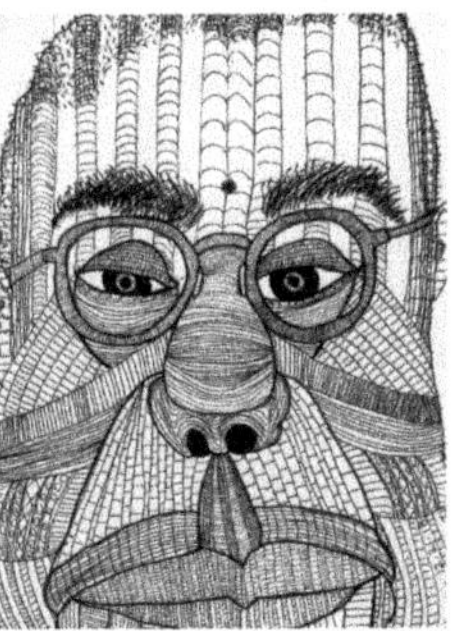
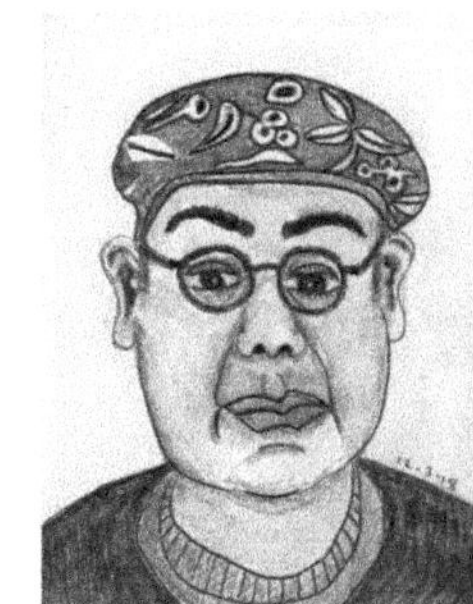
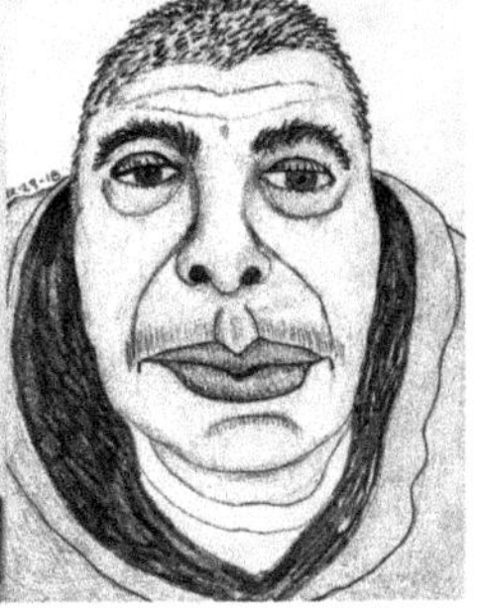

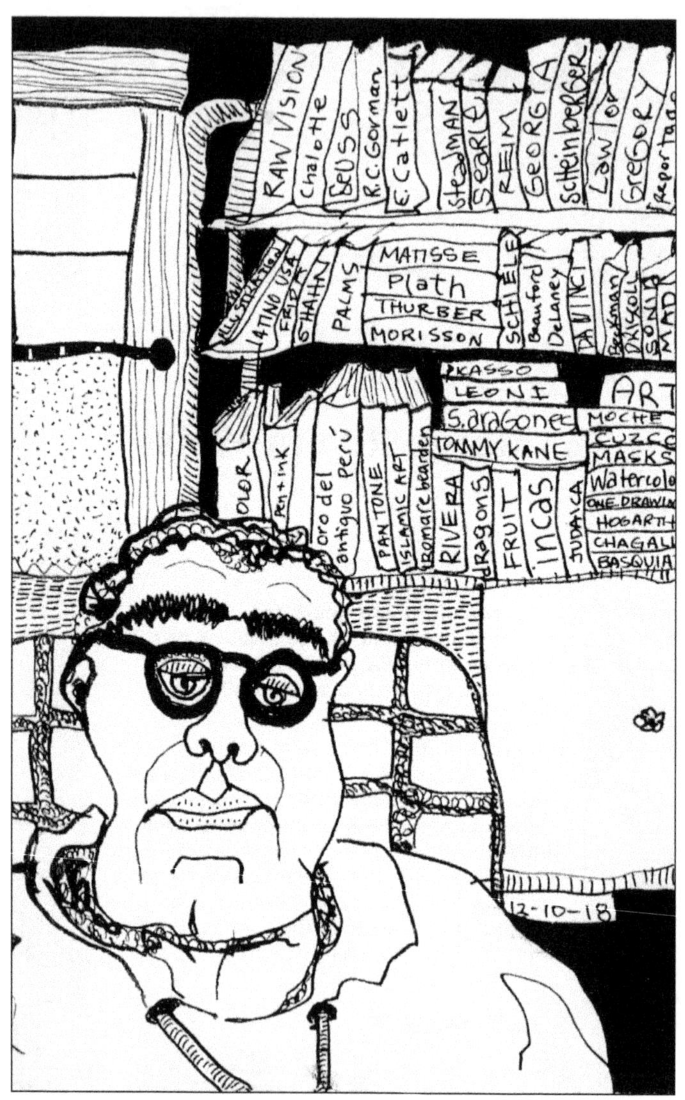
RAW VISION
Chalotte
SEUSS
R.C.Gorman
E.Catlett
GEORGIA
GREGORY
MATISSE
Plath
THURBER
MORISSON
SCHIELE
Beauford DeLaney
PALMS
LATINO USA
PKASSO
LEONI
S.aragonés
TOMMY KANE
ART
MOCHE
CUZCO
MASKS
Pen+ink
oro del antiguo perú
PANTONE
ISLAMIC ART
Romare bearden
RIVERA
dragons
FRUIT
incas
JUDAICA
HOGARTH
BASQUIAT
12-10-18

TABLE OF CONTENTS

ACKNOWLEDGEMENTS

Many special thanks to the international community of amazing LGBTQ+ artists who illustrated *Masculinities*. They were endlessly patient as I struggled through the past three years of writing this book during the pandemic and a 3,000 mile coast-to-coast move. For me, it's been a literal journey.

Special thanks goes out to Colleen O'Shea, outreach and exhibition manager from Women Make Movies for the link to the film *Rebel Dykes;* Jenni Olson for her generosity and knowledge of queer filmmakers; Hadas Rivera-Weiss for sharing a collection of stunning self-portraits of her spouse, the late Margo Rivera-Weiss; Phranc for her superb enthusiasm about the book—it kept me going; M Rocket for stepping up to illustrate at the drop of a hat; Diane Kanzler for tirelessly copy editing and designing *Masculinities*; Lili Marleen, the cat we rescued in 2022 (she also saved us), who reminds us that cuddles, naps, and snacky snacks are crucial to quality research and writing; and Jenni Olson, Rhoda Williams-Nazanin, Jen Bornemann, Koja Ray, Isaac (Karlyn) Lotney, and Sidney Woodruff for answering our endless, nosey questions about their lives.

INTRODUCTION

Welcome to *Masculinities: boi · bulldagger · butch · masc · MOC · soft butch · stud · tomboy · transmasc*. *Masculinities*, like the San Francisco Pride parade, starts with the Dykes on Bikes®, the thundering roar of gleaming motorcycles, the glorious sight of dozens of exuberant dykes, and Soni Wolf leading the way with her rainbow flag, American flag, and POW flag on poles duct-taped to her bike, unfurling behind her as she zooms down Market Street to City Hall.

You'll find hope, courage, and inspiration from the fascinating subjects within these pages. The statement "these are historic times" is not one to be used lightly, however, it is apropos to the summer of 2023. We're living through a multitude of dramatic, life changing events, some national but many international; a deadly global pandemic with COVID-19, the invasion of Ukraine by Russia, the brutal upheaval of climate change, the rise of fascism, the increase of anti-LGBTQ+ hate crimes and policies which led the Human Rights Campaign to declare a state of emergency for LGBTQ+ people in the U.S., an escalation of gun violence, national attacks on abortion and women's reproductive rights, a rise in book bans, radical conservatives implementing drastic censorship in primary, secondary, and higher education curriculums, and an ex-president who's been indicted for espionage and already been convicted of sexual assault. To note that "these are historic times" feels like a gross understatement.

Masculinities reveals the evolution and perseverance of masculine-presenting women over the past few decades, demonstrates that activism takes many forms, and installs hope and courage. From bulldaggers to butches, in the past few years the gender identities of masculine-presenting women have expanded to include a broad spectrum of possibilities. This glorious galaxy of masculinity is reflected in our subtitle; we are bois, bulldaggers, butches, masc, MOC (masculine of center), soft butches, studs, tomboys, and transmasc folks. Activism is persistence and power in the face of oppression, bullying, malfeasance, and grief.

The theme of coming out runs like a river throughout *Masculinities*, sometimes violently turbulent and sometimes a gentle meander. Families rejected their children or embraced them, with many families accepting them only after the soothing power of time. One public figure came out only to very close friends and died semi-closeted, several lost contact with their parents, and another suffered through conversion therapy. June 28, 1970 was the first Pride march in the US to commemorate the one-year anniversary of the Stonewall riots. Most of the people in *Masculinities* came out during the 1970s, 80s, or 90s, when LGBTQ+ acceptance was starting to flourish. With the current conservative crisis in the US, the battle for LGBTQ+ rights is far from over, and coming out is perilous once again.

Implementing change comes in multiple ways, not only through politics and protests. The act of resistance is not a one-size-fits-all political activity; we must utilize our distinctive, individual talents to resist in creative and timely ways. As feminist Carol Hanisch popularized in an essay written in 1970, "The personal is political." The people featured in this book are all masculine queer activists that have enacted change in unique and powerful ways. They are writers, fire fighters, singers, artists, politicians, social workers, journalists, scientists, performers, academics, filmmakers, athletes, and religious leaders. They are your neighbors, your relatives, your lovers, and they are you.

You are not alone in your struggle. Despite these desperate times, we will remain strong, loving, and creative. We will flourish and we will resist!

Avery Cassell, author
Diane Kanzler, editor and designer
August 2023

FOREWORD

What could be used as a book review is just the truth: I couldn't stop reading. Avery Cassell introduces and adorns each subject with such care, such intimacy, and such faithful research that reading *Masculinities: boi · bulldagger · butch · masc · MOC ·soft butch · stud · tomboy · transmasc* feels like sitting down with an old friend—or a new one who feels instantly familiar: are you sure we haven't met before?

This expansive work provides history that is left out of Women's Studies and Gender Studies textbooks, overlooked in the popularized pursuit of Diversity, Equity, and Inclusion (DEI), obscured by the grip of heteropatriarchy, and entirely left out of bedtime stories for girls. These faithful biographies of Butch hometown heroes, contemporary queer legends, and internationally recognized lesbians should be required reading for classrooms, in the front windows of bookstores dedicated to gender liberation, and stocked (but usually checked out, in one sense or another) at every library across town. This book is for anyone who believes that gender is a construct—and for anyone who believes that self-determination is the best revenge.

Inherently political, ever controversial, and beautifully themselves, the sisters, resisters, and alt-misters in *Masculinities* present a remarkable range of queering masculinity in the 21st century.

Within these pages you will find the sixteenth United States Poet Laureate, the original Grand Slam tennis legend, the first American woman to fly in outer space, a Fire Chief, a minister for Foreign Affairs, a Top Chef, authors and artists, journalists,scientists, activists, professors, and self-professed perverts. If the brave folks within these pages are your friends, your family, your mentors, your community, your inspiration—welcome home. If they and we aren't yet familiar to you, let me welcome you on our behalf.

Hailing from Canada, the Czech Republic, France, Germany, Hawai'i, Iran, Liberia, New Zealand, Northern Ireland, Singapore, South Africa, the United Kingdom, and unceded territories across the United States, *Masculinities*' Bois, Bulldaggers, Masc, Masculine of Center, Soft Butch, Stud, Tomboy, and Transmasc s/heroes share a collective, triumphant cry against borders both imaginary and imposed. Breaking all gendered rules, roles, and expectations against decades of stigmatized, medicalized, and legalized discrimination, this dashing, daring crowd of activists, artists, athletes, filmmakers, musicians, professionals, scientists, and writers will be remembered for charging ahead and changing the world. This collection celebrates their ongoing legacies, and affirms the spirit of collective good.

There is a power in looking, and a power in being seen. May our handsome images populate every corner and every coffee table. Together, now, and forever, may we form an archive of strength, resilience, pride, joy, and persistence.

Dr. Sasha T. Goldberg

Oakland, California
October 2023

ACTIVISTS

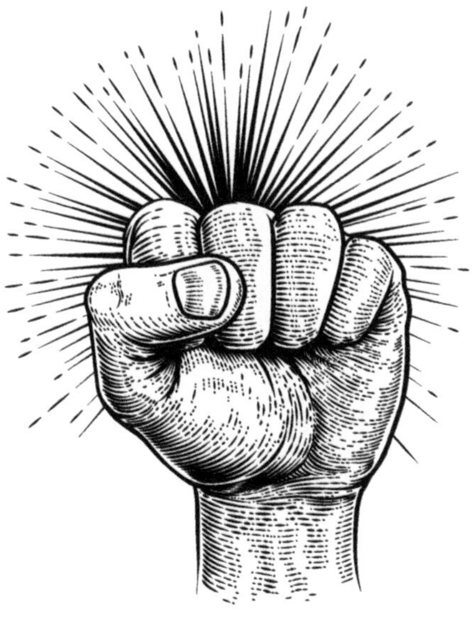

Soni S.H.S. Wolf

Saint Soni Oh So Bright, Dyke on a Bike and Leader of Lesbians, Movements, and Parades
September 1948–April 25, 2018 · USA
drawn by Phoebe Kobabe

The thunderous roar of Dykes on Bikes® riding down Main Street in San Francisco galvanizes and inspires...many spectators. The display of pride exhibited by the Dykes on Bikes® motorcycle contingent in the Pride Parade is literally earth-shaking.[1] –Soni S.H.S. Wolf

Soni Wolf was one of the founders of the nonprofit organization, Dykes on Bikes® (DOB). She fought in the United States Supreme Court for the use of the word "dykes" in the organization's name. The Dykes on Bikes® won the battle.

Soni Wolf grew up in Rhode Island. When able, she enrolled in the United States Air Force, serving in the Vietnam era, working as a medic and treating wounded combat veterans at a hospital in Texas. She refused to talk about her time as a medic due to trauma.

When her time in the US Air Force was up, Soni moved to San Francisco to settle down in that rainbow-colored hub of LGBTQ+ life, the Castro, and got a series of jobs managing copy centers for legal firms.

Soni co-founded Dykes on Bikes® in 1976. The 1960s and 70s were a time when the word "dyke" was still thought of as a slur, even by lesbians. "Dyke" was considered *déclassé*. Misogynists and anti-feminists used the word to intimidate feminists, to discourage and shame them, much as the word "queer" was used as a slur. In the mid to late 1970s, lesbians started reclaiming the word "dyke," but it wasn't until 1983 with the syndicated comic strip "Dykes to Watch Out For" by Alison Bechdel that "dyke" gained steady momentum. The word "dyke" remains contentious by many straight, mainstream people, making it difficult to navigate public messaging and social media. An example is the difficulty with using the word "dyke" in social media posts on Facebook or Instagram. Despite being a member of that group and using "dyke" in a positive manner, often one must disguise "dyke" by substituting symbols for letters to make it less likely to be discovered by censors, thus "d*ke" is often used, and if you're caught, your post will be removed, your dyke wrist will be metaphorically slapped, and you will likely end up in "Facebook jail" for a period of days or weeks.

A contingent of 20–25 motorcycle-riding dykes started off leading the San Francisco Pride parade in 1976. The grand tradition started for pragmatic reasons: dykes were tired of their motorcycles overheating when they rode behind the mostly gay male marchers. An eagle-eyed reporter overheard an ecstatic dyke call the group of hot, leathered-up dykes roaring down the street "dykes on bikes." While the name gained street cred, the group cycled through several name changes before settling on Dykes on Bikes®. First, they called themselves the Women's Motorcycle Contingent, and then The San Francisco Women's Motorcycle Contingent Dykes on Bikes (SFWMC), which was quite the mouthful! Their first organizational meetings were held at members' homes and then moved to a room above the lesbian bar Amelia's, named after the daring aviation pioneer, Amelia Earhart. After Amelia's closed, the meetings moved to the Eagle leather bar in SoMa.

Soni was the organization's secretary and historian. She talked about co-founding Dykes on Bikes® with *Buzzfeed* in 2016, "We are a philanthropic organization that also empowers and educates women riders. We have a board of directors that have voting rights and from which our officers are elected. The active patch holders work to help with fundraising events. To become a patch holder, you must attend six meetings in a row and volunteer with at least one fundraiser. Patch holders are expected to be involved in our meetings and the community as a whole....I've been riding with the Dykes on Bikes® since 1978. The changes since then have been profound. In the beginning, we were perceived as a girl biker gang. Now we are a 501(c)(3) organization."[2]

Soni rode with them at the head of the San Francisco Pride parade each year from 1978 until her death in 2018. Her first bike was a Honda 350 with a custom painted tank depicting the Golden Gate Bridge. Watching Dykes on Bikes® thundering joyously up the street and leading the parade each June was thrilling, a sea of women, leather, glitter, bare breasts, and gleaming machines. Dykes on Bikes® has grown to 16 chapters throughout the United States, Britain, Iceland, and Australia.

Dykes on Bikes® ran into multiple problems with the law in 2003 over their use of the word "dyke" when they filed a trademark application with the United States Patent and Trademark Office (PTO). Straight federal bureaucrats found the word "dyke" in the organization's name contentious, leading to legal issues that were tried in the US Supreme Court. The first case went to the US Supreme Court from 2003 to 2008. Soni guided a team of lawyers led by Brooke Oliver, who donated their hours to fight the battle for Dykes on Bikes®. The PTO said "dyke" was vulgar, offensive, "scandalous" and, according to Webster's dictionary, is "often used disparagingly," although the PTO approved groups named "Crippled Old Biker Bastards" and "Biker Bitch." Brooke Oliver submitted a seven-page letter explaining to the PTO: a) the history and growth of the SFWMC over the last 30 years; b) the re-appropriation of the word "dyke" that had occurred over the last 30 years; c) examples of cities that have Dykes on Bikes® in their Pride parades; d) awards that use the term "dyke" to honor older lesbians that have made contributions to the lesbian, gay, bisexual and transgender (LGBT) communities; and e) evidence about the more recent development of Dyke Marches held around the world and which take place a day before the Pride parades.

Even Alison Bechdel, cartoonist and writer of the strip "Dykes to Watch Out For," was called to testify about the word "dyke": "The San Francisco Dykes on Bikes organization has been trying to register their name with the US Patent and Trademark Office, and recently got their second rejection. The delicate sensibilities of these patent pinheads are offended by the word 'dyke,' despite the best efforts of the National Center for Lesbian Rights to explain it to them. The NCLR got a bunch of activists, scholars, and linguists, including yours truly, (I'm not sure which of those three categories I fall under, though I have been told I'm good with my tongue) to submit declarations outlining the evolution and significance of the word 'dyke,' but to no avail. For what it's worth, 'Queer Eye for the Straight Guy' had no problem registering their name."[3]

Soni stridently testified in her submission before the US Supreme Court about the word "dyke": "If I must be labelled other than as a 'person', 'human being', or 'woman', I choose 'Dyke'. 'Dyke' is a strong word and I say it with pride. 'Dyke' expresses my pride in myself, my existence, and in what I have accomplished. I am gay—I am a lesbian—I AM A DYKE!"[4] After winning the right to call themselves Dykes on Bikes®, they returned to the PTO to register their logo, a triangle overlaid with a gear and the words Dykes on Bikes®. The PTO denied the logo application because it included the same nefarious phrase, Dykes on Bikes®. Dykes on Bikes® won that case in 2018.

Soni just rolled her eyes and said of the use of the word "dyke" in Dykes on Bikes®, "It rhymes. Just kind of rolls off the tongue."[5] At the 40th anniversary of Dykes on Bikes®, Soni, as one of the oldest standing members, commented, "Having ridden with Dykes on Bikes® to start the parade for 38 years, celebrating our 40th anniversary is realizing half of my dream/vision for this group of wonderful women has happened. I am extremely honored to be part of this extraordinary organization."[6]

Dr. Kate Brown, Dykes on Bikes® patch holder and President, spoke at the LGBT Fallen Heroes Memorial Service, Women In Military Service For America Memorial for Soni, "On the morning of Pride Sunday between 8 and 10 a.m. we register, line up, and prepare hundreds of motorcyclists for the shortest, the best ride of the year. The riders are bursting with excitement and sometimes we have to remind them to put their kick stands down because they're so excited. For two hours the Dykes on Bikes® patch holders do our best to organize the chaos as everything moves around us for what seems like a hundred miles an hour. For decades, at the very top of Market Street next to the Dykes on Bikes® pace bikes was Soni's motorcycle, her gay pride flag, American flag, and POW flag on poles duct-taped to her bike. And there is Soni sitting on her bike, calm as can be, and anyone who wears or has worn this pin that says 'President' can tell you what Soni's advice is to them on that morning, in the midst of that chaos 'One way or the other we'll all make it down Market Street.' For years and years she created a small circle of space that was the quiet in the midst of the storm, a place where anyone could stop and be still before returning to the madness of the world."[7]

Soni lived in Daly City in the Bay Area. She died of complications from chronic obstructive pulmonary disease (COPD) and pneumonia at age 69 surrounded by friends and family.

Soni was well-loved, and in March of 2016 Soni joined other queer luminaries such as Harvey Milk, Lily Tomlin, Margaret Cho, Tom Amianno, and Carol Queen when she was Sainted by The Sisters of Perpetual Indulgence® as Saint Soni Oh So Bright, Dyke on a Bike and Leader of Lesbians, Movements, and Parades, for living her life dedicated fundraising, activism, and human rights. Soni was named the community Grand Marshal for the 2018 San Francisco Pride parade, but died before she could ride. Her close friends carried her in absentia by marching with her historic and beautifully painted gas tank from the motorcycle that Soni rode in the first San Francisco Dykes on Bikes® contingent. The US Air Force Honor Guard honored Soni at her memorial service.

Soni Wolf

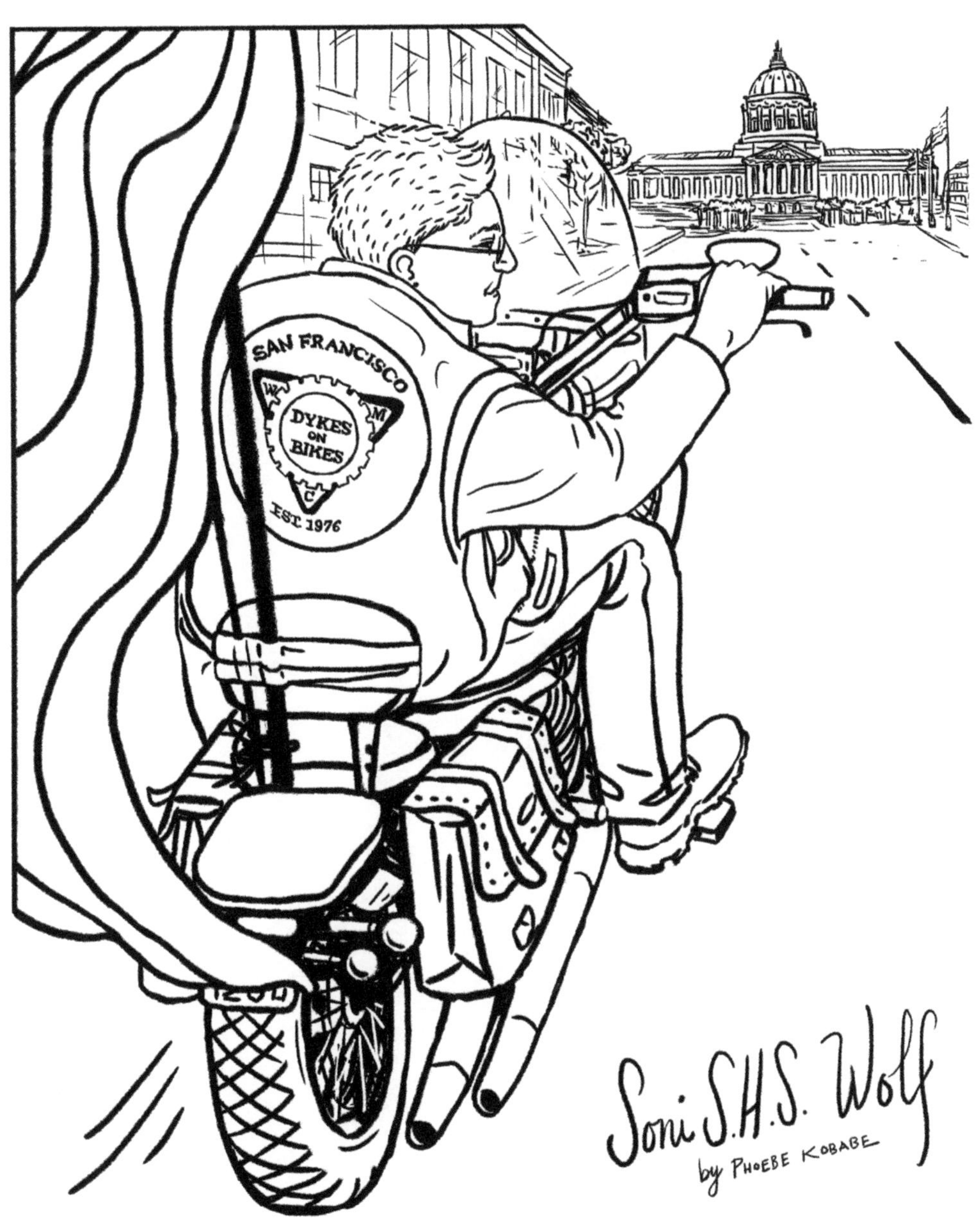

drawn by Phoebe Kobabe

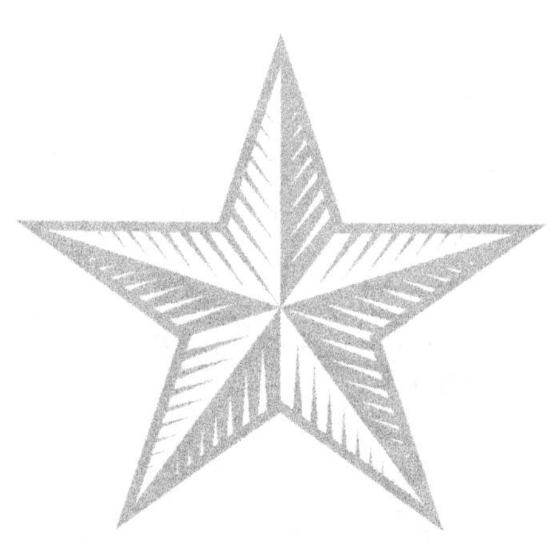

Rhoda Williams-Nazanin

b. 1985 · Iranian-American
drawn by Avery Cassell

It is extremely important to me to love the people who come into my life, even if it is a short period of time. I was raised on Christian beliefs and as I went through seminary to become a pastor, I learned a lot about unconditional love. However, the people who I thought would love me, who promised to be on my side no matter what, were unable to love me unconditionally when I came out publicly in 2019. I realized most people are unable to practice unconditional love. I made it my life's goal to leave people better than when I first met them by being present, listening, opening up my home as a place of refuge and helping them where I am able to. [1]
–Rhoda Williams-Nazanin

Rhoda Williams-Nazanin is a pastor, an activist, and was a 2021 Democratic Congressional Candidate for California's 25th District.

Rhoda was born in Isfahan, Iran, a city so architecturally stunning that it is known in Iran as *Esfahān nesf-e-jahān ast* (Isfahan is half [of] the world). Her family were conservative Assyrian-Iranian Christians, and her father was a pastor, while her mother was a homemaker. One of her parents' missions was to assist people who'd been disowned due to their alcoholism and drug addictions, often giving them shelter in their home. Soon after her birth, the family moved to the capital city, Tehran, where they lived until they emigrated to the United States to escape religious persecution. The Iranian Revolution or the Islamic Revolution culminated in 1979, so by the time Rhoda was born in 1985, everything had changed in Iran. Unlike under the Shah's regime, the Islamic Republic of Iran was a conservative, religious regime that was not friendly toward women or Christians. Prior to the revolution, there were 200,000 Christian Assyrians in the country, but most of them fled to the US, leaving fewer than 20,000 living in Iran now.

Rhoda recalls attending elementary school in Tehran, "I remember on the first day of school in the first grade, I attended an all-girls public school. We had lined up in the schoolyard with all the girls in the school. All of us were in our uniforms, which included wearing 'maghnae' or hijab. We had to be completely covered, even at age 6. I remember the students were encouraged to chant '*Marg bar America*' which means 'death to America.' At that time, my dad was in the States preparing for us to move there and I had this instant feeling of fear for my dad." [2]

Rhoda explained how life in Iran changed for her family and many others after the 1979 revolution, "You know Iran was a free country. At one point you wouldn't be able to tell the difference between Iran and France, and then after the insurrection [the 1979 Iranian revolution] everything changed. My father was forced to wear a priest's collar so that it could be noticed that that's a pastor, he's a person of faith, he's a Christian, he's not a Muslim. And then it was harassing him. He was threatened. He was punched in the face. He was taken by the secret police for weeks without us ever knowing where he was. Why? Because this regime had changed and there was only one belief, Islam. It was very extreme. It wasn't the Islamic people that I've known, you know, it was just a form of control."[3]

Rhoda's father had visited the US before they emigrated and filled their heads with stories of his visit to "Amerkah," but leaving Iran was perilous and not everyone managed to escape. In 1993, Rhoda and her family fled Iran via neighboring country Turkey, where they waited for three weeks for their green cards to be issued. In July, eight-year-old Rhoda, her brother and sister, and her parents flew to Los Angeles, where they were picked up by a family friend and taken to their new apartment. Rhoda was excited to move to the States, but already missed her cousins, aunts, uncles, and grandparents. Rhoda taught herself English in the time-honored method of many immigrant children, by scrutinizing shows and movies on television.

Even with a positive and adventurous attitude, it was difficult, "Growing up in Northridge, I had a lot of Hispanic friends. It was very diverse. Very, very diverse, and so I never noticed the difference until people started making fun of me because of my accent, and making fun of me because I had a unibrow, making fun of me because I had hair on my arm, more than they did, and I was okay, I'm okay. I'm different, so I made a promise to myself that I'm going to learn English so well that you will never know that I was born in another country and I'd speak two other languages as well."[4]

In 2006, Rhoda earned her BS in Business Administration and Management, and in 2018 she earned her B.A. in Communication, both at California State University, Northridge.

Rhoda's father continued his pastoral work in the US until he became sick when Rhoda was in her sophomore year of college. He had not seen a doctor for years because they couldn't afford insurance or medical bills. Unfortunately, he had an aggressive form of pancreatic cancer and died only three months after his diagnosis. One month after her beloved father's death, the family received a bill for $200,000. This experience left a deep impression on Rhoda and caused her to become a strong advocate for Medicare for All when she ran for Congress in 2021.

In 2015, Rhoda got her long hair cut off to reveal the dapper butch that was yearning to be released. Her journey towards butchness was exhilarating, "Identifying as butch has played a huge part in my life. It's who I am. As a kid I was always a 'tomboy,' but as I got older I had to hide my 'queerness.' I was the most feminine closeted lesbian you'd meet. However, inside I wanted nothing more than to be able to wear a suit and tie, hang with the boys and crush on the ladies. In 2015 I decided to cut my hair, and slowly live out how I felt most comfortable. Being able to style my hair the way I wanted, wear the clothes I was comfortable in and be true to myself. I have never felt more confident and comfortable as a woman, than I do today. Embracing my butch identity has led me to new friends, opportunities, and connections." [5]

In 2017, Rhoda's sister outed her to their mother. Her mother was dismayed. Many of her friends turned their backs on Rhoda, saying that she was disgusting or a sinner. Deeply despondent over her sexual orientation, Rhoda talked it over with her pastor and decided to get spiritual therapy in order to free her from the shame of lesbianism. It wasn't until years later and after watching *Boy Erased* that Rhoda realized that she'd experienced conversion therapy and how damaging it was to her mental health. Rhoda's family gradually came around, but it took time. In 2019, Rhoda came out publicly.

In 2016, Donald Trump was elected as President of the United States. The following day felt bleak and mournful, while the period between election night and the Inauguration was excruciating. The GOP was prepared to efficiently and cold-bloodedly dismantle democracy. The Inauguration took place on January 20th. Despite the largest protest to take place in the US with between 3.3 and 4.6 million protestors in the US Women's March against Trump, his nefarious plans continued. On the day of his Inauguration, all mentions of LGBTQ+ rights, climate change, and global warming disappeared from the White House website. One week later, on January 27th, the Protecting the Nation from Foreign Terrorist Entry into the United States, a.k.a. the "Muslim ban" was enacted. When the ban was enacted, a call went out for bilingual folks to help people that were stranded at airports, many times without access to their cell phones or legal aid. Immigration lawyers also flocked to airports to assist. Rhoda and her fluffy, white Maltipoo, Claire went to Los Angeles International Airport (LAX) to offer their translation services and support to anyone speaking Farsi or Assyrian.

In 2020, Joe Biden was elected 46th President of the United States, and in 2021 he was inaugurated. In the two months between his election and his Inauguration, the GOP and their supporters planned an insurrection to prevent Biden from being sworn in as President. The insurrection occurred on January 6, 2021. It was spectacular and violent, and reminded Rhoda of the militarized Iranian college students who overtook the US Embassy in Tehran in 1979. The 200+ Iranian students who stormed the US Embassy were followers of the radical conservative Muslim Students of the Imam Khomeini Line, and the January 6th 2,000+ insurrectionists were followers of US radical conservative groups, including the Oath Keepers and the Proud Boys.

She said, "It reminded me of when the [Iranian] students who decided to protest in front of the US embassy, and then they invaded the building. They got in. There's an interview with some of the students that are still alive. It was asked of them, 'what was your plan?'" She continued, "Some people will brush January 6th off as 'Like it was just a riot, it's fine.' No, that was dangerous. I'm sure you've seen photos and videos of nooses. The noose was for Mike Pence. You know what happened after the regime changed in Iran? There were nooses being hung in the city centers from cranes, and anyone who had loyalty to the Shah was being hung in the city square. So for me it was difficult not to see the similarities."[6]

Rhoda and her fiancée, Sarah, had flown into Washington, DC to attend Biden's Inauguration, excited to welcome the first female vice-president, who was also a woman of color. They were horrified that the uprising had marred this glorious day, so she decided to protect our democracy and joined thousands of American women who were inspired by the attack on democracy to run for office.

In 2021, Rhoda ran as the Democratic candidate for the 25th Congressional District with the promises to address health care as a human right, bold action on climate change, affordable college tuition for everyone, and to preserve the promise of America. She withdrew from the race but remains passionate about helping the community. Inspired by her parents' service to their community and her ten years as a pastor, Rhoda wants to follow in her parents' footsteps, "Hearing their stories while growing up, I wanted to serve and help people too. My dream is to eventually get to a point where I can start an organization that helps LGBTQIA+ teens and young adults find a safe space to turn to, those who have been turned away by family members. For the time being, Sarah and I have opened our home for any LGBTQIA+ folks we meet who need community, safe space, or just a warm place to feel welcomed."[7]

In 2022, Rhoda and Sarah, like so many during the pandemic, chose to move across the country from Southern California to St. Louis, Missouri to be closer to Sarah's family. In November of that year, they were married on their front porch. They live with their Maltipoo named Claire, a black and white tuxedo cat named Leo, and two Pekin ducks named Abigail and Amelia.

Rhoda Williams-Nazanin

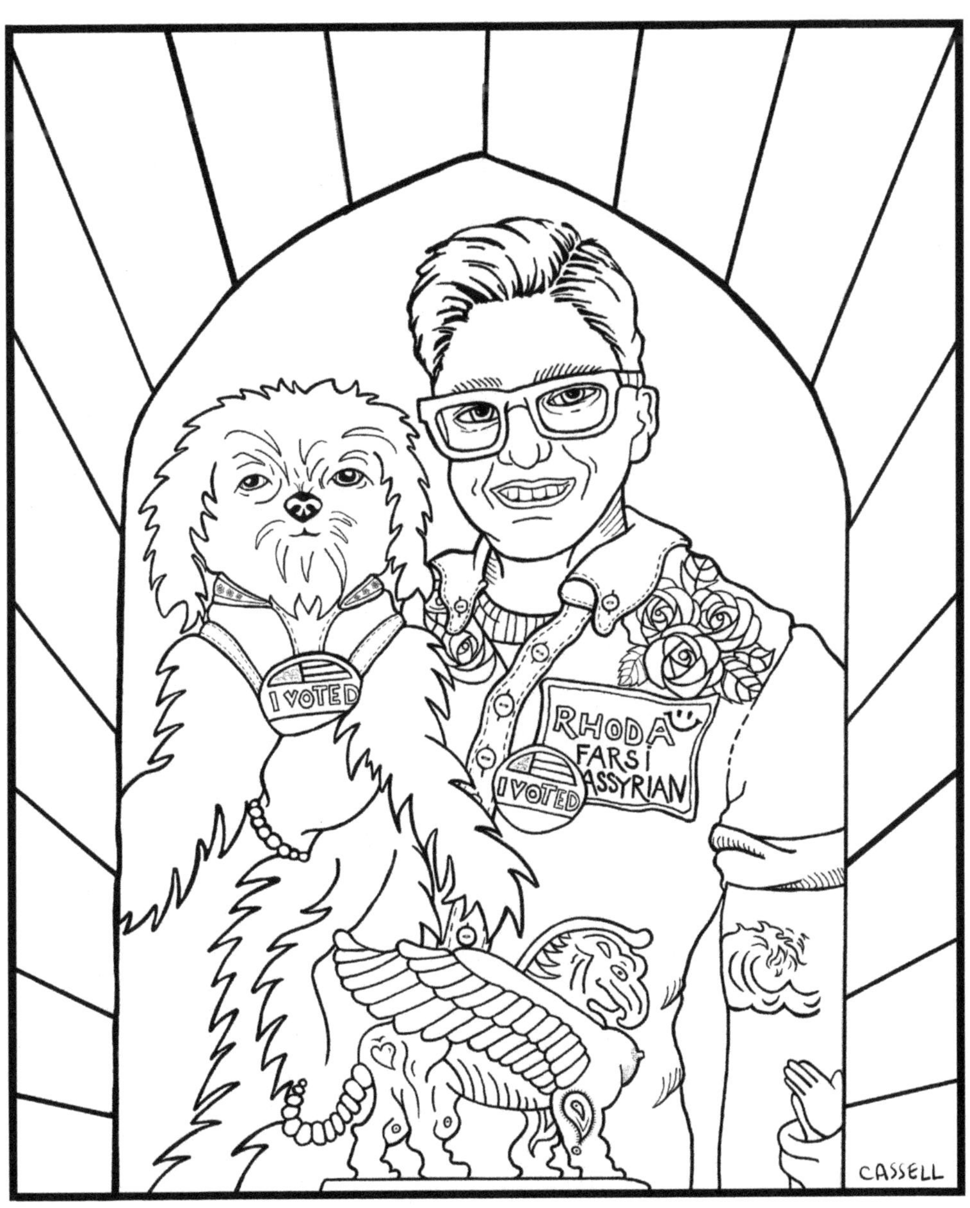

drawn by Avery Cassell

Del Martin

May 5, 1921–Aug. 27, 2008 · USA
drawn by Leslie Ewing

Women needed privacy...not only from the watchful eye of the police, but from gaping tourists in the bars and from inquisitive parents and families.[1] –Del Martin and Phyllis Lyon

Del Martin and her wife, Phyllis Lyon, were groundbreaking icons in the United States lesbian community. Del Martin started the nationally distributed lesbian publication *The Ladder* in the United States in 1956, and she and Phyllis Lyon were the first same-sex couple in the USA to legally marry. In addition, Del and her wife were community organizers, political activists, feminists, and educators.

Del Martin was raised in the Richmond district in San Francisco, California. Del was a tomboy, however, her favorite game was playing house. Del would be the husband, playing the part by wearing her father's pants with the pant legs rolled up, "then she preened in front of the full-length mirror and strutted around in her child's eye-view of what it meant to be a man."[2]

After graduating from high school, Del attended the University of California, Berkeley and San Francisco State College, where she studied journalism and met her future husband, James. The birth control pill would not be invented or approved for another twenty years, and in the early 1940s, diaphragms were just starting to be prescribed. Del became pregnant and dropped out of college. Del married James at age 19 and gave birth to a daughter, Kendra. The marriage did not last long, and after Del fell in love with another housewife, Del and James divorced. When James remarried, he persuaded Del that Kendra would thrive if she was raised in a heteronormative, two-parent home, and Del relinquished custody.

The bombing of Pearl Harbor on December 7, 1941, ushered the US into WWII. The war didn't end until late 1945 with the aftermath taking years to resolve. Del knew she was attracted to women but couldn't find much support. A co-worker turned her onto *The Well of Loneliness* (1928), a depressing novel by British butch Radcliffe Hall. Del was ecstatic to find out she wasn't alone but couldn't find any social groups or other literature. The flurry of lesbian novels by authors such as Valerie Taylor, Marijane Meaker, and Ann Bannon would not be published until the late 1950s.

When they met in 1950, Del and Phyllis were both journalists for a construction trade magazine in Seattle, Washington. Phyllis, who identified as straight at the time, thought Del was the most handsome woman she'd ever seen. Her crush on Del heightened at an office party as Phyllis surreptitiously watched Del bond with male co-workers over martinis, cigars, and necktie knot-tying. Phyllis explained her sexual awakening, "And then when I thought about it, [it] explained a lot about the fact that I had been really attracted to women in high school, etc., etc., but I didn't, and still was, but I didn't really have a clue as to what that was all about." [3]

The desire between the two women became undeniable; in 1952 they became lovers, and a few months later, they moved to the Castro District in San Francisco. Little did they know that this was their first step toward becoming lesbian activists. The 1950s, encompassing the McCarthy era, was a conservative period known for its punishing laws towards LGBTQ+ folks. Homosexuals suffered for their differences and were considered sexual deviants. They were purged from federal employment because of their perceived sexual perversity, writers and artists were jailed for obscenity, employers fired them, and their families frequently shunned them. Police raids on queer bars were a constant fear, same-sex couples dancing together in public was illegal, lesbians were legally obliged to wear at least three feminine garments while in public or risk arrest, and meeting other gay folks was difficult. The LGBTQ+ community went underground; almost all socializing was dangerous and occurred in gay bars and private homes.

Neither Del nor Phyllis had come out to their parents due to the stigma of being gay. Fellow gay rights activist Wiggsy Sivertsen described the cultural climate around being gay in the 1950s, "It was very scary in 1955. The police were actively finding ways to harass the community. There was no hugging, no holding hands in public, nothing at work that said you were gay or lesbian." [4]

When Del and Phyllis got together, they attempted to model a classic butch/femme relationship but discovered that their dynamics didn't fit into the stereotypical mold. Phyllis explained their frustration: "It didn't work for us no matter how we tried. It was true that Del tended to light my cigarettes, okay? But that was as butch as she got sometimes. She doesn't drive, and I did. You know, she didn't drive the nails in and I did. She didn't do any of these butch things. I remember thinking, well, now, let's see, I've got to get Del's breakfast every morning, because that's what mother did for dad. So I did that for a week. Forget it. None of these things really worked for us, and I suspect that was true for most couples." [5]

In 1953, Del and Phyllis bought a home in the Noe Valley neighborhood of San Francisco and were desperate for a community of lesbians. Phyllis described the phone call that changed their life and eventually the lives of lesbians across the country: "September of 1955, I was vacuuming this living room, and the phone rang. It was that woman that we had met at the party, and she said would we be interested in joining her and her partner and three or four other couples in starting an organization for lesbians. I said, 'OF COURSE.' We just wanted to meet some lesbians."[6]

They joined forces with three other lesbian couples, Rose and Rosemary, Marcia and June, and Noni and Mary, to form the Daughters of Bilitis (DOB), the name a reference to lesbian love from 19th century poet Pierre Loüys, who invented Bilitis out of thin air and his imagination. DOB was a "secret social club for lesbians." They wanted a place to safely dance, flirt, and socialize with other lesbians. Del and Phyllis recalled, "Women needed privacy...not only from the watchful eye of the police, but from gaping tourists in the bars and from inquisitive parents and families."[7]

Although Del and Phyllis are often credited as being the main founders of DOB, Phyllis clarified, "WE ARE erroneously given credit as the founders of the Daughters of Bilitis in San Francisco in 1955. It wasn't even our idea. Founders included Del, Phyllis, a young Filipina immigrant named Rose, and her Chicana friend, Mary. They envisioned a club for lesbians here in the States that would allow us to meet and socialize (and especially to dance) outside of the gay bars that were frequently raided by police. Meeting in each other's homes provided us with privacy and a sense of safety from the police and gawking tourists in the bars. Personally, our motivation was simply to meet other lesbians. There were eight of us in the beginning: four couples, four blue-collar and four white-collar workers, two lesbian mothers, and two women of color."[8] By 1960, the DOB had national chapters, including ones in Los Angeles, Chicago, and New York.

After forming the DOB, Del and Phyllis started publishing a newsletter in 1956 called *The Ladder*, the first nationally distributed lesbian publication in the United States. *The Ladder* featured poetry, biographies of notable historical lesbians, book reviews, legal information, articles on self-acceptance, and advice columns. Unfortunately, in the early 1970s, *The Ladder* stopped publishing due to infighting within the lesbian community about whether to continue alliances with gay men, feminism, and disagreements about organization.

When *The Ladder* disbanded, Del and Phyllis continued to organize. They were the first lesbian couple to join the National Organization for Women (NOW) during a time when lesbianism was frowned upon by straight feminists. Partnering with Glide Memorial Methodist Church, they founded the Council on Religion and the Homosexual, which worked to encourage ministers to accept homosexuals into churches and to decriminalize homosexuality.

Del and Phyllis were dedicated to lesbian rights and continued to expand their activist activities. This is merely a short list of their work toward freedom. In 1960, the DOB held its first National Lesbian Conference in San Francisco. 200 women attended, and when the police showed up to make sure they were wearing the requisite three items of women's attire, they were met with lesbians in skirts, lipstick, and heels. In the early 1970s, Del challenged the American Psychiatric Association, successfully lobbying to remove homosexuality from the Diagnostic and Statistical Manual (DSM) of mental disorders. Homosexuality was removed by name as a psychiatric disorder in DSM-II, seventh printing, in 1974, but continued to exist by other names in that and following editions until any diagnosis that might be construed as homosexuality was completely removed in DSM-5 in 2013. Del was a co-founder of OLOC (Old Lesbians Organizing for Change). They also wrote books; *Lesbian/Woman* (1972), *Lesbian Love and Liberation* (1973), and *Battered Wives* (1979) by Del Martin, who argued that domestic violence was part of a larger social issue. In 1971, Del, Phyllis, Beth Elliott, and Jim Foster founded the Alice B. Toklas Democratic Club, the first gay political club in the United States.

After 50 years together, in a glorious San Francisco City Hall ceremony on February 12, 2004, Del and Phyllis became the first same-sex couple to legally marry in San Francisco. They re-married in 2008 when same-sex marriage was made legal in the state of California. Mayor Gavin Newsome presided over the 2008 ceremony, with Del wearing a mauve pantsuit while Phyllis wore a sky-blue pantsuit. Del's daughter, Kendra attended with her husband and said of the wedding, "This is bigger, more profound, more overwhelming than I ever imagined."[9]

Their awards are numerous. Both women are included on the National LGBTQ Wall of Honor, an American memorial wall dedicated to LGBTQ+ "pioneers, trailblazers, and heroes." Del was included in the inaugural fifty American "pioneers, trailblazers, and heroes" inducted on the National LGBTQ Wall of Honor within the Stonewall National Monument in New York City's Stonewall Inn. Del was named an inaugural honoree in the Rainbow Honor Walk, a walk of fame in San Francisco's Castro neighborhood. Del's papers are archived at the GLBT Historical Society in San Francisco. Their home at 651 Duncan Street, where they helped found the DOB, has been assigned landmark status, with the hope to preserve the interior and use it as a research facility and an LGBTQ+ community center. In 1995, they were named delegates to the White House Conference on Aging. Their wedding pantsuits are in the permanent collection of the GLBT Historical Society in San Francisco.

Del died in 2009 after suffering a broken arm, and Phyllis died in 2020.

Del Martin

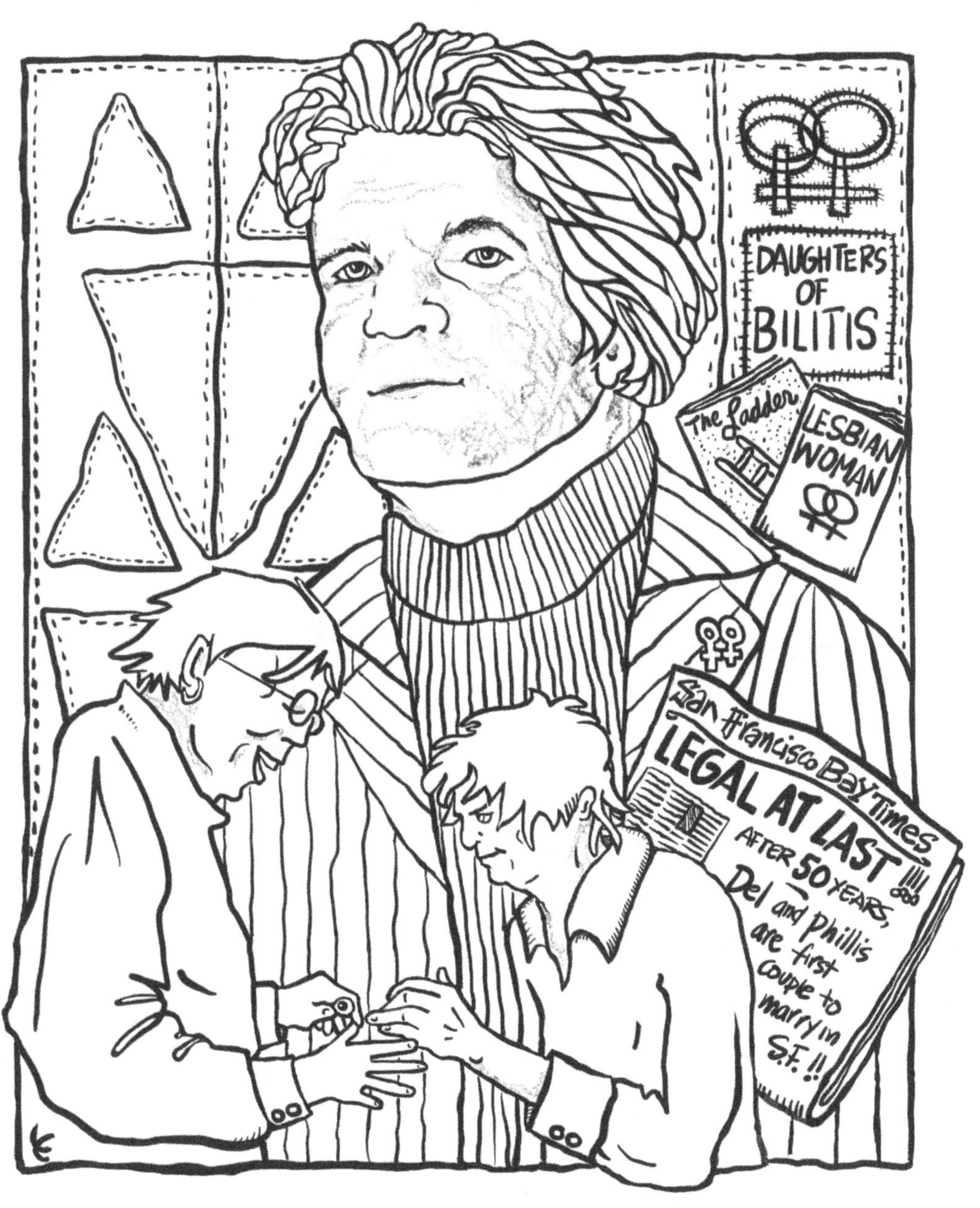

drawn by Leslie Ewing

Koja Ray

USA/Indigenous, Oglala Lakota
written by Tijanna Eaton and Koja Ray
drawn by Jessica Bogac-Moore

I know that everything comes back to this: the personal is all of it political. Where we stand and whose land we're on. –Koja Ray.

Koja hit the ground running, a young broke, Indigenous (Oglala Lakota) butch dyke in San Francisco in 1999. But she'd been more than ready. "I grew up in the depths of the depths of evangelical church, but by 9 years old, I was solidly atheist." However, that was a whole lot easier to keep under wraps than what the adults around her were desperately trying to write off as being "just a tomboy;" later conversion attempts never did stick. Butch wasn't a word she'd hear until she was called one and not affectionately or neutrally. "I'd been called 'he-she' and 'bulldyke' before I had context for what those things meant. Being a masculine girl-child attracted a lot of attention. Negative attention. But I also began finding freedom in it when no one was looking. The center of me that feels like home is still in that spot. In that place where slurs can name us before we can."

A California native, she split her time between the Northern and Southern parts of the state; up north in a tiny town with one stop-light and down south in Los Angeles, where she was born. While it may not have provided a life of ease, she does credit it with having both street smarts and country skill. "I'm no 'butch-off-all-trades,' but you could say I'm handy to have around in a wide range of capacities." At 13, she began sneaking off to "Take Back the Night" rallies, which would have proved a wildly punishable offense, and she was already more than suspect.

Attempts at using her athletics to fly under the radar? No such luck. Still too... butch. "I mean looking back, being a baby dyke was pretty undeniable. I was the only girl in my high school graduating class to wear pants, for christ sake. It was an intensely high price to pay, being the only then-rumored lesbian in school. It was violent. Honestly, I still don't quite know how I pulled it off, even securing myself a spot as one of the 'cool kids.' Though I imagine smoking, drugs, and a whole lot of cutting class didn't hurt. So, I guess I got a strong head start in rebellion before I found use for it politically!"

But at 15, she met two other lesbians for the first time, two mountain women who took her in and called her daughter. "And frankly, just in the nick of time. I can say without hyperbole that they saved my life. And they shaped an enormous part of who I am today as a butch woman. I was becoming awfully reckless at that point and was starved for guidance, but more than anything I just couldn't picture a future for myself. I'd never seen an adult anything like me and I was so desperate to know there were women like me to grow into." Koja remains very close to those two women today, her "Dyke Moms."

When she landed in the Bay, several years away from drinking age, intent on finding her people and creating home, she did so with little more than a few hundred bucks, a couple of suitcases, and a shitty old truck.

The butches she met there became her family. "We shaved each other's heads. You have to remember those were still days when it wasn't unusual for barber shops to turn women away. I got pretty good at a fade." Most were older, wiser, and willing to tell their stories to a younger butch eager to listen, to put stock in the worth of those stories, and to count lived experience as priceless. "I realize now that my herstory as a butch started when I first heard that word. Butch. Finding language and community tied to a part of me that existed even before I had a name for it was, IS necessary to my survival. And I've them to thank for that, really."

Flash forward to now, Koja is blue-collar to the bone, having spent her career as a first responder in fire and emergency medicine. "I'm at my best under extreme pressure when things are just at a fever pitch of chaos and adrenaline. But I'm also a public servant by nature. I've built a lot of my life around service, and I intend to keep that as my focus." Koja is a long-time activist, narrowing in on BIWOC (Black and Indigenous Women of Color), Dykes and Elders, and looking for tangible ways to extend and improve the quality of life of those whose shoulders we stand on. She's a founder and an organizer of several orgs and spaces catering to these populations, including the "Dykes Only Space" at the San Francisco Dyke March. "We created this out of righteous anger at the loss of our spaces and it just took off! We grow larger and stronger with each and every year and it's really such an honor to facilitate and just get to watch the intergenerational connections being made, especially between butches. It's definitely one of my projects I'd say I'm most proud of." Later in the summer, Koja runs "The Playground," a space for women, trans, and non-binary people attracting 15,000+ out of the 150,000 attendees at San Francisco's annual Folsom Street Fair (the largest leather and alt-sex community event worldwide).

Koja has penned a critical piece rebuking the hypocritical practice of so-called land acknowledgements. She's read from her Indigenous children's book, *47,000 Beads*, available worldwide, taught workshops, given keynotes, and been a panelist across Turtle Island. "I don't care if it's a tiny independent bookstore or NYU, it's not

Koja Ray

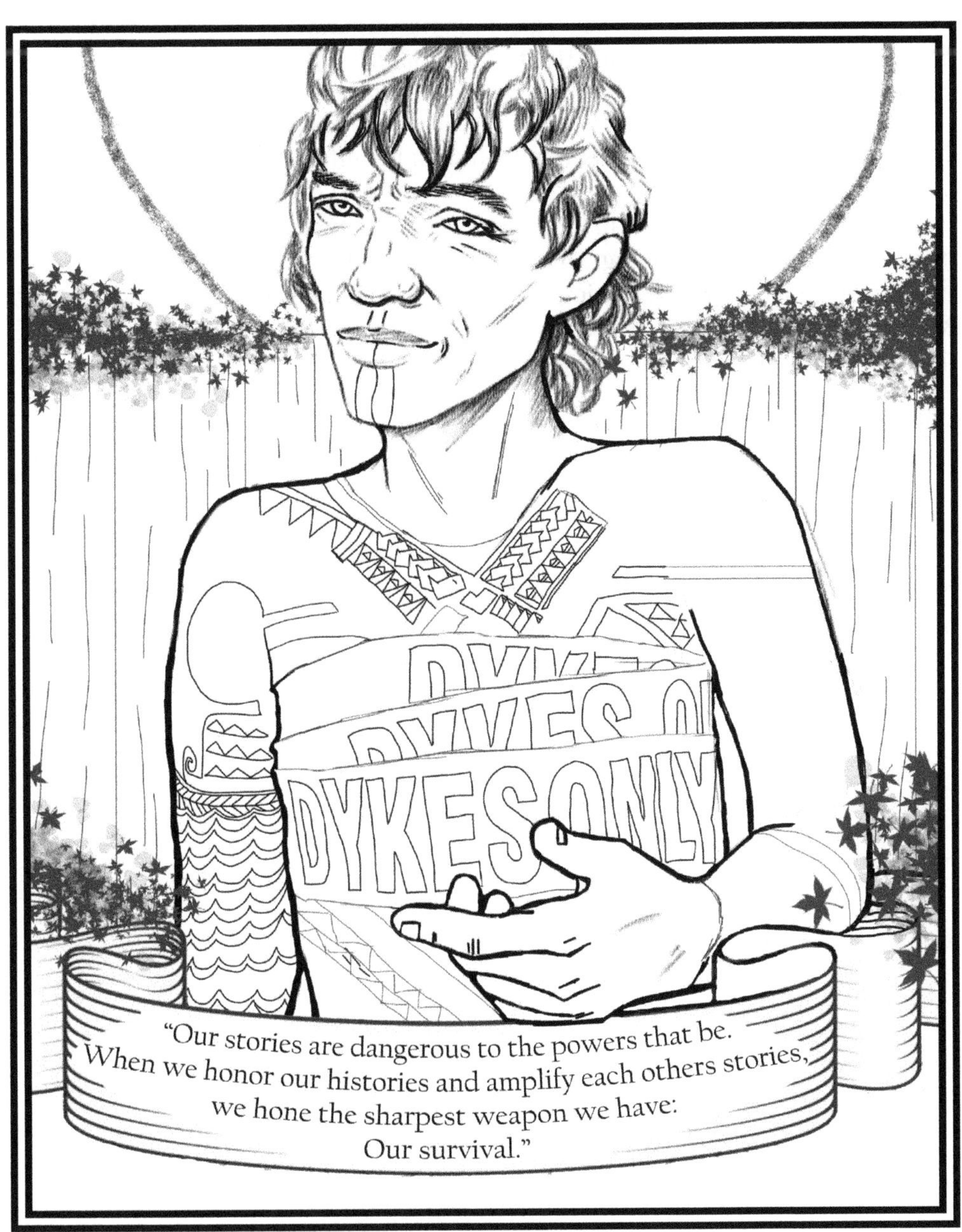

drawn by Jessica Bogac-Moore

about a resume, it's about the people. I'm not an academic. I don't have a degree. And it's important to me that people know that when I show up to talk to them."

Koja describes herself as a socialist, a communist, a staunch feminist, and sober addict. She's a surfer with strong ties to the *Mni* (Water), the lessons it brings and stories it tells.

These days Koja, in her early 40s, admits that in her efforts towards stoicism, she was unnecessarily hard on her body and mind and often feels old for her age as a result. But even so, she can be found getting her hands dirty, reading five books concurrently, drumming, forever singing and dancing to the Indigo Girls, obsessively practicing calisthenics, self-restraint, and hard truths. And, admittedly, Koja is still fulfilling butch stereotypes galore, but the more comfortable sort, like living in 501s and her favorite old boots.

Koja still calls the Bay Area of northern California home, in a 300-square-foot house she shares with an ancient Betta fish named Joni Mitchell and far too many plants, but very stoked to own nothing she doesn't love or need.

"Reject this 'butches are extinct' party line. I will not be erased. WE will not be erased. I'm so tired of hearing this dinosaur bullshit. We are not extinct. But we are still endangered and if we want to survive, we have to look to our history and MAKE IT our responsibility to carry that history forward."

Lyra McKee

March 31, 1990–April 18, 2019 · Northern Ireland
drawn by Rachael House

It's better to go down fighting. Do not fucking listen to bullshitters and naysayers. See if you want to do it? You go do it. And don't let anyone tell you that you can't do it.[1] –Lyra McKee

Lyra McKee was an investigative journalist, writer, and editor in Northern Ireland. She was murdered during a riot in Derry at the age of 29.

Lyra was raised in Belfast, Northern Ireland by her working-class Catholic mother, her grandmother, and her oldest sister. Lyra was the youngest of six, a feisty runt. She had to wear an eye patch as a child due to faulty vision and needed remedial reading classes. Teachers took an interest in Lyra, mentoring her with book recommendations. Lyra started her journalism career young and wrote for her high school newspaper.

Lyra realized that she was a lesbian at a young age but, being raised Catholic, was tormented by visions of hell to the point of contemplating suicide. She came out to a schoolmate, was rejected, and was taunted by her classmates as a "lesbo" and "weird."[2]

When she came out as a lesbian to her mother, she was a university student in her early 20s, but it was nothing like she had expected. As Lyra wrote on her blog in a piece entitled "Lyra McKee: a letter to my 14-year-old self," "Three months before your 21st birthday, you will tell Mum the secret. You will be sobbing and shaking and she will be frightened because she doesn't know what's wrong. Christmas will be just a couple of weeks away. You have to tell her because you've met someone you like and you can't live with the guilt anymore. You can't get the words out so she says it: 'Are you gay?' And you will say, 'Yes Mummy, I'm so sorry.' And instead of getting mad, she will reply, 'Thank God you're not pregnant.' You will crawl into her lap, sobbing, as she holds you and tells you that you are her little girl and how could you ever think that anything would make her love you any less? You will feel like a prisoner who has been given their freedom. You will remember all the times you pleaded with God to help you because you were so afraid, and you will feel so foolish because you had nothing to worry about."[3]

The Troubles was a 30-year-long war that lasted from the late 1960s until the 1998 Good Friday Agreement. The Troubles resulted from disagreements over whether Northern Ireland should remain part of the United Kingdom as per the Protestant unionists, or split off and become part of the Republic of Ireland as per the Roman Catholic nationalists. Lyra was eight years old when the Good Friday Agreement was signed in 1998, a pact intended to end The Troubles with its attendant years of bloodshed in the region. She and her family lived near Belfast's Murder Mile, named thus because of the number of casualties during The Troubles. Although not officially a civil war, The Troubles were embodied by violent street fighting, city bombings, sniper attacks, roadblocks, and trial-less jailings.

Trauma from The Troubles marked Lyra's generation with the nickname the Ceasefire Babies, and despair ran through their lives. Suicide was epidemic among Lyra's friends. Suicide rates in Northern Ireland doubled between the peace agreement in 1998 and 2008. Anecdotally, intergenerational transmission of trauma due to war can result in PTSD and suicidal ideation. This has been seen in families of Holocaust survivors and with families of people that lived through The Troubles. In an article that Lyra had published in *The Atlantic* magazine in 2016, sociologist Mike Tomlinson talked to her about intergenerational transmission of trauma: "Tomlinson recounted a time he was interviewed on the BBC World Service about his research. At the end of the interview, a fellow interviewee from the US asked him, 'Where is the evidence from other countries?' The problem is, there's very little. In war, the ruling government usually collapses—and with it any form of meaningful record-keeping. Northern Ireland was unique: the Troubles were an internal conflict throughout which the state remained strong, even when the mainland was being bombed. To borrow a scientific term, it's the best dataset we have to prove that the problems faced in a war-torn country do not end with the arrival of peace." [4]

Lyra was in the thick of The Troubles: raised near an area where there were particularly brutal street skirmishes, and had friends who commited suicide because of war trauma. Lyra became a journalist in order to document the surrounding chaos. She was an idealist and determined, "There are wrongs you cannot fix. As a younger reporter, I found this so hard to stomach. For me, journalism was about saving the world; if I told the terrible stories, someone would have to do something about them. Someone would sit up and notice." [5]

In 2011, Lyra started working for the news aggregator, Mediagazer, and numerous local and international journals and newspapers. In 2014, her article, "Lyra McKee's Letter To My 14 Year Old Self" was made into a short film by Stay Beautiful Films. In 2017, Lyra gave a TEDx talk, "How uncomfortable conversations can save lives" about the LGBTQ+ Orlando nightclub shooting in 2016. She was working on two

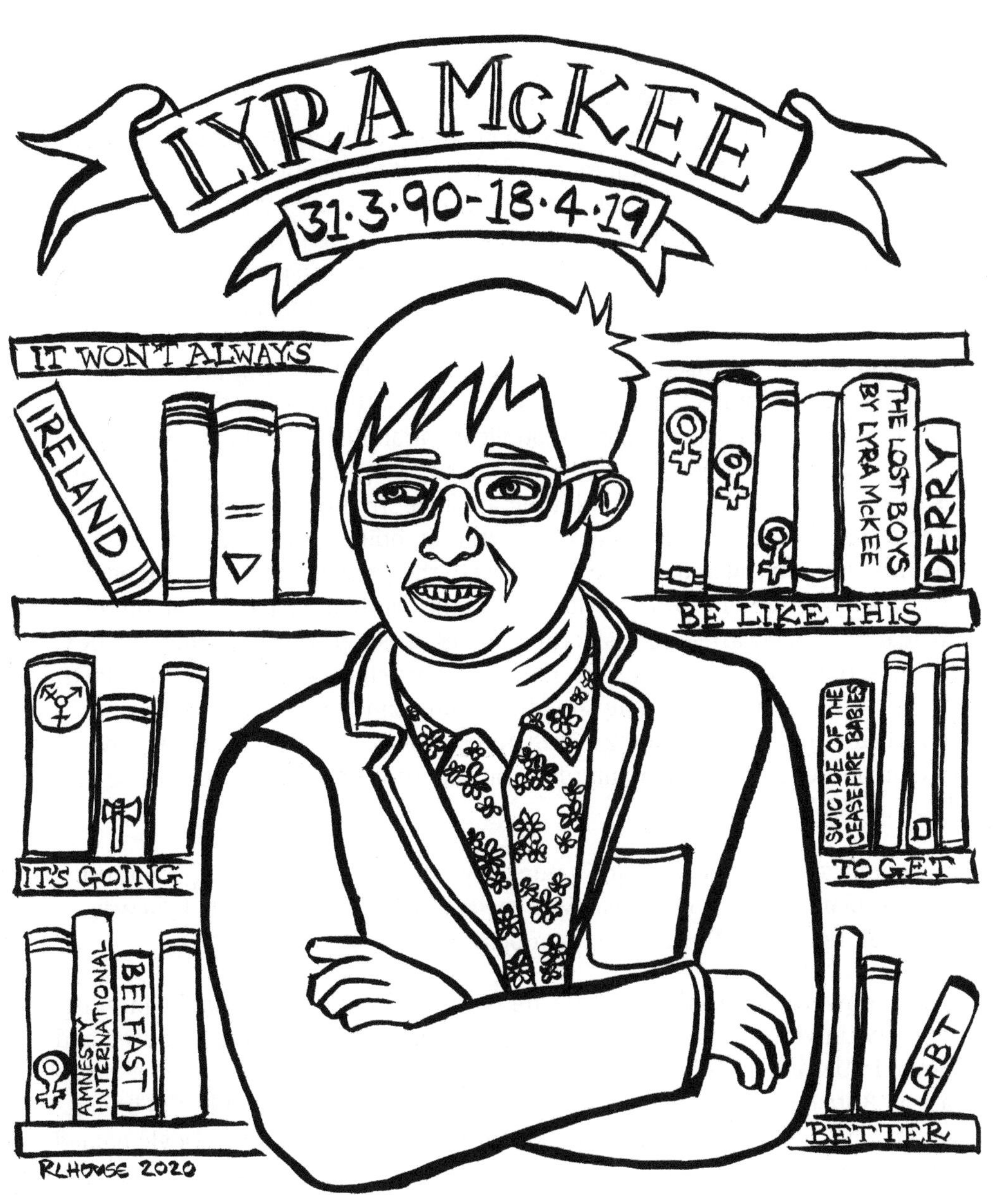

drawn by Rachael House

investigative books, *Angels with Blue Faces*, about the Provos IRA killing of Belfast MP Robert Bradford, and *The Lost Boys*, about the November 1974 disappearances of Thomas Spence and John Rodgers from Falls Road in Belfast.

In April of 2019, Lyra was covering the anticipated street riots in Derry; Easter Sunday was when the 1916 Rising against British rule was traditionally commemorated. That April, the Easter rioting seemed casual. Folks were filming documentaries, mothers brought their children, and people stood about watching and talking. As the evening progressed, masked New IRA members and other rioters started shooting guns. During the mass confusion, rioters torched cars, tossed Molotov cocktails, and opened fire at the police. Lyra was there as a journalist, standing near the officers, and was shot in the head by a masked gunman.

The owner of the gun used to kill Lyra was Niall Sheerin. He was prosecuted; however, a clear connection between ownership of the gun and the shooting was not established. The dissident republican paramilitary group, the New IRA, had confessed anonymously to killing Lyra, but charges were not filed. They sent a statement to *The Irish News* with their apology, "In the course of attacking the enemy Lyra McKee was tragically killed while standing beside [the] enemy. The IRA offer our full and sincere apologies to the partner, family and friends of Lyra McKee for her death. On Thursday night, following an incursion on the Creggan by heavily armed British crown forces which provoked rioting, the IRA deployed our volunteers to engage. We have instructed our volunteers to take the utmost care in future when engaging the enemy and put in place measures to help ensure this." [6] On January 23, 2023, the police charged Peter Gearóid Cavanagh and Jordan Devine with Lyra's murder, and six other Derry men with rioting and throwing Molotov cocktails.

Lyra's domestic partner was Sara, a nurse. Lyra had bought an engagement ring and was planning to propose marriage to Sara the following month. Lyra was killed before she had the chance to propose.

Lyra was awarded a posthumous Master of Arts in online journalism by Birmingham City University. The award-winning film about her, *Lyra*, was produced and shown in UK and Irish theaters in November 2022, and it is expected to be broadcast on British public television in 2023. She was named as one of its "30 under 30 in media" by *Forbes* magazine. In 2019, *Irish Times* writer Martin Doyle named Lyra "Best of Irish: 10 rising stars of Irish writing." Lyra had two non-fiction books published posthumously, *Angels With Blue Faces*, an investigation into the death of Northern Ireland MP Robert Bradford in 1981 (Excalibur Press, 2020), and *Lost, Found, Remembered: In Her Own Words*, a selection of journalistic articles (Faber & Faber, 2021).

Dr. Jamaica Heolimeleikalani Osorio

b. 1990 · USA
drawn by Jessica Bogac-Moore

The first thing that comes to mind when you ask that question is capitalism because it's wrapped up into everything. It's wrapped up into white supremacy, and the displacement of Natives from our land. But it's also this really seductive thing that is constantly trying to pull us into its gravity. As a way for capitalism to survive it tries to convince us that we can make it pono to serve our needs. But the truth is that there's no way that you can make capitalism and the commodification and exploitation of our 'āina and kanaka, pono. As my good friend Ilima Long says, 'Capitalism is antithetical to Aloha 'Aina.' [1] –Jamaica Heolimeleikalani Osorio

Jamaica Heolimeleikalani Osorio is a Kanaka Maoli wahine poet, artist, professor, and activist from Hawai'i.

Jamaica grew up surrounded by artists, educators, and activists. Her father was a professor, poet, and musician, and through him she met the activists Haunani-Kay Trask, a leading figure of the Hawaiian Sovereignty movement, and Lilikalā Kame'eleihiwa, historian and professor at the University of Hawai'i's Kamakakūokalani Center for Hawaiian Studies.

Jamaica got involved with the Hawaiian spoken word community, seeing the connection between the oral traditions that she grew up with and sharing poetry on stage. She told an interviewer at *'Aina Momona*, "The writing side came on much later. As a kaiāpuni student, I really didn't feel comfortable in my ability to write. But I kind of fell into the spoken word community in Hawai'i, because I got dragged along by a friend. And as I fell in love with that art form, it felt so similar to the practices of our kūpuna and our oral traditions and how similar I felt sharing a poem on stage as I felt as a child, chanting the kumulipo with my classmates. It felt like the same thing." [2]

Jamaica is heavily influenced by aloha 'āina or "love of the land", although the concept of aloha 'āina is wider and more nebulous than that simplified translation into English. Aloha 'āina can be found in Kumulipo (creation chants), an adoration of the land, hula dance, storytelling, and community activism. Aloha 'āina is not patriotism, but it is connected to a broader, spiritual practice.

The film *Jamaica Heolimeleikalani Osorio: This Is the Way We Rise* (2021) was about her activism and writing. Jamaica spoke in the award-winning VR (virtual reality) documentary, *On the Morning You Wake (To the end of the world)* (2022) about what it was like to live through an early morning text warning of a (false) nuclear strike that occurred in Hawaiʻi on Saturday, January 13, 2018. Divided into three acts, each part of the documentary is framed by a poem written by Jamaica. In an interview with Agnese Pietrobon from *XRMagazine*, Osorio urges us to pay attention, "This is the biggest problem of the society we live in: disconnection and the normalization of disconnection. Even before COVID and Zoom....In this society dominated by American values, what we ask ourselves is how we can compartmentalize our lives outside of their impact and connection with others, so that we can justify any behavior we want to have. But I come from a culture where our values couldn't be more different than that, as a Native Hawaiian I know that all my choices and how I move through the world not only impact my family, but impact every person my family loves, and every person who loves the land I live in, both past, present and future."[3]

Jamaica earned her Ph.D. in English (Hawaiian literature) from the University of Hawaiʻi and currently teaches Indigenous and Native Hawaiian Politics at the University of Hawai'i at Mānoa. Her dissertation was titled "(Re)membering 'Upena of Intimacies: A Kanaka Maoli Moʻolelo Beyond Queer Theory." She wrote in her dissertation's abstract that she was exploring the "ʻŌiwi concepts of aloha ʻāina and pilina at the intersections of ʻike Hawaiʻi, Indigenous queer theory, and Indigenous feminisms."[4]

Her book, *Remembering Our Intimacies: Moʻolelo, Aloha 'Aina, and Ea*, was published in 2021. In it, Jamaica discusses forms of intimacy, including pre-colonial intimacy. She talks about the meaning of Aloha, "So before, as some might say in kāwā ʻōiwi wale, at the time of just the natives, before the arrival of people like Captain Cook and all his homies and then, of course, the ABCFM mission. My people practice a really, as you say, expansive practice of aloha and intimacy and care. We were not heteronormative by any stretch of the imagination, we did not practice compulsory monogamy or compulsory heteronormativity. We practice what folks like Lilikalā Kameʻelehiwa, who's a brilliant Hawaiian scholar, she calls it moe aku moe mai, the sleeping here or there. There were a lot of things about Hawaiian society that were heavily regulated and spiritually regulated. But pleasure was never one of them, there was no expectation for you to have one partner of a particular sex. In fact, the only expectation there was that you enter into consensual relationships and that you respect those relationships. And you respect whatever boundaries you set up with the people you are in relation to. And that's important because those Pilina, those intimacies we shared between people, we shared them in that way because it was also reflected in the ʻāina. Right, in the land, and that which fed us we, we learned how to give each other pleasure through pleasuring the land, or through watching our other than human kin pleasure each other, or the land," she continued the discussion to creating space for an expansive practice of Aloha, "And when we talk about this more expensive practice of Aloha, whether it is to wahine, seeking pleasure from each other, or to kāne to women to men seeking pleasure from each other, or multiple women and men or people who do not fit anywhere near this very strange gender binary, seeking pleasure with each other in ways that are ethical, and then reflecting the intimacy of our land with each other. When we talk about that, we not only make room for so many more of us who have kind of been cast aside by society really intentionally, we also recognize that the way that Hawaiians and other Native people...have been removed from our land, displaced from our land, alienated from our land, that happened at the same time that they were removing us from each other." [5]

Jamaica reflected upon COVID-19, how lies about the vaccines have affected our relationships with one another, polarization between the left and the right, and her frustration with anti-vaxers and the far right, "And, at the center of this idea that our relationships with each other are going to save us or destroy us, at the center of this is a real desire, as a Kanaka, to not forsake any of my people. Because I am a Kanaka who, because of Western ideology that had been imported into my community, had been forsaken. There is, to me, a direct correlation between the ways that many Hawaiians have bought into the idea of heterosexuality as virtue and the only way to be in relation is for a man and a wife to have a child, all that BS. There's a correlation between that, and the way that these other very strange anti-Vax, anti-science, anti-collective care, alt-right centering of American freedom and rights have gotten also strangely imported into my community," she continued, "I kind of stepped all the way into the polarized mud around to vaccinate or not to vaccinate because I was getting so frustrated, not just with what is certainly a large group of new age, strange cross-over white supremacy groups in Hawaiʻi kind of creating their own misinformation about COVID and the vaccine. But what I was really troubled by was how many Hawaiians were repeating those same narratives. And I got so frustrated, instead of being in conversation and community with lāhui, I just started shaming people who did not think the way that I did. And that was in direct opposition to these larger, more important ideal ideas around how important our relationships are." [6]

Jamaica lives with her partner and their young child in Wahiawā. She is an assistant professor of Native Hawaiian and Indigenous Politics at the University of Hawaiʻi, including Introduction to Indigenous Politics, Hawaiʻi Politics, Native Hawaiian Politics, and Contemporary Native Hawaiian Politics.

Jamaica was a Ford Fellow, and when she was only 18 read her poem "Kumulipo" about Hawaiian identity, colonization, and American imperialism before President Barack Obama and the First Family.

Jamaica describes her scholarly research, "As an educator committed to the decolonization in Hawai'i and beyond, I believe it is my kuleana to produce research that actively (re)members the personal, genealogical, and scholarly relationship between Hawai'i and our 'ohana in Oceania. While much of my academic background is rooted in a respectful study of an Indigenous politics and theory primarily rooted in Turtle Island and Hawai'i, I recognize that our own decolonization will demand re-situating Hawai'i back home in Oceania, rather than within an American political context, and therefore a context of occupation."[7]

Dr. Jamaica Heolimeleikalani Osorio

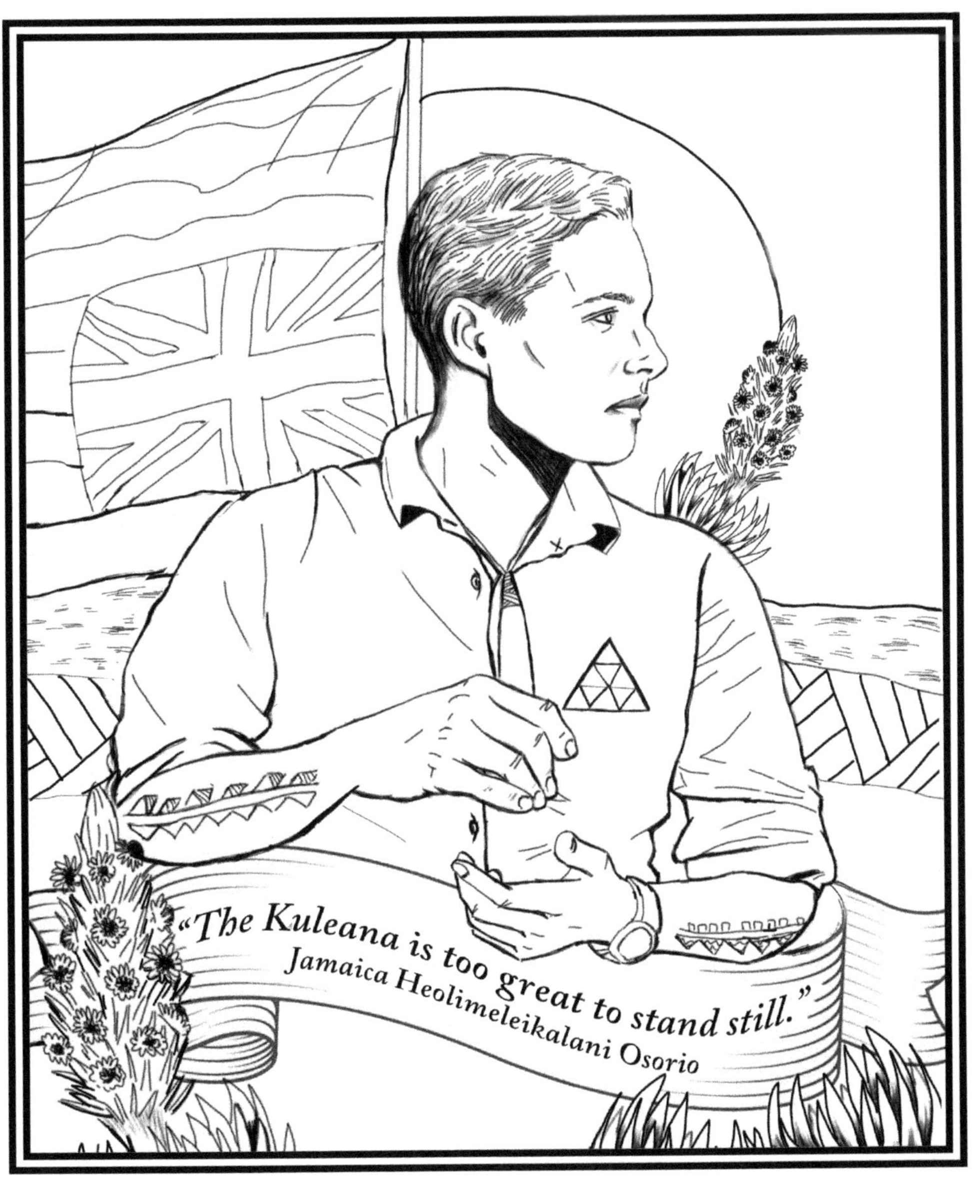

drawn by Jessica Bogac-Moore

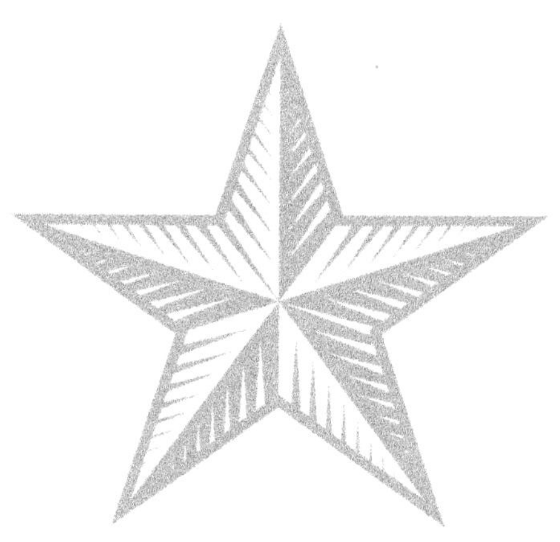

ARTISTS

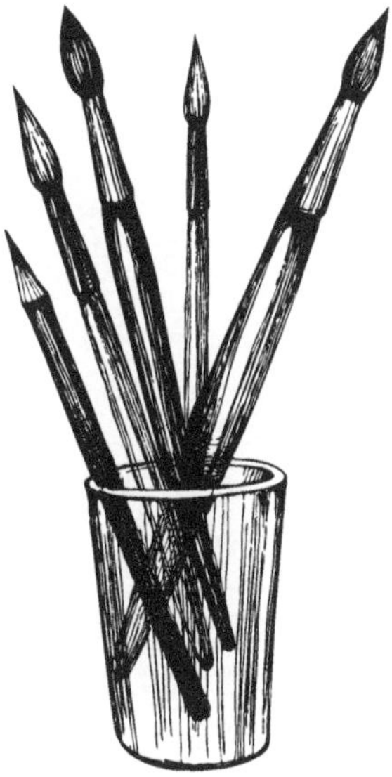

Ajuan Mance

b. September 19, 1966 · USA
drawn by Justin Hall

In the summer of 2020, as Americans crowded the street to protest the death of George Floyd, Breonna Taylor, and other Black people that lost their lives at the hands of police, I could not help but look back to earlier generations of African-Americans. What would they think, not of the death of unarmed Black people at the hands of police, but of the persistent harassment of Black people by non-Blacks, whose discomfort was their presence in community settings like libraries, swimming pools, and shopping malls to often ending in demeaning conversations and 911 calls. How would they respond to this continuing crisis? As a Black artist living through this moment in reckoning, how would I?[1] –Ajuan Mance

Ajuan Mance is an artist, author, and editor. She is a professor of Ethnic Studies and English and the Dean of Digital Learning and Innovation at Mills College in Oakland, California.

Ajuan grew up in the village of Freeport on the South Shore of New York's Long Island. Ajuan's father was a chemistry teacher, and her mother taught, too. Her parents exposed her to books, culture, and art, making frequent family outings to The Metropolitan Museum of Art in New York City. Her mother was careful to choose books written and illustrated by and about Black people, providing the groundwork for Ajuan to see herself as an artist and a writer. Ajuan was fond of creating illustrated books and drawing, and she also started playing the piano in kindergarten. Ajuan described her life as a juvenile artist, "I always gravitated towards art—my mother has kept drawings that I did when I was three or four years old. My parents would take me to stores where art students bought supplies and to museums in Manhattan, where I'd walk around with a notebook writing down the paintings that I liked best. I was very serious."[2]

After graduating from high school, she attended Brown University; however, she didn't take any art classes despite loving to draw and paint. She explains, "Like a lot of Black people, or people who don't come from privilege, art as a profession felt inaccessible to me, like something that only rich people would do."[3]

After earning a B.A. in English at Brown University, she went on to earn an M.A. in English and a Ph.D. in Literature, both from the University of Michigan. There, she became engrossed by archival work and 19th-century American literature.

Her dissertation evolved into her first book, *Inventing Black Women: African American Women Poets and Self-Representation, 1877–2000*, and in 2008 the American Library Association (ALA) awarded *Inventing Black Women* Outstanding Academic Title.

In the early 2000s, Ajuan started becoming involved with the queer comics scene, discovering a community of LGBTQ+ artists who encouraged her to make work about her experiences as a Black, queer woman. The support and sustenance were thrilling: "Queer comics have really created a space for complexity that didn't exist in a lot of other comics. The space for different ways of being a person of color, different ways of being gendered. It's really amazing. It's like nothing I've ever seen before." [4]

In 2014, Ajuan produced her first zine, *Gender Studies*, an autobiographical depiction of discovering her butch masculinity in college while navigating dating men, then discovering that coming out as a lesbian didn't necessarily clarify things. *Gender Studies* ends with, "Looking back, I'm not sure my friends saw anything in me that I hadn't seen in myself. It's just that no one had ever really named it. Somehow, I'd managed to out myself as masculine—wonderfully, queerly masculine—without even trying." [5]

Ajuan spoke with Prism Comics Queer Press Grant member and fellow artist Jon Macy about her visual inspirations: "My main inspirations are other figurative artists. As a child, I could spend hours paging through books of paintings by Norman Rockwell, Pieter Bruegel the Elder, Otto Dix, and the Dutch Masters. Their breadth of subjects, distinct styles, and rich use of color are part of my creative DNA. As an adult, though, I have been drawn to artists who make use of heavy lines and ink on walls or paper, like George Grosz, the Hernandez Brothers, and the street artists Swoon and Doze Green. I also just adore the audacity, honesty, and stylistic vocabulary of African American and Afro-European artists like Kara Walker, Kerry James Marshall, Whitfield Lovell, Chris Ofili, Archibald Motley, and Njideka Akunyili-Crosby, whose work is just beautiful. I'm also interested in the way that stained glass windows use thick black lines, simple geometric shapes, and multiple shades of a single color to depict complex figures and landscapes. I have those kinds of shapes in mind when I sit down to draw a portrait or even an imaginary person. Almost all of my subjects are Black people, and I usually begin with the nose and lips of my figures. I've just always started with those features of African American faces that I love the most, which also happen to be those features for which we have traditionally been maligned. I start in the center of the face and work outward." [6]

Ajuan Mance

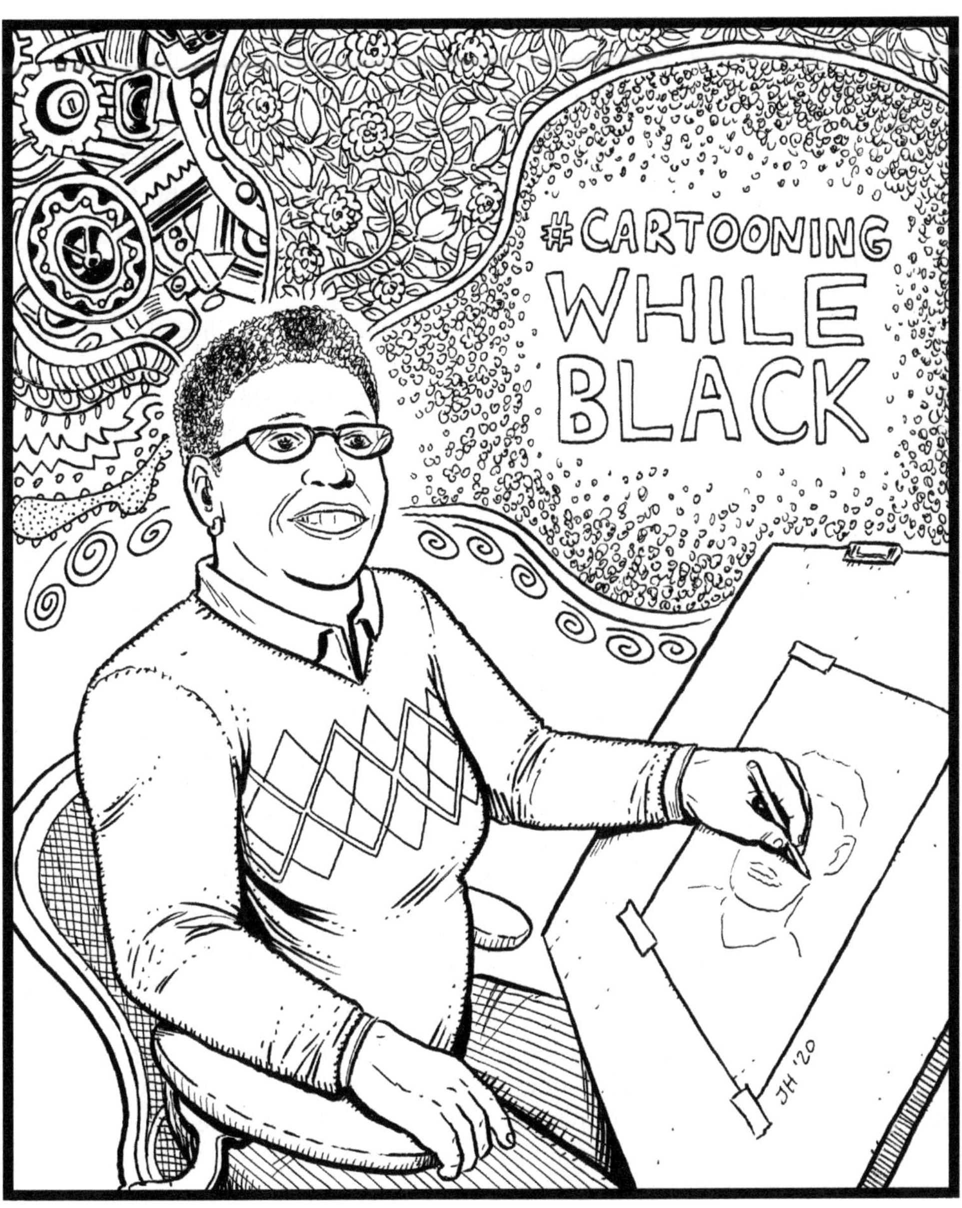

drawn by Justin Hall

From 2010 to 2016, Ajuan worked on a uniquely new project. Inspired by her love of Black men, Ajuan started a project called "1001 Black Men," drawing those that she encountered during her daily life in Oakland and in her travels. 300 drawings into the project, she realized that she was only drawing men that she felt comfortably familiar with and that reminded her of her family and friends; elders, nerds, academics, and men in suits, rather than the diversity of the larger population of Black men. This was a startling realization for Ajuan, and she rectified it by becoming more inclusive in her choices of subjects. In 2021, *1001 Black Men: Portraits of Masculinity at the Intersections* was published. A stranger she saw on the street and her beloved father bookend the portraits in *1001 Black Men*.

During the isolation of the COVID-19 pandemic and inspired by Black Lives Matter (BLM) protests, Ajuan started drawing portraits of Black people doing ordinary things. After posting twenty of the drawings on Instagram, she was contacted by an editor at Chronicle Books about turning her new project into a book. Some activities included driving a car, a child selling water at a stand without a permit, a teen wearing a hoodie in the mall, and an adult bicycling. Ajuan included a timeline with actual events in the book and talked about how distressing the research process was: "It was kind of an intense process, looking up all of these incidents. It was really depressing, so I kept having to step away for a little while, then come back. Even as a professor who teaches African American literature, I didn't realize the scope, magnitude, and severity of some of these incidents."[7] With a foreword written by BLM co-founder Alicia Garza, *Living While Black: Portraits of Everyday Resistance* was published in 2022. A visually beautiful book, *Living While Black* is a tool for teachers, students, activists, and parents navigating conversations about racism and resistance.

Ajuan continues to focus her art on Black representation, fortitude, and beauty. In another visit to the Metropolitan Museum of Art, this time as an adult, she talked about the awe she felt when viewing the Gee's Bend quilt collection, "...that the Gee's Bend quilters, these African-American women from a tiny Southern town that you have to reach by ferry, that 25 of their quilts are now part of the Metropolitan Museum's permanent collection, and when I learned that, I just felt like someone else could see that Black people make beautiful things," Ajuan continues, "Black people are beautiful, and then the notion, the acknowledgment, that Black people create beautiful work. It matters. Representation matters. To see yourself expands your sense of possibilities."[8]

Ajuan and her wife, Cassandra, live in Oakland, California.

Alison Bechdel

b. September 10, 1960 · USA
drawn by Diego Gomez

Honestly, drawing a landscape is just baffling to me. Trees make me want to kill myself. How does anyone ever draw a tree? It's difficult unless you really enter into it, you know? So I set my challenge in this book of doing these occasional scenes, where I'm not even using a pen, I'm using a brush, and I'm just drawing. I'm not actually using a Sumi-e technique but I just sort of fake a Sumi-e kind of painting, which does require a great deal of presence. I can't be listening to a podcast when I'm doing one of those drawings. I've really gotta be at the tip of that paintbrush, all aware of myself to be there. Anyhow, I'm still not very good at landscapes, but I did push myself to do them in this book. And it somehow feels like a good stretch. [1] –Alison Bechdel

Alison Bechdel is a cartoonist and writer. She is the creator of *Dykes to Watch Out For* (*DTWOF*), a syndicated comic strip that started in the 1980s that provided a lifeline to lesbians across the United States.

Alison grew up in the small town of Beech Creek, Pennsylvania. Her father was a part-time mortician, a closeted bisexual man, and an English literature teacher at the local high school. Her mother was active in the local little theater group and taught high school English literature. Alison was a tomboy, an avid reader, and an artist from a young age, carrying a penknife, sporting shorter hair, and roughing it with her two brothers. "I continued using the girls' bathroom and checking the female box on questionnaires. But in my head I occupied my own private Switzerland, where I spent the remainder of my childhood in splendid neutrality." [2]

Alison started manifesting obsessive-compulsive disorder (OCD) when she was 10. It showed itself in several ways, including counting the drips in the bathtub and not turning the tap off unless they were an even number, kissing her stuffed animals goodnight in a specific order, and having rules about how she wrote about herself in her diary.

Her father was obsessed with restoring their home, a 4,000-square-foot, Gothic Revival mansion to its former grand glory: "He was an alchemist of appearance, a savant of surface, a Daedalus of décor." [3] Alison and her siblings spent their childhood helping their father hunt for antiques and tiptoeing around fragile objects in their home. Alison described growing up "in a house full of antiques, where there were secrets, and appearances were important." [4] The hidden sex life of her father with young men cast a pall over the childhood home, "This embarrassment on my part was a tiny scale model of my father's more fully developed self-loathing. His shame inhabited our house as pervasively and invisibly as the aromatic musk of aging mahogany." [5]

After earning an A.A. degree from Bard College in 1979, Alison went on to earn a B.A. in studio arts and art history from Oberlin College in Ohio. In 1980, she came out to her parents via a phone call while away at college. Their reactions were noncommittal. In reflecting upon this, Alison stated, "In many ways, my life, my professional career, has been a reaction to my father's life, his life of secrecy. I threw myself into the gay community, into this life as a lesbian cartoonist, deciding I was going to be a professional lesbian. In a way, that was all my way of healing myself." [6] Eventually, Alison moved to New York City.

Alison applied to graduate school but was rejected by all she applied to. She moved from NYC to Hadley in Western Massachusetts and then back to NYC. All the while, Alison sketched. Her start as a real live lesbian cartoonist began casually: "I had a series of boring, awful office jobs after I got out of college in 1981, and to while away the time I wrote letters to a friend who was still in school. One day I drew a picture in the margin of a deranged naked woman holding a coffee pot and called it, 'Marianne, dissatisfied with the breakfast brew. Dykes To Watch Out For, Plate no. 27.' Then I drew some more deranged women doing different things, in hopes that one day I really would rack up twenty-seven of them." [7]

In 1983, her first comic strip was published in the feminist newspaper, *WomaNews*, where she also volunteered as a book and film reviewer and did design and layout. The strip was a series of drawings of lesbians writing letters. The women were depicted as they smoked cigarettes, chewed on their pens, contorted themselves, vigorously typed, daydreamed, and chomped on candy. It doesn't take much sleuthing to see the beloved *DTWOF* characters inching their way to the surface in these early drawings.

In 1986, Alison and her girlfriend moved to Minneapolis, Minnesota, where she worked as a production manager for the lesbian and gay periodical *Equal Time* between 1986 and 1990. The same year, she drew "The Amazon's Bedside Companion: A Sapphisticated Alphabet" with such iconic lesbians of dubious distinction as "T is for Tess, at the 4 a.m. feeding" depicting a couple dozing in bed with a suckling baby; "N is for Noelle, who liked to wear leather" of a couple walking hand-in-hand on the beach, one in a swimsuit and the other in full leather gear; "Q is for Queenie, who raced in her chair" with a dyke speeding along in her wheelchair during a marathon.[8]

In 1986, Alison published the first official installment of *DTWOF*, titled "One Enchanted Evening," which introduced overly-analytical Mo and the cavalier Lois discussing Mo's celibacy and included such culturally relevant, queer dialog as, "Lo: Right...what about Naomi from the food co-op. Mo: Are you crazy? I'm way too crushed out! I can't even ask her where the bulghur is without hyperventilating!" [9] Alison explained why she chose to create a lesbian comic, "I didn't think of myself as an activist or a lesbian separatist, though many of my friends were. I just felt the vital importance of seeing an accurate reflection of me and us in the cultural mirror, so I decided to create one." [10] The same year, Firebrand Books published the first collection of *DTWOF*.

It wasn't until 1990 that Alison could move back to NYC, earn enough money with her comics to quit her day job, and devote herself to making art full time. *DTWOF* had become syndicated, picked up nationally by the myriad of gay publications that sprouted up post-Stonewall. *DTWOF* featured a diverse cast of punchy, smart characters and politically relevant commentary while providing joy, gossip, and role models to LGBTQ+ readers nationally. Alison called the strip, "half op-ed column and half endless, serialized Victorian novel."[11]

Alison and her pal Liz Wallace are known for introducing the Bechdel-Wallace Test into popular lexicon. The Bechdel-Wallace Test examines movies using three criteria: (1) it has to have at least two women in it, (2) who talk to each other, (3) about something besides a man. Of course, the Bechdel-Wallace Test can be applied to other media or used intersectionally.

Alison's childhood art influences were Chas. Addams (creator of the Addams Family), the humor magazine *Mad Magazine*, and popular illustrators Norman Rockwell and Edward Gorey. At age twenty-two, Alison read *Gay Comix*, an anthology comic book edited by the late Howard Cruse (Howard Cruse was the creator of *Stuck Rubber Baby*, the amazing graphic novel about coming out during the Southern civil rights movement in the 1960s...read it!). She said that it was seeing Howard's work in *Gay Comix*, along with work by other gay and lesbian cartoonists like Mary Wings, Jennifer Camper, Cheela Smith, and Jerry Mills, that made her realize she could draw cartoons about queer life. As a result, Alison's *DTWOF* exploded into the growing gay rights movement.

Stylistically, Alison's cartoon idols are Hergé, the creator of the charming French comic series *Tintin*, starring boy reporter Tintin, his faithful white Wire Fox Terrier named Snowy, and the well-pickled Captain Haddock, and R. Crumb, founder of the underground comics publication *Zap Comix* and known for his illustrations of women with powerfully strong legs and asses.

In addition to *DTWOF*, Alison has written three graphic memoirs to date, *Fun Home*, *Are You My Mother?*, and *The Secret to Superhuman Strength*. *Fun Home* details Alison's childhood, her coming out, and her father's likely suicide at age 44 when hit by a Sunbeam bread truck. In *Are You My Mother?*, Alison talks about her fraught relationship with her distant mother, all through the eyes of Virginia Woolf and the psychoanalysts Alice Miller and Donald Winnicott. Alison describes *The Secret to Superhuman Strength* as, "It's about physical fitness and...mortality—and that's the hard part, the mortality. It's about what it's like to live in an aging body, knowing you're going to die. The exercise part is like the sugar to make the medicine go down, the medicine being all these big questions of life."[12]

In 2012, *Fun Home* was made into a hit musical which features the butch anthem "Ring of Keys," with its loving observations about butch hair, dungarees, swagger, lace-up boots, and iconic ring of keys attached to the belt. The song is sung by the young Alison character upon spotting a working-class butch in a diner and is based on an experience that Alison had as a child, "We were in Philadelphia...a much larger city than where we lived, and we were having lunch in a diner, and this woman came in—this big, burly woman with short hair and men's clothes—and I was spellbound. My jaw dropped. My father saw me looking at this woman, and he whipped his head around and said, 'Is that how you want to look?' And there was so much going [on] in that exchange. In that moment, I recognized that woman: I identified with her; I wanted her; I wanted to be her. And I knew that that was completely unacceptable."[13] The musical "Fun Home" opened Off-Broadway in 2013 at The Public Theater, then on Broadway in 2015 at Circle in the Square Theatre and was nominated for—and won—numerous awards. The musical moved on to a national US tour and overseas productions. "Fun Home" has won many awards, including five Tony awards and two Obies. There is hope that "Fun Home" may be made into a movie.

In 1996, Alison inherited enough money for the down payment for a 1980s cedar-sided home in rural Vermont, where she and a friend constructed an art studio. At the time, she was living off royalties from *DTWOF* and its accompanying swag. Why Vermont? Alison explained, "In many ways I'm your typical Vermonter—chai-sipping, artisanal-cheese-eating, NPR-listening, Subaru-driving, left-wing-freak-show-who-came-from-somewhere-else homosexual."[14]

In 2008, The last *DTWOF* strip appeared in print, and Alison met her wife-to-be, Holly Rae Taylor, first at a bike swap, then again at the Onion River Co-op in Burlington. They soon moved in together. Alison talked about what her therapist said about Holly, "She said Holly helped me 'cathect' real life, to live in reality instead of in my head and work. Cathect is a crazy psychological term that is the opposite of catharsis, which is the release of energy. Cathexis is taking it in. Relationships are not my strong suit, but somehow it's very important for me to be in one." She continued, "They've been my weak suit because of the family I came from. I grew up in a family where there was no evident warmth or love expressed between my parents. I know that they had a very powerful bond, but mostly saw them fighting and never touching. I had to learn how to do that on my own, and it took a long time."[15]

DTWOF was released as an audio adaptation by Audible in the summer of 2023, with a dyke-o-licious soundtrack by the likes of Joan Jett, Faith Soloway, Holly Near, and Sweet Honey in the Rock, and voicework by LGBTQ+ stars including Jane Lynch, Robert Colindrez, Carrie Brownstein, Roxane Gay, and Jenn Collela.

Alison Bechdel lives in rural Bolton, Vermont with Holly, an abstract artist, botanist, and compost maven, and their cat Donald. Holly and Alison collaborated on *The Secret to Superhuman Strength*, with Holly doing the coloring. Alison's papers are kept at the Sophia Smith Collection of Women's History at Smith College in Northampton, Massachusetts.

Alison is the humble recipient of several awards, including an Eisner Award, a MacArthur Fellowship, a Guggenheim Fellowship, and a Stonewall Book Award. In 2017, she was named the Vermont Cartoonist Laureate.

Alison Bechdel

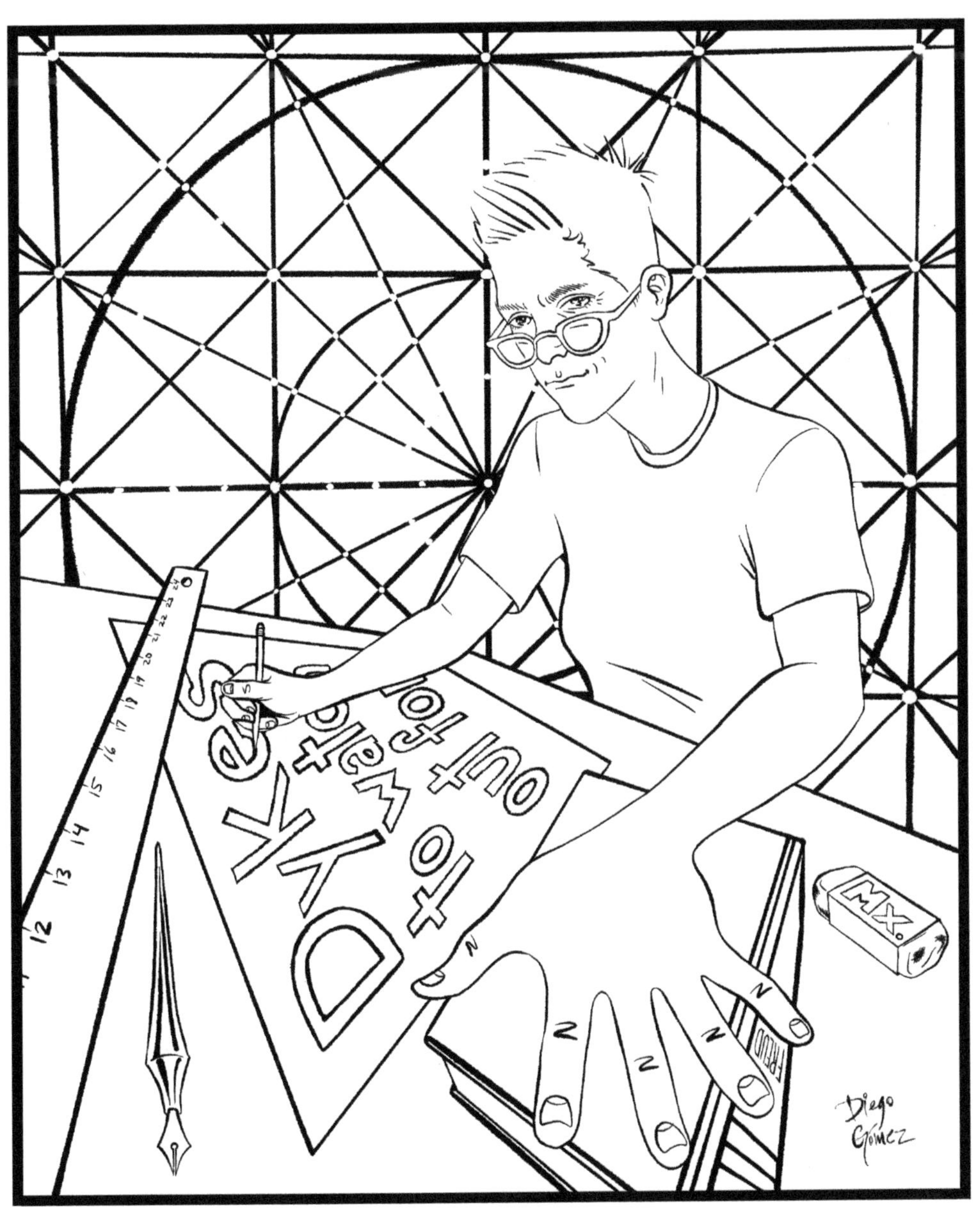

drawn by Diego Gomez

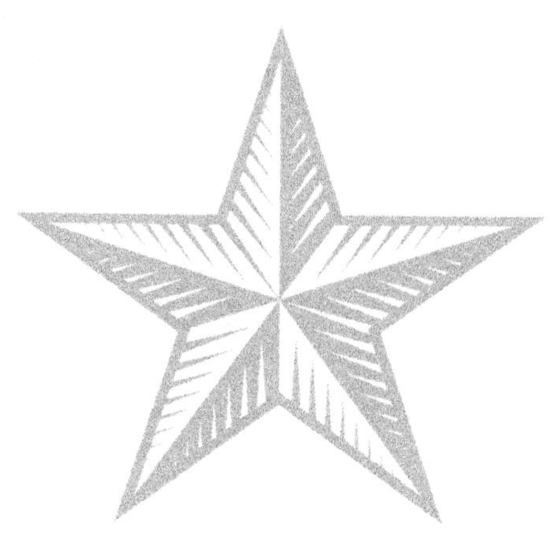

Gabby Rivera

b. September 1, 1982 · USA
drawn by Jessica Bogac-Moore

So much of the Evangelical Christianity that I experienced growing up was about making sure women knew their place. Women had to be obedient to their husbands and let them lead the house. You know all that stuff. And of course the real deep homophobia, sex-shaming, and rigid rules about gender presentation. Women wear skirts and men wear suits etc. All that stuff that's designed to keep everyone in place cuz apparently, God can't handle it otherwise.[1] –Gabby Rivera

Gabby Rivera is a queer Latina writer, poet, teacher, LGBTQ+ youth activist, and comic artist. Gabby's pronouns are she/her, and her identities include loverboi, nerd, and Butch Tia.

Gabby was born and raised in the Bronx, New York City. Her mother was a kindergarten teacher, her father was a salesman for Cafe Bustelo Coffee, and her family are Pentecostal Evangelicals. Although she loved attending church as a child, her feelings shifted as she got older. Gabby was a tomboy, the church disapproved of her masculine ways, and she prayed to be delivered from lesbianism every night. Her mother warned her that being a lesbian was not an option. When she came out, her mother was unhappy, "Coming out to my parents was insane. I thought God was going to strike me dead as the words came out of my mouth. My dad was cool, but my mom flipped like it was the end of her world. The world that had me as a straight woman that would give her grandkids. I also thought God would just turn his back on me. I asked him through prayer every night to take my life, seeing as though I was a deviant homosexual. God never took my life. And so I viewed that as a sign to carry on."[2] Eventually, her mother evolved into acceptance with the help of being exposed to more gay folks, specifically when she had a Black gay couple that had a son in her classroom.

By age 17, Gabby was reading at the iconic and award-winning Nuyorican Poets Café open mics. The Nuyorican Poets Café has been operating since 1973. It provided a platform for POC writers, playwrights, poets, and musicians whose work was rejected by the mainstream and White academic, entertainment, or publishing industries.

Gabby's award-winning debut novel, *Juliet Takes a Breath,* is about a NYC Puerto Rican baby dyke discovering herself during a summer internship with a White feminist writer in Portland, Oregon. Gabby describes Juliet as "someone who is thick-bodied, a little nerdy and pretty queer and still totally confident."[3] *Juliet Takes a Breath* is semi-autobiographical, "I was 19 in the early 2000s, right? When I was coming out during this time, I was very much a part of white lesbian circles and trying to understand what is a Tegan and Sara and an Ani DiFranco. And, like, what is this world? And we didn't have gay marriage yet....I never in my mind would have imagined that I would be out and talking about my book and talking about me as an artist in this way. I wasn't in the closet, but I just imagined that the way that queerness sometimes is like a secret society, that I would always be in my secret society."[4]

In talking about her process of finding herself as a Puerto Rican queer butch, "There were moments in my life where I have aligned myself with white lesbian feminists. And all of that was super good, and there was a lot of uplifting in our queerness and coming together. And then, when racist shit would happen, these chicks would scatter. Or there would be some gaslighting. We're, like, so and so didn't really mean it. And you got to understand where they're coming from, instead of addressing the harm that their racism actually enacted on all of us. And when you start to see that kind of shit, when you start to see, for lack of a better term, you start to see bitches acting funny like that. It really makes you reevaluate who you are aligning yourself with. And I was pushed to find more of my own people, I was pushed in the best way to read Audre Lorde, I was pushed in the best way to read books like *Queer Brown Voices*, talking about LGBTQ Latinx activists from the 40s, 50s, and 60s, and really finding the root of where my people are, people [that] have been doing this work. And it is a work that will actually continuously show up for who I am at all times."[5]

In 2017, Gabby became the first Latina to write for Marvel Comics with the *America* (America Chavez) series published by Marvel, drawn by Joe Quinones, and starring a lesbian Latina superhero. Although Gabby knew nothing about writing comics, she hit the ground running when Marvel made their offer to her. She said, "I had never written a comic before, and I was momentarily overwhelmed, but also Trump had just been elected. So in my mind I was like, well, if I take any inspiration from him is that you don't have to have any experience to do the thing that you want to do....So why should I hold myself back from this opportunity? I slap that impostor syndrome so quick just smacked it right down."[6] Gabby made America Chavez into a superhero, but also accessible—goofy and relatable, not just tough like so many Latino characters. Gabby says of America Chavez and the comic, "It's important to talk about the intersecting identities and her being queer and Latina...but so much of content around people of color is centered in oppression or political conversations."[7]

In the summer of 2017, Heather Antos, an assistant editor at Marvel, posted a selfie of a group of female co-workers on social media. This drew the ire of members of an alt-right group called #comicsgate, who strongly opposed the comic book industry's efforts to include more women, BIPOC, and LGBTQ+ characters in their work. Gabby became the recipient of a frightening online harassment campaign from men at #comicsgate. They took their homophobia, sexism, and anger out on Gabby by doxing her, sending threats, and harassing her at speaking engagements. Gabby became so disillusioned that she considered not writing more comics, but then reconsidered: "What really saved me and turned all of this into big love was when I went into individual comic books shops. I shut off the internet, I shut off Twitter for a year." [8]

In 2019, Gabby released the first of a Young Adult (YA) graphic series through BOOM! Studios about a 15-year-old named b.b. and her best friend, Chulitast, titled, *b.b. free and the plague that ate greed.* Post-plague and eco-dystopian, "*b.b. free* is a bouncy love letter to queer kids everywhere, especially the chubby Puerto Rican ones." [9]

Gabby is a strong advocate for queer youth, happiness, creativity, and telling one's authentic story. In a talk titled "Writing your Heritage is Radical Creativity," she was passionate about youth, "So for me, part of the disruption is I am gonna put folks that mean the world to me in my work. These references, Sonia Sotomayor, please tell me do y'all know who Sonia is? Can we give it up for the first Puerto Rican Supreme Court justice from the Bronx?" Gabby continued, "We are important. Why not put Sonya in that place [America Marvel comic] and if you read the comic and you kind of see it a little bit here, she's a hologram. She is a giant rogue hologram that welcomes students from all across the galaxy into school to learn. And to me again, this is disruption. This is also life-changing. This also saves lives. The more faces and stories that you include in the work that you do, the examples of people's magic out in the world. You are saving lives. There's no other way to put it out there again." [10]

Gabby started thinking deeply about joy when we faced the agony of Trump's election in 2016, "Joy is interesting because I never had it as a personal concept. I think I understood happiness, that I could be happy if I caught the train at the right time and made it to work on time and had a good lunch. I could feel happy. You know what I mean? But joy as deep-rooted radical politics, and spiritual practice. That is something that I have been working on in the last ten years or so," Gabby continued, "So for me to see him become president. I was just, wow, this is the dupe of the century. This shyster. This con man from birth has just swindled the country. And I saw the devastation and people everywhere riding the subway that morning when he was elected. It was fucking silence. People were devastated and pissed. And what I noticed was when I was traveling for my work, gigs, talking to students, talking to teachers, talking to librarians, talking to corporate leaders, that people were gutted. This started during the Muslim ban. Then he started talking about the wall. Then all the White folks started coming out of the woodworks with their White supremacist protests and their tiki torches. And people in my circles were [this is] a fucking scam...I'm scared because he called Mexicans this. I'm scared because he's rallying the white people. I'm scared because everything that I believed in that would keep me and my family safe is ready to crumble. And it was this circle of commiserating. And it was killing me. I could see it draining people. And I started asking folks, yo, what brought you joy this week? Because I need some joy," she continued, "In my whole life, no one has ever asked me about joy, and my joy, and how they can help me experience more joy. And so that's when it really started to take off for me, that this was something not only that I needed, but that I could in my own way offer to others and invite people into the conversation right? So with the Joy Uprising podcast, I talk to queer and trans people of color and our ally supporters." [11]

Gabby Rivera lives in Oakland, California, with her partner and their child. Gabby loved being pregnant, "For all the body shaming people have thrown my way over the years for being chubby, butch, and free, I've always loved my body. I love my soft belly, thick thighs, and perfect magic delicious *tetas* 😁😁😁🥰🥰. And growing a tiny human inside of me has just made me fall in love with my body all over again. I am body and fortress, Altar, and infinite universe. I'm safe within myself, and my baby is safe within me." [12]

She was a silver medalist in the 2017 Independent Publisher Book Award for *Juliet Takes a Breath*, and *America* was a nominee for the 29th GLAAD Media Awards for Outstanding Comic Book. She was a keynote speaker for the 2017 Butch Voices Conference. Gabby was given a 2017 NBC Out #Pride30 innovators award. She is a 2022 Sundance Screenwriters Fellow.

Gabby Rivera

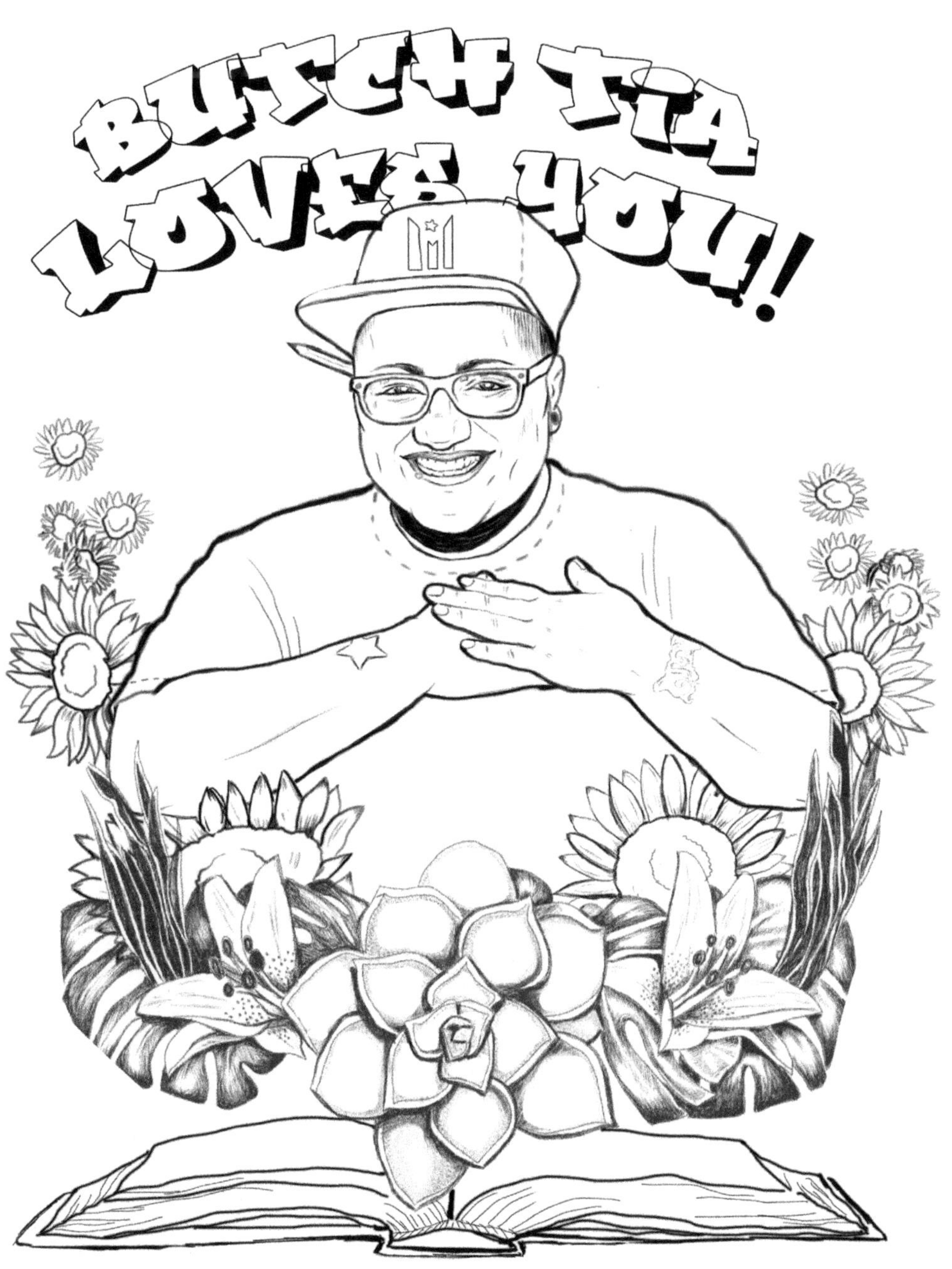

drawn by Jessica Bogac-Moore

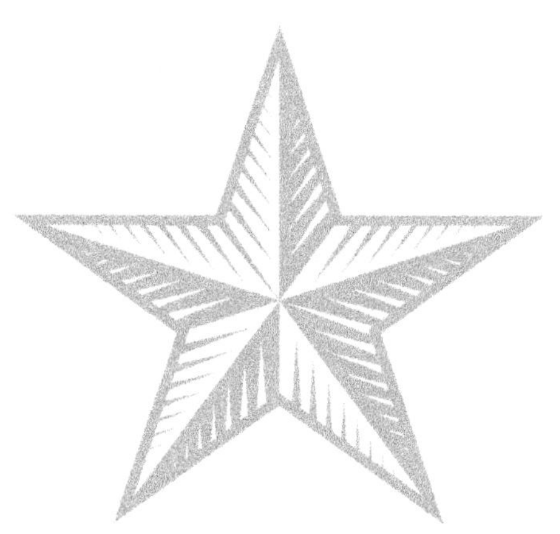

Storme Webber

b. 1969 · USA/Sugpiaq (Alutiiq), Black, and Choctaw
drawn by Burton Clarke

There's a lot of imagination [needed] to place ourselves in places where people lived. A lot of poor people don't have archives—archives have been reserved for the powerful, and people were forced to be in hiding at times, so it became a habit to consider [keeping records] dangerous.[1] –Storme Webber

Storme Webber is a Two-Spirit writer, artist, educator, poet, and curator. Descended from Sugpiaq (Alutiiq) women with origins in Seldovia, Alaska, and from Black and Choctaw men from Texas and Louisiana, Storme grew up in Seattle, Washington.

Storme was born in Seattle's Skid Row, now renamed Pioneer Square. In the beginning of the 20th century, the neighborhood was the home to Blacks, Indigenous people, working-class families, Chinese immigrants, and LGBTQ+ folks. Her parents met at a neighborhood bar, The Casino, a combination pool hall, dance club, and gay bar. Her mother was a lesbian and a descendant of the Sugpiaq (Alutiiq) people of Seldovia, Alaska, and her father was a drag-wearing, Black Choctaw bisexual from Texas.

Until she was 11 years old, Storme was raised by her maternal grandmother, Maxine. Maxine was Sugpiaq and originally from Seldovia, Alaska, but moved to Seattle when she was eight years old. Maxine taught Storme to read before she started elementary school and installed in her a love of music, storytelling, and the arts, singing along to Billie Holiday, Dakota Staton, and Ray Charles. At age 11, Storme left her home due to family problems, spending the rest of her childhood in the foster system. Storme was academically and artistically advanced, which earned her a full scholarship to the prestigious private Lakeside School.

Storme came out as a lesbian at age 16. In a burst of teenage activism, Storme started a social group for Black, Indigenous, and people of color (BIPOC) lesbians. Although her mother had also come out as a teenager, she was distraught with the news that Storme was a lesbian, fearing that she would have a hard life and suffer from homophobia. Storme explained her mother's fears, "When [my mother] was younger, the police would raid the gay bars, and they would beat everyone. I am thankful for all the change. Sometimes the things that can be our burdens can be our blessing, too. I am a Black Indian Two-Spirit. There have been instances everywhere I turned where I've not been enough something."[2] Storme's grandmother was not fazed when Storme came out to her, "I was going to the Michigan Women's Music Festival and a friend of mine was coming to pick me up, but I'll rewind back to the other part. So I came in one day and I said, 'Grandma, how are you doing?' And she said, 'Hmm, everybody comin' out.' She had a Texas accent. It was so beautiful and very slow. I said, because this was the time of Ellen [DeGeneres] coming out on nationwide television, so I thought this is my chance because I hadn't come out to my grandmother, and I said, 'Grandma, you always know when people are gay, don't you?' And she said, 'Um-hum.' And she answered real fast. She was just sad, kind of startled, you know? Then I said, 'Well, did you know I was gay?' And she said, 'Hmm, I knew since you knew.' So that was that. There was no judgment. There was no shaming. She just was totally accepting. And then a funny thing happened is that a friend of mine came to drive me to the airport to go to the festival and grandma grabbed on to her hand and grabbed onto my hand—she was about 89 then—and she held both of our hands, she looked into our eyes, and she said, 'Now listen, I don't usually get involved in young folks cotin' [courting], but I just want to tell you one thing. I don't judge you. I don't judge you because when I die, God ain't gonna ask me what you did.'"[3]

In 1977, Storme graduated from Lakeside, then relocated to the East Coast, attending The New School in New York City (NYC) where she earned a B.A. She then earned her M.F.A. from Goddard College in Plainfield, Vermont. After graduating, Storme moved back to NYC, where she became involved with the art and performance scene, showing in national galleries and publishing erotica and poetry. In 2007, Storme founded Voices Rising: Northwest LGBTQ Artists of Color, with a mission to nurture and provide community to BIPOC artists, producing events that involved mentoring, bringing in emerging artists with established artists into each show, and encouraging support and the sharing of knowledge.

In 2017, Storme curated a documentary exhibit called "Casino: A Palimpsest" for the Frye Art Museum in Seattle. The show documented The Casino and Skid Row with historical artifacts, along with Storm's family memorabilia and poetry, but its meaning went deeper. The exhibit of the now gentrified neighborhood was important historical documentation, "As with a palimpsest, on which writing that has been erased remains visible under new script, the historical documents in this exhibition reveal some of the many histories that lie beneath Seattle's streets. Beginning in the late 19th century, saloons, bars, and diners on Seattle's Skid Row (present-day Pioneer Square) provided a haven for poor folks, lesbian mothers, urban and displaced Indigenous people, gay servicemen, working girls, hustlers, achnucek (two spirits), butches, femmes, drag queens, and the city's working class, long before the creation of 'safe spaces' for LGBTQ people. Establishments such as the Double Header, the Busy Bee Café, and the Casino—all located near the corner of South Washington Street and Second Avenue South—provided refuge for many, including Webber's own family. In a city where history is vanishing daily, Webber's work stands as a corrective witness, seeking to restore narratives that have been lost in the evolving myth of Seattle." [4]

Storme spoke about growing up in the neighborhood with her family, "By the time I spent time there, and this was the 1960s, it was a bar and grill, and it was a gay bar. I think of being in these spaces as a child was somewhat like a child artist's residency. I learned about how people made community when they were considered outsiders. I learned how people could love one another and care for one another, even under oppressive situations. I learned how delicious Filipino food is. I learned about the ways in which people are soulful that help them to survive." [5]

Storme continued as she described a family snapshot in the exhibit called "Our American Dream" (1963/1964) of her femme lesbian mother, her mother's butch girlfriend, her newborn baby sister, and herself gathered together on the bed and feeding the baby, everyone pleased and happy. Storme commented, "*This is a family portrait* [italics added by this author for emphasis]. Our country is in a moment of great challenge and great opportunity. [This photo] holds hope for us. I would hope that that would be something that would be useful about images like this, because it's a very uncommon image, and also sometimes when LGBTQ history is presented it's presented to us all White, and often all middle-class and often all-male." [6]

Art in America critic Minh Nyguyen, wrote of the show, "Rather than erect divisions between personal art and historical archives, 'Casino' considered the intangible properties by which art and poetry are connected to family, ancestry, language, and public memory, revealing intergenerational, underground histories of resilience." [7] Storme's performance pieces have toured internationally and include "Buddy Rabbit," "Noirish Lesbiana: A Night at the Sub Room," and "Wild Takes of Renegade Halfbreed Bulldagger." She has toured England, Ireland, Germany, and the Netherlands with her poetry.

Storme is deeply involved with education, creativity, and the indigenous community, attending Two-Spirit gatherings nationally and creating workshops. She describes her work as cross-genre, "incorporating text, performance, audio and altar installation; archival photographs and collaboration in order to engage with ideas of history, lineage, gender, race, and sexuality." [8]

When asked by Afuwa Granger of *Kindling* how her Indigenous identity influences her artistically, Storme replied. "Well, I read something lately from

Ma-Nee Chacaby. I'm not sure if I'm saying her name right, but she's a wonderful writer from there in Canada. A Two-Spirit Elder and I read her book when I was doing one of those residencies up at Banff. And she said something that really was resonant for me, and she said that the role for Two-Spirit people is to keep the fire going in the village. I feel like there's a connection between making art and our family and our community, and it should be something that is healing, inspiring, helps people as we struggle against all the things that we're struggling against at the moment. You know, we've just come out of four-year despotic rule, but we're not free; we're still struggling so much against fascism and racism and all the oppressive forces that are so frightened of us becoming the majority of the world. Of course, we've always been the majority of the world. They are just sort of catching onto it. So I would say it affects me in that way that I feel that it is not just for me, it is something for community. It is something that should be of service."[9]

In 2014, Storme published *Blues Divine*, a self-described ancestral mix tape which combines a book of poetry with an audiobook read by Webber. Storme describes the book and mixtape as, "These poems have been creative salvations, signposts, people's history, and testimonies. Inside is a journey of many intersections and switchbacks, fast-running rivers and swamplands, as well as those sacred places where sun splits the sky wide open."[10]

In 2022, Storme, along with six other Black-Indigenous women artists, exhibited her work in the Smithsonian Institution's National Museum of the American Indian's first exhibit to feature Black-Indigenous women artists, "Ancestors Know Who We Are." Focusing on issues of race, gender, multiracial identity, and intergenerational knowledge, some of the show is also available online.

Storme lives in Duwamish territory in Seattle, Washington.

Storme has received numerous grants and awards, including being named a Seattle Living Legacy for building global awareness of the LGBTQ+, Indigenous, Two Spirit, and Black populations of Seattle through her art in 2019, a grant from the Raynier Institute & Foundation for her show at the Frye Art Museum in 2017, and the James W. Ray Venture Project Literary Award in 2015.

Storme Webber

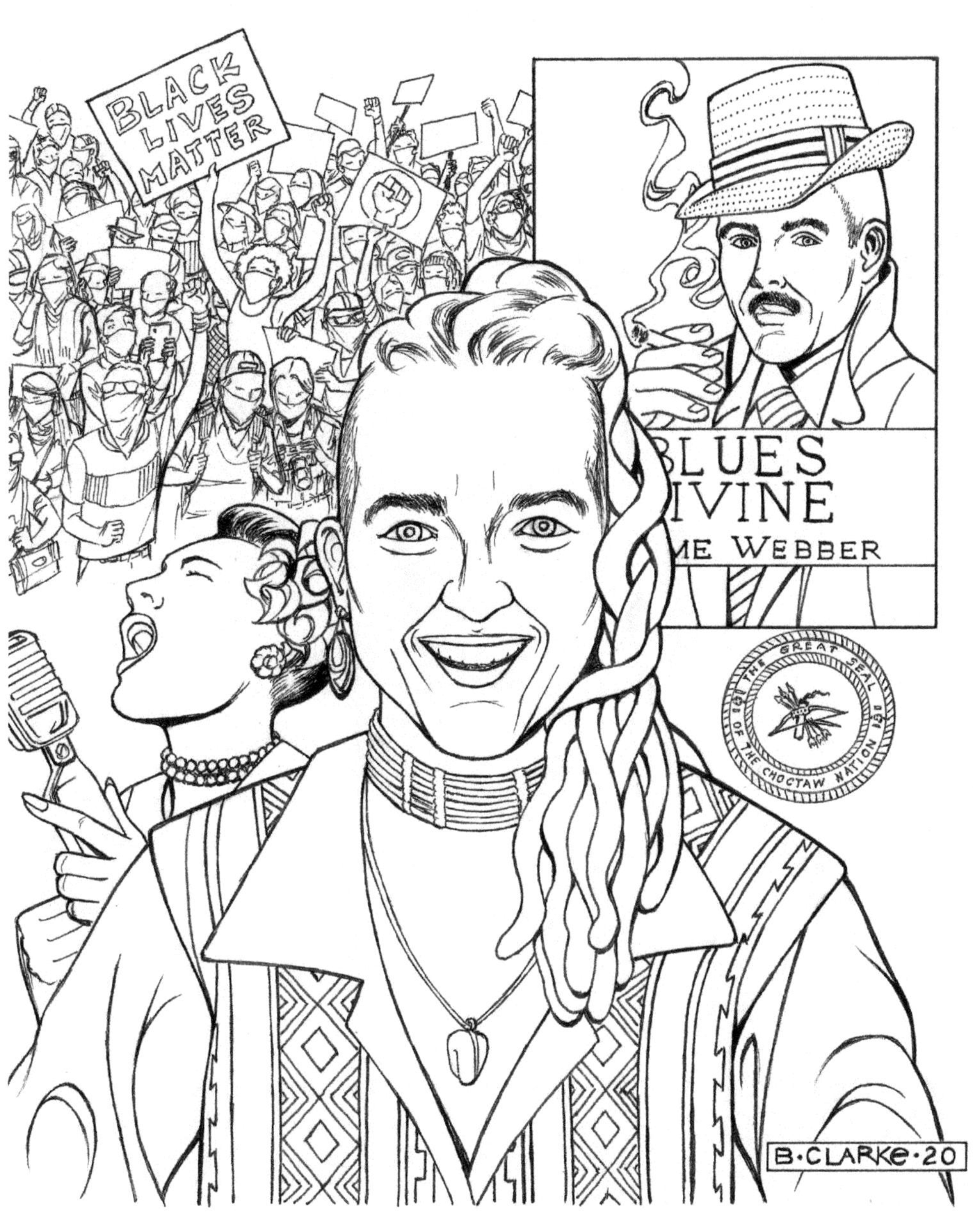

drawn by Burton Clarke

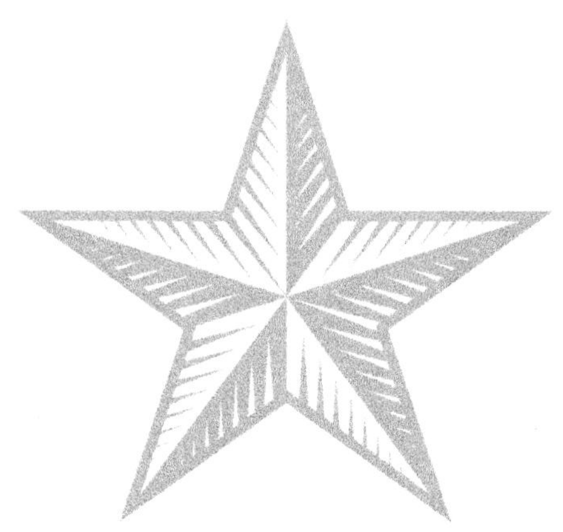

ATHLETES

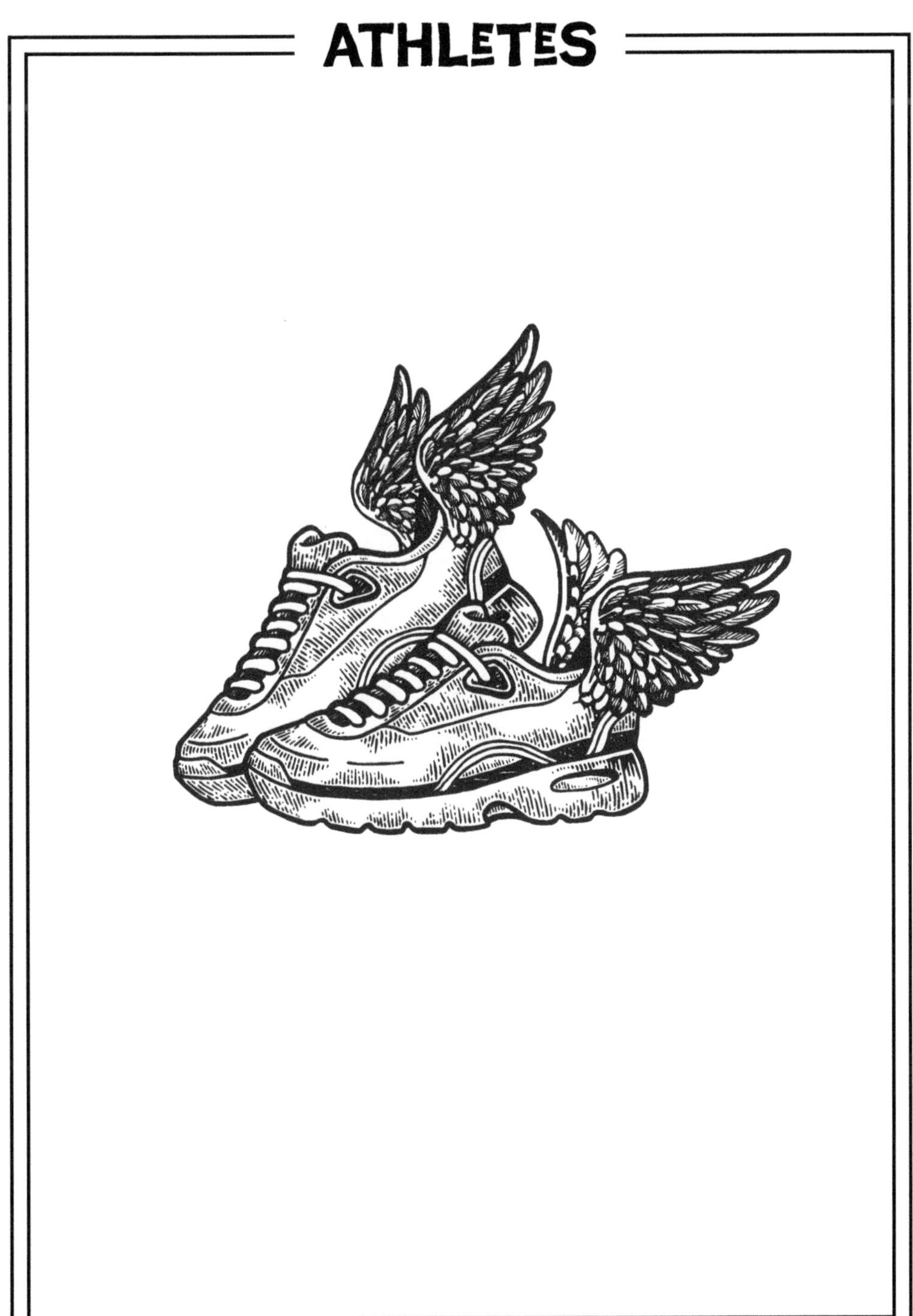

Brittney "BG" Griner

b. October 18, 1990 · USA
drawn by M Rocket

I think that's a big reason why a lot of people go overseas. That's why I was there. As much as I'd love to pay my light bill for a love of the game, I can't.[1] –Brittney "BG" Griner

Brittney Griner is a basketball player for the Phoenix Mercury of the Women's National Basketball Association (WNBA) and an activist. In 2022, she was a political prisoner in Russia.

BG was born and raised in a close-knit family with two sisters and one brother in Houston, Texas. Her mother, Sandra, is a homemaker who enjoys cooking and crafting, while her father, Raymond, is a Vietnam veteran and a deputy sheriff. As a child, she was a lanky tomboy. She learned to fix cars with her father and altered the Barbie dolls that her mother bought her by cutting off their hair and painting them green and black. She was incessantly bullied in school for her lack of femininity, deep voice, flat chest, and height. BG quickly developed a tough veneer, along with intense anger at the world. Her father was distrustful of outsiders. BG explained what it was like growing up: "At first I would ask my dad for permission to join them: 'Can I go to my friend's house?' And he would quickly say no, without even really considering it, his voice like a rock dropping. 'I don't know anything about that family,' he would tell me. 'They could be killers.' He actually said this; that's how much he distrusted other people and wanted me to learn to do the same."[2]

BG came out as a lesbian when she was a high school freshman to her mother's acceptance and love, but she was hesitant to come out to her father because she feared his anger. When she finally came out to him as a high school senior, he was livid, telling BG, "You can pack your bags and get the fuck out!"[3] He eventually threw her out of the house, and BG spent the next seven weeks living at her assistant coach's home. However, her father has since come around and has become supportive, saying that he now understands that BG wants to be accepted for who she is rather than who he wanted her to be.

In 2009, BG started attending Baylor College, a strict Baptist-affiliated school, chosen so that she could work with Olympic gold medalist Kim Mulkey. BG didn't realize the extent to which she would be required to remain officially closeted by her coach and while at Baylor. Kim advised BG to tone it down: to hide her tattoos, delete any Twitter posts containing references to her girlfriend or LBGTQ+ issues, and remain closeted to not hurt recruitment at the college. BG told ESPN, "It was a recruiting thing. The coaches thought that if it seemed like they condoned it, people wouldn't let their kids come play for Baylor." [4] BG met her wife-to-be, Cherelle, at Mooyah Burgers on the Baylor campus when BG accidentally grabbed Cherelle's milkshake; however, even though BG was immediately blown away by Cherelle, they didn't start dating until years later.

After graduating from college, BG was selected by the Phoenix Mercury during the 2013 WNBA draft. She started her career with the team with two dunks in a game against the Chicago Sky, breaking WNBA records for the number of dunks in one game. BG continued playing for the Phoenix Mercury and garnered numerous awards as the years progressed.

In 2013, BG was cornered, along with two of her teammates, during a *Sports Illustrated* interview conducted by Maggie Grey. Although Maggie had been told explicitly that BG's sexuality was off limits during the interview, she went there anyway under the innocuous guise of asking why it was easier for female athletes than male athletes to come out. After the interview, BG got blow-back on social media about being a lesbian, but she also received support. A week later, BG was visiting Waco, Texas, at the same time President Obama was there for a memorial service for victims of a deadly fertilizer plant explosion. The EMTs were in BG's neighborhood and spotted her. As BG described it in her book, "One of the stations seemed to have a number of gays and lesbians on staff, and a man came up to me and started thanking me. He was almost crying. He told me my 'coming out' was going to make things better. He also told me there was a local church that was giving him a hard time for being gay," she continued, "I thought 'Okay, what I'm doing really does matter. I'm helping in some way.'" [5]

In 2014, BG accepted an endorsement proposal from Nike, making her the first openly gay athlete with a Nike endorsement deal and perhaps the only female athlete where it's written into their contract that they can model clothing intended for men. Nike was ecstatic to have BG represent them, telling ESPN, "It's safe to say we jumped at the opportunity to work with her because she breaks the mold," [6] and BG was just as overjoyed that her style and butchness were recognized and valued. "I want to print that quote and put it on the wall! For a company like Nike to say that I'm breaking the mold! I was extremely happy. I'm not the only female that wears men's clothes, so I'm not one in a million. But someone told me I was kinda pioneering it—for it to be okay, to be accepted." [7] BG praised both Nike and the WNBA for creating an atmosphere where being LGBTQ+ was more acceptable in professional sports, "It is easier now; 10 years ago it wasn't easy to come out.

I remember going to a game and it wasn't a friendly atmosphere. Now you see lesbian families, gay families, with the pride nights—I give a lot of credit to the WNBA. I want to see what is next and what we're going to do." [8] BG also published her memoir that year, *In My Skin: My Life On and Off The Basketball Court.*

The same year, BG became engaged to fellow player, Glory Johnson. It was a turbulent relationship, resulting in both women being arrested on charges of assault and disorderly conduct before their wedding. The marriage was brief but long enough for the couple to have twin daughters. They divorced in 2016. BG and Cherelle had remained friends over the years and started dating. In 2018, GB proposed to Cherelle, and a year later they married.

In 2020, in response to the murders of Black people at the hands of the police and specifically Breonna Taylor, who'd been killed just months before, BG protested the playing of the national anthem, "The Star-Spangled Banner," before games and stated she would not be on the court while the national anthem was played during game openers. She also wore Breonna's name on her uniform to pay her respects. BG said, "We don't get asked enough what's going on in our communities, and I think that's a shame. Yeah, we're here to play basketball. But basketball doesn't mean anything in a world where we can't just live. We can't wake up and do whatever we want to do. Go for a run, go to the store to buy some candy, drive your car without the fear of being wrongfully pulled over. I just want to challenge everybody to do more. Write the story that might be tough. Take a chance. Ask a question that's tough. Don't let it be silent." [9]

Like nearly half of WNBA players and many female professional athletes, BG played off-season to supplement her income to come closer to male professional athletes' income. Sexism in professional sports affects many things, including pay scales, with women in the WNBA earning between $60,000 and $229,000 annually, while men playing in the National Basketball Association (NBA) earn upward of $40 million annually. Female athletes also were more highly regarded in Russia, receiving the amenities and resources men receive in the US, but that women do not. For instance, men in the NBA fly to games on luxurious chartered flights, while women in the WNBA fly Economy Plus, although that may be changing. It's hard to imagine 6'8" BG with her long legs flying in the cramped seats of economy class. BG had been playing with the Russian UMMC Ekaterinburg team for several seasons and was fond of her teammates in Russia, as they were of her.

The US issued a "do not travel" advisory for Russia on January 23rd, 2022, prior to Russia's invasion of Ukraine on February 24th. On February 17, BG was detained by Russian customs officers for having THC vape cartridges that her doctor had prescribed for pain management. After several detainment extensions, BG went to trial, explaining to the court that she'd been recovering from COVID-19, accidentally packed the vapes in her luggage, and had no intention of breaking Russian law. BG was sentenced on August 4th to nine years in a remote penal colony, even though the average sentence for Russians was five years, and many defendants were granted parole. All the while, the Biden administration was negotiating with Russia for BG's release. On October 25th, she lost an appeal to reduce the excessively harsh sentence, and in November, she was transported to IK-2 female penal colony in Yavas, a penal colony that was unusually barbaric, even by Russian standards, with routine brutality, torture, beatings from the staff, lack of medical care, and rampant malnutrition. On December 8th, BG was released to US soil in exchange for a Russian arms dealer, thanks to President Biden's negotiations.

When BG was returned to the US from Russia, Cherelle sobbed as GB descended from the plane. Cherelle described their reunion after BG's arrest and imprisonment in Russia, "The first night, we didn't sleep at all. We just talked all night long and all morning. And it was so good to be able to do it without three weeks in between the conversation because for 10 months we were passing letters. It was great to have that dialogue back and forth."[10] In 2023, BG and Cherelle marched together in Phoenix, Arizona's Martin Luther King Day parade, happy to be home and reunited.

During BG's first WNBA game after her return from Russian prison, BG stood for the US national anthem, "One thing that's good about this country is our right to protest. You have a right to be able to speak out, question, to challenge, and do all these things. [After] what I went through, it just means a little bit more to me now. I was literally in a cage and could not stand the way I wanted to...and a lot of other situations. Just being able to hear my national anthem, see my flag, I definitely wanted to stand."[11]

BG and Cherelle live together in Phoenix, Arizona. Cherelle holds a Juris Doctor degree, having graduated with honors while BG was imprisoned in Russia. Prior to studying and practicing law, she was a math teacher. BG is playing with the Phoenix Mercury in the 2023 WNBA season.

BG earned two Olympic gold medals in 2016 and 2021 and is a six-time WNBA All-Star. In 2014 and 2018, BG won the FIBA Women's World Cup with Team USA. She holds the NCAA record for dunks in a career, with 18 total dunks. In 2021, she was included as one of the WNBA The W25.

Brittney Griner

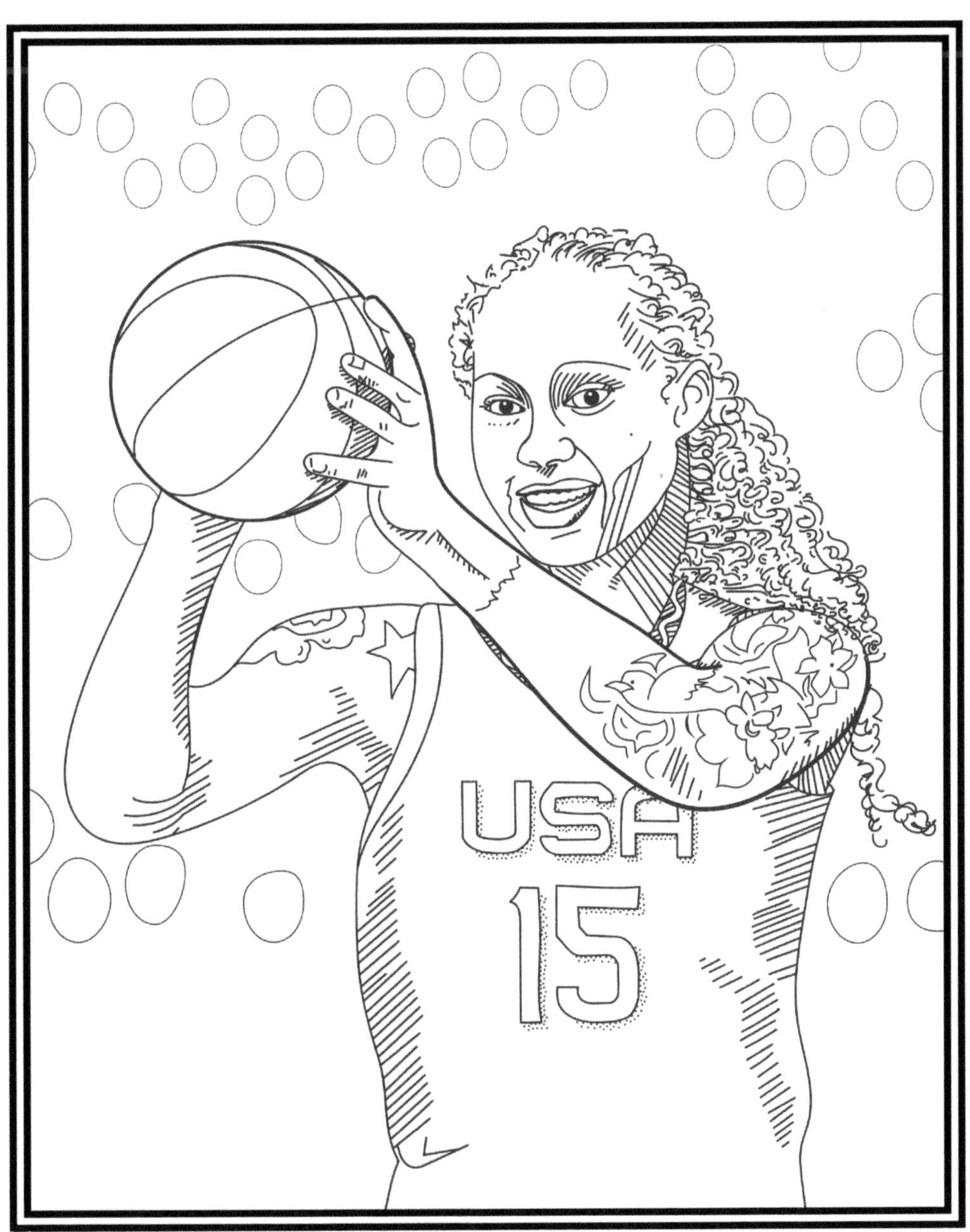

drawn by M Rocket

Amélie Mauresmo

b. July 5, 1979 · Saint-Germain-en-Laye, France
drawn by Soizick Jaffre

His death [her father's] really changed me. You look back and realize that the priorities are the ones you love—family, friends. But on the other hand tennis helped me to get over it, to focus on something else. To survive the grief and get my life back. Some times were easier than others, but it made me grow up faster than anything else.[1] –Amélie Mauresmo

Amélie Mauresmo is a French tennis player, surfer, motorcycle lover, wine aficionado, muscular lesbian idol, and runner.

Amélie was born in the suburbs of Paris, France, to Francis and Françoise Mauresmo. Her mother was a homemaker, and her father was an engineer in a paint factory; however, neither parent was athletic. Amélie was a tomboy as a child, playing sports and running around. In 1983, 4-year-old Amélie watched Cameroonian-French tennis player Yannick Noah win the French Open, and she set her sights on learning to play tennis. Her parents enrolled her in lessons, and after four years, she joined a local tennis league.

Amélie came out as a lesbian at age 19, early in her tennis career. She was distressed about how she handled coming out. Years later, she confessed, "It was tough. It was hard. I have never regretted the fact that I came out, but I do regret how I said it. It was too brutal. I could have done it in a much easier way. [Being gay] was no big deal for me. But I didn't realize what a huge story it was going to be."[2]

During the same time period, she started seeing her first girlfriend, Sylvie Bourdon, a Saint Tropez restaurateur who ran a tennis bar called *Le Gorille* (The Gorilla) and was ten years older than Amélie. Her parents did not react well to the news that Amélie was a lesbian and did not approve of Sylvie. They stopped speaking to Amélie, and they remained estranged for several years, only reconciling just before her father's death from cancer in 2003.

Amélie didn't lose sponsorships when she came out the way Martina Navratilova did in 1981. Notably, she was the first lesbian tennis player to come out without losing any major sponsors; however, she quickly faced homophobia from other players. Amélie's girlfriend was cheering her from the stands at the Australian

Open semifinals in 1999. An opponent at the semifinals, German player Martina Hingis, was asked whether Amélie played differently than she did a year previously before coming out. Martina sneered and cattily replied, "She's here with her girlfriend. She's half a man."[3] Later, Martina tried to defend herself by maintaining that her comment referred to Amélie's muscular body, her strength, broad shoulders, strong one-handed topspin backhands, and powerful shots rather than her lesbianism. Others in the world of tennis were more supportive, and she received a long encouraging message from Martina Navratilova.

Academics Pamela Forman and Darcy Plymire discussed Amélie's muscular, butch body in an article in *Women's Studies Quarterly* titled "Amélie Mauresmo's Muscles: The Lesbian Heroic in Women's Professional Tennis," calling her a "butch hero" for coming out as a lesbian while butch and muscular, thus fitting specific stereotypical butch lesbian attributes. The press supported Amélie during the fallout, but tennis fans were disdainful, mocking Amélie's strength and muscles, "Honest to God, I watched the final and saw her for the first time...and surely this IS a man? Seriously! Her shoulders, her walk, her 'gate' [sic], her face! Her chin! Her swing and her HANDS! Does tennis have sex tests like women's athletics [track and field]? Because I think there's something 'fishy' going on here." [4] At that moment, Amélie was a tennis racket swinging, powerful, brawny gender trouble icon, and the mention of her large hands was the clincher, pointing to her obvious lesbianism. The confluence of well-developed muscles and gender caused confusion for fans. Pamela and Darcy maintained that "this move domesticates and trivializes the butch hero, enclosing her within the boundaries of a niche market and thereby containing the threat of lesbian sexuality and identity."[5]

The media joined her detractors in lampooning her for her looks, with a popular French satirical television show creating a puppet with a woman's head on top of Arnold Schwarzenegger's body combined with the words, "It's the first time in the history of French sport that a man says he is a lesbian."[6] Amélie was handsome, not pretty, more broad-shouldered and square-jawed than was considered acceptable for a woman. She wore practical, brightly-colored tennis attire rather than more feminine clothing, rebuking many currently held stereotypes for female athletes.

Amélie retired from professional tennis in December 2009. In early 2010, she was honored with a special video retrospective of the highlights of her career during the GDF Suez Open tournament. Amélie's mother joined Amélie, former and current members of the women's tennis tour, and other celebrities for the salutary ceremony.

After retirement, she broke new ground when she started coaching leading Scottish male tennis player Andy Murray in 2014. She was the first female tennis

Amélie Mauresmo

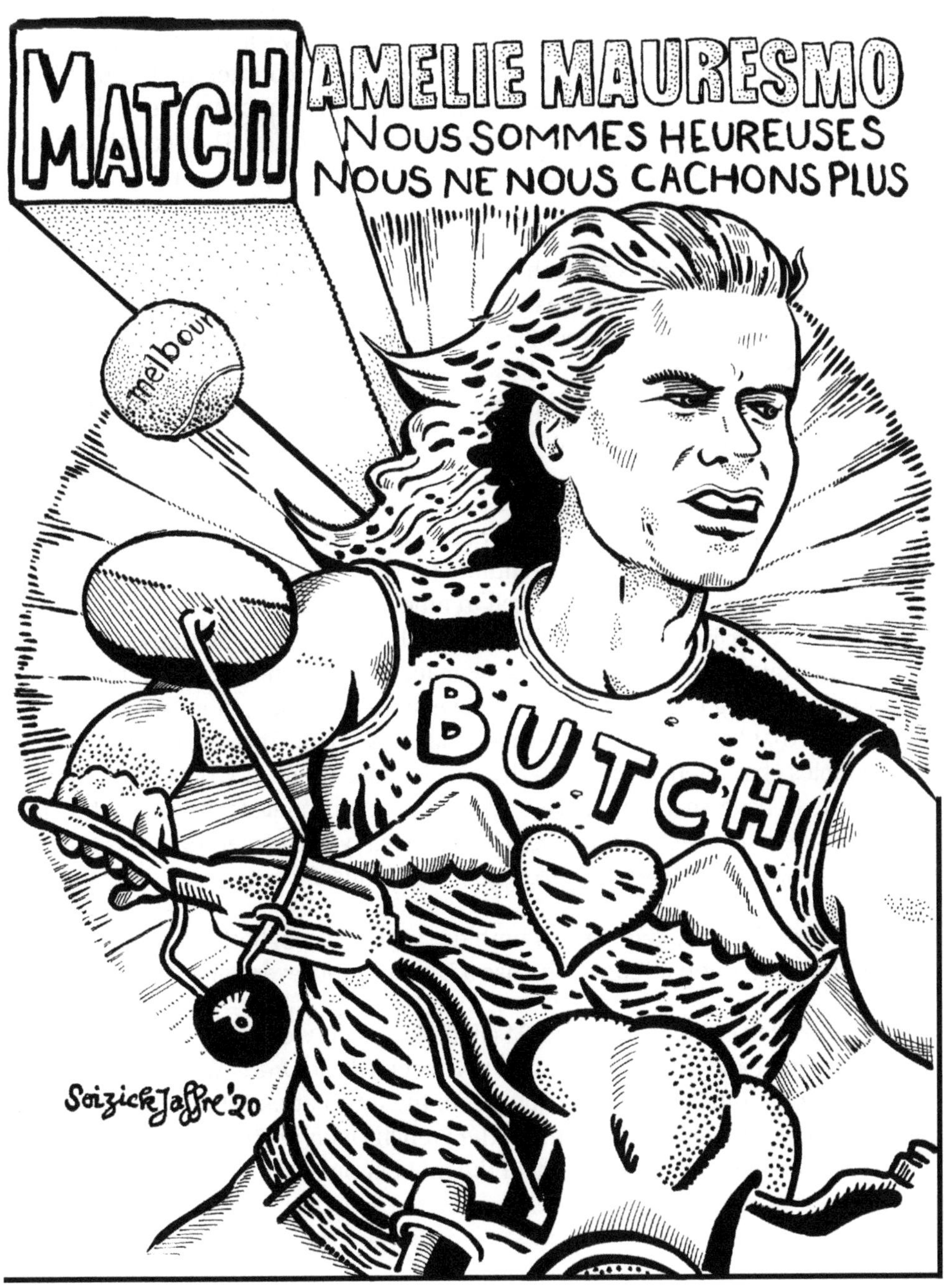

drawn by Soizick Jaffre

player hired to coach a male tennis player by a woman outside his immediate family. It wasn't much better in women's tennis. Shockingly, at this time there was only one top 50 player on the women's tour that had a woman coach. Andy was surprised by the degree of misogyny and criticism that exploded from within the tennis community for a woman coaching a man. Andy's mother, who was a Scottish tennis coach and British Fed Cup Team Captain, countered, "I think it's really important that there are more female coaches in tennis. We need role models to give younger female coaches inspiration and belief. They certainly have softer skills than male coaches. They are probably better listeners and there is less ego with women than men." [7]

In 2019, Amélie was hired as a coach by French player Lucas Pouille. By then, the decision to hire a female coach was not as outrageous to tennis fans as it was in 2014. When criticized about his choice to hire Amélie, Lucas said, "A lot of people have asked me: 'Is it different that she's a woman? What do you do—can she come in the locker room?' But what is important is what's happening on court, what's happening to get ready for the match, and what happens after the match. I don't care who is in the locker room." [8]

In 2021, Amélie was hired as the director of the French Open. In 2022, Amélie took some heat for her choices when scheduling for the French Open tournament when she scheduled only one women's match to nine men's matches for the widely watched night sessions. Amélie defended her choices, saying, "In this era that we are in right now, I don't feel—and as a woman, former women's player, I don't feel bad or unfair saying that right now you have more attraction, more attractivity—Can you say that? Appeal?—for the men's matches." [9] Pam Shriver, a 22-time Grand Slam doubles champion, retorted, "Why did she have to insult women's tennis? It really hurts to have an alumni player, who's now a tournament director, who made history as a female coach of a top men's player, really diss women's tennis the way she did. Her words today were inexcusable for a leader." [10]

Amélie lives in Geneva, Switzerland with her two children, both born after she retired from professional tennis. She has a Labrador retriever named Spinee.

Amélie won a Silver Medal at the 2004 Olympics, won two Grand Slam titles—the Australian Open and Wimbledon—in 2006, received the *Ordre National de la Légion d'honneur* in 2007, was accepted into the International Tennis Hall of Fame in 2015, and was named the director of the French Open in 2021. She has almost twenty tournament titles and has held the number one ranking of the Women's Tennis Association.

Caster Semenya, Order of Ikhamanga

b. January 7, 1991 · South Africa
drawn by Phoebe Kobabe

This fight is not just about me; it's about taking a stand and fighting for dignity, equality and the human rights of women in sports. All we ask is to be able to run free as the strong and fearless women we are!! Thank you to all of those who have stood behind me.[1] –Caster Semenya

Caster Semenya is an award-winning Olympic athlete. A middle-distance runner, she has won several gold medals for her strength, agility, and speed. Caster is an intersex, cisgender, assigned female at birth (AFAB) woman with XY chromosomes and naturally higher testosterone levels. Her testosterone levels, masculine running gear, muscular build, deep voice, unshaved armpits, and natural athletic talents caused an uproar in the world championships community, leading people to question whether she should be allowed to compete with other women.

Caster is originally from the small town of Ga-Masehlong, South Africa. Caster traveled to a nearby village to live with her grandmother, Maphuthi Sekgala, when she was young and grew up in a home without running water or electricity. A tomboy, Caster enjoyed running and soccer and was teased by her conservative, rural classmates for her boyish mannerisms and attire. Her school principal said, "I have never seen her in a skirt or dress, always trousers. Initially, we doubted her gender, but eventually we realized she's a girl. We've seen her birth certificate and her file from primary school. At about the age of 16 she started to associate with other girls and try different hairstyles. But she never developed breasts."[2]

Caster won several medals in 2009. She broke national records running in the African Junior Championships and won a gold medal in the 800-meter World Championships. She was named the 2009 Number One Women's 800-meter runner of the year by *Track and Field News*. There were cries that she had won unfairly. In the same year, the organization World Athletics (IAAF) forced Caster to take a gender verification test, claiming that she won by unnatural means. Her family stood behind Caster when the IAAF demanded that she undergo the test, defending her against claims from the organization that she was not all woman. Her mother scoffed at the authorities, "If you go to my home village and ask any of my neighbors, they would tell you that Mokgadi [Caster] is a girl. They know because they helped raise her. People can say whatever they like, but the truth will remain, which is that my child is a girl. I am not concerned about such things."[3] Her father said much of the same, "She is my little girl. I raised her, and I have never doubted her gender. She is a woman, and I can repeat that a million times. For the first time, South Africans have someone to be proud of, and detractors are already shouting wolf. It is unfair. I wish they would leave my daughter alone," [4] and her grandmother was just as indignant, "I know she's a woman—I raised her myself. She called me after [the heats] and told me that they think she's a man. What can I do when they call her a man when she's really not a man? It is God who made her look that way." [5]

Confirmation that muscular female professional athletes are actually women has gone through several iterations in the last few decades. In the early 1940s, the International Olympic Committee (IOC) had countries swear that their female athletes were indeed women. In 1966, they demanded that female athletes disrobe and undergo a genital inspection, nick-named the "nude parade." In the late 1960s, this changed to a chromosome test, with several notable female athletes being disqualified due to atypical results. After pressure and years later, they stopped testing all female professional athletes; however, they still performed a chromosomes test when they deemed a woman was too muscular or masculine, followed by a hormone test, a gynecological exam, and a psychological evaluation if they felt there were any additional doubts. In 2011, the International Association of Athletics Federations (IAAF) decided to stop using the nebulous terminology "gender verification" or "gender policy," but would test for "hyperandrogenism" (high testosterone). Women with higher testosterone levels would be barred from competing unless they underwent hormone therapy and, if necessary, have their undescended testes surgically removed. Several women agreed to the testes removal surgery, and in some cases, it included a clitoral reduction in order for their clits to appear smaller and more womanly. Women's natural testosterone levels are typically .12–1.79 nanomoles per liter of blood, while men's natural testosterone levels are typically 7.7–29.4 nanomoles per liter of blood. Under the IAAF rules, female athletes must keep the natural testosterone level under 5.0 nanomoles per liter through Hormone Replacement Therapy (HRT).

Caster talked to reporters about what went on behind the scenes before and after an exam discovered that she had internal testes and after she took hormone therapy medication to lower her testosterone levels so she could run in competitions: "They thought I had a penis. I told them, 'It's okay. I'm a woman. I don't care. If you want to see that I'm a woman, I'll show you my vagina. Do you agree?' That medication made me sick. It made me gain weight, I had panic attacks, I didn't know if I was even going to have a heart attack. It's like stabbing yourself with a knife every day. I had no choice. I was 18, I wanted to run, I wanted to get to the Olympics, it was the only option for me." [6] Despite the horrific side effects, Caster continued to take the medication for several years before she confronted the IAAF.

Shocked that the IAAF ordered gender testing for Caster, South Africans accused the IAAF of racism and imperialism. "Such comments can only serve to portray women as being weak," said the African National Congress (ANC) in a statement. "Caster is not the only woman athlete with a masculine build and the International Association of Athletics Federations should know better," and urged all South Africans to "rally behind our golden girl and shrug off negative and unwarranted questions about her gender."[7] Her coach, Michael Seme, said, "Then she has to explain that she can't help the fact that her voice is so gruff and that she really is a girl. The remarkable thing is that Caster remains completely calm and never loses her dignity when she is questioned about her gender."[8] Although she was cleared of any doping or wrongdoing and retained her medal, these issues continued to plague her.

In 2018, the IAAF announced new rules concerning Differences of Sex Development (DSD). Now, athletes that were competing in the 400m, 800m, and 1500m runs and had specific disorders of sex development, higher testosterone levels, and particular androgen sensitivity were required to take medication to lower their testosterone levels. It appeared that Caster was being singled out and punished by the IAAF for her masculinity. Two months later, Caster legally challenged the new ruling, stating, "I am a woman and I am a world-class athlete. The IAAF will not drug me or stop me from being who I am."[9] Dr. Eric Vilain testified that "sex is not defined by one particular parameter...for many human reasons, it's so difficult to exclude women who've always lived their entire lives as women—to suddenly tell them 'you just don't belong here.'"[10] Unfortunately, Caster lost that round, but she continued to fight in the courts.

In 2019, Caster appealed the decision to the Federal Supreme Court of Switzerland and lost again. She filed an appeal with the European Court of Human Rights in February 2021. Caster said, "I hope the European court will put an end to the long-standing human rights violations by the World Athletics against women athletes. All we ask for is to run free, for once and for all, as the strong and fearless women we are and have always been....This fight is not just about me, it's about taking a stand and fighting for dignity, equality, and the human rights of women in sports. All we ask is to be able to run free as the strong and fearless women we are!! Thank you to all of those who have stood behind me."[11]

As of this writing in March 2023, all female athletes with higher testosterone levels and a difference in sex development must reduce their blood testosterone to below 5.0 nmol/L for at least six months and then maintain the lower level of testosterone during their athletic career in order to compete in events from 400 meters to a mile. Caster retorted, "I am very disappointed to be kept from defending my hard-earned title, but this will not deter me from continuing my fight for the human rights of all of the female athletes concerned."[12]

Disallowed from competing as a professional runner, Caster joined the South African SAFA Sasol Women's League football (soccer) club JVW F.C. It is unknown when she will play her first game.

Caster has married fellow runner Violet Raseboya twice, once in a traditional ceremony in 2015 and also in a glamorous second wedding in 2017. They have two children that were conceived through IVF. Caster is writing a memoir tentatively titled *Silence All the Noise*, with an anticipated release date in the autumn of 2023.

Caster has won numerous gold medals, including the Olympics in 2012 and 2016; the World Championship in 2009, 2011, and 2017; Commonwealth Games for 800 and 1500 meters in 2018; African Games in 2015; African Championships in 2016 and 2018 in 400 and 800 meters; and the Continental Cup in 2018.

The British magazine *New Statesman* included Caster in its annual list of "50 People That Matter" in 2010 for unintentionally instigating "an international and often ill-tempered debate on gender politics, feminism, and race, becoming an inspiration to gender campaigners around the world." [13] Caster was chosen to carry South Africa's flag during the opening ceremony of the 2012 Summer Olympics. Caster was named one of *Time* magazine's 100 Most Influential People of 2019 for making a singular historical contribution to our understanding of biological sex. She was awarded the 2012 South African Sportswoman of the Year Award. In 2018, the bronze Order of Ikhamanga was bestowed on Olympic runner Caster Semenya by President Jacob Zuma, who stated, "In this class we honour our celebrated athlete Mokgadi Caster Semenya, who stood firm and resolute against prejudice and went on to become an Olympic gold medalist," [14] and described her as "one of the most well-loved daughters of the soil who won hearts of many by making running look like poetry in motion." [15]

Caster Semenya

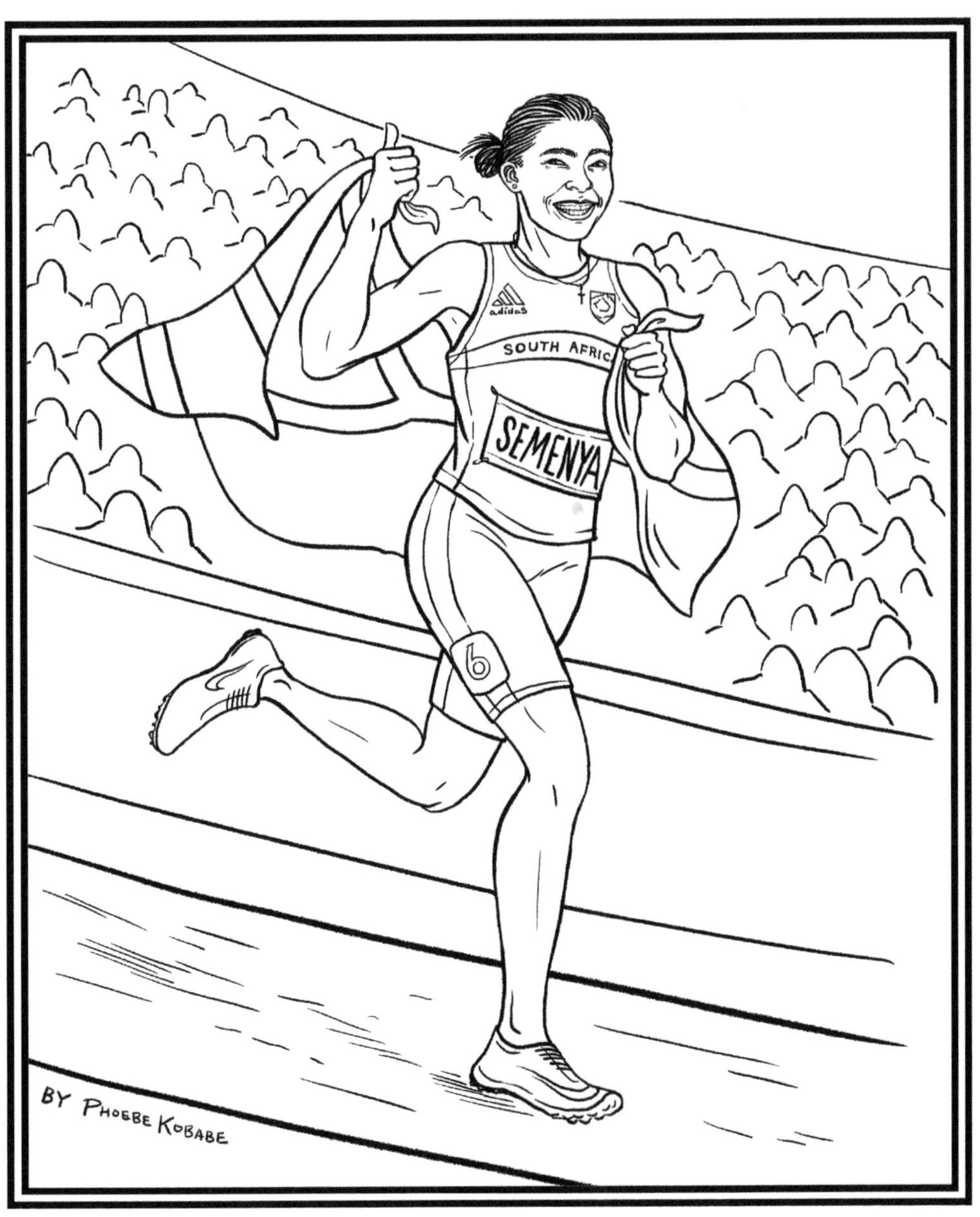

drawn by Phoebe Kobabe

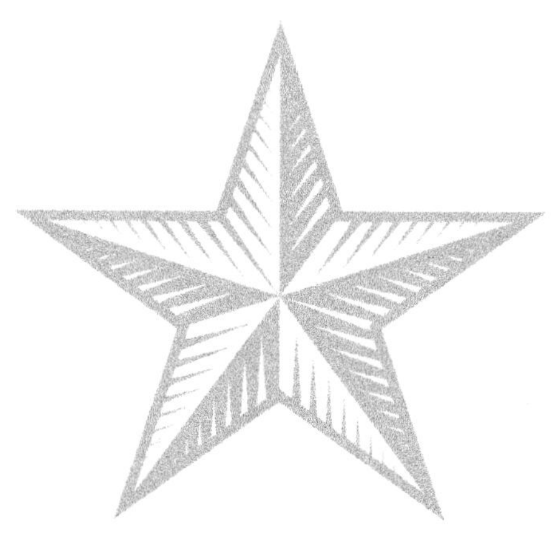

Martina Navratilova

b. October 18, 1956 · Czech-American
drawn by Soizick Jaffre

I mean, it's shocking. It's still the good old boys' network. And you know and at the bottom line is that male voices are valued more than women's voices. Overall it was a shock because John McEnroe makes at least £150,000 [$210,000 US]. I get about £15,000 [$21,000 US] for Wimbledon, and unless John McEnroe's doing a whole bunch of stuff outside of Wimbledon, he's getting at least 10 times as much money. It adds up over a lifetime, it adds up to an extraordinary amount of money. So it's extremely unfair and you know, it makes me angry for the other women that go through this.[1] –Martina Navratilova

Martina Navratilova is a champion tennis player. Czech-American, she once confessed that she feels more like an American than a Czech.

Martina Navratilova was born in Prague in the former Czechoslovakia (now the Czech Republic) and holds a dual Czech-USA citizenship. Martina's parents, Jana and Mirek, divorced when she was a toddler. Mirek committed suicide several years after the divorce, and a few years later, her mother married the man who would become Martina's first tennis coach. Athleticism ran in the family; her father was a professional ski instructor, her mother was a gymnast, tennis player, and ski instructor. Martina's grandmother, Agnes Semanska, was a player for the Czechoslovakian Federation before WWII, and Martina was skiing at age two.

Martina played tennis for the first time around age six or seven. She wrote in her autobiography, "I remember the first time I played tennis on a real court. The moment I stepped onto that crunchy red clay, felt the grit under my sneakers, felt the joy of smacking a ball over the net, I knew I was in the right place. I was probably about six years old when that happened, but I can remember it as if it was yesterday."[2]

Martina won the Czechoslovakian national championship at age 15 in 1972 after playing tennis for only eight years. She started playing professionally when she turned 18 in 1975, playing the French Open. Left-handed Martina played professionally, with an all-time women's winning record of 167 singles championships, and was ranked No. 1 in the world for seven different years, including consecutively from 1982 to 1986. She has won 18 Grand Slam singles titles, along with 31 doubles and 10 mixed doubles titles. She retired from professional tennis in 2006 at the age of 49.

Fellow champion tennis player, friend off the court, and rival on the court, Chris Evert said of Martina's abilities, "Martina revolutionized the game by her superb athleticism and aggressiveness, not to mention her outspokenness and her candor. She brought athleticism to a whole new level with her training techniques—particularly cross-training, the idea that you could go to the gym or play basketball to get in shape for tennis. She had everything down to a science, including her diet, and that was an inspiration to me. I really think she helped me to be a better athlete. And then I always admired her maturity, her wisdom and her ability to transcend the sport. You could ask her about her forehand or about world peace and she always had an answer. She really is a world figure, not just a sports figure." [3]

Matina defected to the United States of America after competing in the 1975 US Open, meeting with lawyers, FBI agents, and the Immigration and Naturalization Service in her hotel room on Manhattan's Lower West Side. She says, "I was so stubborn, so independent, that I was more American than Czech, even as a little kid. I didn't feel I belonged anywhere until I came to America for the first time when I was 16. I'm not a mystic about many things—I tend to be pretty pragmatic about life—but I honestly believe I was born to be American." [4]

Although Martina was one of the first international athletes to come out to the media and the public as gay, the timing was nonconsensual. In 1981 Martina and tennis player Billie King were outed in the same month. Martina was outed when she told a reporter that she was bisexual but asked him not to write about it because she was afraid it would interfere with her pending US citizenship application and was concerned that the Women's Tennis Association (WTA) could lose an Avon sponsorship if they knew she was gay. At the time of her outing, Martina was living openly in Virginia with lesbian writer and horsewoman, Rita Mae Brown. Being publicly LGBTQ+ was uncommon in the early 1980s, and people often faced severe legal and personal repercussions. After being outed, Martina ended up losing $12M in sponsorships and had to design her own tennis clothes because she couldn't find a brand to dress her.

Despite being outed as gay ten years earlier, eventually some companies courted the outspoken tennis star as a spokeswoman. In 1991, Subaru launched the first national advertising campaign aimed at lesbians, and in 2000 Martina and fellow champion athletes Juli Inkster, Meg Mallon, and Diann Roffe-Steinrotter became spokeswomen for the iconic lesbian-favored cars, with the playful voice-over, "What do I know about performance?" and then at the end of the advertisement with a smirky "What do we know? We're just girls?"[5] As one Subaru focus-group participant put it, "Martina Navratilova is a spokesperson. What more do you want?"[6]

In 2018, Martina publicly called out the British Broadcasting Cooperation (BBC) in an interview for the show, "Panorama: Britain's Equal Pay Scandal" as they investigated why women are still being paid far less than men, even nearly 50 years after the passing of the Equal Pay Act, which theoretically prohibited any less favorable treatment between men and women regarding pay and employment conditions. Martina was furious once she discovered the hothead tennis player John McEnroe was paid three times what she was paid.

This pay discrepancy between women and men continues to be a significant problem in professional sports, however, confronting the issue with anger, facts, and if necessary, legal action can affect changes. In 2019, the US Women's National Soccer team filed suit against the US Soccer Federation, winning a lump sum and promising to pay women's and men's national senior teams equally. Like many of her colleagues in the Woman's National Basketball Association (WNBA), professional basketball player Brittney Griner, an eight-time WNBA all-star and winner of two Olympic gold medals, supplemented her income by playing overseas during the offseason and earning a significant amount of income playing for the Russian team, UMKC Ekaterinburg. The quick and dirty difference between the National Basketball Association (NBA) and the WNBA average player salaries is $5.3 million a year versus $130,000 a year.

In 2019, Martina criticized trans women competing against cis women in professional sports in an article in *The Sunday Times*, "Simply reducing hormone levels—the prescription most sports have adopted—does not solve the problem. A man builds up muscle and bone density, as well as a greater number of oxygen-carrying red blood cells, from childhood. Training increases the discrepancy. Indeed, if a male were to change gender in such a way as to eliminate any accumulated advantage, he would have to begin hormone treatment before puberty. For me, that is unthinkable,"[7] and at the same time acknowledging that there are exceptions, "[cis woman with hyperandrogenism and runner, Castor] Semenya, [trans woman and tennis player, Renée] Richards and many others have been subject to vilification, ostracism and the awful human inclination to identify anyone who is different and start a witch hunt. I had problems of that kind myself when I came out as gay in 1981, and it hurt terribly."[8] After facing a storm of blowback for her statement, Martina apologized to the LGBTQ+ community and made a documentary with the BBC called *The Trans Women Athlete Dispute with Martina Navratilova*, where she met and discussed trans women in sports with athletes, trans women, and scientists. She was contrite, "What I have come to realize, the biggest thing for me, is just the level of difficulty trans people go through cannot be underestimated. The fight for equality and recognition is just huge. I hurt people with my comments—that bothers me. I campaigned all my life for LGBT rights."[9]

A lesbian icon, Martina has frolicked through pop culture. Phranc wrote and recorded a tender homage to Martina, titled "M-A-R-T-I-N-A," and Martina appeared in the show *Portlandia* as a Yelp reviewer of the fictional bookstore Women & Woman First, invoking the ire of bookstore owners Toni and Candace.

Martina met her girlfriend, the Russian model and actress Julia Lemigova, at a Parisian gay bar in 2006. They started dating eight years later and got married in New York City in 2014. Martina has two stepdaughters with Julia, and the couple lives with five cockatoos, including a parrot named Coco. After being treated for breast cancer in 2010, Martina's breast cancer reappeared in 2023, along with HPV-related throat cancer. She is currently being treated for both cancers. She is active with organizations that work for the rights of animals, children, and LGBTQ+ people.

Martina has garnered a mountain of honors. In 2000, she received a National Equality Award from the Human Rights Campaign, and in 2003 she received the BBC Sports Personality of the Year Lifetime Achievement Award. In 2013 she was inducted into the National Gay and Lesbian Sports Hall of Fame.

Martina Navratilova

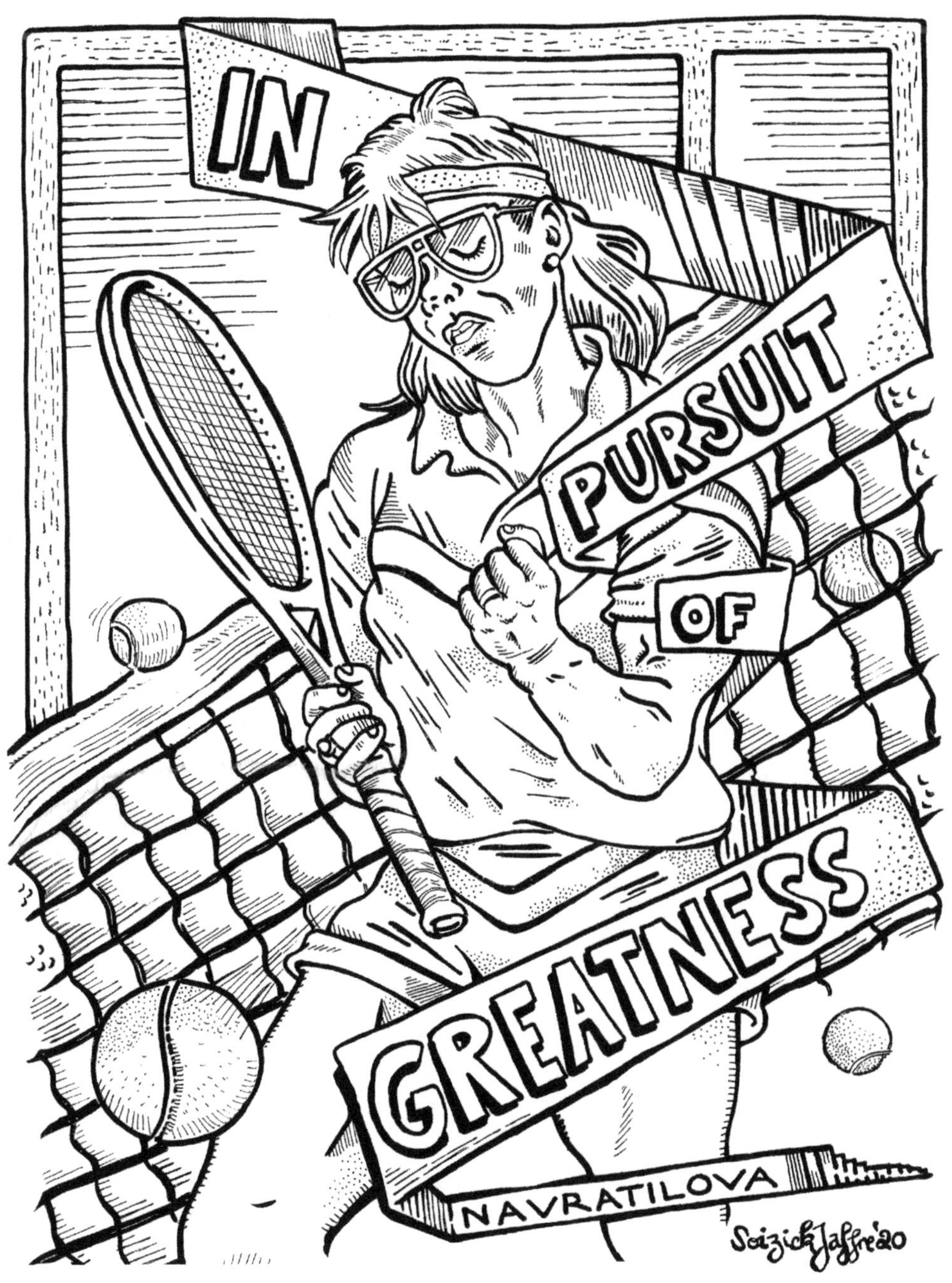

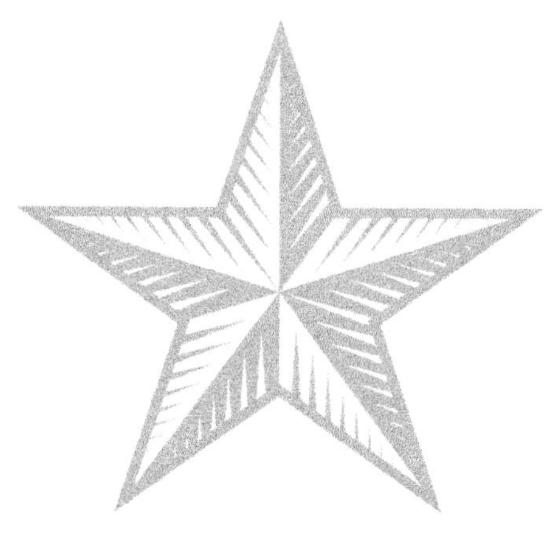

FILMMAKERS

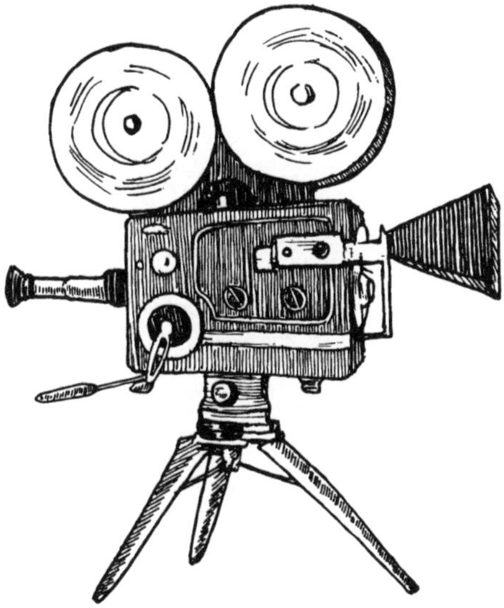

Jenni Olson

b. October 6, 1962 · USA
drawn by M Rocket

I always say that telling butch stories or the butch experience is one of the most important things to me. Not just as a person, but also as a queer film historian, I've always had the sense of the importance of seeing ourselves on screen. In terms of butch representation, there is just so little out there. To see ourselves on screen is pleasurable and validating...there's not a strong enough word to say how valuable and important it is. It makes us feel less alone, and those kinds of representations, especially in cinema, help us connect with others and community.[1] –Jenni Olson

Jenni Olson is a butch queer writer, archivist, LGBTQ+ film historian, film curator, consultant, activist, and experimental filmmaker. Over the years, most of her films have been fundamentally informed by her perspective as a butch lesbian.

Jenni was raised in Falcon Heights, Minnesota, a suburb of St. Paul. Her mother was a professor of political science, and her father was a veterinarian. Her stepfather was an usher at the local Varsity Theater, and Jenni loved classic Hollywood films, even as a child. James Cagney, Buster Keaton, The Marx Brothers, and Fred Astaire were some of her favorite actors, and she had a fondness for Spaghetti Westerns, imagining herself as the heroic cowboy. Jenni talked about how movies were a lifeline as a child, "Growing up in the Midwest, as a gender dysphoric tomboy. Watching movies was a cherished relief from the awkward realities of daily life. Emulating the actors in my favorite Hollywood films, I happily acquired a new borrowed masculine persona. Experiencing myself as a fictional character has been a mode of survival for me ever since."[2]

Jenni started attending the University of Minnesota in the early 1980s, and eventually came out in 1986 when she devoured the classic book, *The Celluloid Closet: Homosexuality in the Movies*. It changed her life. The same year, Jenni co-founded a LGBTQ+ film series called Lavender Images, later rechristened as the Minneapolis/St. Paul Lesbian, Gay, Bisexual and Transgender Film Festival. At the same time, Jenni started collecting LGBTQ+ film memorabilia such as posters and press kits.

In 1991, Jenni graduated from the University of Minnesota with a degree in film studies. The same year, Jenni met her wife-to-be (now ex-wife), international LGBTQ+ human rights advocate Julie Dorf at Creating Change, the annual conference of the National Gay and Lesbian Task Force, but they did not start dating at that time. By 1994, they had fallen in love with one another.

In the early 1990s, Jenni moved to San Francisco where she applied for and got the job of guest curator at the legendary Frameline Festival in San Francisco, the *crème de la crème* job for queer film curators as it is the oldest and largest LGBTQ+ film festival in the world. It was the birth of New Queer Cinema with young LGBTQ+ directors producing shorts, features, and documentaries. It was a mere three years before Cheryl Dunye's *The Watermelon Woman* was released, and despite the deadly AIDS epidemic that started decimating gay folks in San Francisco in the early 1980s, the city was a vibrant LGBTQ+ oasis.

In the early 1990s, Jenni started curating and compiling her vintage, LGBTQ+ 35mm film trailers into curated presentations leading to *Homo Promo* (1993), *Jodie Promo*, and *Neo Homo Promo*. *Trailer Camp* and *Bride of Trailer Camp* followed. She worked with Karl Knapper to produce *Afro Promo* (1997), a compilation of trailers from Black films of the 1940s to the early 1970s. *Trailers Schmailers* (1997) documented Jewish people in films utilizing trailers from the 1930s to the 1990s. The evolution from curating LBGTQ+ trailers to curating trailers from other marginalized groups was a natural progression, "Recognizing the importance of gay films for gay audiences, I also became interested in the general under-representation of so many other audiences/identity-based groups, and have always been interested in unearthing historical representations of those groups for contemporary audiences."[3]

After watching *Massillon* (1991), a coming-of-age documentary movie that takes place mostly in the depressed Rust Belt city of Massillon, Ohio, directed by William E. Jones and filmed as a landscape with a voiceover, Jenni decided that she wanted to go beyond curating movies and also wanted to produce them, specifically 16mm, urban landscape, voiceover essay films. Another film influence for Jenni was the documentary *Sherman's March* (1986), directed by Ross McElwee, which started out as a documentary about Sherman's March through Georgia and the Carolinas but evolved into a rambling, hilarious narrative on life, love, futility, religion, General Sherman, and the Cold War. Her early shorts include *Sometimes*, *Blue Diary*, and *Meep Meep*. This led to several full-length films, including *The Joy of Life* (2005) and *The Royal Road* (2015). Her feature-length films are all written as poetic first-person accounts focusing on butch identity and longing. In these essay films, Jenni engages with themes of butch identity, a central focus of her work as a writer-director and a unique perspective that queer academic Tina Takemoto has described as "a butch poetics."

Jenni also started writing books about LGBTQ+ films, including the chapter, "Butch Icons of the Silver Screen" in *Dagger: On Butch Women*, where Jenni offers up her reflections on the history of butch characters in cinema ranging from the tomboys of the 1970s and 80s to masculine lesbians of 1990s cinema. She also talks about her beginnings as a curator of LGBTQ+ films, "I wanted to see the films Vito [in *The Celluloid Closet*] wrote about. Not just on video in the privacy of my home, but with an audience full of people who wanted to see them as badly as I did. With the lists of film titles in my hand, I approached the student film committee with my proposal for 'Lavender Images: A Lesbian and Gay Film Retrospective.' Their unenthusiastic approval left me alone and uncertain in front of a shelf full of 16mm film distribution catalogs. Finding the source for *The Killing of Sister George* after hours of searching, I begin my career as a film programmer." [4]

Jenni worked at Frameline for three years. Her colleague, co-director, and close buddy at Frameline was the brilliant British raconteur and LGBTQ+ film expert, Mark Finch. On January 14, 1995, at the age of 33, Mark, who had struggled with depression since his teens, ended his life by jumping off the Golden Gate Bridge. Witty, irreverent, and driven, Mark was also a mentally ill depressive who'd been attempting suicide since he was a teenager. Jenni said of Mark, "During our three glorious years at the helm of the oldest and largest LGBT film festival on the planet, Mark was colleague, friend, mentor, neighbor, copy editor/co-writer, and my fictional twin sister, Bree—short for Sabrina, his favorite Charlie's Angel (really he just adored Kate Jackson). I was his twin brother Jim—short for Jimbo Stark, James Dean's character in 'Rebel Without a Cause.' With his loving, effusive support of everything I did in my work and my personal life, he made it feel like he was also my biggest fan. Twenty-five years later, Mark's suicide is still incomprehensible to me." [5]

Ten years after Mark's suicide, Jenni created *The Joy of Life*, an experimental, voiceover, urban landscape documentary about the life of a butch dyke in San Francisco who's looking for love and understanding, along with the history of the Golden Gate Bridge and suicide. *The Joy of Life*, and her 2015 follow-up *The Royal Road*, offers a deep first-person reflection on gender identity, butch vulnerability, and pining over unavailable women all set against a backdrop of melancholic San Francisco city landscapes.

Jenni became a tireless advocate for adding a suicide barrier to the Golden Gate Bridge, providing local newspapers with excerpts from the script of her film, and sending video copies of *The Joy of Life* to the Bridge District board of directors. In March 2005, the Golden Gate Bridge District board of directors voted 15-1 to approve a two-year, $2 million study to explore the feasibility of a barrier. A plan was devised, and construction of the barrier began in 2018. The barrier is expected to be completed in 2023.

Jenni's creativity has always been focused on her butch identity, "There is a line in [her film] *Blue Diary* that talks about, 'always having crushes on girls and never being able to do anything about it.' Growing up with this kind of experience as a young tomboy was formative for me. Over the years, my work has been about grappling with my butch self, my gender identity, and my discomfort in the world. It has to do with a kind of longing that resides in a perpetual state of desire and trying to find ways to savor that experience on an erotic, emotional, intellectual, and even philosophical or spiritual level. Transforming these emotional resonances into a poetic language has helped me work through some of these experiences. Nowadays, even though I still feel very uncomfortable in the world, I have developed a strong connection to the landscape component of my work that is about being in the moment and being spiritually present in the physical world." [6]

Jenni's other work in the queer film world has included working for the LGBTQ+ film distributor Wolfe Video, as well as serving as consulting producer on many queer films and as an archival producer on numerous queer documentaries. In 2018, Jenni and Roe Bressan created The Bressan Project to preserve and release the films of gay, independent filmmaker Arthur J. Bressan, Jr. The films *Buddies* (1985), the first American film about AIDS, and *Gay USA* (1977), the first documentary about LGBTQ+ life in America, including tantalizing and profound glimpses into early Gay Freedom Day marches, a.k.a. Pride marches, have been restored and released.

In 2021 Jenni was honored with the prestigious Special TEDDY Award at the Berlin Film Festival for embodying, living, and creating queer culture in the world of film. The recognition was deeply touching for Jenni, "I know it's the industry side of it, connecting filmmakers and festivals and distributors and all that, but it's also been all about friendship. These people are my friends. They're my life," she continued while dabbing at her tears with a hanky, "'I'm a little emotional. I was just thinking of Mark and how this is what he did. I learned it all from him. And I think that lives on in me." [7]

Jenni lives in Berkeley, California and is the parent of two adult kids. She is currently the director of the Social Media Safety Program at GLAAD, the national LGBTQ+ media advocacy organization. Her latest work in progress is *The Quiet World*, about what it was like to be a queer, gender-non-conforming child in Minnesota.

Jenni co-founded the now-defunct PlanetOut.com, and she is also the proprietor of Butch.org. Jenni's LGBTQ+ film memorabilia collection from her book, *The Queer Movie Poster Book*, her films, her writing, and her enormous collection of film and video material documenting LGBTQ+ film history are archived at Harvard University. In addition to her TEDDY award and numerous other honors from various film festivals and cultural institutions, her films (including *The Royal Road* and *The Joy of Life*) have garnered acclaim and awards.

Jenni Olson

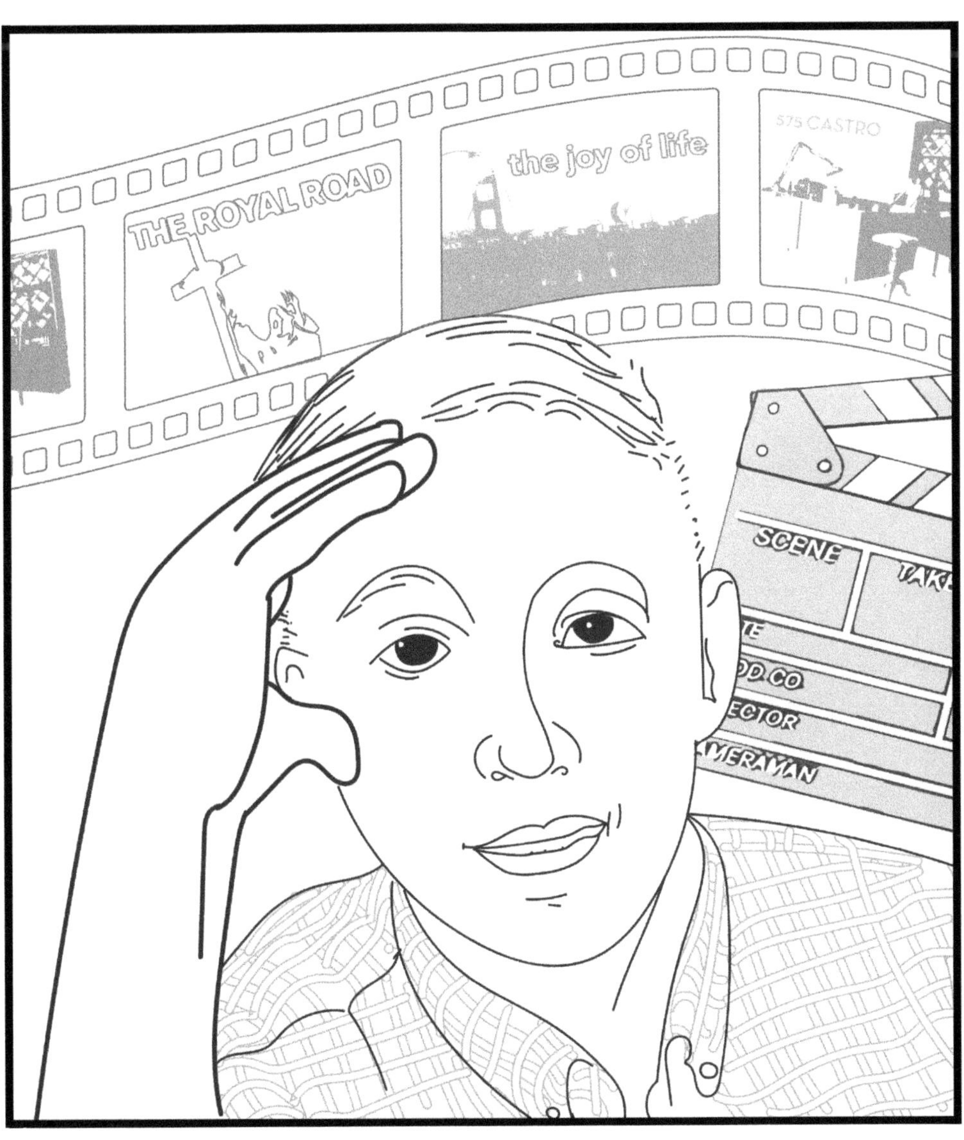

drawn by M Rocket

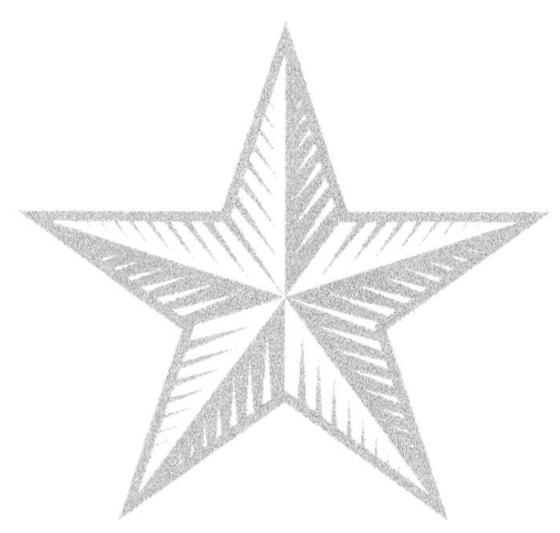

Madeleine Lim

b. May 11, 1964 · Republic of Singapore-USA
drawn by Ajuan Mance

Well I grew up in a mixed race/culture, racially I'm mixed and also with my stepfather who is German and Spanish, but I think that my ethnic and racial identity is obviously a part of me. I mean in terms of films that I make, someone said to me, "Are all of your films going to be about Asian lesbians?" and I said, "Well, why not? That's who I am." Woody Allen's films are about Jewish men in Manhattan, so what's wrong with that? It's definitely a big part of who I am along with being queer and being a filmmaker, they're all my different identities, along with being an immigrant to this country.[1] –Madeleine Lim

Madeleine Lim is an LGBTQ+ activist, documentary filmmaker, and university professor. She founded and is the executive director of the Queer Women of Color Media Arts Project (QWOCMAP) and co-founded SAMBAL (Singaporean & Malaysian Bisexual Women and Lesbians). Her films address address POC lesbians, survivors of domestic violence, and immigrants living in America.

Madeleine was born to a Chinese mother and a father with a mixed Chinese, Malay, Indian, and Portuguese heritage. When her parents divorced, her mother remarried a man who was half German and half Spanish. Madeleine practiced both European and Chinese customs at home, and attended the all-girl Convent of the Holy Infant Jesus school, where she started dating her first girlfriend at age 15. Outed by the vice-principal, she was firmly scolded for being a lesbian, nearly expelled, and told that she was too intelligent and studious to be gay, then forced to break up with her girlfriend. This experience laid the foundation for her life of activism. Madeline became so depressed about being outed and the repercussions that she became suicidal. She said of this bleak period in her teenage life, "I felt so isolated and alienated. That time in my life really fueled my commitment to build community, to feel like I had some place or some space where I belonged."[2]

In 1984, after graduating from high school, Madeleine attended Catholic Junior College in Singapore where she started her career as a lesbian activist, organizing monthly potlucks, and publishing an underground lesbian feminist newsletter. In 1985, she became involved with a group formed at the National University of Singapore called the NUS weekly tea group for womyn.

In 1987, Singapore was not a safe place to be LGBTQ+. Madeleine described living there as a young lesbian, "Institutionally, in Singapore, homophobia is legal and enforceable by the powers that be. And that fear gets trickled down to the individual in complex ways. I think that internalized homophobia is an extremely destructive force. I have many lesbian friends in Singapore who are very much afraid and closeted, and they sometimes are the ones who attempt to censor me for being an 'out' lesbian. The most traumatic homophobic experience is still when I was 16 years old, and coming out and coming to terms with my lesbian identity as a teenager, in an all-girls Catholic convent school. The pressure from the school, the church, the teachers, the principal, my parents, my girlfriend's parents, was tremendous, intense, and daily." [3]

Around this time, Madeleine co-wrote and directed a skit called the "Myth Pageant Beauty Contest" (a spoof on the Miss Pageant Beauty Contest), which was performed at a dinner to celebrate International Women's Day. This playful skit caught the eye of the Singapore authorities, who arrested the skit's co-writer and imprisoned her without a trial. This was a period of government crackdowns in Singapore, with intellectuals, artists, and writers being especially targeted for arrest.

Madeleine said of her decision to escape Singapore after the arrest, "I had been fairly fearless in my lesbian community organizing efforts up to that point, but the second round of arrests struck a little too close to home for me. And that was the whole point of those arrests, to instill fear and effectively clamp down on organizing efforts and dissenting voices of any sort. My parents feared that I would be arrested. So, once I was done with College of Physical Education and graduation was over, I left Singapore for the US." [4]

Madelaine traveled for a while before settling in San Francisco in 1988. In 2000 she founded the Queer Women of Color Media Arts Project (QWOCMAP) with funding from the California Arts Council. QWOCMAP was inclusive of a wide range of POC, stating that QWOCMAP "creates, exhibits, and distributes films that authentically reflect the lives and address the social justice issues that concern African Descent/Black; Native American; First Nations & Indigenous; Native Hawaiian & Pacific Islander; Southwest Asian, Middle Eastern, Arab, North African, South Asian; Asian, Southeast Asian, Central Asian; Latinx including *indígena* and *afrodescendiente*; and multi-ethnic lesbian, bisexual women, queer women of color (both cisgender & transgender), Two Spirit, intersex, and nonbinary, gender nonconforming, and transgender people of color (of any orientation)." [5] QWOCMAP has been behind the creation of over 450 films through their Filmmaker Training Program, the largest catalog of LGBTQ+ BIPOC films in existence.

Madelaine's transnational identity has shaped her, and her multi-national parents may have at least partially prepared her for the difficulties of living in the

US while also having deep roots in Singapore, the beloved country she left behind. She quickly began organizing. In 1994, a good friend moved to San Francisco from Singapore, giving Madeleine a buddy to share with her feelings of being caught between two countries, "She instantly added an amazing sense of family to my daily life that I hadn't felt since leaving Singapore. Up to that point, I had been living in San Francisco for six years. My lesbian identity was totally validated but not my Singaporean identity. After my friend moved to SF, we talked constantly about belonging and about what home meant to us, where that was, whether it was geographically based, etc. That was when the idea of making a film that reflected our daily lives began to germinate."[6]

In 1996, Madelaine produced a short film, *Shades of Grey*, about lesbian domestic violence, and in 1996 she produced a film, *Youth Organizing, Power Through Art*, about 15 homeless youth organizing through art.

In 1997, Madeleine produced the award-winning short film *Sambal Belacan in San Francisco,* a movie about transnational identity, race, sexuality, and nationality. In the documentary, three first-generation immigrant Asian lesbians from Singapore work at creating home; exploring how cultural identity, lesbian sexuality, and immigration status affect belonging. *Sambal Belacan in San Francisco* has proven to be relatable and well received by expatriates of many stripes, not only lesbians from Singapore. In 1998, Singapore banned the film, but in 2020 they made a one-time exception and allowed it to be shown in San Francisco at the Singapore International Film Festival in their heavily regulated pre-festival program New Waves. *Sambal Belacan in San Francisco* has been screened internationally and has won numerous awards.

Along with the three themes of transnational identity, race, sexuality, and nationality in *Sambal Belacan in San Francisco,* Madeleine stresses that "Feminism is also an important part of this film. There is this scene in the film where I shot two women's naked and entwined bodies from the foot slowly up to the head. While this is happening, the audience is seeing these female bodies as sex objects, but when the camera reaches their heads, they look back at the audience as if they had been interrupted and intruded upon. This act of looking back at the audience makes the audience aware that they themselves had been caught in the process of objectifying the bodies on the screen." She continues, describing how she uses nontraditional and non-narrative methods in *Sambal Belacan in San Francisco,* "In this film, I try to expand the boundary of traditional documentary film making by making it more intimate, less like a formal interviewer-interviewee format, and by including scripted scene, poetry and newsreel footage."[7]

Madeleine lives and works in the Bay Area, teaching as an adjunct professor at the University of San Francisco and working as the executive director of QWOCMAP.

Her most recent release, *The Worlds of Bernice Bing*, explores the art, activism, and life of Abstract Expressionist painter, Beat-era Existentialist, Buddhist, feminist, and Chinese American lesbian Bernice Bing.

In 2016, Madeleine was diagnosed with breast cancer. Although the cancer was successfully treated, it reoccurred in 2019 and is being treated again.

In 2001, Madeleine became the first local lesbian to be featured in *Fridae*, the popular Asian English-language LGBTQ+ portal. She has won a large handful of local awards, including the Award of Excellence from the San Jose Film & Video Commission's Joey Awards in 1997, the National Educational Media Network Bronze Apple Award the following year, the LGBT Local Hero Award from KQED-TV for her leadership of QWOCMAP and her dedicated service to queer women of color in 2005, the Phoenix Award from Asian Pacific Islander Women & Transgender Community (APIQWTC) in 2010, and was awarded the San Francisco Arts Council Individual Artist Commission twice.

Madeline Lim

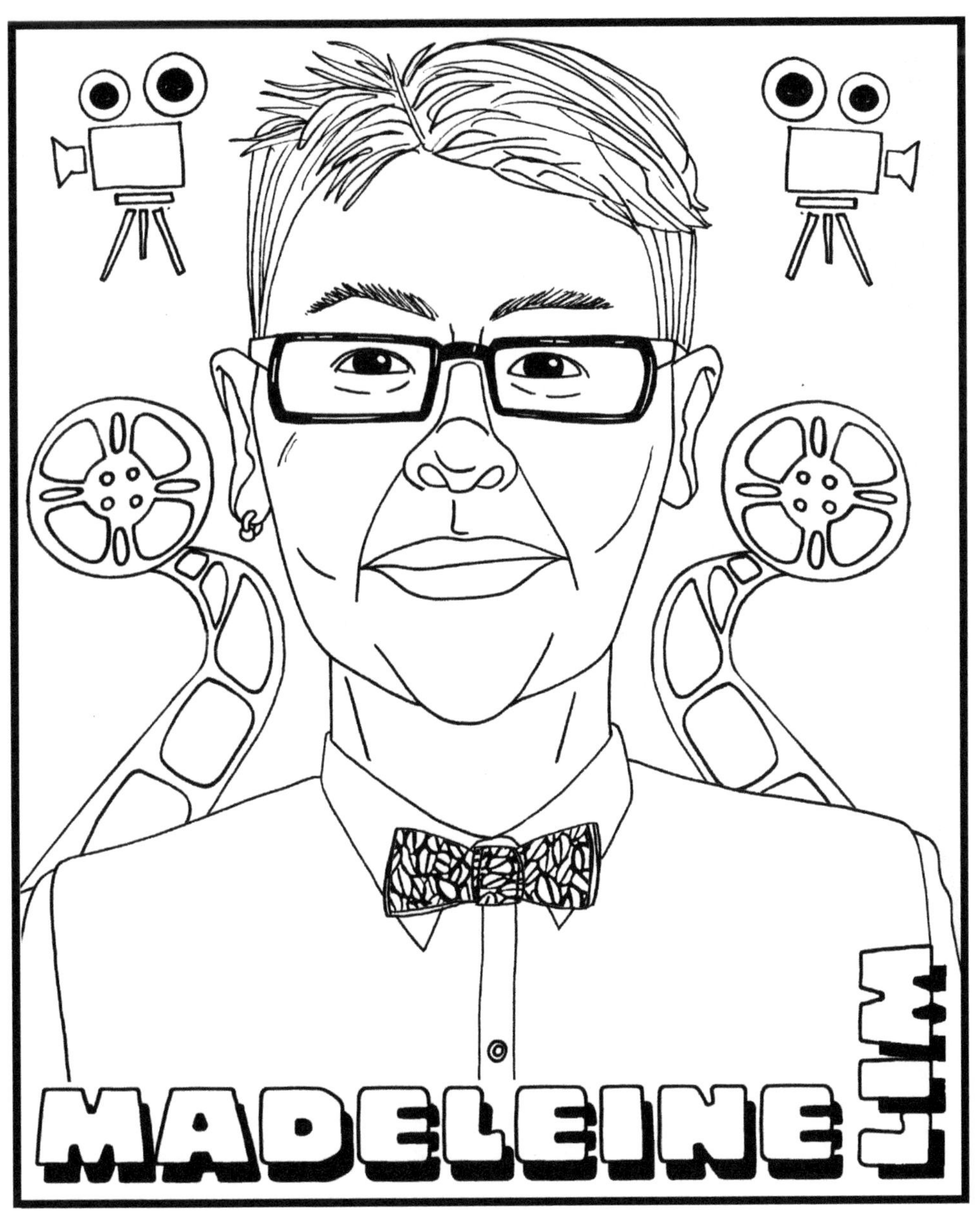

drawn by Ajuan Mance

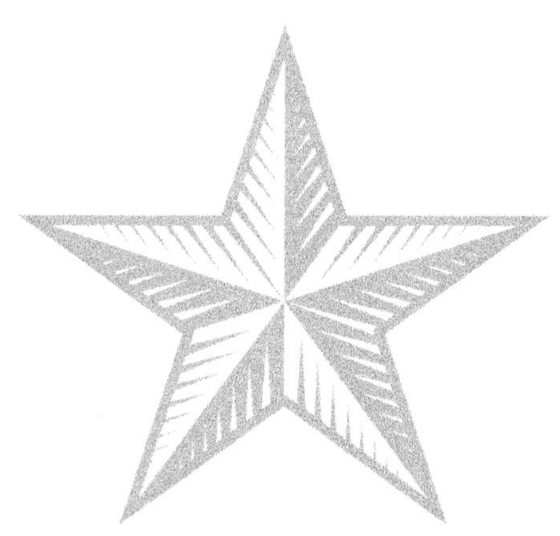

Shine Louise Houston

1975 (?) · USA
drawn by Tyler Cohen

Race and class are so fused together, that from the get-go people need to have economic freedom as that leads to freedom to make choices not impacted by economic pressures. Then there's also pressure from respectability politics saying that being a sex worker is not ok, that it wasn't a choice because of economics, and you have to rise up above that.[1] –Shine Louise Houston

Shine Louise Houston is a film producer, a painter, and has started several companies including Pink & White Productions and PinkLabel.tv.

Shine was raised by her mother in southern California. Her father was legendary jazz double-bassist Clint Houston, while her mother is proud and supportive of her daughter's accomplishments.

In the late 1990s, Shine was a painting major at San Francisco Arts Institute when she suffered a painting block, so on a whim she switched her major to filmmaking. That decision proved to be life changing.

After graduating from the Institute, Shine got a job at Good Vibrations, a worker cooperative, woman-founded sex shop in the Mission district of San Francisco. By 2005, Shine had worked on the floor as a salesperson for over five years. Shine had just turned 30 and became reflective about her lack of a career. She mulled things over, "OMG, I'm 30, and I'm still doing retail. Well, why not make porn? It was one of the avenues I explored as I was reinventing myself—including thoughts of furniture making, finishing my welding certification, or going back to grad school. I was checking out a lot of stuff, and the doors that opened at that time were for porn."[2]

Customers came into Good Vibrations and asked Shine for queer porn recommendations, and she was flummoxed for answers, "It gets really personal with people when you're selling them these types of products. What was also interesting is that as far as video, I would get the same questions over and over again: 'What can I watch with my girlfriend that's not going to piss her off?' And queer women who would ask, 'What can I watch that's not all long hair and long nails? I want somebody who actually looks like they come from the [LGBTQ+] community.'"[3]

In 2005, Shine decided to take matters into her own very competent hands and started the queer porn film company, Pink & White Productions, with funding from Blowfish.com, a Bay Area online sex toy store. Her first film was "Crash Pad" a gritty realistic queer film starring Jiz Lee, who at that time was beginning their career in porn. Over the summer of 2005, Houston put together a crew, rented film equipment, and cast local Bay Area women in a five-day shoot at a friend's loaned apartment. Shine mused about her first day of shooting "Crash Pad," "For the first time in my life I'm managing a crew of six or seven people at a time, and then three or four actors on set at a time. In the middle of production I'm watching all this shit happen, and then that's when it hits me: I'm making all this shit happen: I'm making a film."[4] "Crash Pad" won the Feminist Porn Award's "Hottest Dyke Sex Scene," and evolved into a series of over 360 *Crash Pad* films and still counting.

Crash Pad started off by being uniquely queer and female-centric. There are many things that differentiate Shine's porn from most mainstream porn including a decidedly queer aesthetic, deliberately choosing people that are not typically shown in mainstream porn, a style of directing which focuses on the performer's natural chemistry and intimacy, non-choreographed sex, and showing performers that have a diverse range of ages, shapes and sizes, abilities, colors, racial and gender identities, and sexual expressions. Butches? Check! Strap-ons? Check! Black femmes? Check! Nonbinary folx? Check! Real orgasms? Check! Fat daddies? Check!

Shine advocates for consent between all employees, everyone is paid prior to being filmed in order to remove any cash incentive to perform in ways they may not want to, there is food on the set, it's a sober environment, and everyone is cognizant of employees' pronouns. This is not what we think of as a typical porn studio environment but is feminist and queer-centric. Shine talked to the women at *Curve* magazine about charges that there is an innate degree of exploitation of women in pornography, "That's lending itself to a lot of assumptions about porn. I mean, who's to say that the men in porn aren't also being exploited? There is power in creating images, and for...a woman of color and [a] queer to take that power....I don't find it exploitative; I think it's necessary. This film genre is so stunted, compared to all other genres. I want [my films to be] as good as independent films. I want that film language to grow."[5]

Shine is also careful to treat her employees ethically and does not give her work away, "If you're patronizing places that have free porn, basically you're making it so producers and talent can't get paid. That's true no matter what kind of porn you're watching for free, even the straight stuff has likely been pirated. Often, whether or not the performers get paid is the difference between 'ethical' or 'feminist' porn and porn that's not ethical. A lot of times, companies will slap a 'feminist' label on their porn, but it doesn't really mean anything."[6]

In 2012, Shine started PinkLabel.tv in order to support emerging, independent porn producers. She was inspired to start PinkLabel.tv after seeing stupendous films during Pornfilmfestival Berlin and realized that unless someone stepped up, these films and shorts would sink into oblivion. Shine explained, "I want young producers to get a good chance, it's kind of like an incubator. We have a shared revenue model, and we usually give 40%, which means we usually break even. They don't have to deal with processing fees, don't have to incorporate, or start a website as they might not have the cash."[7]

The Bay Area queer porn scene was booming, and in the summer of 2020, the San Francisco PornFilmFestival held its inaugural festival. It was the beginning of the COVID-19 pandemic, vaccines had not yet been developed and released, and much of the world was masking and on some variation of lockdown. California was also suffering from a record-breaking season of brutal wildfires. Like so much during that first pandemic year of lockdowns and the rise of the use of Zoom, the festival was conducted online, so filmmakers were able to show their work internationally.

In 2020, Shine released *Chemistry Eases the Pain*, a crowd-funded, straight-curious romantic comedy that was inspired by a man that Shine knew. Some of the themes in *Chemistry Eases the Pain* are biphobia, changing sexual and social identities, fear and ambivalence about unexpected sexual attraction, and the difficulties of being in an interracial couple.

Shine is frustrated by the cultural and business challenges that the porn industry faces in the US, "...what I would change is the 'ghettoizing' of the porn industry, because that is what leads people to make bad decisions. Even if you're on the side of trying to be a 100% legit business, it's hard to find people who will work with you. It's tenuous to get bank accounts, it's tenuous to get a merchant's account, and investors. It's even hard to have electricians come to your building. That's awkward, and it shouldn't be awkward. You hire movers, and they look at you funny. Once you get big enough, I think people may not give a shit, but for small and mid-sized companies, it's a big problem."[8]

In 2022, Shine stopped directing the *Crash Pad* series to focus on more personal work. She handed over the camera to Ava LaPrima, a trans woman of color who'd worked with Shine for several years.

Shine's films have been screened internationally and have been featured in numerous publications, institutions, conferences, and museums, including National Public Radio (NPR), British Broadcasting Cooperation (BBC), *The New York Times*, *Rolling Stone* magazine, *The Village Voice*, Princeton University, the Butch Voices 2001 Conference, and the Tate Modern Museum. She has garnered several awards including the 2014 Feminist Porn Award's "Best Boygasm" for the film *Bed Party*, PorYes Europe's 1st Feminist Porn Awards Honored Filmmaker in 2009, International Ms Leather Keynote Speaker, and the 2015 Sylvester Pride in the Arts Award from the Harvey Milk LGBT Democratic Club for "providing many of us with the opportunity to see ourselves and our desires reflected in her films. We appreciate the multi-gender inclusivity of her work and the political lens behind it."[9] As she accepted her award, Shine responded, "We need stories about this intimate part of our lives because stories help us understand who we are and who we can be. I want to hold this space, like those who held this space before me, for future generations to tell their stories. I make porn because queer bodies, trans bodies, brown bodies, and fat bodies are beautiful. I make porn to make our voices heard. I make queer porn to set the story straight."[10]

Shine Louise Houston

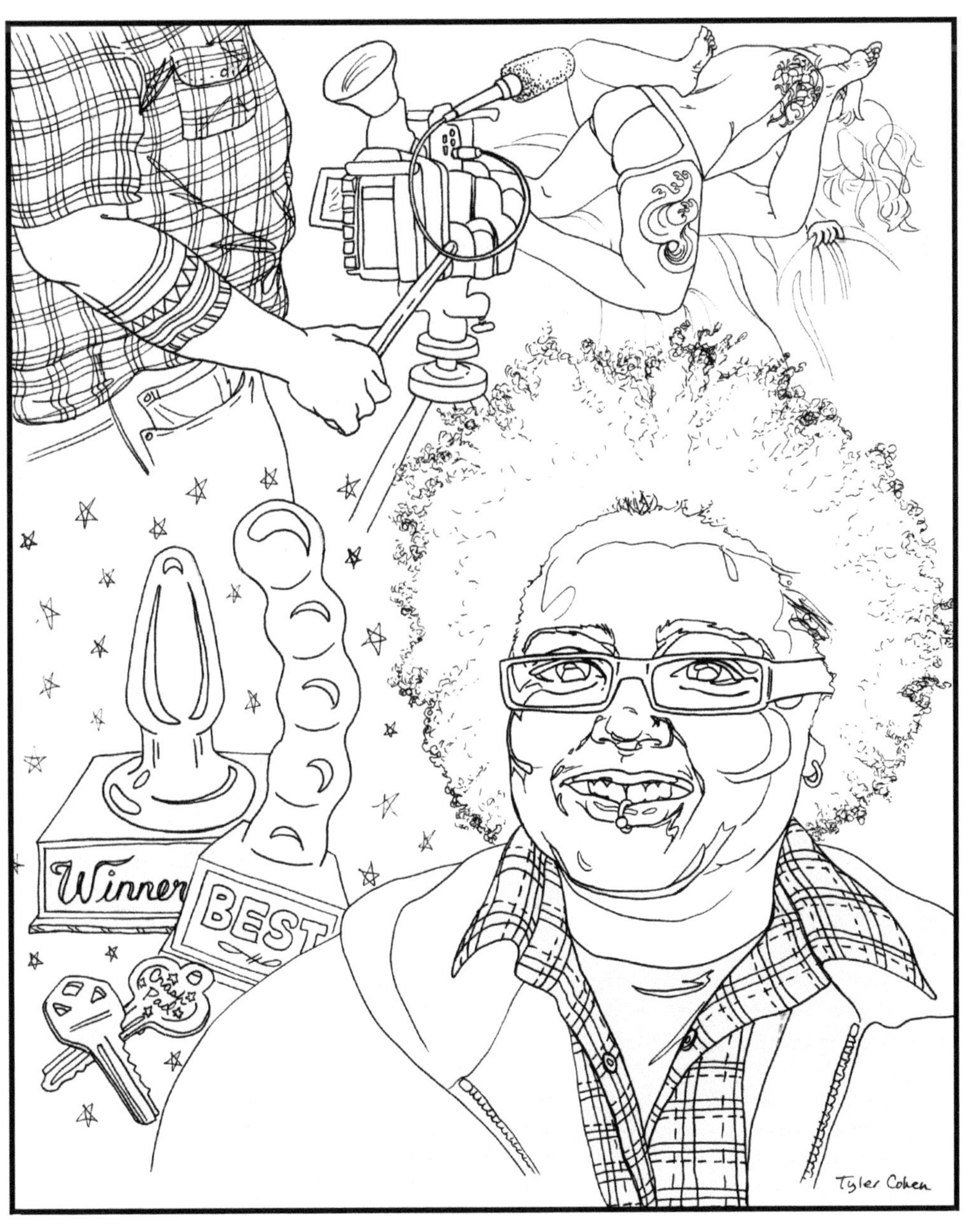

drawn by Tyler Cohen

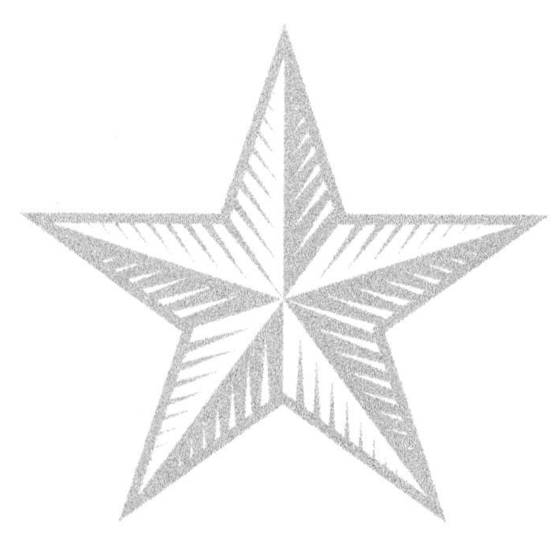

Cheryl Dunye

b. May 13, 1966 · Liberian-American
drawn by Ajuan Mance

It's different for black lesbians. It is a space where a part of your identity can feel reclaimed, and I think that's what The Watermelon Woman *really talks about, this reclamation of the pluralities that we hold in our identity.*[1] –Cheryl Dunye

Cheryl Dunye is an innovative film director, producer, screenwriter, editor, mother, and actress whose work often centers around race, sexuality, and identity. Cheryl is known for creating what she calls "dunyementaries"—works that blend the personal and the political.

Cheryl Dunye was born in Liberia and moved to Philadelphia, Pennsylvania as a young child. Her father worked for the Polaroid company, which manufactured cameras. Cheryl was interested in documenting from a young age and was the family's designated cameraperson: "I got interested in making films, I would say when I was a child. I'm African on my father's side of the family and African-American on my mother's side of the family, so there was always this real interesting texture in the family photo album, so I always would look at it seeing you know how varied those pictures were, lining things up, moving things around, creating my own sort of visual familial timeline with my photographs of my family. And my father actually worked for Polaroid. There was a little button on it that came all the way out with those first Instamatic cameras where you could allow with a long string somebody to take make a selfie, so my father would let me be the one to push the family selfie picture so documenting was the way that it began."[2]

Cheryl described how meaningful it was to read the Combahee River Collective Statement that was written in 1977, "As a baby dyke in Philly in the 80s, I came across a manifesto written by the Combahee River Collective…and it changed my life forever. This group of Black feminists and Black lesbians wrote about how race, gender, and sexual orientation were woven together in the lives of queer Black women. They used the term 'intersectionality' as a way to describe how these multiple identities can be constantly and simultaneously present within one person's body."[3] The manifesto discussed four major topics, "(1) the genesis of contemporary Black feminism; (2) what we believe, i.e., the specific province of our politics; (3) the problems in organizing Black feminists, including a brief herstory of our collective; and (4) Black feminist issues and practice," and ended with,

"As Black feminists and Lesbians we know that we have a very definite revolutionary task to perform and we are ready for the lifetime of work and struggle before us." [4]

In 1990, she received her undergraduate degree from Temple University, and in 1992, her M.F.A. from Rutgers University's Mason Gross School of Art.

OutFest Los Angeles said of her early works, "Dunye's delightful early short films—her 'Dunyementaries'—fuse humor, intelligence, and drama in the world of urban, young black lesbians as they make their way through the murky waters of love, friendship, and dating." [5]

In an interview with *Time* magazine in 2020, Cheryl said, "One of the most important films to me, that made me start making work, was *She's Gotta Have It,* by Spike Lee. I was a budding filmmaker, I hadn't decided what I was going to do with my career. I was at Temple University, and I was already queer. I was political, but I hadn't committed to filmmaking as the form of expression that I was going to have. A woman went up, got the mic, and said, 'Why did you make Nola like that, such a weak woman? Why couldn't she have choices? Your portrayal of her was wrong.' And Spike's only response to her was, 'You know, I wanted to make this movie. If you want to go make movies that answer all those things, then go make your own movie.' And upon that, I figured it out. I was going to make movies." [6]

In 1996, Cheryl produced the seminal *The Watermelon Woman,* which was the first narrative film produced by a Black lesbian. Inspired by *Swoon* (1992) and *Norman... Is That You?* (1976), *The Watermelon Woman* stars Cheryl as a filmmaker who's attempting to make a documentary about an anonymous Black actress from the 1930s who was known only as the "watermelon woman." While researching "watermelon woman," Cheryl discovered that the unidentified actress's name was Fae Richards and that, in addition to being an actress, Fae was a lesbian torch singer with a penchant for stone butches. The movie follows Cheryl as she makes her documentary about Fae seeking identity, community, and love. Cheryl talked about how because she could not afford to pay for actual clips, she and her pal and photographer, Zoe Leonard, recreated history in the film by dressing up themselves: "When I started to look at purchasing archives to use technically in the film, they were out of our budget and out of our range—we had no money at that time. That pushed me closer to collaborating with my friend, the photographer Zoe Leonard, and bringing together a troupe of people to reinvigorate and put a lens on this project within the queer community as something that's happening. It really did this twofold thing and allowed me to create, in the pre-Kickstarter days, an object to auction off later. We put the pictures up and people came and got to buy a print to help support the film for fifty bucks. It was something really inexpensive, and now those pictures are worth thousands in permanent collections, so it's quite interesting that way." [7]

In 1996, the movie premiered in the Panorama Section of the Berlin International Film Festival (Berlinale) in Berlin, Germany, an international film festival where it earned a Teddy Award. Cheryl stated, "It was amazing. I hadn't been to a film festival in competition in the world of cinema. It was the first place where I felt like a filmmaker, in a way, and not somebody who's struggling or hustling, because there are filmmakers all over, from around the world, pushing their film in the market or screening in the competition. It was amazeballs to be part of that, let alone to win. They actually gave me a Teddy bear. This is before they had the big award that they have now, a piece of glass or whatever it is." [8]

In 1995, the GOP assumed the majority in the United States Congress, leading them to attempt to eliminate monies for National Endowment for the Arts (NEA) in 1997. They chose to attack arts that they found offensive, including LGBTQ+-centered arts. *The Watermelon Woman* was blasted by former Congressman Piet "Pete" Hoekstra (R-MI), who complained in a letter to the NEA that *The Watermelon Woman* "is one of several gay- and lesbian-themed works cited by the *Michigan Republican* as evidence of 'the serious possibility that taxpayer money is being used to fund the production and distribution of patently offensive and possibly pornographic movies.'" The *Advocate* article about the letter and the NEA continued, "Meanwhile, Hoekstra and his allies are on the warpath, and they're finding ammunition in the 25th anniversary catalog of Women Make Movies Inc., an independent producer and distributor of films and videotapes that received about $112,700 in NEA grants over three years. Besides *The Watermelon Woman*, Hoekstra's letter cites catalog listings for *Seventeen Rooms*, a comedy about what lesbians do in bed; *Ten Cents a Dance*, a three-part film that includes a segment depicting anonymous bathroom sex between two men; and *BloodSisters*, a look at the lesbian S/M community. 'I do not believe the above videos, as described, are the type of "art" Congress intended to fund through the NEA,' Hoekstra said in the letter. 'In fact, these listings have the appearance of a veritable "taxpayer-funded peep show."'" [9]

In 2002, Cheryl was hired by Miramax Films to direct *My Baby's Daddy*. She described how disregarded she felt in Hollywood: "It was odd, man. I was just completely invisible, even in the process of me making the film. My film was edited completely over. It wasn't my film. That's what you really learn." [10]

By 2004, when *My Baby's Daddy* was released, Cheryl's relationship with her partner had dissolved, and she moved to Amsterdam for the next few years. In 2010, she moved to Oakland, California.

In 2014, Cheryl produced the short film *Black is Blue*, about a Black trans man. *Black is Blue* premiered at the San Francisco LGBTQ+ Frameline Film Festival in June 2014. In 2016, Cheryl was asked about *Black is Blue*, "I had just moved to

Oakland a couple years ago to teach at San Francisco State, and do a few other things, and was looking for myself in a community, and it was the trans men of color and trans people of color community that I embraced and reflected a lot of what I was going through as a new masculine of center looking person, but their stories are invisible. So here again, as something that I want to do, is like, put the spotlight on our margins. Our marginality is our strength. Storytelling is filled there. And so in looking at that story, you know, I made up a story and do what I do, which is called the doing the Dunyementory now, which is that mixing of documentary and fiction, and tell this life of this guy who had to live in his car because he doesn't have the right papers, and he's not able to get a job, and so the short film ends with one period there, and so we're making it a comma, and adding on to it to make a feature film and expanding it to look, not only just a black trans man, but also looking at a black trans woman and sort of a love story between the two of them. A tragic love story."[11]

In 2016, a restored version of *The Watermelon Woman* was shown at the Berlinale. In an interview, she talked about marginality, activism, and filmmaking, "I feel like what one of my teachers, mentors in literature, Audre Lorde, said: 'The Master's tools will never break up the Master's house,' you have to create your own thing. My marginality is my strength. I need to speak my truth. So by doing that and by putting myself in the picture, and by telling stories about that, I'm not only just making work about and putting my identity out there, but I'm also trying to entertain and also trying to not say I'm just like everyone, but definitely show all the facets, an equalizer, and to say I belong, and I'm in that spectrum of media, which somehow we forget, you know, we definitely forget. I think that's going on a lot right now with the internet and identities just popping out left and right, so I want to be in that pool or show who I am."[12]

Cheryl launched Jingletown Films in Oakland in 2018. Jingletown Films features storytellers and filmmakers that are people of color and/or queer. She has also done extensive work for television, including "Queen Sugar," "Claws," "Love Is," "Dear White People," "The Umbrella Academy," and "Lovecraft Country."

Cheryl lives in Oakland, California with her two children and her wife, Karina, who is a professor and an academic.

Cheryl has taught at numerous institutions, including University of California, Los Angeles, University of California, Santa Cruz, Claremont Graduate University, California Institute of the Arts, The New School of Social Research, the School of the Art Institute of Chicago, and San Francisco State University. She has received grants from Frameline, was a NEA grantee, a Rockefeller Foundation fellow, and was awarded a 2016 Guggenheim Fellowship. In 2021, *The Watermelon Woman* was selected to be in the Library of Congress's National Film Registry. Cheryl donated her collection of queer history to the ONE Archives at USC Libraries.

Cheryl Dunye

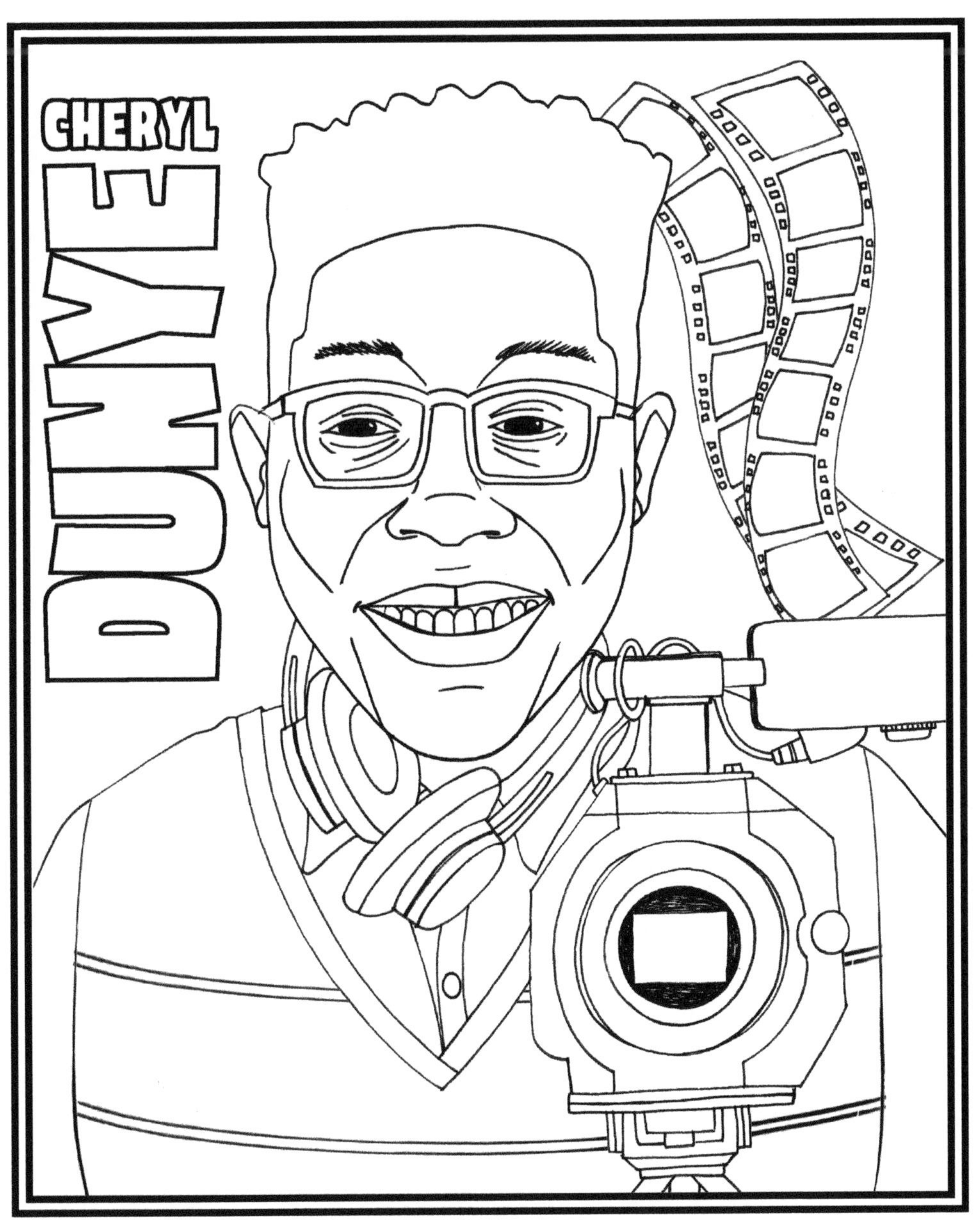

drawn by Ajuan Mance

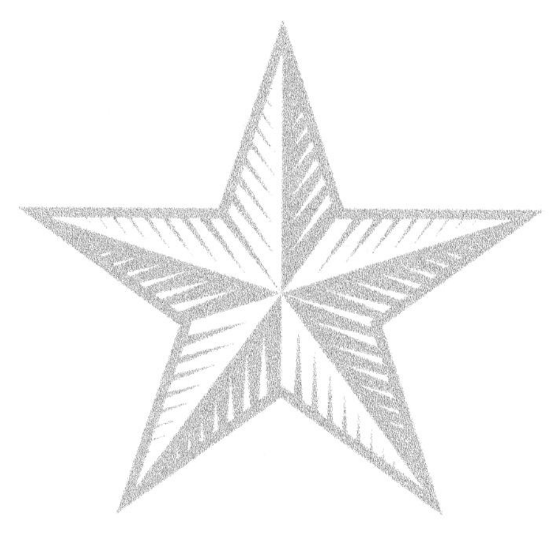

Barbara Hammer

May 15, 1939-March 16, 2019 · USA
drawn by M Rocket

Her leg touched my own, and I felt this incredible rush, erotic rush, just through our knees, and I thought, 'Oh, my God, I've never felt this for a woman before,'...or even that much for a man as I can remember. And I decided right then I can act on this or ignore it. I decided to act on it. And so, Marie A. Shaw and I went back to my place in Santa Rosa and spent the night and were still up to see the dawn. I became a lesbian. At that moment on that night, my whole sense of touch increased. I began to be more aware of the follicles of hair on my body, the way they told me what space I was moving through, the way I was reinforced by touching a body similar to my own. So, this reinforced my own outline of the body and became the mode of my lesbian aesthetic, so that in my films I want the viewer to feel in their bodies what they see on the screen.[1] –Barbara Hammer

Barbara Hammer was a ground-breaking, avant-garde lesbian filmmaker.

Barbara was born in Los Angeles, California, into a blue-collar family; her father was an alcoholic who worked at a Mobil gas station, and her mother was an art-museum-hopping, well-read secretary in Hollywood. Barbara's Ukrainian-immigrant maternal grandmother was a self-taught painter, a one-time cook for American actress Lillian Gish, and worked as a live-in cook for the film director D.W. Griffith. Barbara saw her force-of-nature grandmother as a role model, "She used to live with my father and mother, much to my father's discontent. But she would paint at the kitchen table with oil paints, and she would use Styrofoam packaging for meat as her canvas. She was very creative. She would make things out of ceramics and paint them and do her own firing."[2]

A cheerleader in high school, Barbara went on to attend University of California, Los Angeles, and earned a B.A. in psychology. She married a classmate the day after her graduation, but on the condition that he would travel around the world with her on a Lambretta motor scooter, which they did. Her husband ended up becoming another significant cultural influence. He introduced Barbara to subtitled films, public radio, and San Francisco, where Barbara earned an M.A. in English Literature. In the early 1970s, she studied film at San Francisco State University. After going back to the land, opening up their marriage to include other lovers, and building a home in Sonoma County, Barbara started making art and dropping acid. Frustrated with being delegated to making coffee for her husband's artsy friends, his anger issues, and jealous of a woman that her husband was flirting with, Barbara took her Super-8 camera and a motorcycle, leaving him and rural life in the mid-70s, saying, "It's too much for me to be stuck here in the woods being a housewife without any art community around." [3]

After leaving her husband, Barbara got a job teaching at Santa Rosa Junior Community College. Although she knew she was a feminist and had inklings that she might be a lesbian, Barbara continued to date men. A year or so later, after watching *One Flew Over the Cuckoo's Nest* together, Barbara fortuitously went home with Marie Shaw. Marie and Barbara became lovers and collaborators for the next two years. Barbara continued to make art, get high, and paint the sides of windmills and murals.

After coming out, Barbara decided to dedicate her life to lesbian film. She made what is considered the first lesbian experimental film, *Dyketactics*, about nature, dyke nudity, and lovemaking. With 110 images in four minutes, *Dyketactics* is influenced by her attraction to the language of touch as defined by Carl Jung. Sexuality and touch remained a driving force for her: "I have never separated my sexuality from my art, even if the film has nothing to do with lesbian representation." [4]

Barbara experimented with musical soundtracks in her short films. She initially used music from iconic 1970s lesbian-separatist musician Alix Dopkin's album *Lavender Jane Loves Women* for the soundtrack for *Dyketactics*, however, once Alix caught wind that men might watch the short, Alix forbade her from using her songs in the film. This led Barbara to Mills College, where she learned to use a Moog synthesizer, and that became the film's soundtrack. Eventually, in the late 1990s, Alix let Barbara use her music for a reissue of *Dyketactics*. By then, Alix had softened her stance towards men: "Alix lived in Woodstock, and I ran into her, and she had two little boy grandchildren. And I said, 'Alix, I'm—you know, might be re-releasing this film. Would you give me permission now?' And she said yes, and 'I've got, you know, boys in my family'—boy children. And so, I made a new film that hardly anybody's seen called *Dyketactics X 2*. And I only have one print of it, but I could make more. So, it has both soundtracks on it." [5]

Synesthesia-adjacent and sensual, Barbara described how images affected her physically: "A more abstract situation might be—and I speak about this with audiences often, describing the sensational—in driving in a car, looking out, and seeing a plowed field, a farmer's field, nothing growing in it, I can feel that earth and those furrows in my body. I can look at a puff of cotton and feel it, the sharp edges around it. It's very visceral for me." [6]

Nature and lesbian sex became the lodestone of Barbara's filmmaking, and the 1970s was a rich time for lesbian politics. Barbara was driven, producing film after film. In 1977, she released *Multiple Orgasm*, with footage of rock formations and trees overlaying close-up images of a woman masturbating and her ecstatic face. As the woman in the film becomes more aroused, the rocky terrain and cervices seem to mimic the shape of her vulva as it contracts with orgasms, a predecessor to performance artists and ecosexuals Annie Sprinkle's and Beth Stephens' work.

Barbara's subjects in her films eventually included the aging body, AIDS, menstruation, lesbian history and culture, woman shellfish harvesters in Jeju-do, men's view of women's sexuality vs. women's view of their own sexuality, Ukraine, dying and cancer, and the artists Henri Matisse's and Henri Bonnard's artwork during World War II combined with the French Resistance Movement.

At age 48, Barbara's life changed when she met Florrie Burke at the West Coast Women's Music Festival in Yosemite National Park, California. Both were stark naked, and Florrie was prepared for a fling, but something more permanent was in the works. Barbara had been in a 3-month-long relationship in San Francisco; however, goaded by her therapist, she decided to try for something more sustained with Florrie, who ultimately became her life partner. Florrie was an activist who specialized in combating human trafficking. Barbara's therapist said, "'No reason you can't continue this bed-hopping life. Nothing morally against it. But there is, you know, long-term relationships that you're not having.' And I thought I'd take something new for a change, which was the long-term relationship. That would be the adventure—to see how that unfolded."[7] Barbara had evolved and was ready for a committed relationship, "...that was solid. Then, finding out that her work meant as much to her as mine. This is the first time. Lots of other lovers had kind of tagged onto me or they had work, but it wasn't as compelling in their life as mine was, which meant it would take more time away from me and my work. So, I needed somebody who was my same age who wasn't interested in being taken care of or admired by a younger woman, and I wasn't interested in an old—I had been interested in older women earlier, like Gloria Churchman, 11 years my senior, because they had experiences that I hadn't had, and I could learn from them."[8] Barbara and Florrie lived together, dividing their time between the West Village, Manhattan, New York, and a cabin upstate in Woodstock, New York. They remained together for 31 years until Barbara's death.

In 1992, Barbara produced her first feature-length film, *Nitrate Kisses*. *Nitrate Kisses* was another ground-breaking film. It consisted of historical images, interviews with gay couples, and scenes from the 1933 movie *Lot in Sodom* in a montage that portrayed how LGBTQ+ people were marginalized in the 20th century.

Diagnosed with endometrioid ovarian cancer in 2006, she decided to give fellow filmmakers her outtakes of footage to edit into films. One of the filmmakers was Joey Carducci, who had made *Generations* (2010) with Barbara when Joey was a dyke. Joey had not produced any new work in five years, and Barbara hoped that, with this gift, he would power through his artistic block and create again. The generous gesture had the desired effect, and Joey made a trans coming-out film with imagery from *Tender Fiction* outtakes. Barbara was satisfied: "She caught the spark, became a guy, and now is going on in this trans work. So, as much as you plan something, the thrill, openness of something new happening and coming in is always an option and to be embraced—not denied. And I hope I die embracing new options, not denying them."[9] Barbara died of cancer in 2019. Barbara, a right-to-die movement advocate, fought for the New York Medical Aid in Dying Act.

Wildly prolific, Barbara made over 100 films in her 79 years and garnered a slew of awards including a 2013 Guggenheim Fellowship, three Teddy Awards, and the Grand Jury Prize at the 1993 Sundance Festival. Her work has been shown extensively at festivals and in museums internationally, including retrospectives at the Museum of Modern Art, the Tate Modern, the Jeu de Paume in Paris, and the Hammer Museum in Los Angeles. Her archives are held at Yale University's Beinecke Rare Book and Manuscript Library in New Haven, Connecticut.

Barbara Hammer

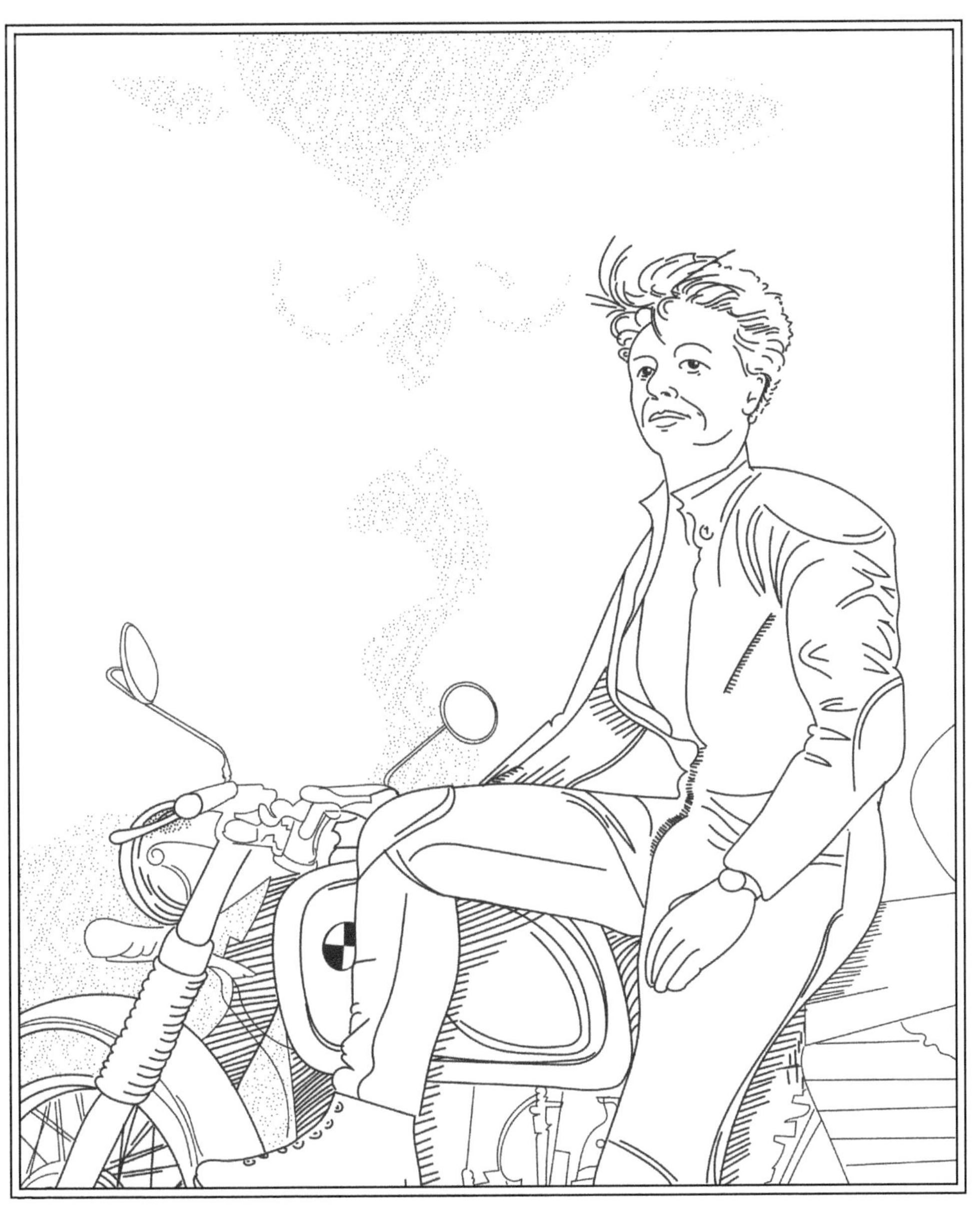

drawn by M Rocket

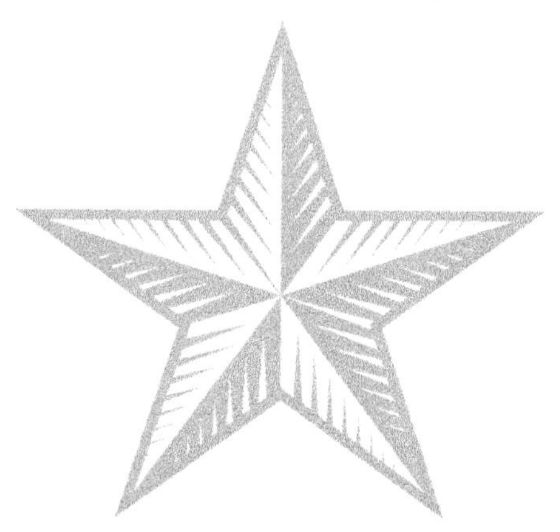

MUSICIANS

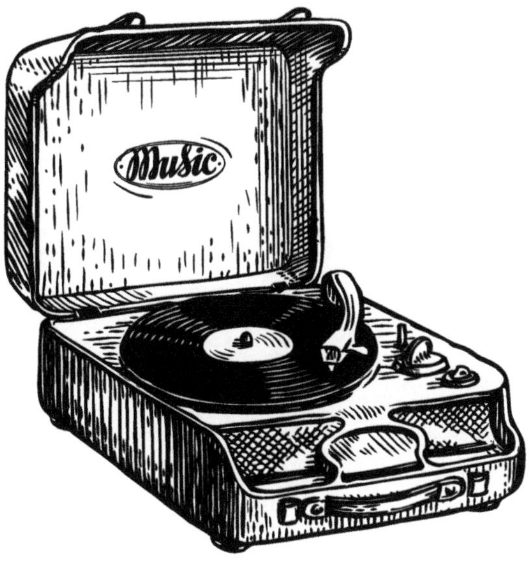

Meshell Ndegeocello, a.k.a. Meshell Suhaila Bashir-Shakur

b. August 29, 1968 · USA
drawn by Ajuan Mance

I'm curious about the seed of what makes a person want to react to their bigotry, disdain, discomfort, lack of familiarity, lack of education, that makes them want to engage in violence. I'm more interested in the seed that's in someone that wants to annihilate the other. It says much more about that person than it does about me.[1]
–Meshell Ndegeocello

Meshell Ndegeocello is a writer, composer, activist, and musician who identifies as a Two-Spirit bisexual. She is known for her wide range of styles and as a kick-starter of the neo-soul movement.

She was born in West Berlin, Germany. Her father, Jacques, was a musician who played in a military band, and her mother, Helen, was a domestic. They moved when Meshell was young and raised her in Washington, D.C. Obsessed with the album *Dirty Mind* by Prince, she played it on repeat to the distress of her religiously devout mother. Meshell started playing the bass guitar when she was 14 years old so that she could play alongside her brother. Meshell had a difficult childhood, and her conservative, religious parents were deeply disappointed when she came out as queer.

When she was in her late teens, Meshell changed her first name from Michelle to Meshall and her surname to Ndegeocello which is Swahili for "free as a bird" to honor her queer identity and to distance herself from her parents.

In 1994, when Meshell was in her mid-20s, she met Midwestern singer-songwriter John Mellencamp, and this unlikely pairing changed her life. They played a session together in John's hometown of Bloomington, Indiana, producing a co-billed cover of Van Morrison's "Wild Night." The song became a hit, peaked at number three on the Billboard Hot 100, and resulted in an explosion of popularity for Meshell.

Two years later, in 1996, Meshell recorded "Leviticus: Faggot" for her second album, *Peace Beyond Passion*. "Leviticus: Faggot" was shocking and remains so. The song tells the story of a young Black gay man who's thrown from his parental home at age 16 for being gay, his grief at losing his family, and his (implied) suicide. Martha Mockus writes in *Unmaking Race, Remaking Soul: Transformative Aesthetics and the Practice of Freedom*, "Ndegeocello claims that 'Leviticus: Faggot' is a reference to Funkadelic's 'Jimmy's Got a Little Bit of Bitch in Him' from their 1974 album *Standing on the Verge of Getting It On* (Powell, 1996). 'Jimmy' is a playful, flamboyant tune about the unconventional gender traits of a gay man. However, the political courage and lyrical-musical complexities of 'Leviticus: Faggot' far surpass those of 'Jimmy.'" Many music video stations refused to air it unless it was toned down to remove the hint of suicide, the word "faggot," and the topic of homosexuality. [2]

Decades later, the song still resonates. Photographer and journalist Johnnie Ray Kornegay III talked about hearing "Leviticus: Faggot" when he was a 19-year-old closeted gay Black man, "I am sure I'd seen the word faggot written before, and I am very sure I'd heard it in music before, but not in a context like this. In 1996, I hadn't yet come out, and I was searching for a connection to explain who I was in a way that felt genuine. Ndegeocello's use of the loaded f-word in this song in a way that wasn't being used to hurt or taunt me, but as a means to introduce me to a story about someone who I might know was life-altering. This time, the hurtful slur was inspirational." [3]

Between 1999 and 2014, Meshell released one album around every other year, starting with *Bitter* (1999) with its themes of heartbreak and rebirth and including collaborators and former Prince band members Wendy and Lisa; *Cookie: The Anthropological Mixtape* (2002) drawing on the mixtapes of her youth and features recorded samples of speeches by Black activists, poets, and musicians; *Comfort Woman* (2003), sensuous and reggae-influenced; *The Spirit Music Jamia: Dance of the Infidel* (2005) full of jazz deliciousness and #4 on Billboard's Top Contemporary Jazz Albums chart in the US. These were followed by *The World Has Made Me the Man of My Dreams* (2007) which intertwined identity, politics, misogyny, and religion and hit #60 on Billboard's Top R&B Album chart; *Devil's Halo* (2009) influenced by musicians she listened to during a trip to Ireland, "I got to go to Ireland. I went to a couple of pubs and there were much older gentlemen playing the guitar and just singing these amazing, simple songs—and I really admired that. I wanted to get to that kind of place where the song could just exist with a guitar and a vocal" [4]; *Weather* (2011), soulful and intimately erotic, with husky whispers of "Who's your daddy?" on "La Petite Mort," which garnered wide praise; *Pour une Âme Souveraine: A Dedication to Nina Simone* (2012), a compilation of soulful classics including "Please Don't Let Me Be Misunderstood," "Black Is the Color of My True Love's Hair," and "To Be Young, Gifted and Black"; and *Comet, Come to Me* (2014) which was subdued and soulful.

In 2018, Meshell's father had leukemia and was reaching the end of his life, while her mother was suffering from dementia. During this difficult time, she recorded *Ventriloquism*, an album that consisted of covers of eleven 1980s and 1990s R&B

and pop tracks, including George Clinton's "Atomic Dog," Prince's "Sometimes it Snows in April," and Sade's "Smooth Operator." *Ventriloquism* was nominated for Best Urban Contemporary Album at the 2019 Grammy Awards. Music has always been a salve to Meshell, "I recorded the album after my father died and while my mother was ill. I have always loved recording and love to be in the studio. It was a comfort to consider making something, but I had nothing to say myself. I was just depleted. Revisiting songs that I grew up with, in a time when my parents were still my parents, helped me focus positively on the present via reimagining the past."[5] In speaking more about grief, inspiration, and creation during the making of *Ventriloquism*, Meshell said, "I was mourning that my father was about to journey to the next realm, and I would drive back and forth to the hospital. My mother's old car only got one [radio] station. The soundtrack to that experience was listening to the oldies. That was my joy. So a lot of those covers are just something that was coloring my experience. Something that gave me transcendence during the hard time."[6]

Meshell has played session work with such musical icons as the Rolling Stones, Chaka Khan, John Mellencamp, Madonna, Alanis Morissette, Robert Glasper, Herbie Hancock, The Blind Boys of Alabama, and the Indigo Girls. She was the first queer woman to appear on the cover of *Bass Player Magazine* and is an eleven-time Grammy nominee and one-time Grammy winner for Best R&B Song "Better Than I Imagined" in 2021.

Her play, *Can I Get a Witness? The Gospel of James Baldwin*, a musical theatrical work set as a pan-African church service and inspired by James Baldwin's *The Fire Next Time*, opened in Harlem in 2016. Meshell talked about the long-running, evolving show in 2020, "It's a community-specific kind of thing. It shape shifts based on city and venue, and it's based on Baldwin's timeless wisdom and warnings, so much of which is as true now as then, as ever. The first thing I finished was the album of music from the project. I am working on how that will come into the world now. I'd want people to know that even though he is seen as this divisive firebrand, he was really trying to bring us back to our most elemental humanity and to love. He worked to dismantle the delusion and mythology of race and gender and masculinity and sexuality to find what's human. Despite familial abuse and the abuses of society for his race or because he was gay, I am always amazed by his ability to conclude that love was imperative to our survival."[7]

In preparation for an upcoming album based upon James Baldwin's book of collected essays, *The Fire Next Time* (1963), Meshell gathered collaborators to work on the piece, "Before Covid-19, a group of us—including Staceyann Chin, Justin Hicks, Chris Bruce, Jebin Bruni, Abe Rounds, Jake Sherman, Julius Rodriguez, and Kenita Miller—spent 10 days together at Dreamland Studios near Woodstock,

New York. We did our cooking and our sleeping there, and we all sang out in the room together, sort of like a choir. Baldwin was a child preacher, and I used the church as the foundation of the music because I also come from that."[8] The piece includes songs written by Meshell, queer musician Toshi Reagon, Justin Hicks, and lesbian poet Staceyann Chin.

Meshell put in an appearance in *Queer Country* by Shana Goldin-Perschbacher that addresses the intersections of country music, the writers' personal experience, and interviews with LGBTQ+ musicians. Shana wrote about the difficulties people had navigating Meshell's queer identity with her Black identity, "She was the only Black musician at her label. And yet executives were calling her album *Bitter* 'too white.' And she was saying, 'I'm the only Black person in this building except for the security guard, and all these white people are saying that my album sounds white and I'm a Black person and I made it.' She plays jazz, she plays neo-soul, she's sort of dabbled with hip hop elements, is a singer songwriter and also does chamber pop. She's really all over the map musically. She's really versatile and creative. And being bisexual, and Black, and a woman—that has all worked against her musical career. People don't know how to frame her and they constantly ask about her identity rather than her music. The genre and the gender and sexuality and the race piece is just absolutely critical and completely linked."[9]

In 2007, Meshell moved to Hudson, New York, an artsy, progressive small town, saying, "I hate New York, I tried to live there several times and it's not my bag, but I love Hudson. It's a red-light town, a small town but really culturally diverse."[10] Since moving to Hudson, Meshell has gotten entrenched in the local arts scene, playing with the Bunnybrains and getting involved with WGXC, a community radio station. She lives part-time on a farm, has a son with Rebecca Walker, Alice Walker's daughter, and a second son with her wife, designer and wordsmith Alison Riley.

Meshell Ndegeocello

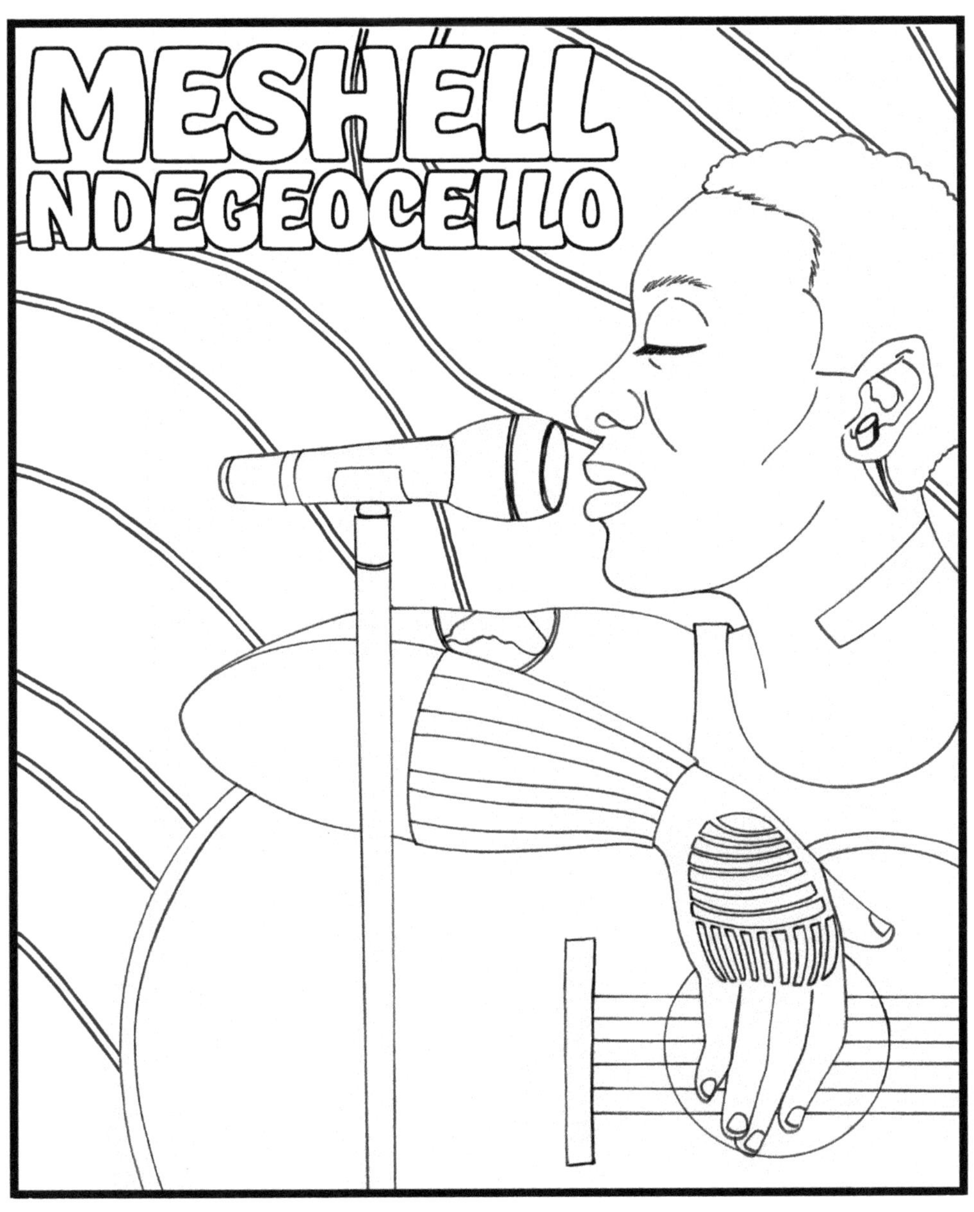

drawn by Ajuan Mance

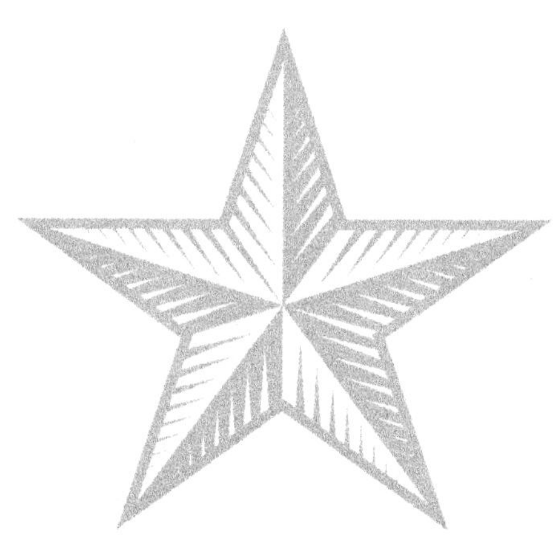

Phranc

b. August 28, 1957 · USA
drawn by Miriam Stahl

Most of the songs were terribly misogynist things, really abstract or really angry, and so noisy, but I wanted to be in a band real bad...till '77 I had been living in almost exclusively women's communities, and all of a sudden here I was in like punk rock land.[1] –Phranc

Like Cher or Prince, Phranc is mononymous and simply known as Phranc. Phranc is a singer, songwriter, visual artist, swimmer, and surfer, and a self-described "your basic all-American, Jewish, lesbian, folksinger."[2]

Born in Santa Monica, California, Susie was raised in nearby Mar Vista. She started entertaining when she was 14, performing during a family Succot celebration, "My grandfather is a cantor. Every year when I was growing up we would celebrate Succot, the festival of the autumn harvest, at his home. It was a very big event, maybe 60 people, and he would always hire entertainment. When I was 14, he hired me. I sang 'Zum Gali Gali' and other Jewish folk songs. And you could say it all started that Succot evening."[3] Her grandmother, Mariam, was a painter and took young Susie to art museums and made sure she had art lessons. She grew up listening to folk music, show tunes, and Jewish comedy. Janis Ian and Pete Seeger were favorites.

After telling her mom that she was going to the library, 17-year-old Susie rode her bike to the lesbian feminist drop-in rap session at the women's center on Hill Street in Venice, CA. Lesbian feminism was a far cry from the apathy of early 1970s high school, and Susie was entranced, so she grabbed her guitar, dropped out of high school, and moved to Venice to be a lesbian.

It was the mid-1970s, an exciting time to become involved in the radical lesbian feminist movement, and Susie got involved quickly. In 1975, Susie went to a retreat called The Lesbian History Exploration, held at Camp JCA Shalom near Malibu, CA.

She arrived at the retreat as Susie, with shoulder-length hair. Once at the retreat, she had her mind blown by the entertainers, including Alix Dobkins' music; a slideshow of orgasming women by Magic Wand and masturbation devotee Betty Dodson; a presentation called "What the Well Dressed Dyke Will Wear" by Lisa Cowan which cited overalls, short hair, and comfortable pants; and participated in a rooftop make-out session with *Village Voice* columnist and author of the iconic book *Lesbian Nation*, Jill Johnston. Inspired by French romanticism, Susie became "Franc" and inspired by Lisa Cowan, the freshly named "Franc" skedaddled to the barbershop next to the Safeway on Santa Monica Boulevard for the first of her legendary crew cuts. Afterward, she went to visit a friend to show off her new lesbian 'do, told her friend her new name, and her pal said, "Oh, perfect—I've got just the thing for you,"[4] and gave Franc a blue baseball cap with a "P" on it, which is how "Franc" became "Phranc."

In the mid to late 1970s, Phranc traveled 350 miles north to San Francisco because she'd heard that there were lots of dykes there. For the most part, the dykes she met in San Francisco were cliquish and aloof, until she was introduced to a warehouse of punks. Phranc moved in with them, made the transition from lesbian feminist separatist folksinger to modeling nude at the Art Institute, listened to angry loud punk music, and lived with leather fags and dykes and punks of all genders. The energy was electric, she made some close pals and decided she was a punk, but after four months she moved back to LA. The first punk band that she was in was Nervous Gender, followed by Castration Squad, which was a feminist, all-female punk band, and then Catholic Discipline.

Phranc came into punk with a lesbian feminist background, hoping that the two oppressed communities would get along, but the lesbian feminists felt that the punks were misogynistic, and the punks found the lesbians to be humorless. Unfortunately, the lesbian feminist community and the mixed-gender, scruffy punk community did not play well together, and Nervous Gender had their sound pulled and were hustled off stage when they played a benefit for the Women's Video Center at the Women's Building in Southern California. It wasn't until queercore became a thing in the mid-1980s that the two worlds finally made peace with one another.

Soon, things changed in the punk movement, becoming darker and more violent. Some punks and skinheads became entranced with wearing swastikas, mostly as an aesthetic statement to prove how tough and anti-establishment they were. Phranc became angry by this rash fascist fashion statement and wrote the beautifully blunt "Take Off Your Swastika" with the refrain "fascism isn't anarchy," playing it solo with just an acoustic guitar because she wanted people to hear each and every word in her lyrics.

Soon after "Take Off Your Swastika," Phranc started performing solo as the all-American, Jewish, lesbian folksinger, even starting a folk-punk hootenanny folk night with her punk friends at the dive bar Whisky a Go Go in Los Angeles, where John Exxine sang "Jackson" and the Circle Jerks performed "He's Got the

Whole World in His Hands." Some of Phranc's more memorable cover songs were an enthusiastic rendition of "I Enjoy Being a Girl" and a sweetly sung "Mrs. Brown, You've Got a Lovely Daughter," both of which take on sparkly new meanings when sung by the the butch, crew-cutted Phranc. And there's always, "Bulldagger Swagger," with lyrics about public bathrooms and being butch.

During this period, Phranc worked as a printer silk-screening gym clothes, but it was never enough to pay the rent. She started painting on cardboard that she foraged from the trash, blew her money on expensive tubes of gouache, and sold her work from home to raise money to pay the bills. Phranc moved from Hollywood to the west side, saved $1,200 teaching swimming and lifeguarding at Santa Monica College, and in 1983 made her first record, *Folksinger*, which was put out by Rhino in 1985, resulting in touring, then the record being reissued by Stiff Records. Phranc was touring and opening for well-known bands such as The Violent Femmes, The Smiths, Hüsker Dü, and the Pogues.

In July of 1991, Phranc's brother was murdered. She walked away from her upcoming show at Madison Square Garden and flew home. Devastated and depressed, she stopped making music, and for the next few years she surfed to soothe her pain.

Painting became her creative outlet when a studio space opened up for Phranc, and that was the beginning of her career as The Cardboard Cobbler, creating work on kraft paper and discarded cardboard, eventually utilizing a hot glue gun and her Nana's old Singer sewing machine. Currently, her works are three-dimensional wall-hung constructions, mostly depicting clothing such as swimwear, sailing flags, life vests, or creatures made of Kraft paper, thread, paint, and cardboard. The colors are deep yet have a vintage look. A typical work is *Red Dress (Please Don't Make Me Wear This Dress)* (2018). This piece is a 36" x 42" x 37" sculpture of a tomato red, sleeveless shirtwaist dress with a white Peter Pan collar and a thin black belt. The full skirt stands out stiffly, inviting the viewer to keep their distance. *Junior* (2015) is a painted Kraft paper construction of a faux Steiff grey tabby cat puppet, complete with a distinctive round "Original Phranc" tag. Phranc's artwork is shown nationally, and she is represented at the Craig Krull Gallery in Santa Monica.

In 1994 Phranc started performing again, and in 1995 the record *Goofyfoot* was released. Around the same time, seeking a part-time side gig that would allow her to make art and be with her growing family, Phranc started selling Tupperware, rose to senior executive manager, became a national top salesperson, created a special butch Tupperware uniform, and had her Tupperware career documented in "Lifetime Guarantee: Phranc's Adventures in Plastics." Phranc loved the unique

Tupperware women's community, "Tupperware acknowledges women in a way that's very special. You're self-sufficient, making great money....It really builds self-esteem. I have seen some of the shyest women become exuberant."[5] Phranc stopped selling Tupperware when the internet came along, causing Tupperware to change procedures and deflating the magical comradery she'd loved.

Phranc makes art and lives in Santa Monica with her 20+ year lifelong partner, the Young Adult (YA) writer Lisa Freeman and their parakeet, Pickles. They have two daughters. As Phranc sings on "Old in LA" (2017), she loves living in LA where you can surf every day and where you have a great barber who'll give you a fresh flattop.

Phranc

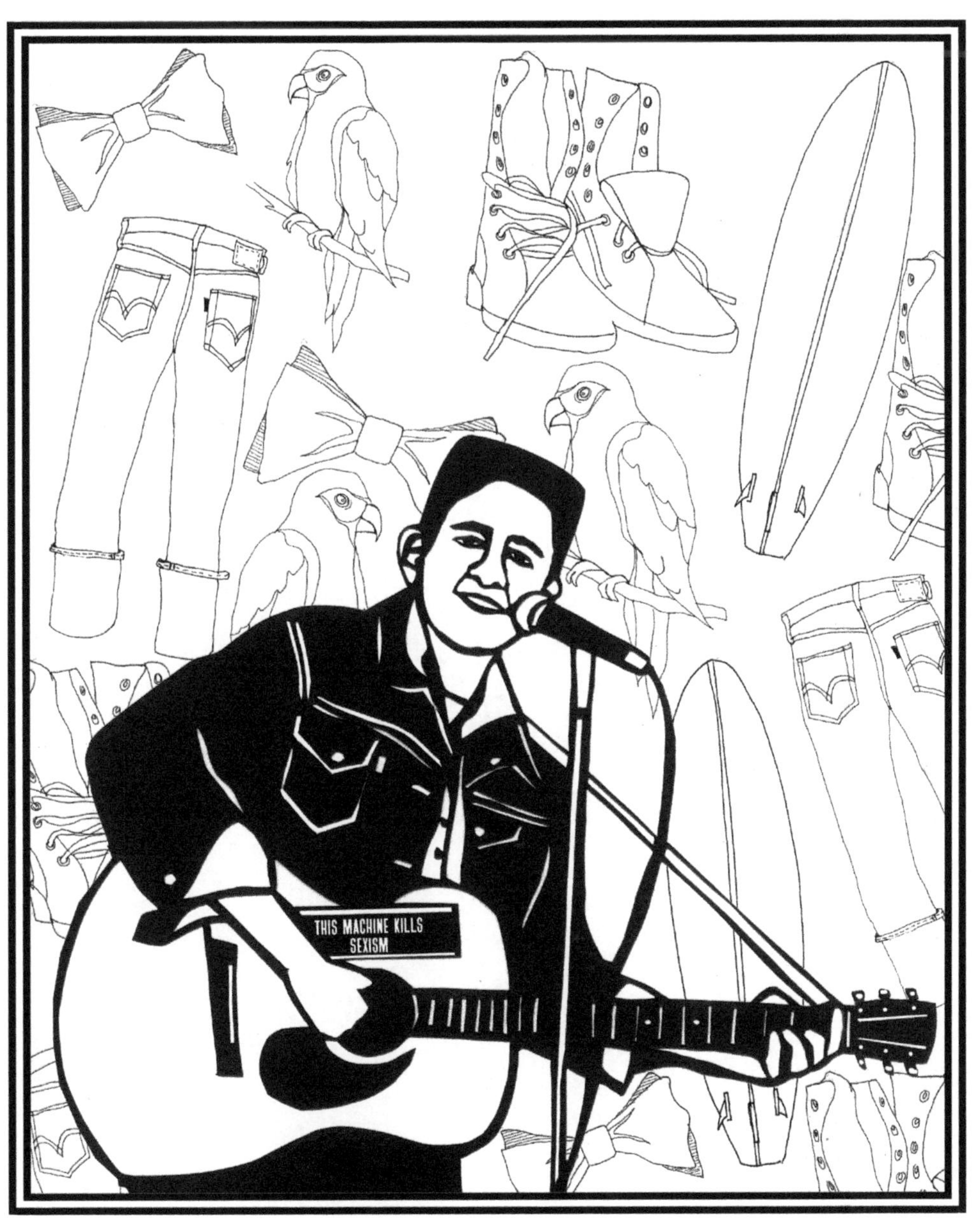

drawn by Miriam Stahl

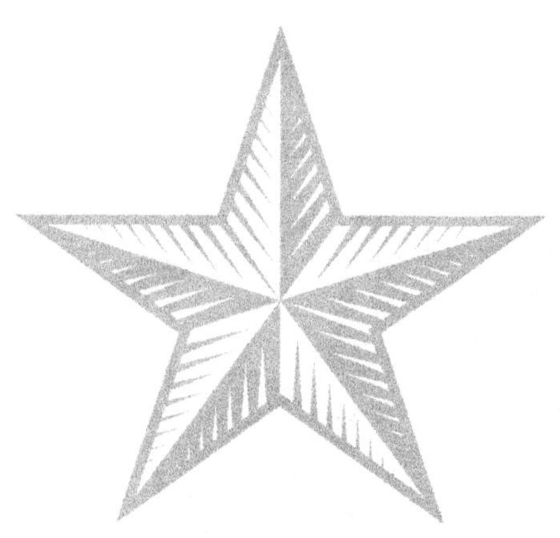

Dame Julie Bethridge Topp and Dame Lynda Bethridge Topp

a.k.a. The Topp Twins, Jools and Lynda Topp
b. May 14, 1958 · New Zealand
drawn by Cheela Smith

Quite a lot of the country songs we used to do had lines in them that we didn't like as lesbians, they were a put-down of women or had men as heroes, so we actually changed the lines. There's a song sung by Slim Dusty called 'Boundary Rider Blues' that was a really chauvinist, sexist song. It says, 'I wish I could see my girl again, I've got the boundary rider blues.' Although not all the songs we sing have a distinctively feminist message, we never sing about a man. It's about a woman or a thing."[1] –Jools Topp

The Topp Twins are identical twin sisters named Jools and Lynda Topp. They are performers, musicians, yodelers, vaudevillians, spoon-players, and activists. As activists, they've worked for women's rights, unions, the anti-apartheid movement, a nuclear-free New Zealand, Māori land rights issues, environmental issues, and the homosexual law reform bill.

Jools and Lynda, along with their brother, Bruce, were raised on a dairy farm in rural Waikato, New Zealand. Their parents, Jean and Peter, encouraged their creativity and were musical themselves. Jules and Lynda explained, their voices merging, that their upbringing was surrounded by music, "Mum's always been a closet opera singer and Dad's always sung. If we had a party at our house we'd always end up singing. Our country music background came from the farm because most of the music we did at home was country music. We didn't put on the record player, we'd sing. When we came home from school, we used to sing every night for two hours, grab the guitar and play. We never went to concerts or dances. We were just home on the farm, milking the cows. In fact, the cows had a lot to do with our singing. Cows are really into singing."[2]

Bruce, who is also gay, bought them their first musical instrument, a guitar with a songbook titled *Play in a Day*. In true anarchist fashion, Jools read the book in a day, memorized the chords, then promptly threw away the book. The twins were obsessed with music; Jools talked about how they developed their distinct style, "I do play the guitar simply, but I had a wonderful upbringing in the sense that I spent a lot of time down the back of the bus going home from Huntly College with the Māori kids in the back, where they would teach me the Māori strum. To play the Māori strum is pretty out there. You're playing the drums, the harmonica, and a guitar all at the same time. Because you're dampening the string, you're using your hands, [Lynda: "You're playing the rhythm as well."] So I learnt it, and the thing is, when the Topp Twins sing there is no drums, there is no bass, we've just got one guitar and two vocals. So I've been playing percussion and guitar and finding different ways of how I would play that guitar." [3]

Lynda also learned to yodel as a child, "I went into a 'yodel coma' I call it, and I just thought I gotta learn how to do that. I was absolutely mesmerized by the sound. There was no musical teacher that could teach me yodeling." [4] Jools laughed about Lynda's early efforts, "For a long time it sounded like a strangled cat. There was a lot of practicing, probably about five or six years before she actually sang publicly with a yodel. I had no great desire to yodel whatsoever. I just tagged along on the coattails of Lynda's fame about yodeling. It's worn off on me. At a certain point now I can yodel, but only if Lynda's yodeling." [5]

When Lynda and Jools were 17, they enrolled in the New Zealand Territorial Army's Signals Platoon, eager to see the world. The charms of the Army were fleeting though, and the sisters jumped train, guitars in hand, and landed in Christchurch, population 200,000+. Once in the big city, they started busking and playing music in cafes, interspersing their music with political repertoire and comedy. There, they met many radical lesbian feminists and the musician, Nancy Kiel, a redheaded rock performer known as "the Janis Joplin of Christchurch." The sisters came out as lesbians during this period in a "Ring of Keys" moment. Lynda said, "Coming out as lesbians for us was never ever a big deal. It was just something that happened. Nancy had invited us to a party after a pub gig, and we were so excited that we were going out with a rock star, to a party. And everyone else got in their cars and drove off, and Jools and I were still walking at that stage, so we arrived a little bit late. There was a group of women, these short-haired women, wearing guardsmen's jackets and stuff, in the corner. And I said to Jools, 'Look at them, over there—we're just like them.' And Jools said, 'Yeah, we're just like them.' And then somebody said to us, 'Oh come over and meet the lesbians…' And we were like, lesbians? Lesbians? We must be lesbians! They're just like us!' And you know what, from that day on afterwards, we identified as lesbians. There was no kind of angst or, 'Oh my god what's our parents going to do?', or do we have to fall in love first." [6]

In the late 1970s, they were spotted and recruited by a staff member of the Students' Arts Council who ran national tours. The sisters set off on a national tour and quickly became well-known for their incredible harmonies, strong political stances, and joyfulness. In 1978, they wrote their first feminist song, "Freedom" to be sung at International Women's Day, followed by "Paradise," a tribute to lesbian love. "Paradise" was not always well-received, earning such dastardly headlines as "Men Hating Mickey Taking Lesbians," and causing the US to stamp their Visa applications "Check for Deviance."

From there on out, they joined protests and wrote and performed movement songs on topics including nuclear-free New Zealand and the homosexual law reform bill. They were members of the Web Women's Collective who made New Zealand's first feminist record, *Out of The Corners*, in 1982. "Untouchable Girls" was one of their well-known songs about strong women and went on to become the subtitle of a documentary about Lynda and Jools.

Over the years, Lynda and Jools have developed a small village of outrageous characters in their act, including Ken and Ken, a sheep farmer and a failed sports-caster; New Zealand favorites, Camp Mother and Camp Leader; Posh Socialites and ladies who lunch, Pru and Dilly; The Ginghams, spoon-playing farmgirls; the Bowling Ladies, widows, gardeners, and bowlers; and Brenda and Rarline, wanna-be hairdressers with attitude who want to open a salon called 'Cuts for Sluts.' They saw humor as something that drew people together. Jools said, "There's something quite beautiful about having a green-haired punk rocker sitting next to a 90-year-old grandmother, and they are all laughing at the same thing. We made ourselves look ridiculous... we asked them to laugh at us, not to laugh at someone else's misfortune."[7]

In 1998, Lynda, in her persona as Camp Mother, won 3.75% of the votes for mayor of Auckland, running for an integrated public transport plan, a celebration of New Zealand culture, common sense values, and a gay and vibrant Auckland.

In 2009, the documentary *The Topp Twins: Untouchable Girls* about Linda and Jools was released to acclaim, and it won numerous awards. The documentary broke all New Zealand records for opening day and opening weekend and was a nominee at the 21st GLAAD Media Awards for Outstanding Documentary.

The sisters had a television cooking show between 2014 and 2016 in which they traveled about New Zealand talking to passionate cooks and foodies, rather like twin, yodeling, lesbian Anthony Bourdains.

In 2006, Jools was diagnosed with breast cancer and underwent chemotherapy and a mastectomy. In 2022, Lynda was diagnosed with breast cancer, and at the same time, it was discovered that Jools' cancer had now metastasized throughout her body. Lynda started chemo, but had to stop due to the side effects and severe peripheral neuropathy. They were undergoing treatment for cancer and staying apart due to the risk of catching COVID-19, when they decided to celebrate their birthday together and both caught COVID-19.

The people of New Zealand came through for the beloved sisters, including putting on a concert in November 2022 called Topp Class, in which various performers paid tribute to their vibrance, political activism, good natures, and talent. Lynda and Jools were dapper in suits, sashes, and their New Zealand Order of Merit badges, and they brought their mother to the show. Jools praised their family, "Our family is so tight and so loving. Our mum is 92 and quite amazing. She was at the tribute concert. She got dressed up to the nines. She's so beautiful and I couldn't ask for a better mum. She's a glam chick. She's probably asked herself, 'Why the hell did I have two lesbians who dress up as men?'" [8]

In 2013, Lynda married her longtime partner, Donna. Lynda and Donna run the Topp Country Café in Methven, Canterbury. Donna's son recently had a child, making Lynda a grandmother and Jools a great auntie. Lynda has been busy teaching her granddaughter to yodel, but success has been elusive.

Jools is a talented horsewoman and used to shoe horses professionally, but now lives on a farm in South Head, Auckland.

They have received many accolades. In 2018, Jules and Lynda were named Dames Companion of the New Zealand Order of Merit for services to entertainment. They received the Lifetime Achievement Award at the NEXT Woman of the Year 2019 Awards. In 2018, they were inducted into the New Zealand Music Hall of Fame.

The Topp Twins

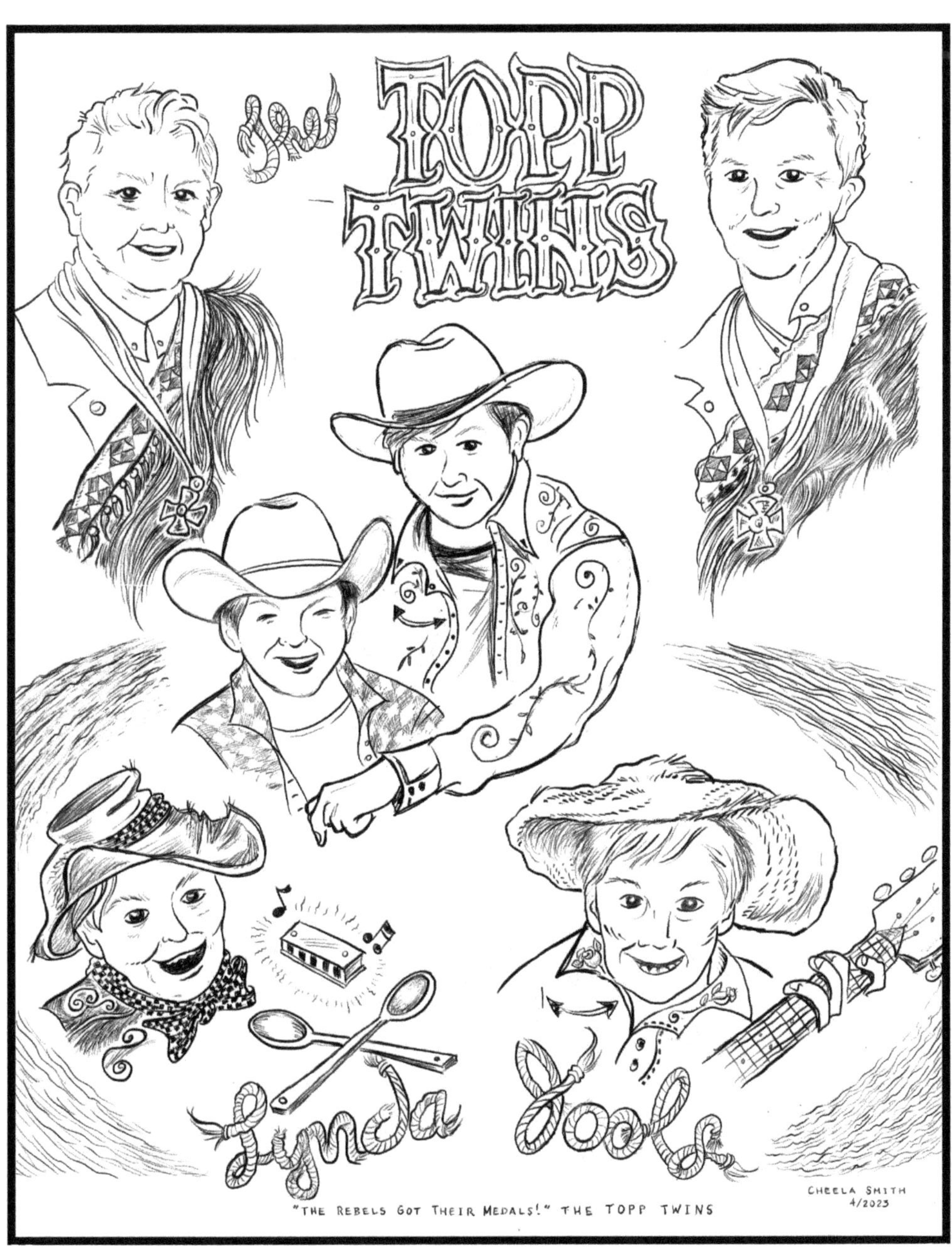

drawn by Cheela Smith

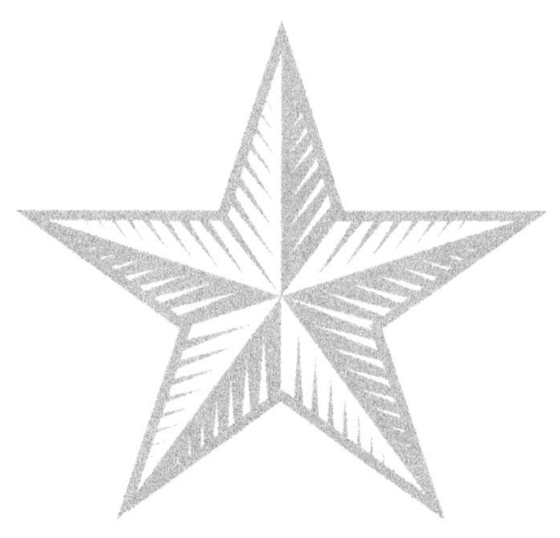

Debbie Smith

UK/Anglo-Caribbean
drawn by Rachael House

You can speak to women of color who are into punk today, and they will tell you exactly the same thing—there are no black women there. It's a white teenage, male scene. Maybe black people think it doesn't have anything to say to them, but I only have two words for them: Bad Brains [all-Black punk band formed in Washington, D.C. in 1976]."[1] –Debbie Smith

Debbie Smith is a DJ and a musician who has played in several punk bands, including Curve, Echobelly, Nightnurse, Snowpony, Bows, Ye Nuns, SPC ECO, Blindness, and The London Dirthole Company. She plays guitar, bass, and banjo. Debbie is self-described as "The finest practitioner of 'Debbie Smith' type guitar playing in the known universe."[2]

Debbie's father played jazz saxophone, passed on his love of music, and encouraged Debbie to play guitar. Although she loved music, she was too wild to settle down with an instrument. "At 14, my dad had given up buying me guitars after my brother and I would literally tie them up into the tree at the bottom of the garden and shoot arrows at them. But at 14 I decided, 'Right, I'll try now'"[3] The impetus for Debbie's change of heart about learning to play the guitar was finding a discarded cassette tape one rainy morning during her newspaper route. It was a mix tape filled with clips from John Peel's radio show, Blondie, the Au Pairs, and Television. From there, Smith discovered Siouxsie and the Banshees, the Ramones, and The Birthday Party. Self-taught, Debbie bought an Argos guitar, a cheap amp, and an oversized Ibanez guitar pedal. She practiced to Siouxsie and the Banshees' album in her bedroom with the door shut, "I've forgotten a lot of them now, but give me a couple of drinks and a guitar, and I will go Banshees on you. I learned 'Mirage' because it had bar chords, but they were all A shapes so I just moved the A shape up and down. I still play like that. I don't do the correct chord shapes. I just play the way I taught myself, wrongly, when I was 14."[4]

Debbie loved punk music from the start, "For myself, I didn't really think of trying to find a Black or queer community within the music scene. It was all about the music. Any Black friends that I had at school listened to Black music—soul, reggae, jazz, funk—which I listened to a bit but wasn't my main area of interest. I was kind of 'freaky deaky' because I liked white people's music."[5]

Debbie always knew she was a lesbian but hid it from her parents. She accidentally and dramatically came out as a dyke to her parents at age 16 when her mother found her *in flagrante delicto* with another woman and dragged her out of bed, stark naked. "I knew from as long as I had memory that I was a lesbian. I even knew what the word meant and everything. She dragged me out and drove me to my father's house—it must have been 6:30 in the morning—and she was screaming 'Your daughter's a lesbian!' And he said, 'Tell me in the morning'" [6]

Debbie played in a scattering of punk bands during and after college, including a several year stint with her all-dyke Scottish-London band Mouth Almighty. Mouth Almighty consisted of two members called Debbie plus a set of identical twins with a penchant for Joy Division, The Cure, The Proclaimers, and Lloyd Cole, and a thirst for whiskey. They tore up the house, toured Europe and sang about heartbreak interspersed with passionate, drunken rants about conservative politics.

The 1980s was an exuberant time to be a punk dyke, and Debbie was in the thick of it. Dashing and rebellious, she protested, played music, and partied. The time period was pre-riot grrrl, an underground feminist movement that was started in Washington state in the early 1990s. The movement in the 1980s was scruffy, hedonistic, and wrapped snugly in leather and spikes.

The USA was being dismantled by Ronald Reagan, and the UK had Margaret Thatcher. In 1982, the Feminist Sex Wars were ignited at the infamous Barnard Conference on Sexuality when the sex-positive Lesbian Sex Mafia and the feminist-led Women Against Pornography nearly came to blows. The AIDS epidemic had just started; Section 28, the UK legislation prohibiting homosexuality was being debated and ended up being law from 1988 to 2000. Nihilism was rampant. Getting drunk and high, raunchy sex, and dancing were survival strategies, and queer family formed in the midst of squats and leather clubs.

In 1987, punk dykes in the UK opened the first lesbian S&M leather club night, called Chain Reaction. Chain Reaction was held on Tuesday nights in a gay men's bar called The Market. This was a period when many lesbians were stridently vanilla, and S&M was considered to have harsh overtones of pandering to the patriarchy. *Rebel Dykes* producer Siobhan Fahey talked about the Chain Reaction's first few weeks, "I was a stripper on the first night and I remember there was lots of live sex and experimenting with S&M. Lots of leather! Someone did a sex show on a motorbike. There's no way you'd get away with that now. It was wild. And a real community—people met lovers and friends who they have stayed lovers and friends with 'til today....On the first night, they [mainstream lesbians] protested outside it. On the next one, they came in and smashed the place up in balaclavas. They got chased out by leather dykes and never came back, but it hit the papers, and as we say in the film, from that moment on, the club became even more popular. Looking back, I don't think it was all about the S&M. I think people just finally wanted to be sexual in a world where being a lesbian had become extraordinarily celibate, feminist, and right on. People wanted to put a finger up to that and create something more outrageous. The night only lasted a couple of years, but it had a big influence on sex-positive feminism, Riot Grrrl culture, queer core—all of those movements came out of it."[7]

In 1991, Debbie fortuitously answered an ad for a guitarist and was hired to play with the band Curve. This was her introduction to the official music business, and she played with them until 1994. In 1994, Debbie started performing with Echobelly, a band fronted by Indian-born Sonya Madan, whose style was compared to Morrissey. Then, as it is now, the music scene was dominated by White men, and most of the women in rock dressed in a seductive femme style. Debbie did not pander to the male gaze while on stage. She was a butch dyke with a shaved head, suave in a waistcoat, a vintage necktie, a pinkie ring, Docs, and pinstriped pants. "Britpop was a bit lady, but a lot of great women did get into the limelight. It was just a little tokenistic. The women were always objectified; Louise Wener was objectified, Justine [Frischmann] was objectified, Sonya was objectified. Women are generally judged on how they look, or if they're not good-looking, it's all, 'Oh, but she writes brilliant songs.' What do you mean, but she writes brilliant songs? She does write brilliant songs. There's always a double standard for women."[8]

Debbie is in the film *Rebel Dykes*, which was first shown as a work-in-progress in 2016, then as a finished movie in 2021. *Rebel Dykes* is a documentary about UK punk dykes in the 1980s. Jack Thompson wrote about watching *Rebel Dykes* for the first time and laments the current lack of queer spaces, "Watching the preview surrounded by the dykes that were part of it, it was plain how close they've remained, how they're family, despite having gone separate ways. Thinking about that screening now, from the anxious end of another long coronavirus lockdown, gives me a little gut twist; so many of us have been separated from our queer family for so long now, have gone through (and are still going through) not only a pandemic but the horror of virulent transphobia, institutional racism, sexual violence, abuse of police power. We've watched this horror unfold from screens in our individual homes, the most vulnerable among us unable to join protests, the protests that do happen broken up with violence. And we're not able to come together in pubs or kitchens or clubs in the same way we would have pre-pandemic, to decompress and find comfort in one another. It's strange watching a film so much about togetherness, when togetherness feels so alien."[9]

Debbie is sought after and has played with many other musicians including David Bowie, bassist Gail Ann Dorsey, Alanis Morrisette, and Foo Fighters drummer Taylor Hawkins. From 2017 until the present, she has hosted and DJed for the Club Nitty Gritty Radio Show as DJ Dapper D and Dappa D. She still plays in bands, most currently the all-woman tribute band Ye Nuns. She has been interviewed in several books about women and rock, including, *Never Mind the Bollocks: Women Rewrite Rock* and *Frock Rock: Women Performing Popular Music*.

Debbie lives in London with her greyhounds. She works as a DJ and promoter at The Nitty Gritty Club and as the Heritage Coordinator at a local library and archives.

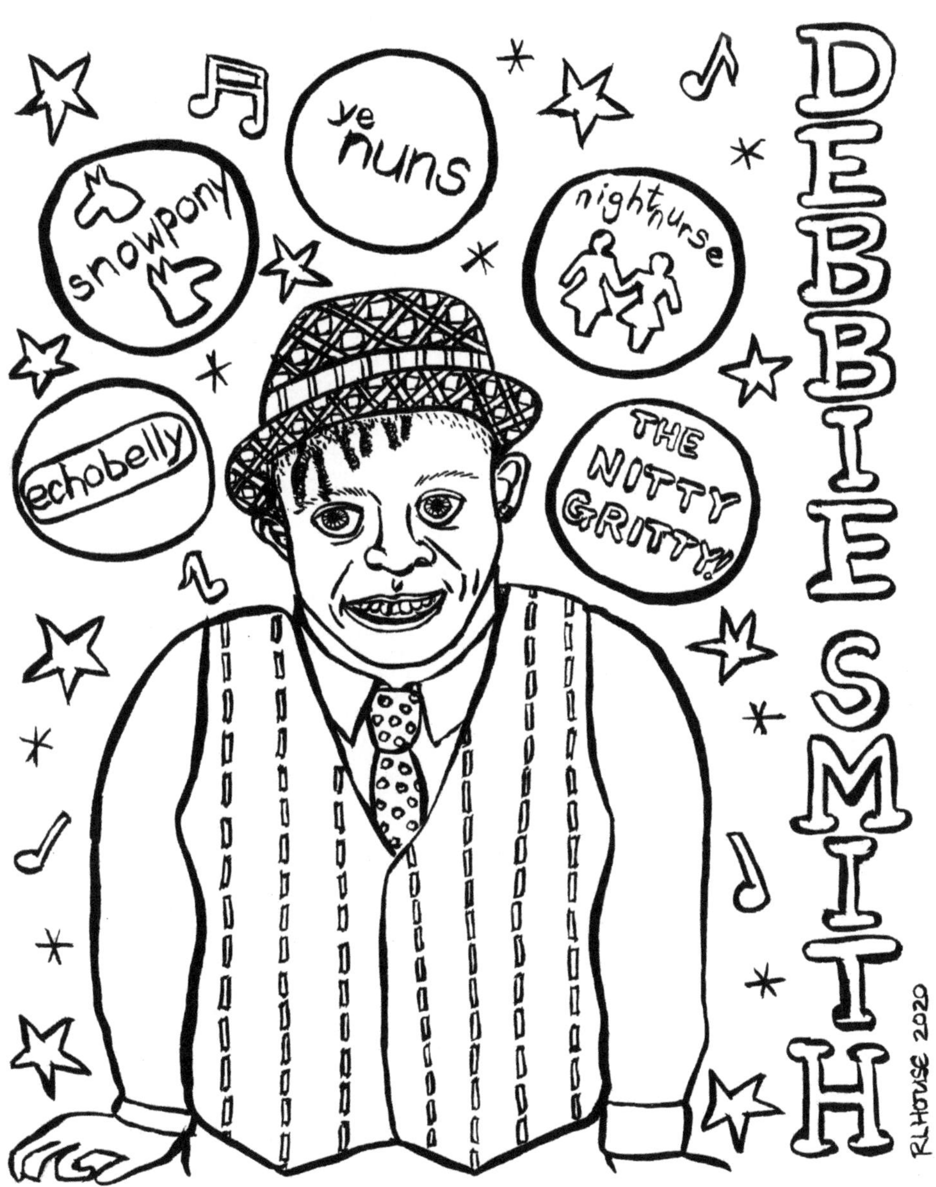

drawn by Rachael House

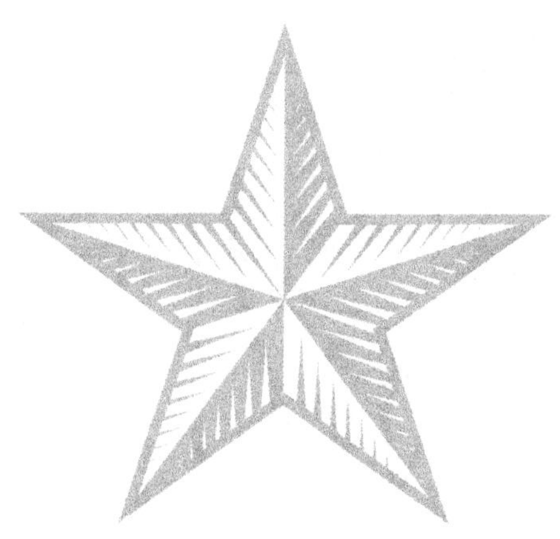

Toshi Reagon

b. January 27, 1964 · USA
drawn by Miriam Stahl

Sometimes people get overwhelmed with this idea about how they can participate in things, and I was just saying that you can have a voice and a focus from within. Sometimes making change is doing something very good in a small way. Or having better communication with your neighbors. Sometimes little steps are the hardest things, and when we sometimes focus too much on the big picture, it's overwhelming. For example, in terms of our elections, we hardly focus on our community judges that we get to elect, the school people that we can elect, and we focus only on the bigger campaigns. I'm guilty of this too. But from within our small places we have so many opportunities to affect things. Just investing a little time from within where you are in your everyday life. For me, my kid didn't have a music teacher. So I volunteered to be a music teacher at her school. I did it as much as I could before I started touring, just went and sang with the kids. Small things can influence you and your community in a positive way.[1] –Toshi Reagon

Toshi Reagon is a musician, composer, curator, instructor, and producer. She plays a wide variety of genres including protest music, rock, soul, gospel, blues, and funk, stamping each song with her distinctive voice and guitar style. She currently performs solo and with her band BIGLovely.

Toshi was born in Atlanta, Georgia, but grew up in Washington, DC. Her parents were Bernice, a progressive civil rights activist and founder of the ensemble Sweet Honey in the Rock, and Cordell, a civil rights activist, freedom rider, and founder of The Freedom Singers. Collaborators and friends with activists and folk singers, Bernice and Cordell named their daughter after Pete Seeger's wife, Toshi, who was also little Toshi's godmother. When Toshi was two, her parents divorced, and shortly afterwards Toshi, her brother Kwan, and Bernice moved north to Washington DC. Bernice eventually worked for the Smithsonian Institution as a folklore specialist.

Raised with music from around the world, Toshi listened to everything starting at age two, from Jimi Hendrix, to Big Mama Thornton, to KISS. KISS was her first concert at age 13, and she's still a fan of their music. In 1973 Toshi's mother founded the *à capella* group Sweet Honey in the Rock, right around the same time 11-year-old Toshi swiped her brother's drum set, jamming at home while listening to the all-female group Labelle's *Nightbirds* album. When Toshi was 13, a fall on the concrete pavement while playing softball derailed Toshi's ambition to play football, leading to multiple surgeries, lifelong hip pain, and the use of a cane to help her get around.

Toshi threw herself into music with enthusiasm, teaching herself guitar, bass, and drums. The only formal training she had was the voice lessons that her mother made her take when she was 14 after she injured her vocal cords. Toshi went into voice lessons reluctantly but persisted: "Now, when I work with vocalists and their grownups, a lot of vocalists still don't have that understanding. And so they'll say, 'I get really tired in my throat,' or, 'My shoulders hurt,' or, 'My lower back hurts.' And it's like their body trying to figure out how to make the sound that they wanted to make, but they're not activating the systems, the physical systems. At some point, you have to learn how to use that, or you will not have your voice. Your voice will quit." [2]

At age 17, Toshi was playing at folk festivals, then dropped out of college when up-and-coming singer-guitarist Lenny Kravitz asked her to tour with him on his first world tour. In 1990, her first record, *Justice*, was released. In 1996, her band BIGLovely, named after an endearment from her girlfriend, started performing.

Toshi came out to her mother while in her teens when she started having sex with her girlfriend; however, her mother was unperturbed. When Toshi's mom asked her, " 'Who are you fooling around with?' Toshi replied 'Oh, this girl...' to which her mother said, 'Okay.' She didn't say, 'A girl!?!' It was just, 'Oh, Okay.'" However, when Toshi pushed the envelope and asked if the girlfriend could sleep over, her mother declined her request. [3]

Toshi is raising a daughter, and when asked about parenting as her daughter gets older said, "I think you have to fall in love with whom you fall in love with. There are a bazillion people on the planet. I don't know what my daughter is going to do, but whatever she wants to do, as long as it is healthy for her, is fine with me. We're not going to be telling her who to be with. Our worst thought is that she falls in love with a disgusting person. We don't care what sex or color the person is." [4]

Shortly after the destruction of the World Trade Center in 2001, Toshi—like many folks who lived in or near New York City—developed a trauma-induced fear of flying. Her reaction was to embrace her fear, recognize her need for control, and learn about the technicalities of flying so that she could understand what was happening in the air at any given moment.

In 1993, Toshi and her mother, unbeknownst to one another, bought copies of award-winning Octavia Butler's post-apocalyptic novel, *The Parable of the Sower*, for each other, never guessing that the gift would lead to an opera and a podcast.

In 2015, Toshi and her mother created a congregational opera based on *The Parable of the Sower*. The book, *The Parable of the Sower*, starts in 2024 and touches on climate change, corporate greed, religion-fueled violence, and homelessness, which are sadly all too relevant to us in these turbulent times.

Performing again in March 2020 during the start of the pandemic, Toshi exhorted, "Octavia made it very clear in her predicting: it'd be our disinterest with our civic duties that'd move very lame people into powerful positions, and with those powerful positions they'd take up a lot of resources and a lot of space. If you make decisions based on your biases—and by the time *Parable* happens, which is just four years from now, right on track—we have such a horrific situation in terms of administration of the United States of America...We all have the potential to be refugees in America, and that's very real. And this particular virus is an opportunity for us to really flip that narrative into the speculative fiction world where it needs to live—and actually, in our real world, turn things around in our own ways." [5]

In 2019/2020, Toshi collaborated with writer adrienne maree brown on a podcast called "The Parable of the Sower," a reading and discussion of Octavia Butler's work. The podcast "summarizes the storyline, places it in a strategic context for those intending to change the world and provides questions to help bring Butler's ideas to life." [6] The podcast is available on multiple platforms.

Toshi is known for her collaborations with other artists, including Meshell Ndegeocello, Nona Hendryx, Pete Seeger, Elvis Costello, Chocolate Genius, Dar Williams, and Ani DiFranco. She has played internationally and on stage at Carnegie Hall, the Paris Opera House, and Madison Square Garden. Although she's not been a member of her mother's group, Sweet Honey in the Rock, she has worked closely with them, producing songs on their records and shows and co-producing her mother's 1985 solo album.

Toshi lives in Brooklyn, New York with her partner of over 11 years, filmmaker J. Bob Alotta. Together, they've raised Toshi's brother's daughter as their adopted child. When not creating music and community, Toshi collects flashlights, watches Bollywood movies, and makes jam, "I don't know. I carry a backpack, but I always use them. And then I bought flashlights, and then, I just like, see an interesting one, I get it. And then my mother-in-law, Marlene, she gives me a new flashlight, so she's actually really responsible for this. She gives me a new flashlight for Christmas every year, and she has found so many forms of light, it's pretty amazing. They're always different. They're always pretty interesting. And now it's a thing between us, so for the last, I don't know how long, she's been giving all these cool flashlights." [7]

Toshi has earned numerous awards, including the 2021 Religion and the Arts Award by the American Academy of Religion, the 2021 Herb Alpert Award in the Arts, the 2004 New York Foundation for the Arts award for music composition, and the 2009 Out Music Award. She was awarded a Ford Foundation Art of Change Fellow in 2015 and is a National Women's History Month Honoree. Toshi has contributed to Smithsonian Folkways, the nonprofit record label of the Smithsonian Institution.

Toshi Reagon

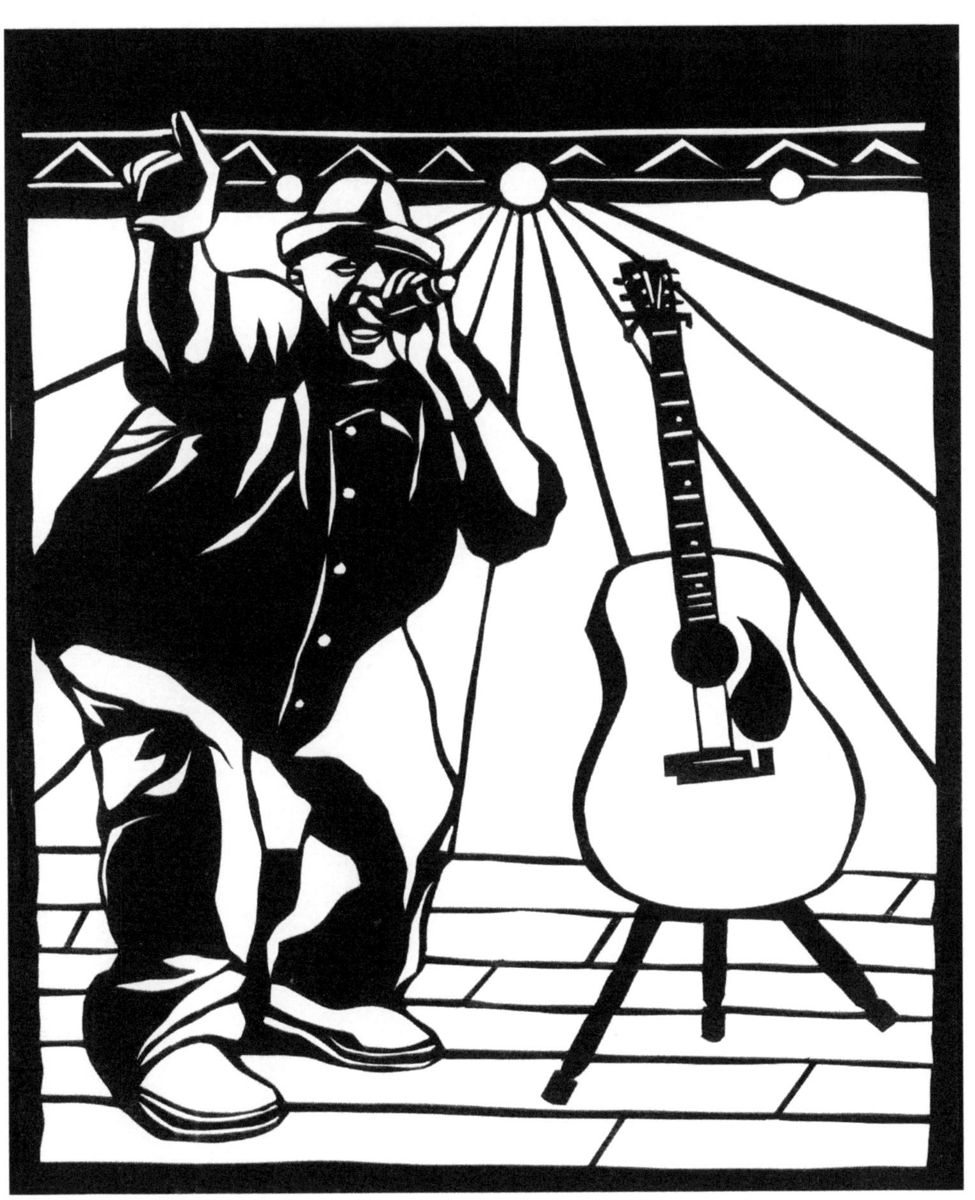

drawn by Miriam Stahl

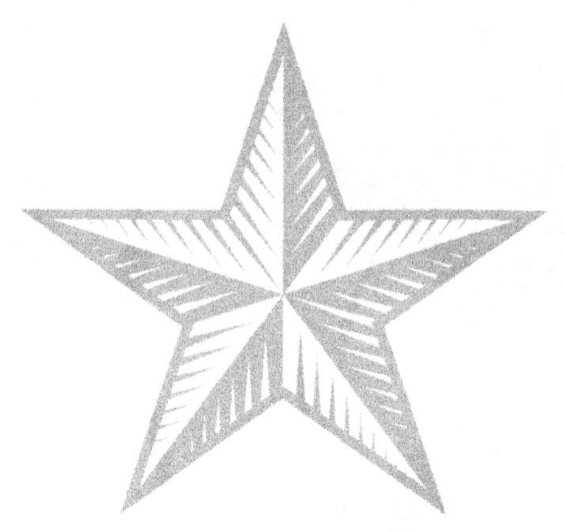

PROFESSIONALS

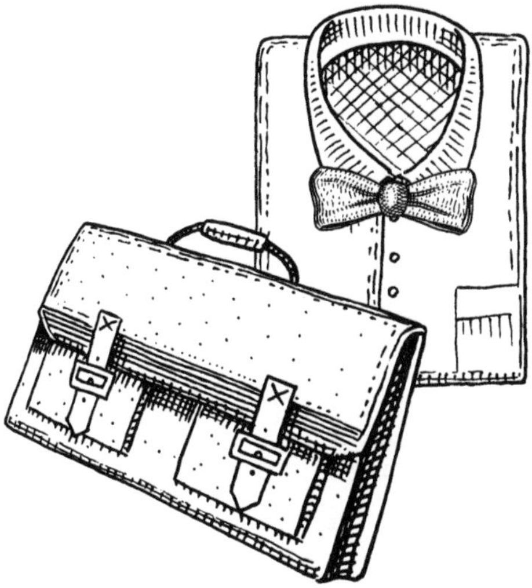

Captain Jennifer Bornemann, United States Public Health Service (USPHS)

b. December 1972 · USA
written and drawn by Diane Kanzler

If my picture in the CDC Emergency Operations Center was able to provide an ounce of hope during such an uncertain and difficult time, then I am incredibly lucky.[1] –CAPT Jennifer Bornemann

At the beginning of the COVID-19 pandemic, Jennifer Bornemann was serving as the Center for Disease Control and Prevention's Resilience Officer. She provided leadership and support in the areas of programs and communication strategies for public health emergency responders throughout the CDC. In early March 2020, Twitter user @taber (Taber Bain) re-tweeted an image of Jen and a colleague at the CDC Emergency Operations Center. Wrote Taber: "First relief I've felt on the US COVID-19 response is the CDC posting this picture from their emergency operations center showing there is at least one lesbian with a keychain neck lanyard that jangles when she walks on the job."[2] It was at this very point in time that the photo of Jen and her lanyard went viral on Twitter and in online journals. The photo of "a competent-appearing woman involved in coronavirus response"[3] certainly instilled hope in the hearts of many as the image was shared widely and rapidly throughout social media.

Jen describes the experience thus: "While focusing on the early days of the COVID-19 response at the CDC, my only breaks were taken to walk my rescue pup around midtown Atlanta. On one of those walks, a friend and fellow officer stationed in San Francisco messaged me that I was 'trending on gay Twitter.' Of course, my initial reaction was 'Huh?!?' as well as that I just don't have time for this, but when I actually looked at the tweet and subsequent comments, it put a much-needed smile on my face. I was so moved by the incredibly positive and hopeful comments as a lesbian, social worker, officer in the US Public Health Service."[4]

Some Twitter users objected to the fact that Taber had described Jen as a lesbian. In an interview with *The Pink News*, Taber said, "...every person that's been like 'how do you know she's a lesbian how DARE you make assu-' has been promptly met by a firm butch going, 'Hon, she's family. I am not going to explain this to you.'"[5]

Jennifer Bornemann was born in 1972 in Riverdale, Georgia. She is one of a pair of identical twin sisters and has a sister who is ten years younger. Jen's father was enlisted in the US Army at the time of the twins' birth. The family moved around the US over the course of Jen's childhood, starting in Atlanta, then they moved to Florida, and on to New Orleans, Louisiana where Jen's father earned his Master's degree in Social Work from Tulane University. Jen was always athletic and very much a tomboy, so the family's next move was formative. Jen's father was commissioned by the United States Public Health Service, and they moved to San Francisco, California where her father worked at the Public Health Service Hospital in the Presidio district. Jen enjoyed playing catch with her father, and she became the first girl to play in Little League in the Presidio. Jen's mother earned her undergraduate degree in healthcare administration while raising the twins. She worked in the private sector as a Federal contractor, running the primary care clinic at the U.S. Naval Academy for a number of years.

After the Public Health Service Hospital was closed during the Reagan era, Jen's family headed back east crammed into a two-door, orange Volvo sedan for the cross-country trip. They settled in northern Virginia where Jen's younger sister was born. Eventually, Jen's father retired from the military with the rank of rear admiral.

Jen worked her way through college and received her B.A. from the University of Maryland. After college, she was employed in the office of a Congressman in Washington, DC, but soon she and her spouse moved to New York City when he landed a job there. They lived in the city for 12 years, during which time Jen earned her M.S.W. from Columbia University's School of Social Work in 2000. Jen was working as a social worker in corporate philanthropy at an investment bank when she met and fell for a woman. Jen reflects upon those times: "I realized I had feelings for a woman but not sure what that meant beyond that. It was a time that changed everything for me and made me realize that I had actually had feelings for women for as long as I could remember. It was a surreal (and kinda scary) time for me. But I then became more comfortable in my new skin and identified as a gay woman." [6]

After a number of years working in corporate philanthropy on Wall Street, and after a conversation with her father, Jen realized she wanted to follow in her beloved father's footsteps and proudly serve her country in uniform. In 2010, Jen commissioned in the United States Public Health Service around disaster behavioral health, working to keep deployed staff safe and healthy. She has deployed in multiple locations/events, including the Camp Fire wildfire in Paradise, CA, Hurricane Recovery in St. Croix, the Ebola epidemic in Liberia (2014–16), the Washington Navy Yard shooting, Superstorm Sandy in New Jersey,

CAPT Jennifer Bornemann, USPHS

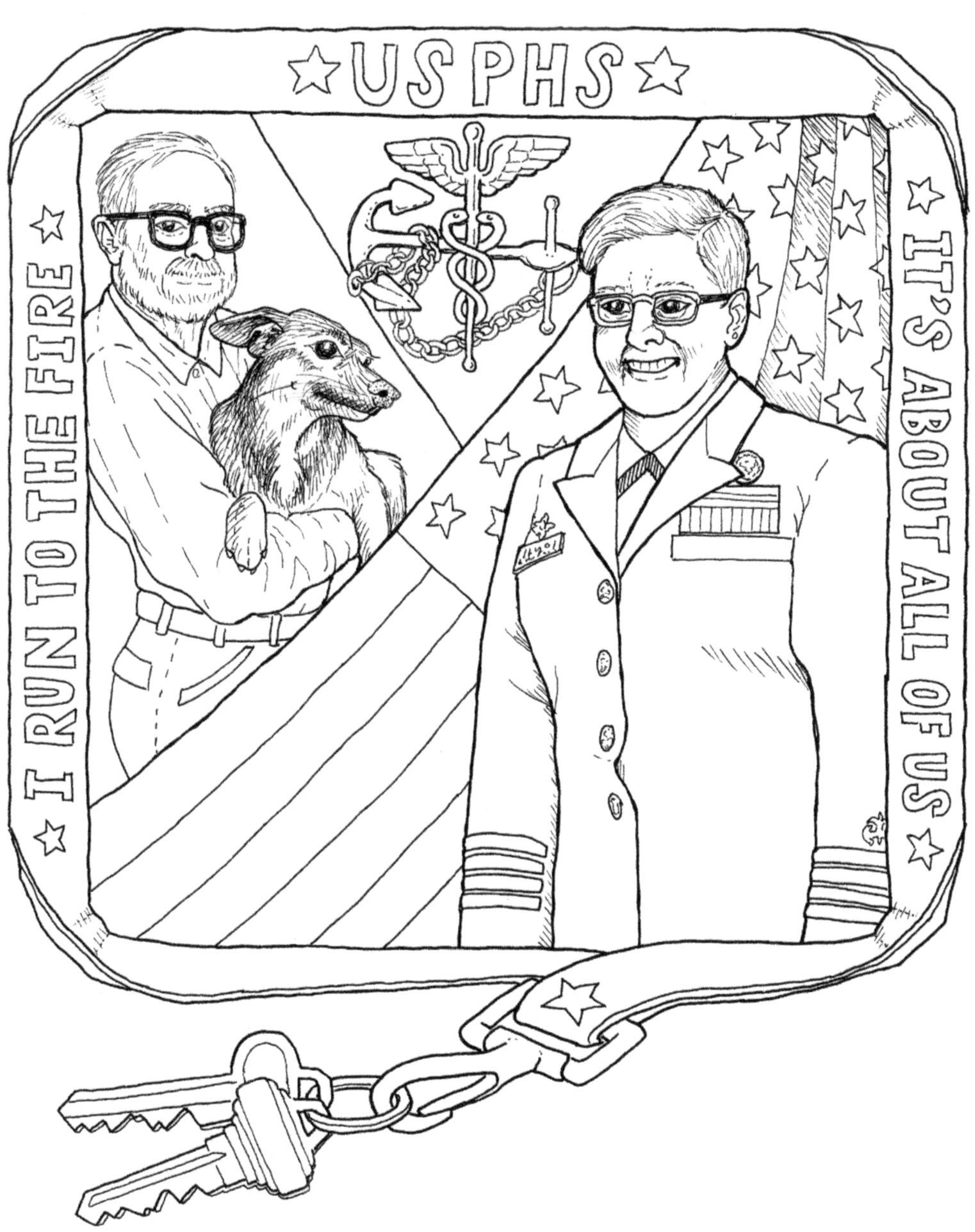

drawn by Diane Kanzler

the Umpqua Community College shooting in Oregon, and severe flooding in Baton Rouge, Louisiana and eastern Kentucky. In her own words, "I like to run to the fire instead of away from." [7]

Working for the CDC during the COVID-19 pandemic put all of Jen's and her coworkers' skill and experience to the test. As scientists and doctors in the US and around the world scrambled to understand, learn to treat, and advise the public about this novel, deadly coronavirus, the CDC has been tasked with providing up-to-date, and sometimes changing, information. People either embraced or turned away from the CDC's advice, and, sadly, this seems to have fallen along political lines rather than one and all looking out for each other in a unified front which certainly would have shortened the pandemic (as of this writing, is in its third year). In an interview Jen gave in 2020, she stated, "What I'm hoping is that folks can really, truly recognize that this world isn't about them. It's not about each and every one of us, it's about ALL of us, and that we are only as good as our sickest or weakest or most vulnerable person. We need to live our lives in a way that is more gentle, more thoughtful with each other." [8] Jen also spoke about the unfortunateness of the term "social distancing," preferring to describe it thus: "It's more about physical distancing with social connectedness." [9]

Jen currently serves as the Team Lead within the Division of Community Mitigation & Recovery for the United States Department of Health & Human Services (HHS) Office of the Administration for Strategic Preparedness and Response (ASPR). She is a licensed clinical social worker in the state of Maryland, and a board-certified Diplomate in Clinical Social Work. As Jen has said, "This is what I was put on this earth to do...living a life of service...this is what makes me tick, this is what inspires me." [10]

Jen is very close to her parents, sisters, and nieces. Both of her parents serve as role models for Jen and her sisters, teaching by word and example how to have compassion for others. She lives with her rescue dog, Indie, and she and her partner are in the process of building a home. Jen is still very athletic and is a three-time Ironman triathlon finisher.

Chef Melissa King

b. October 11, 1983 · Cantonese-American
drawn by Ajuan Mance

Each year, I look forward to pride month and celebrating who I am. Some of you have asked how I identify myself and I realize it's a big question for me—I am a passionate chef, a strong woman, an outspoken Asian American, a Californian, an artist, an entrepreneur, a Libra, a romantic, a proud lesbian, and a queer, androgynous, gender-fluid human. I am an Auntie and an Uncle. Some days I feel like a grandma, and other days I embrace my inner grandpa. I use the pronouns she/her, but am also comfortable with they/them. I cringe a little when I'm sir'ed or ma'amed but understand it's often said out of politeness. I am highly uncomfortable when I walk into a women's public restroom and get mistaken for a man (cannot tell you how many times this happens) and appreciate a gender-neutral bathroom. I never shop in the women's section and find it difficult in the men's. I blush in the best way when my 4-year-old nieces call me "handsome" or respond with "a prince!" when asked what I should be for Halloween...I am a King and not just because it's my last name, but somedays there's a Queen in me that just wants to wear her damn crown. I am masculine, I am feminine, and I am unapologetically all the in between. I am me.[1] –Melissa King

Melissa King is a professional chef. She competed in the television series, *Top Chef*, developed a line of condiments, teaches cooking workshops, and recently started hosting the cooking show, *Tasting Wild*. Her trademark flavors include an inventive blend of modern Californian cuisine with traditional East and Southeast Asian flavors.

Melissa King is a first-generation Cantonese-American who was raised in Los Angeles, California. Her parents were engineers and immigrated to LA from Hong Kong in the late 1960s. Her mother was Cantonese and her father was from Shanghai. Melissa was fascinated by food and cooking as a child. She learned the basics of Chinese cooking from her mother, such as how to steam white rice, properly wash bok choy and other vegetables, and handle a Chinese meat cleaver. She received her first cooking knife for her 10th birthday, "I started helping my mother put dinner on the table by age 6 and watched cooking shows while other children watched *Sesame Street*. I wanted to be a chef since I could remember, but my family suggested I explore it as a hobby in hopes that college would shift my career focus. I guess their master plan didn't work out as intended."[2]

She started cooking in restaurant kitchens at age 17, when she worked as a pastry assistant at the Getty Museum in LA. She assisted with making beloved chef Julia Child's birthday cake at the Getty. "I remember piping out the profiteroles and putting them on the cakes." [3]

After earning a B.A. in psychology, Melissa followed her childhood dream of becoming a professional chef by attending The Culinary Institute of America in Hyde Park, NY, developing her craft in countless restaurants, and appearing on the popular television series, *Top Chef*. She is a certified level 1 sommelier and specializes in combining modern California cuisine with Asian flavors.

After competing in *Top Chef: Boston* in 2014, Melissa returned to the program in 2020 as one of three chefs appearing in *Top Chef: All-Stars LA*, winning both Top Chef and Fan Favorite. She says that competing on *Top Chef* was draining and she had doubts about returning for *Top Chef: All-Stars LA*, "To be truthful, I didn't want to do the second time either," they said, "I was exhausted from competing. It can be a traumatic experience. It's very emotional and physically draining," she continued to talk about her impetus to represent, "I recognized the impact on the Asian American and LGBTQ communities and how important representation was. A lot of that fueled my decision to go back for a second time. I remember watching Martin Yan when I was five on TV and seeing how much that influenced my career." [4]

In a trip down memory lane for Melissa, the "Strokes of Genius" portion of the program took place at the Getty Museum, where Melissa created and won with a dish inspired by the Rococo art movement: a Michelin-star-worthy dish of lobster wonton with shellfish consommé and charred allium oil with vegetables. In the season 17 finale, Melissa created a culturally blended tiramisu by replacing espresso with Hong Kong milk tea flavorings from her childhood via 8-1/2 table-spoons of instant Hong Kong milk tea powder. Melissa described her cooking style thus, "I'm a Chinese American, queer chef that's been classically trained in French Michelin kitchens, as well as Japanese and rustic Italian kitchens. There are many layers to what defines me and my identity, all of which you can feel when you taste my food. I want my Met Gala creations to feel nostalgic for what America was, yet highlight the diverse cultures, flavors, and progressive techniques we find in today's America." [5]

Melissa worked with the producers of *Sesame Street* in 2021 when the show introduced their first Asian-American Muppet, Ji-Young. Melissa was excited to inspire children with the wide and beautiful array of Asian cultures and to cook dumplings with Ji-Young, giving junior chefs cooking advice such as how to get curious in the kitchen, to be like Cookie Monster and not be afraid to try new flavors, and to learn by helping one's parents in the kitchen.

In 2022, Melissa started hosting *National Geographic's Tasting Wild* on Hulu, where she often utilizes unique local ingredients in dishes. *Tasting Wild* adventures have included foraging for mushrooms in Olympic National Park where she hiked through the forest with fungal ecologist Korena Mafune. Melissa is a mushroom enthusiast, "Mushrooms tend to anchor a dish. They carry so much earthiness. They're very versatile as well. You can cook them fresh, use them dried. You can turn them into powders and infuse them into broths, but they add a boost of flavor to your dishes."[6] The two of them gathered mushrooms, and then Melissa cooked them into a rice porridge mushroom kanji, made with caramelized oyster mushrooms, morels, chanterelles, shiitakes, herbs, ginger, garlic, and rice topped with a bit of seaweed and fried shallots. Their most recent culinary *Tasting Wild* adventure was frying up dumplings in a giant wok in a parking lot of Smith Rock State Park in Oregon.

Melissa offers free tutorials on butchering chickens, grilling stone fruits, and poaching lobsters in butter via her website, chefmelissaking.com. She also teaches virtual cooking classes on a range of topics, including how to make seafood chowder, Dutch pancakes, and mapo tofu. She donates prize money and earnings to several disenfranchised communities, including Asian Americans For Equality, Asian Youth Center, The Trevor Project, and National Black Justice Coalition.

In addition to being a professional chef, Melissa is a genderfluid butch style maven who sports couture menswear with glamorous abandon. She wore Thom Browne shorts, a coal-black tuxedo jacket, a white bow tie, and bejeweled gold hand jewelry to the 2022 Gilded Glamour themed Met Gala Red Carpet event. She describes her style this way, "My style right now is androgynous, comfortable, and minimal. I always go for comfortable clothing first before anything else, so lots of flowy printed shirts, sneakers, slides, and we can't forget the quarantine sweatpants. I most always wear menswear or unisex clothing but often have difficulty finding clothes that fit my style and body. I try to seek out slimmer-fitting silhouettes and brands or have items tailored to my proportions. I try to keep things effortless and easygoing."[7]

Melissa lives in San Francisco with her dog, Blanche. Her favorite midnight snack is either a grilled cheese sandwich made with crusty bread and California Cowgirl Wagon Wheel cheese, or instant ramen with a poached egg and kimchi. Aside from hosting *National Geographic's Tasting Wild*, she spends her time modeling for Levi and Gap, speaking on panels, and selling sauces and spice mixes under her company King Sauce, a small-batched sauce and spice line available in her online shop. She also has an apparel line and offers virtual cooking classes.

She says, "I feel very strongly that *Top Chef* has given me more than just a platform for food. I've been really trying to use my voice as much as I can, especially for the people out there that don't have that voice."[8]

In addition to being a *Top Chef* winner and judge, Melissa won "Out 100 List" (OUT, 2020) and "The Best Female Chefs in San Francisco" (*THRILLIST*, 2016). She is a culinary judge for *Top Chef* and The Food Network's *The Julia Child Challenge*. She has been recognized as "one of the best female chefs in San Francisco" and "40 under 40: Rising Star." She was a San Francisco Pride Grand Marshall in 2016.

Chef Melissa King

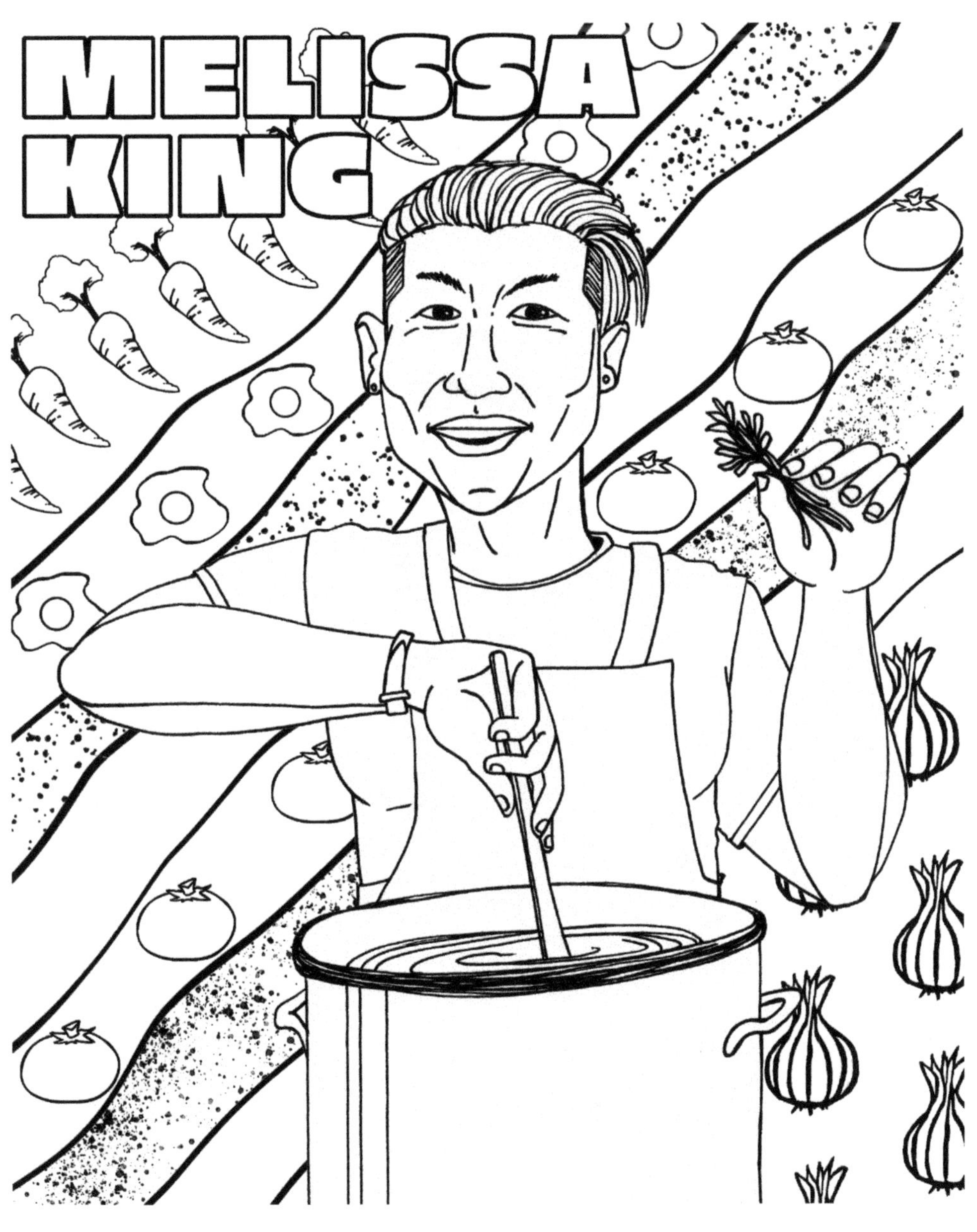

drawn by Ajuan Mance

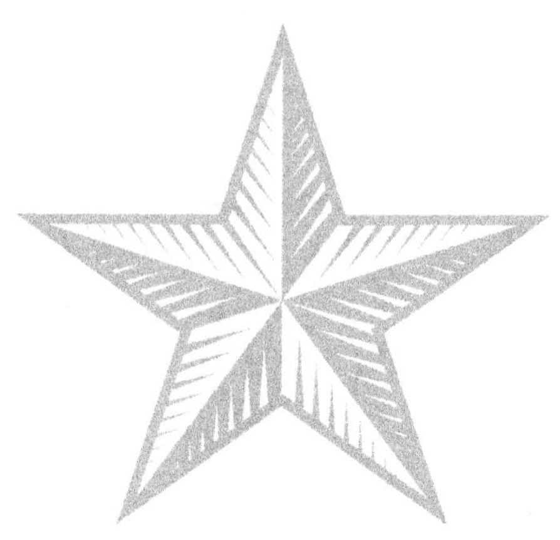

Sandra Lawson, a.k.a. Rabbi Sandra

b. October 14, 1970 · USA
drawn by Jessica Bogac-Moore

I have the Bee Gees on my iPod, and the next thing is Modeh Ani. I'm being chased by zombies and the Shema would come on. It's Saturday morning, [I'm] wearing a Superman shirt, running, being chased by zombies, and I sing along.[1]
–Sandra Lawson

Sandra Lawson was ordained as the world's first Black lesbian rabbi in 2018 and is a member of the Jewish Reconstructionist community. She is also a guitarist, an Army veteran, a social justice activist, a vegan, a personal trainer, and a writer. In many ways, Sandra does not seem like a typical Rabbi. She wears multiple ear hoops, is obviously queer, and is Black. She enjoys comic books and graphic novels.

Sandra grew up poor in a military family. Her mother had been a 1970s Black feminist, and her father worked in recruiting and career counseling. After living in segregated St. Louis, Missouri, the family moved to West Des Moines, Iowa when Sandra was 11. They moved five times before settling down in a suburb in St. Louis. Being a preteen is a socially awkward age, not always receptive to moving, so she became an introvert and a bookworm. She escaped to the local library to bury herself in books and zipped through whatever books she could check out through interlibrary loan.

Her family was Christian, but they were practically non-practicing and did not attend church often. Christianity and spirituality did not appeal to her because the few times she attended church with her family, she was repulsed by the sexism and homophobia that she found there.

Sandra's mother suspected that she was a lesbian long before Sandra had a clue about her sexual orientation. Sandra had made a group of friends during her freshman year at Northeast Missouri State University, but when she returned for her sophomore year, her new friends were all gay. Slowly it dawned on her that she might also be gay. Sandra was 19 years old when she hesitantly came out to a close college friend, then came out to her parents, who were supportive.

Sandra didn't do well in college, so she dropped out and joined the military, eventually earned her degree and became a military police officer investigating child abuse and domestic violence allegations. By then, she was going to LGBTQ+

nightclubs but itching to settle down and attend grad school. During her last months in the military, she traveled to Seoul with some friends who were on the U.S. Army Taekwando team. There she was encouraged by a coach to step up her powerlifting and learn more about training.

In 1996, Sandra moved to Atlanta, Georgia where she started a personal training business. She ended up working with Rabbi Josh Lester as his trainer. By now, Sandra had dated several women and had a Jewish girlfriend, so she went to Josh with all her questions about Jewish culture. She explained her ease and attraction to Josh, "...he was unlike any spiritual leader I'd ever met before," she continued, "But I had never been around a White dude who understood or got people of color and at the time understood his White privilege. Like now it's a little more normal, but he really got it in a way that other people didn't. I didn't know anything about Judaism. And also he was a feminist too, so he understood how racism works. I remember him saying to somebody wait, I'm White—yes, I'm racist. I'm racist because of this, and this is what I'm doing to combat that, and I was just like [that is] so great." [2]

As they became close friends, he invited Sandra to a Hanukkah celebration at Congregation Bet Haverim, which at the time was a small LGBTQ+ synagogue. It was at that service that Sandra fell in love with Judaism, "During the service kids were running around and their parents were listening attentively to the service. I was fascinated by this. The children were dancing and singing just having fun, not being rude....Since the children were doing the things that they enjoyed, this meant that the parents could listen attentively and participate in the service. It seemed to me that everyone was getting what they needed from the service, even Chance the helper dog. Chance, may he rest in peace, during the service was helping himself to the crumbs that were dropped by humans from the potluck. I watched with glee as humans adjusted themselves in the pews so Chance could get the crumbs. The children running around, the dog, all of this, happened during the service. I know this might sound chaotic, but it actually wasn't. There was something special about this service and it was something that made me realize that this community and the people in the community could just be themselves. And then at the end of the service, there was this prayer, a prayer called "A Prayer for the End of Hiding," and it begins, 'We as gay and lesbian Jews' and the entire community was saying it, even the straight folks. I fell in love with that synagogue. I fell in love with the people, the prayers, everything about it for me felt like home, even though I had no understanding of the language, I had no understanding of the prayers and the songs. The community felt like home, and at that moment I fell in love with Bet Haverim. Here was a place where I knew I could be my whole self, I could bring all of me, and I knew I wanted to be a part of the community." [3]

Sandra started attending Congregation Bet Haverim more often and became a member of their community. Gradually, her participation grew as she joined boards and committees until she found herself signing checks and carrying keys. Suddenly, Sandra was a community leader. Wanting to learn more about Judaism, Sandra and a friend started an adult bar mitzvah class, but that wasn't enough for Sandra, and yeshiva, the traditional place of learning for the Jewish layperson, only admitted men. Sandra's solution was to enroll in a Rabbinical school in Philadelphia.

In 2011, Sandra moved to Philadelphia to attend Reconstructionist Rabbinical College. There she honed her understanding of Judaism, "Judaism gave me language and a value system that I didn't have before. So to go back to the homeless metaphor, whatever. Like I would know intellectually that it's wrong to step over a homeless person and not help them, but I would probably have no qualms about continuing to go. Today I have this whole understanding in my tradition about what you are supposed to do when this happens, and modeling what you're supposed to do. I've inherited a tradition that tells me how to talk about gay people in a religious context and explain to people that there is absolutely nothing wrong religiously with being someone married to someone of the same sex or in a relationship with someone of the same sex. And so the faith part sort of married with the social justice part gave me tools I didn't have access to before." [4]

Sandra is currently the Director of Racial Diversity, Equity, and Inclusion at Reconstructing Judaism where she is developing a series of anti-racist policies and trainings for the organization and its affiliate members. She also serves as a mentor to rabbinical students.

Sandra talks about racism in the Jewish community, "As a Black Jew, I understand that Jews of color often do not have opportunities to be fully ourselves in Jewish spaces. When we walk into a community for the first time or maybe after multiple times, many White Jews still treat us as if we are strangers. Many BIPOC Jews are navigating many things at once upon entering Jewish spaces, whether for the first or the 100th time. One of those things is, 'How will they treat me today?' We continue to face microaggressions and just plain old racism in Jewish spaces. When this happens, we must choose whether or not to call a person in to let them know they said or did something harmful that has caused us to feel as if we do not belong," she continues, "Many Jews of color ultimately choose to leave our Jewish community or opt-out of the Jewish experience out of exhaustion. We are tired of White Jews feeling entitled and expecting us to explain our existence and our right to be in our own community." [5]

Sandra is notable for her strong Jewish social media online presence, promoting, entertaining, teaching Torah, and educating on Facebook, Twitter, Snapchat, Instagram, and TikTok. With over 500,000 followers, Rabbi Sandra has expanded people's perceptions of the racial and ethnic diversity within the Jewish community and its leadership.

In 2012, Sandra was propositioned by a woman named Susan on the online dating site OkCupid. It was love at first sight for Susan, but it was three years before Sandra proposed. They married in 2015, the year that Sandra completed her chaplaincy training at Reconstructionist Rabbinical College. Susan is not Jewish, which meant that Sandra was one of the first US rabbis to be ordained while openly in an interfaith relationship.

In December 2022, Sandra and Susan visited The White House for Hanukkah, spending the first night of Hanukkah with Vice President Kamila Harris and Second Gentleman Douglas Emhoff at their home, and the second night of Hanukkah at the White House. It was the first time the White House had its own menorah, made by the White House Carpentry Shop using wood salvaged from a White House Truman-era renovation in 1950.

Sandra and Susan live in North Carolina with three small dogs named Izzy, Bridget, and Simon. Susan bakes a mean vegan lemon meringue pie.

Rabbi Sandra Lawson

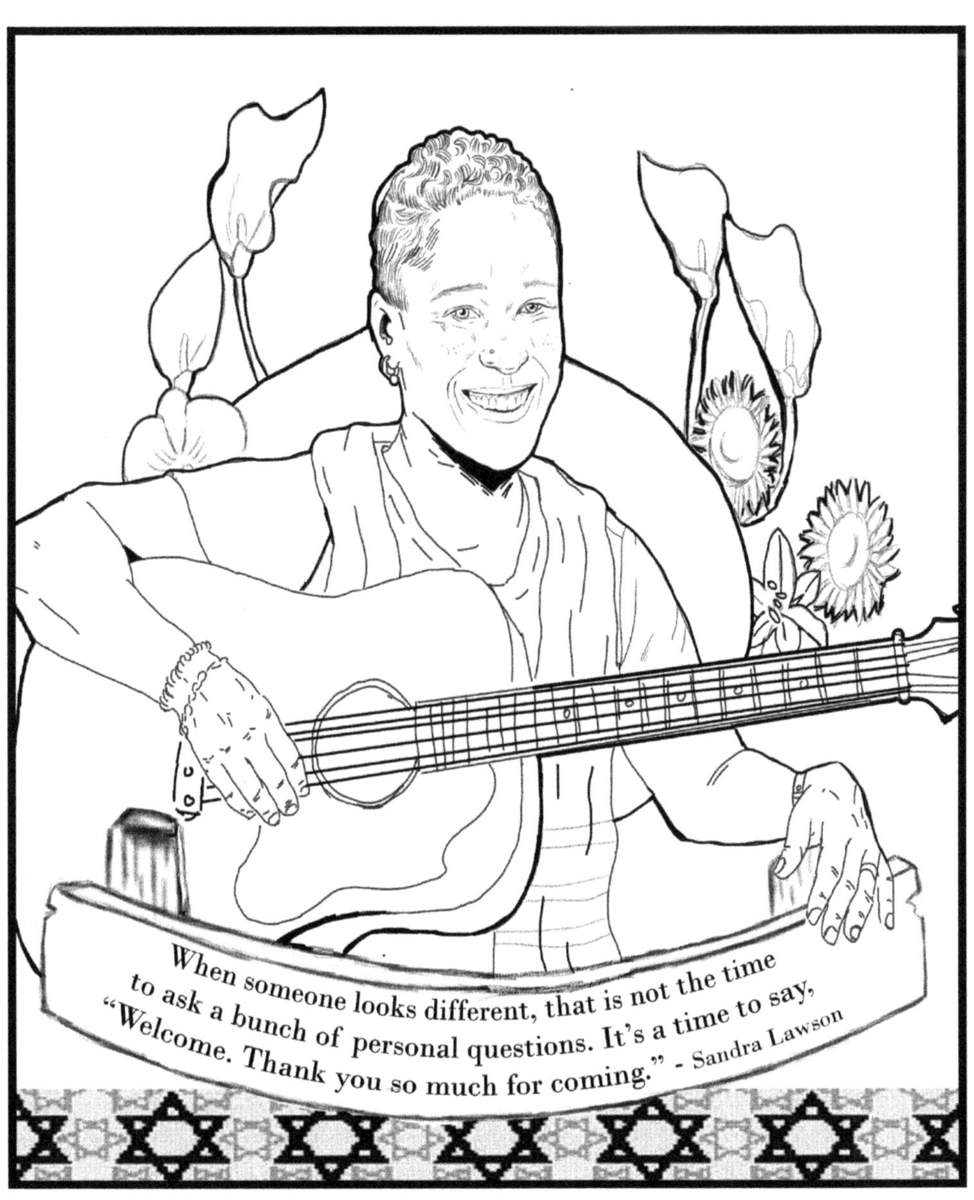

drawn by Jessica Bogac-Moore

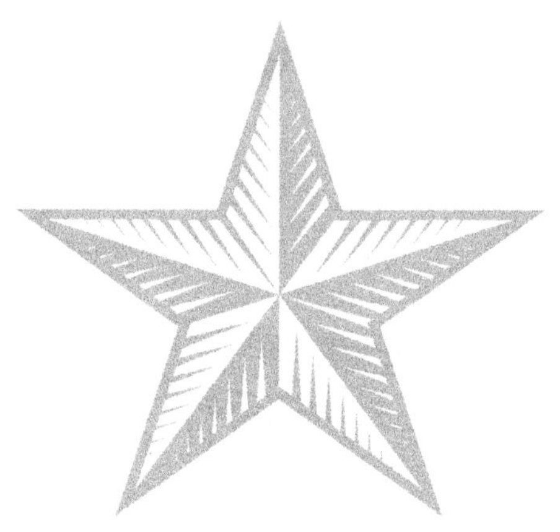

Chief Jeanine Nicholson, SFFD, a.k.a. Neen/Nine

b. late 1960s · USA
drawn by M Rocket

This is about instilling cultural change. We educate our new members on cancer risk and firefighter health in the academy. When we institute new policies and procedures, our leaders in the Department ensure that these are followed. Ultimately these reduce risk and save lives. We need to build on and continue making systemic changes moving forward. So how did occupational cancer change me? It made me more grateful than ever for my life and everything and everyone in it. It made me want to be of more service. It changed my perspective on a lot of things.[1] –Jeanine Nicholson

Nine Nicholson grew up in Pelham, New York. Her family lived across from a fire station. Nine said, "I never saw a female firefighter when I was there and did not have a role model to [inspire me to] even think about the job then. But I was fascinated by all the equipment and the feel of the place. In addition, when there was a fire in town, the horns would sound a particular number, and we would go to our phonebook and look up the number and see what the address was of the fire. I was fascinated by all of this. My father and my grandfather were volunteer firefighters on Long Island, New York. My dad was thrilled when I became a firefighter. My grandfather was also a New York City police officer for many years before he was struck by a drunk driver and could no longer work as a police officer."[2] As a teen, she worked as an all-around employee in a small, family-owned Cape Cod seafood restaurant. Athletic as a child, Nine attempted to sign up for Little League in the early- to mid-1970s but was thwarted because at that time girls were not allowed to play on the team. It was a boys-only club. Little League amended its regulations in 1974, and soon after Nine tried out for the team. Fortunately, her father stood up for her with the league coach and got her in.

Nine attended college at Colgate University, graduating with degrees in anthropology and sociology. Still athletic, she played ice hockey and rugby while at Colgate.

Nine and her three cats moved to San Francisco with a friend in 1990 to find queer community. In 1991, Nine was introduced to the idea that she could become a firefighter during the annual San Francisco Pride celebration when Anita, a firefighter with the San Francisco Fire Department (SFFD), gave her a job interest card and told her that if she could lift heavy objects, then she'd ace it. Anita had started her career as a firefighter in 1989, two years after SFFD began admitting women into the ranks, and there were few women employed by SFFD. Nine was excited by the opportunity. She'd been working construction since her arrival in San Francisco, and firefighting was a career where she could be of service to the community and use her innate skills, explaining that, "I found out that I loved bringing calm and solutions to chaos. Every day brought a different challenge, and I could use both my body and my brain to overcome them."[3]

By 1994, Nine was working for SFFD. She rose in rank from firefighter to firefighter paramedic, splitting her time between the fire engine and the ambulance, and in 2008 was promoted to Lieutenant. In 2012 she was promoted to Captain, and in 2017 to Battalion Chief. On May 6, 2019, Nine was sworn in as the Chief of the SFFD. She is the first openly LGBTQ+ Chief of the SFFD.

In 2012, Nine was diagnosed with breast cancer and underwent a double mastectomy and 16 rounds of chemotherapy. Nine told her cancer story to Firefighters Cancer Support Network, "After 18 years in the SFFD, I heard those three fateful words from my doctor. 'You have cancer.' I was a recently promoted Captain and was focused on learning and growing in that role. But I was diagnosed with an aggressive type of breast cancer. Within two weeks of diagnosis, I had a double mastectomy and a port implanted in my chest. Over the following six months, I endured 16 rounds of chemotherapy. I lost weight, lost my appetite, lost my hair, lost energy, had sores in my mouth and rashes on my body."[4]

As if the debilitation of cancer and cancer treatment wasn't enough, The City's Human Resources Department threw obstacle after obstacle at Nine as she tried to maneuver through fighting cancer and securing workers' compensation leave. One of the issues was that state workers' compensation guidelines automatically designates cancer diagnoses as presumptive and not work-related. Nine told a reporter, "They throw roadblocks after you in the hopes that you just give up. They've asked me to record every single fire I've ever fought. That can be a little difficult to do considering I'm undergoing chemotherapy right now."[5]

Breast cancer changed Nine's life in more ways than she anticipated. A study that took place around the same time as Nine's diagnosis showed that the breast cancer rate among female firefighters is six times higher than in the general population. To put this into perspective, 10 out of 117 female firefighters in San Francisco have had breast cancer. Among female and male firefighters, there were cases of cancers invading the respiratory, digestive, and urinary systems. There were 68 cases of cancer in firefighters within the SFFD in the 4-1/2 years between April 2018 and November 2022.

After recovering from cancer, Nine became an activist fighting for firefighter safety. There were two main issues that contributed to the high rate of cancer in firefighters. One was that smoke and debris from fires had changed over the decades and was more carcinogenic. Nine explained, "What burns these days is very different than what burned 30, 40 years ago. It was wood; it was cotton; it was paper. Now it's all petroleum-based stuff that's burning."[6]

The other problem was the equipment that firefighters used, and a culture that encouraged machismo. Their flame-retardant protective gear, nicknamed "cancer jackets," contains cancer-causing carcinogens, and firefighters tended to wear them longer than necessary, long after the fire was fought. Nine explained that firefighters walked around the station's living quarters wearing their turnout pants and would sleep next to their protective gear at night. Nine talked about the toughness that was present in the firefighter culture, "It used to be a badge of honor if you had soot on your face and your coat was filthy. We would just walk back into the firehouse, take off our coats, and sit at the table to have a meal. So, we've had to institute some new practices."[7]

Additionally, firefighters tended to remove their self-contained breathing apparatus once a fire was put out despite the fact that carcinogens in the smoke lingered at the fire site. The dangerous practices of not wearing self-contained breathing apparatus while on the fire site and continuing to wear their turnout clothing when away from a fire are cultural shifts that are changing. Although SFFD has sought non-carcinogenic protective gear for their firefighters, the main obstacle is financial, as the cost for that gear is higher, and it doesn't last as long.

San Francisco is a vibrant city with a large homeless population and drug use, often going hand-in-hand, and 40% of calls for help to SFFD are from folks without homes. When Nine was promoted to fire chief in 2019, she established several priorities, including disaster preparedness and finding ways to deal with the homelessness, mental health issues, and drug issues that SFFD worked with. In 2021, she established the SFFD Racial Equity Action Plan (REAP) with hiring goals and guidelines for diversity, equity, inclusion, and opportunities for both inward- and outward-facing programs. In 2020, SFFD launched a Street Crisis Response Team. Each team included one community paramedic, one behavioral health clinician, and one behavioral health peer specialist with the goal of helping folks with mental health crises avoid jail or emergency room visits.

Nine has joined the folks at Camp Blaze, a free, one-week camp to encourage girls to pursue a career in firefighting, and the NorCal First Alarm Girls Fire Camp, a free, two-day camp where high school age girls learn about firefighting skills. Nine has been a board member for the San Francisco Firefighters Cancer Prevention Foundation, which assists current and former firefighters with prevention, free cancer screenings, and referrals for medical assistance.

Always looking for more women to join a career as firefighters, Nine has words of encouragement, "Don't doubt yourself. Be prepared physically, psychologically, and mentally. You must believe in yourself and support each other. This is not just for women; I would say that to queer people, people of color, and anyone else that is considering a career as a firefighter. Let me repeat the most important part: support each other."[8]

Nine lives with several rescue animals, including two dogs named Silas and Romeo and a grey cat named Humo, which means smoke in Spanish. She and her pets enjoy rocking out to Marvin Gaye and The Cure.

Chief Jeanine Nicholson, SFFD

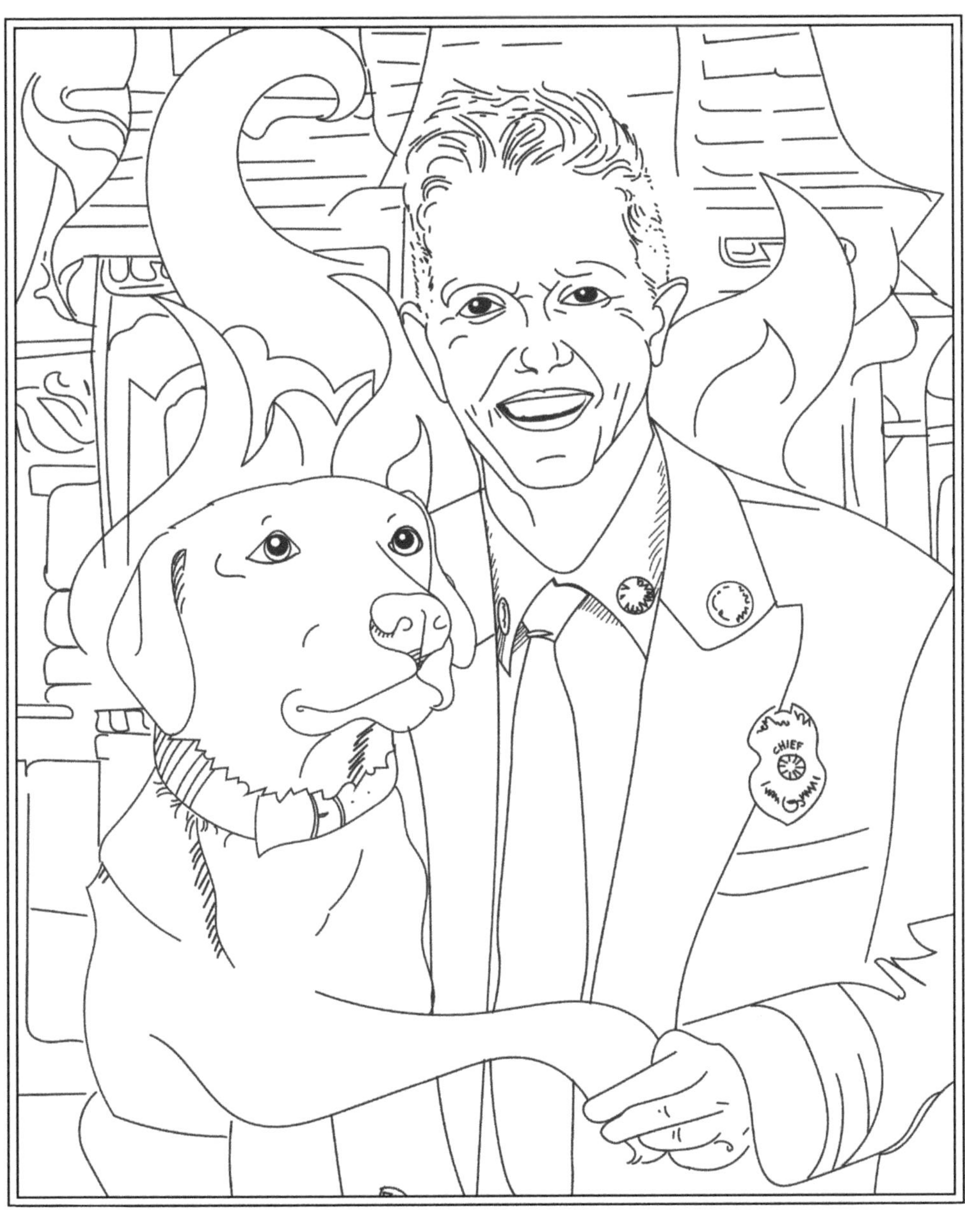

drawn by M Rocket

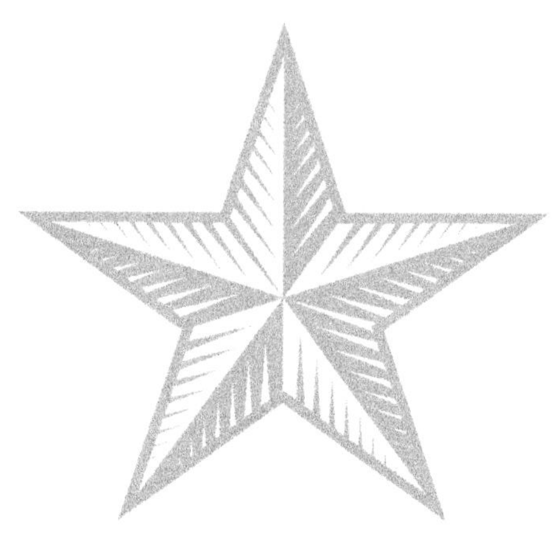

Senator the Honorable Penny Wong

b. November 5, 1968 · Malaysian-Australian
drawn by Pat Tong

I was trying to prove that I could succeed no matter what they said to me, and no matter what they thought of me...I didn't become insular. I've seen that happen with kids, but that wasn't my response. I just pretended to be confident, even when I wasn't. I learned to be steady and still, even when it felt very messy and difficult. You know, to hold yourself steady, even if your reactions are really strong and your emotions confused.[1] –Penny Wong

Penelope Ying-Yen Wong, a.k.a. Penny Wong is a member of the Australian Labor Left Party, with deep political interests in climate change, LGBTQ+ rights, and indigenous and Indo-Pacific issues. She was elected Australia's Foreign Minister in 2022, is the first Asian-born person to hold an Australian cabinet position and is the first out lesbian parliamentarian.

Penny Wong was born in Kota Kinabalu, Malaysia to Jane, an English Australian social worker, and architect Francis Wong, who was Malaysian Chinese. Penny was named after one of her Grandmother "Poh-poh"'s daughters, who was lost while fleeing the Japanese occupation of Borneo in WWII. Penny was trilingual as a child, speaking Malay, Chinese, and English.

When Penny was eight years old, her parents separated, and Penny moved with her mother and brother Toby to Adelaide Hills, South Australia. Penny spoke highly of her upbringing and her parents, "I was really lucky in my parents. I always say they had the most respectful post-divorce relationship I've ever encountered. They are very good friends, she continued, "[I'm] undoubtedly more culturally Australian, but the first thing that most people notice about you is that you are Chinese. That seems to be the way they talk about it. There are some aspects of how I am which I think were probably formed early in Malaysia and with Dad."[2]

Penny and her brother were the only Asians in their school in South Australia and were bullied relentlessly by their schoolmates. The taunting, racism, and physical abuse from their childhood trauma in Adelaide changed both Penny and her brother; Penny became driven toward success and focusing on her studies, while her brother became a respected chef and musician, but he internalized the pain and committed suicide when he was in his 30s.

Penny studied medicine on a scholarship to Scotch College. After realizing that she had a fear of blood, she switched majors and eventually graduated in law and arts at the University of Adelaide with a Graduate Diploma of Legal Practice at the University of South Australia. After graduation, Penny worked for the Construction, Forestry, Mining, and Energy Union (CFMEU), then practiced law with a private firm.

Her first win for office was in 2001 as a Senator and a member of the Labor Left or Progressive Left. There were cultural issues early into her political tenure, as older security staff addressed her as Senator, "I said to them, 'Call me Penny' and they said, 'No we can't'." A Chinese person would address someone much older by a title. "I remember finding it very difficult that older men were calling me Senator and that I didn't have a title to call them."[3] She relaxed into the political post and served as the Minister for Climate Change and the Minister for Finance and Deregulation. In 2022, Penny was sworn in as the Minister for Foreign Affairs. This senior position is responsible for overseeing the international diplomacy section of the Department of Foreign Affairs and Trade.

Penny took a stance against LGBTQ+ marriage rights in 2010 by publicly supporting the Gillard Government's stand against gay marriage and declaring that she respected the Labor's party view of marriage as an institution between a man and a woman. Penny noted, "On the issue of marriage, I think the reality is there is a cultural, religious, historical view around that which we have to respect."[4] The backlash to her denouncement of gay marriage was swift and biting, with the spokesperson for the Australian Marriage Equality retorting that, "It was once the 'cultural, religious and historical view' that women should not be members of Parliament, Asians should not be allowed into Australia, and lesbians shouldn't even exist, yet thankfully all that changed allowing people like Penny Wong to contribute to Australian society at the highest level. By opposing marriage equality, Penny Wong has betrayed gay and lesbian Australians, and by using culture, religion, and history to justify this opposition she has betrayed the principles of tolerance and inclusion that have given her immense opportunities as a lesbian woman of Chinese descent."[5]

Over time, things changed and people evolved. By 2017, Penny was deeply involved with the legalization of same-sex marriage in Australia, stating, "I, for one, am perfectly happy to accept the sacramentality of marriage. A marriage blessed by a member of the clergy is a wonderful thing for those who believe in the sacrament. It is no less a wonderful thing for those whose marriage is celebrated by a civil celebrant, accepting the contractual nature of the affirmation 'I do'," and continuing, "in societies where church and state are constitutionally separate, as they are in Australia and the US, this leads not only to confusion but also to inequity. Religious freedom means being free to worship and to follow your faith without suffering persecution or discrimination for your beliefs. It does not mean imposing your beliefs on everyone else."[6]

A rainbow flag-bedecked Penny wept openly with relief and gratitude when the results of the voluntary postal survey results showed that 61.6% of Australian respondents supported same-sex marriage. At a glitter-sprinkled, gloriously rambunctious, celebratory Australian Marriage Equality street party in Braddon, Penny spoke at Hopscotch Bar and drew applause for her work with LGBTQ+ rights, "I know this has been a tough campaign—I've seen the tears, the pain and the hurt that many people have felt. I want to say to you: take heart from this result because it is a wonderful result. The Australian people have spoken and it is time for Parliament to play its part."[7] The law was passed by Parliament in November 2017. Same-sex marriage legislation was passed on December 7, 2017, and the law took into effect on December 9, 2017.

Under the Labor Party, she had served twice as a federal minister, once each for climate change and for finance. Penny stresses that there is room for growth in the Australian government and that homophobia and misogyny are still prevalent, "I've been cat-called, I've been called a quota girl. There's no doubt that homophobia is still a problem across our community, and the remnants of that are reflected in our Parliament also. I think most politicians—particularly women—will be able to tell you we get some pretty nasty comments on social media. Unfortunately for me, those comments will sometimes have an ugly homophobic undertone."[8]

Penny visited the capital of Sabah and coastal city Kota Kinabalu in 2022 as an act of *balik kampung* (returning home), with affection and respect. In her speech, Penny said that, "Coming here is more than that, too. It is a story that can strengthen the relations between our nations," she continued, "It is the Sabahan childhood, Mamutik Island, Mount Kinabalu, fresh fish and prawns for lunch and Poh-poh's mushroom chicken. These memories stay in my heart."[9]

Penny's brother spoke highly of her ability to inspire folks, "Penny's story should be an inspiration to our young Sabahans. Looking at the rise of a simple Sabahan girl in Australian politics, it means that Sabahans have the potential to succeed and should not underestimate themselves."[10]

Penny lives in Adelaide with her domestic partner and public servant, Sophie, and their two children, Alexander and Hannah, and is a practicing Christian. She relaxes with yoga and poetry. Both children were conceived with IVF with the same man. Penny was determined to keep the second pregnancy private, but her first child Alex had no qualms letting the world know. Penny explained, "Like all families we had to think about whether we tell the toddler because she's notorious—she doesn't know what a secret is. But we decided to tell her because we thought it was important she knew. Which was fine, except at the Labor convention she sat reading *The Gruffalo* to a baby over and over again....I came over and asked how it was going and a friend said 'it's all really good, but she's just told everyone Mummy's got a baby in her tummy.'" [11]

Penny was named as the 2018 McKinnon Political Leader of the Year. She was awarded an Honorary Degree of Doctor from The University of Adelaide for her Parliamentary service and for work with LGBTQ+ rights, gender equality, environmental, multicultural, and economic issues. She is a high-profile spokesperson for the Australian Labor Party.

Senator the Honorable Penny Wong

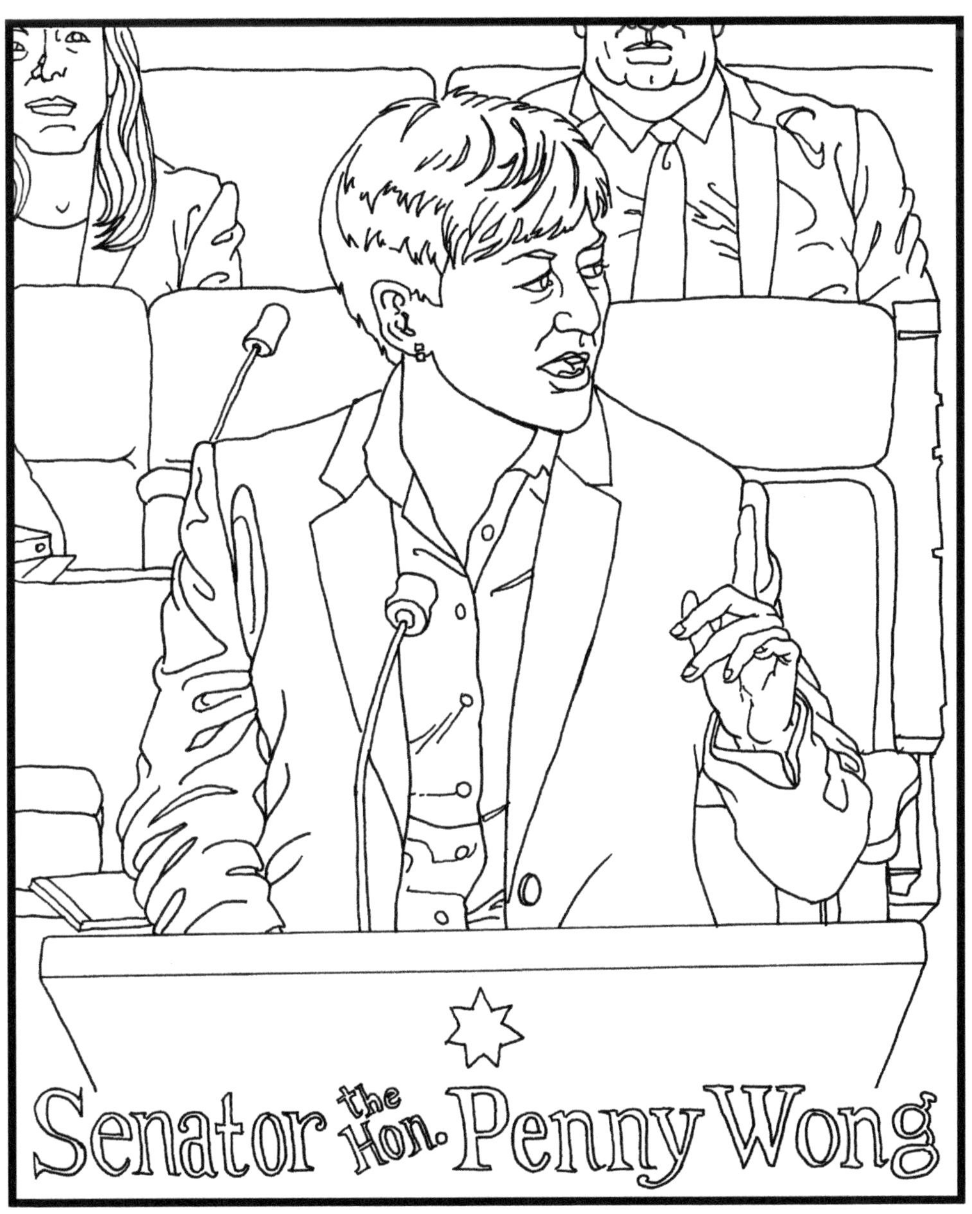

drawn by Pat Tong

SCIENTISTS

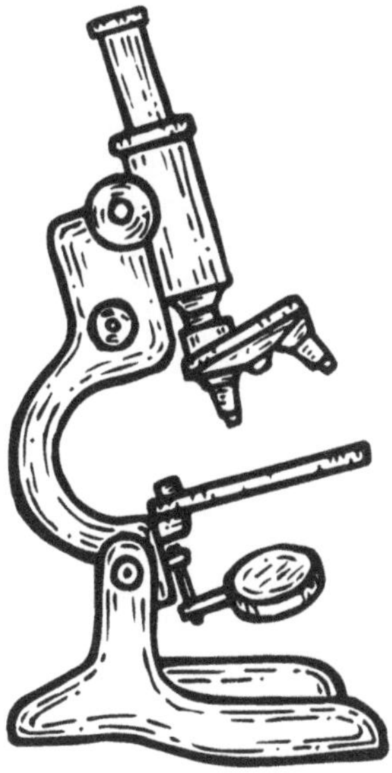

Sidney Woodruff

b. 1994 · USA
drawn by Burton Clarke

One thing I didn't expect to love so much about wildlife was how it didn't always follow the rules! Nature is always changing and moving, so nothing is exact. A common answer in a science classroom is 'Well...it depends.' Even when all of your statistics and models and studies say one thing will happen, nature turns around to say 'Actually, I'm going to do something different.' Herpetology, the study of reptiles and amphibians, I think subconsciously invigorated me. Reptiles and amphibians don't get the same level of love as big mammals or exotic birds, so I think I was partly drawn to it because of the 'outsider' feel to it. Then, learning how frogs can change sex and how salamanders only have paternal care and some male garter snakes can release female pheromones-- all of that disrupts every social norm in humans and I loved that! It makes reptiles and amphibians really awesome animals to me. They don't follow the 'rules.' [1] –Sidney Woodruff

Sidney Woodruff is currently a Ph.D. graduate student in Ecology at the University of California, Davis (UC Davis). They are a turtle aficionado.

Sidney grew up in rural Alabama, the child of a single immigrant mother and with one sibling. Sidney was sporty, but not outdoorsy. Hiking, rock climbing, and other outdoor activities felt like they were reserved for people with time and money for equipment, not for the Black child of an immigrant. As a child, Sidney was a tomboy, getting muddy, digging holes, and climbing trees.

In high school, Sidney thought they were cis and straight, despite not developing crushes on boys or wanting to hang out with female classmates at the mall. When Sidney noted how folks in the community treated effeminate cisgender men and the butch gym teacher, they saw that being queer could lead to lifelong difficulties and heartbreak, so they erased any thoughts they'd entertained about exploring their sexual orientation and gender expression. The exception to this internal self-censorship was Tumblr, the social networking site founded just a few years before Sidney discovered it was a safe place to test-drive their sexuality, gender identity, and gender expression and to connect with people like them. Sidney inadvertently came out to their mother when their mom found their Tumblr page.

Sidney confided, "I am thankful to have a mom who didn't confront me or immediately force me out of the closet. Days flew by, and I didn't even know she had seen it. I can't remember all of the details, but there was one day as a freshman or sophomore in high school where I was having a really rough day, just down in the dumps. My mom, knowing what I was keeping secret and what was weighing on me, mentioned she had seen my page. I immediately broke down and came out to her as bisexual. In my mind, that seemed a safer identity than full lesbian. She supported me through and through and has supported me through my subsequent (and multiple) coming outs later as a lesbian, then questioning transman, and then nonbinary. She's been there supporting me since the beginning, even attending a few Pride parades in Atlanta with me over the years." [2]

Sidney liked animals, and so they decided to become a veterinarian, but high school chemistry stumped them, so they started off in college majoring in psychology. In their junior year, they spotted a flyer for a forestry and wildlife program. They switched over to Wildlife Sciences, explaining how outside of their scope wildlife conservation felt, "Growing up, I didn't have that iconic moment where I was watching Steve Irwin on TV and realized that I wanted to have a career in wildlife conservation. It never even crossed my mind that it was an option for me since Steve Irwin was so different from me (representation is so important at a young age)." [3]

Sidney ended up earning their undergraduate degrees at the University of Georgia in Fisheries and Wildlife Sciences, and a second B.A. in Forestry. While studying for their B.A.s, fate intervened when Sidney accidentally became involved with turtle research. They had a job as a technician in a loggerhead sea turtle genetic-fingerprinting lab, where they ran DNA extractions on eggshells from nesting sea turtles. One thing led to another, and a career was born.

Sidney knows from personal experience how unattainable a career in the sciences would seem to a young Black, Indigenous, and person of color (BIPOC) queer person and uses their status to encourage other BIPOC and queers to go into the field, "It has made me realize why representation in science is so important. So now, I try to be as visible as possible with my various marginalized identities. My queerness is not something I leave at the door. It informs my science, how I look at the world, and how I question things. I hope that someone can see me and realize they want to get into this field and that they can. Science is a White-dominated, affluent, and male-centered field. I've focused my efforts on disrupting that by mentoring students and professionals from underrepresented identities, whether that be in race, gender, sexuality, income, citizenship, etc." [4]

In 2017, Sidney started working as a park ranger at Yosemite National Park, located in California's Sierra Nevada mountains. During this period, they worked outdoors, "...hiking into remote field sites, doing visual surveys for cryptic species, talking to the public about wildlife and ways to protect wildlife biodiversity. The beauty of this field is that it is becoming more and more interdisciplinary and seeing how humans are a part of the equation." [5]

Working as a park ranger was one more step toward equality in what had been a daunting field. People of color (POC) don't visit and vacation at national parks nearly as often as White people, representing less than 25% of visitors in 419 parks. Part of this is due to park entrance fees, difficulty getting time off from work due to lower-paying jobs with fewer benefits, lack of public transportation to the parks, and racism within parks. There are cultural issues, with camping and hiking seen as unattainable by POC, many times park signage is monolingual, and ranger uniforms can feel intimidating to immigrant visitors in light of POC profiling by law enforcement. There are also diversity issues within the parks, with fewer than 20% of park employees being POC. Ambreen Tariq, creator of the "Brown People Camping" social media campaign and an immigrant from India, talked about what it's like to camp in the US, "When I was a child, I felt like an outsider trying to gain entrance, except now I am American and this is my country," she continued, "The future of our country is more and more diverse....we're going to have more people of color in this country than White people, but our parks, our green spaces, our conservation spaces, those demographics are remaining White. What does that mean for the future of our land, for environmentalism? We need everyone to experience and then love the land so that they will stay and fight." [6]

At the time of this writing, Sidney is busy finishing up her Ph.D. in Ecology at UC Davis, with an emphasis on wildlife research, conservation and protection, and examining how climate change and other environmental issues threaten wildlife. She has a passion for how the removal of invasive American bullfrogs, which are not native to western United States but were introduced there, can positively affect Western pond turtle species and how this data can assist conservation decisions and actions in the future.

In their spare time, they enjoy all the outdoor sports that once seemed so unattainable to them as a child, including skiing, hiking, and rock climbing. Although these activities remain overrun by White, well-off men wanting to demonstrate their machismo, Sidney has slowly found pockets of similar sporty BIPOC and queer communities to share their enthusiasm, starting sporting groups as necessary.

No longer a cis bisexual woman, their queer identity remains fluid, "As my language and knowledge in queerness grows, I'm no longer scared or anxious to question my identities because I know they are fluid and can't be defined. I still believe labels are very important for self-recognition and finding community, but I also don't feel as confined by them anymore. I find that I test different identities and pronouns and sexualities often, seeing what makes me tense up and what makes me feel safe. I think I will always feel a level of comfort in butch and stud identities, partly because I know there is still so much variety within those identities. I'm really proud of my growth in accepting myself for all of the various questions and blurry lines that come up with my queerness."[7]

In 2020, Sidney was a panelist for the 2020 Women's Climbing Festival, speaking about the climbing community, racial affinity spaces, and racism in the climbing community. Sidney mentored students through the now inactive organization, M.U.S.E. (Mentorship for Underrepresented STEM Enthusiasts).

In 2022 Sidney won the UC Davis Outstanding Graduate Student Teaching Awards (OGTA).

Sidney Woodruff

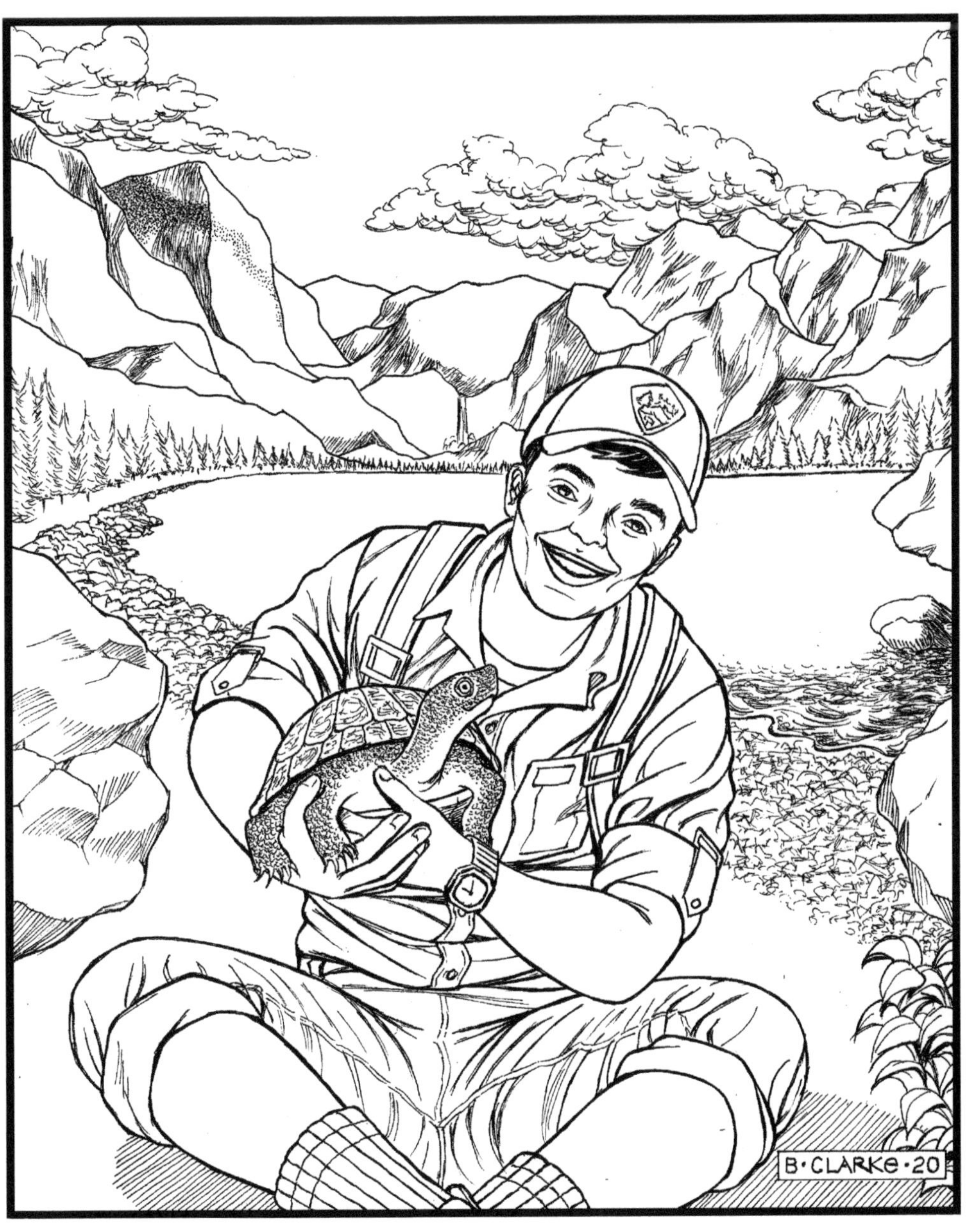

drawn by Burton Clarke

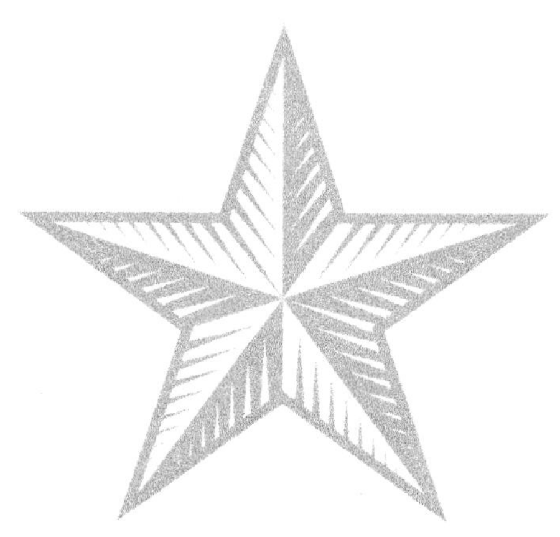

Shelley Diamond

b. 1951 · USA
drawn by Ajuan Mance

In other words, could you get it [AIDs] just like you get COVID? People didn't know. But I was watching the research early on. When I say that, I was still at UCLA, and our lab was across the hallway from Mike Gottlieb's office. Gottlieb was the first physician to report having gay male patients with a condition called Kaposi's sarcoma, later linked to AIDS. He didn't understand why he was only seeing it in gay men. Then one day, we had a discussion about gay sex. Weeks later, Mike asked me if I could pull together some people in the community to form an educational group. AIDS Project Los Angeles [was] taking shape and we formed its first medical advisory board. I was also on the first board for Lesbian and Gay Health and Health Policy Foundation that started at UCLA.[1] –Shelley Diamond

Shelley Diamond is the Managing Director of the Flow Cytometry/Cell Sorting Facility at the California Institute of Technology in Pasadena, California and has been the Lab Manager for Dr. Ellen Rothenberg for 40+ years. She is an LGBTQ+ activist and is the chair emeritus of Out to Innovate (previously the National Organization of Gay and Lesbian Scientists and Technical Professionals, or NOGLSTP) for LGBTQ+ professionals in the fields of science, technology, engineering, and mathematics (STEM).

Shelley was born into an upper-class family in Phoenix, Arizona. Her parents were second-generation Polish Jews and Latvians who set up a series of department stores after emigrating to the USA. The only girl in a family with two brothers, she was a tomboy as a child. Her parents tried to femme her up by sending her to charm school, but when she refused to participate she was expelled. Shelley laughed at the thought, "My father sent me to a modeling school/textile institute in California, and four weeks later, they called him to come and get me and gave him his money back, telling him I had no grace. I was allergic to the makeup—it turned my face orange—and I was horrible in high heels. I kept falling off of them. Literally, he had to come get me."[2] In a last ditch effort to de-tomboy Shelley, her parents paid for her to take cotillion classes to become ladylike. She came out as a debutante at age 16, decked out in white gloves, pearls, a black and white gown, and a matching black brocade evening coat.

In 1969, Shelley started her higher education at Temple Buell College in Denver, a non-academically challenging women's college. Shelley did not do well there; her grades tanked because she was either at antiwar protests or obliviously crushing on her roommates. Then, in the early 1970s, she took a class in developmental biology and embryology at the University of Hawaii which changed her life. She returned to the mainland, aced two semesters at Arizona State, then transferred to the University of California, Santa Barbara, where she graduated in 1974 with dual bachelor's degrees in biochemistry and molecular biology.

By her senior year, Shelley realized that she loved women, but when her high school best friend returned from Vietnam with Crohn's disease from amoebic dysentery and needed medical treatment, she married him so that he could access her health insurance. Her husband, Cliff, knew she was at least bisexual, so they opened their marriage. Ten years into the marriage, Shelley fell in love with her first serious girlfriend. The three of them lived together for a couple of years, but Shelley and Cliff didn't divorce until she met her current wife, Barbara.

After both of her parents died, Shelley finally came out to her brothers. It did not go over well. "I was 26 or something, when I finally decided to tell my [younger] brother. I told him in the car while we were on the freeway—I thought he was going to crash."[3] Her younger brother and his family eventually came around, but her older brother did not. Her older brother was so horrified that she was a lesbian that he wanted to institutionalize Shelley.

In 1978, Shelley was working at City of Hope with the research team that cloned the novel human gene for the first synthetic insulin, which was instrumental to the start of the biotechnology revolution. It was also a sobering brush with sexism and homophobia in science when her name was left off the paper. Working 12-hour days, Shelley recalls the moment they got an active insulin molecule, "I was in charge of assaying that. I was the one actually standing at the scintillation counter when we got it, and I started screaming, and everybody knew that we were successful, and we won the race!"[4] In 1981 her colleagues started sabotaging her equipment because she was seeing another woman in the department. Shelley quit City of Hope soon after the bullying and discrimination took place.

In the early 1980s, Shelley started working at Caltech as the lab manager for Dr. Ellen Rothenberg. Shelley came out to Dr. Rothenberg during the job interview as a lesbian activist, but fortunately Dr. Rothenberg was unperturbed and hired her. Shelley is still managing Dr. Rothenberg's lab.

Shelley specializes in cell separation and analysis. She has managed Dr. Rothenberg's lab for over 40 years, working on various projects, particularly studying the immune system to discover how T-cells and the thymus gland communicate. Shelley explains, "Some people have called me a 'spritzomaniac' meaning I have a lot of different skill sets and different mindsets. I actually think that I think like a cell. In my work with all of my clients, I pretend to be the cell, and sense what it's feeling and try to make things better for the processing."[5]

Shelley also met her wife-to-be, fellow scientist and analytical chemist Barbara Belmont, during this time period. As Shelley tells the story of their meeting, "So the woman that I had the affair with [at City of Hope and later] at the time challenged me to go to a Los Angeles Gay and Lesbian Scientists meeting. And so I went and was there at the beginning of the formation of a lot of the organization. And after about a year, Barbara came to a woman's potluck, and she was a tall drink of water. And one thing led to another."[6] But their relationship was not a linear progression.

As they became closer, Barbara was the brave one to take a chance and nervously tell Shelley that she was in love with her. They'd been visiting, and as Shelley prepared to drive away, she whispered that she was in love too. Barbara said, "So I just put the car in gear and I'm like, 'I have to go now. Should we talk about this?' So as I'm driving away I'm like, 'Callooh! Callay! Oh frabjous day! She loves me too.' But, you know, we had a lot to talk about."[7]

There were obstacles; for one, they were both married to men. Their husbands were supportive of the new romance, but it was obvious that Shelley and Barbara needed to divorce them. In 1987, Shelley and Barbara held a commitment ceremony, wanting as many legal rights and protections as possible, including medical and financial powers of attorney. In 2008, they had a small official marriage ceremony.

Their shared careers as scientists have deepened their marriage. Barbara says, "We understand what we're talking about, and we have got, you know, like a puzzle at work or something weird bugging us and we talk about it, the other one almost always has some insight from their perspective....Being scientists together in a relationship is the very best thing in the world. We geek out on the same things and we solve the world's problems from the same perspectives,"[8] and Shelley, beaming, agrees, "We're the air under each other's wings in terms of our careers. If she's got to stay late in the lab, I understand."[9]

Shelley and Barbara live in southern California. Barbara is an analytical chemist and LGBTQ+ activist. They remain committed to encouraging young LGBTQ+ scientists, "We're out here trying to get other people to come out and not be afraid and push visibility because that's what's going to change the climate."[10]

In 1997 Shelley was awarded the Los Angeles Gay and Lesbian Center LACE Award for Professional Achievement, including her work on AIDS activism and advocating for LGBTQ+ people in the STEM fields. In 2004, Shelley was awarded the first Walt Westmann Award by Out to Innovate. She has represented the LGBTQ+ community for DiscoverE, a nonprofit that celebrates the accomplishments of engineers and encourages an interest in engineering in elementary and secondary school-age students. In 2017, Shelley was the keynote speaker for the National Science Foundation's Pride Celebration. In 2019, she served on the American Association for the Advancement of Science's Societies Consortium on Sexual Harassment.

Rochelle "Shelley" Diamond

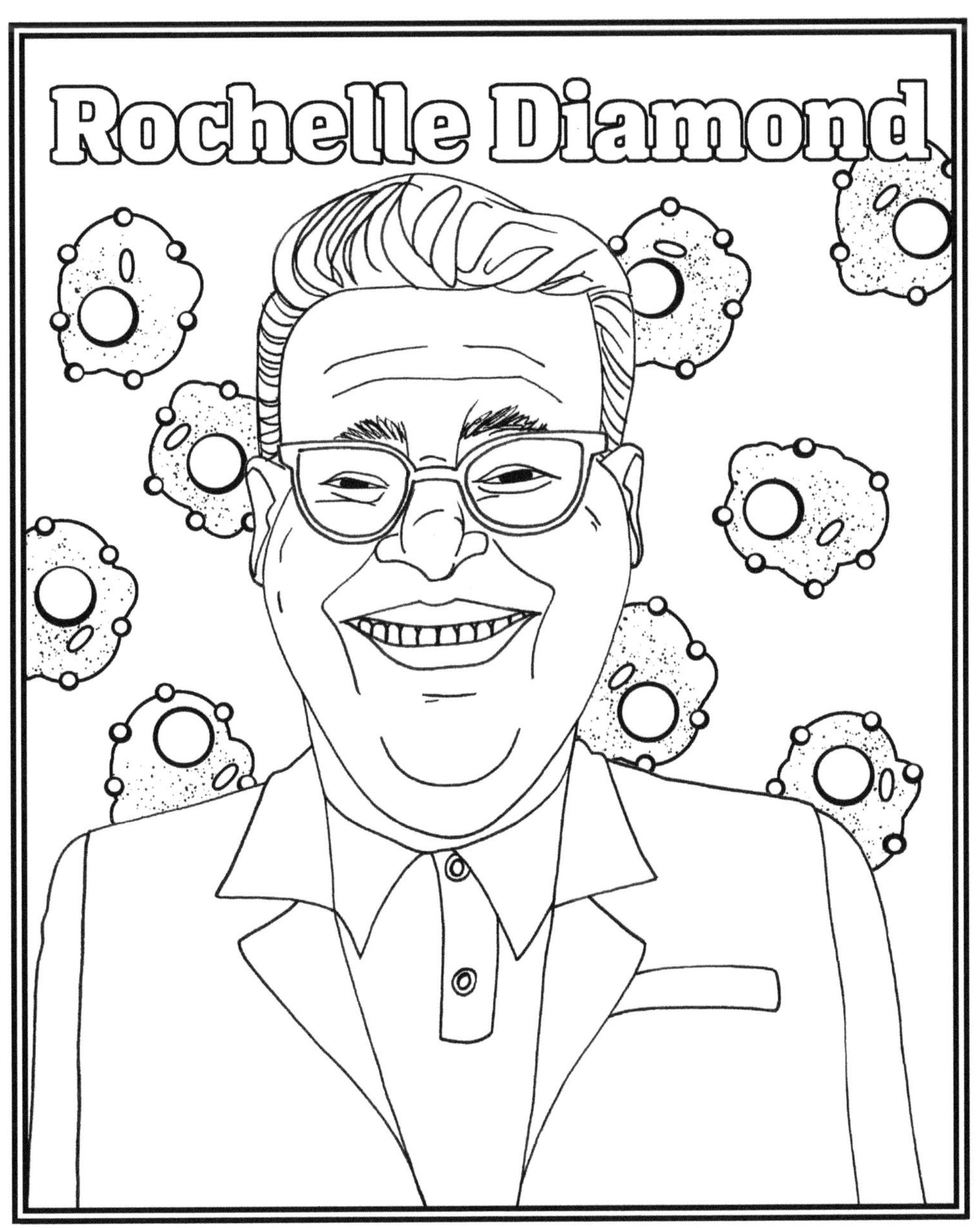

drawn by Ajuan Mance

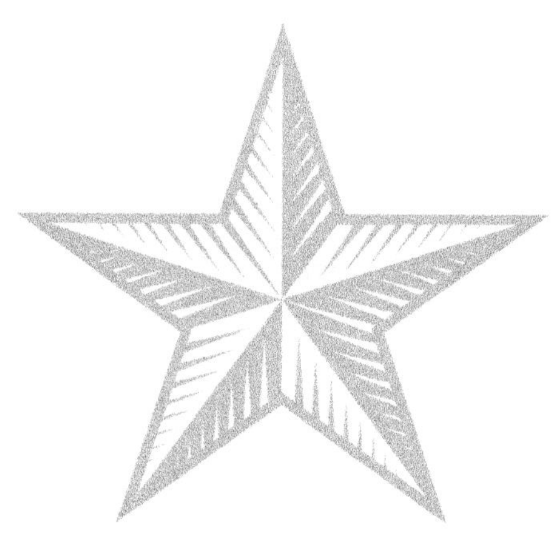

Sally Ride

May 26, 1951–July 23, 2012 · USA
drawn by Jennifer Camper

I am fundamentally an optimist, which is a good thing to be right now. I believe that if people start acting and taking climate change seriously, we can slow it down, turn it around, and have something that looks like the planet that we have all come to know and love. If we have learned anything over the last 30 years, it's that Earth is a complicated place. It might be possible to do something—try some experiment to help solve things—that could actually throw the whole system off, and we might have trouble recovering from it. We have to start working on and developing technologies, and then deploying these technologies. And we need to focus on the science to keep learning more and more. If we start experimenting with the planet, we could get ourselves in trouble. If we are going to be smart, we had better be really smart.[1] –Sally Ride

Sally Ride was the first American woman to fly into outer space. Sally was born in southern California to Joyce and Dale Ride. She had one sibling, a sister nicknamed Bear, who grew up to become a gay Presbyterian minister. Her mother was a counselor at a women's correctional facility, and her father was a political science professor. Both of her parents were elders in the Presbyterian Church. Sally started her love affair with science as a child. Her parents supported her, giving her a chemistry set, a telescope, and a subscription to the magazine *Scientific American*.

Sally was a tomboy and started playing tennis at age nine, ranking 20th in Southern California for girls under the age of 12 and eventually played for Stanford University. Sally met her future life partner, Tam O'Shaughnessy, while playing on the junior tennis circuit in Southern California. Tam went on to become a children's science writer and a professional tennis player, while Sally stopped playing tennis professionally in her early 20s in order to concentrate on studying science and ended up at Stanford University.

In the 1960s, NASA had strict hiring requirements which included graduating from a military jet pilot testing program that disallowed women. Fortunately for Sally, in the 1970s, the military began accepting women into their prerequisite pilot program, leading the way for women to become astronauts. Astronaut John Glenn, the first American to orbit earth, scoffed at the idea that women should be in space in his testimony at the 1962 House Subcommittee Hearings investigating whether NASA was discriminating against women, "It is just a fact. The men go off and fight the wars and fly the airplanes....The fact that women are not in this field is a fact of our social order. It may be undesirable."[2]

In 1977, Sally was enrolled at Stanford and studying physics, astrophysics, and English when she read a newspaper article in *The Stanford Daily* that said that NASA was actively looking for female astronauts. Always adventurous, Sally applied for the position and was accepted. This led to a career with NASA, launching into space on the shuttle Challenger in 1983 and again in 1984. One of the reasons she was chosen for the 1983 space mission was that she was instrumental in the development of a robotic arm for the space shuttle which, ultimately, was used to retrieve a satellite.

Although NASA had hired her, the public and press were unrelenting with their sexist questioning of the appropriateness of a woman in space, asking such questions as whether spaceflight would affect her reproductive organs, whether she would wear a bra or makeup in space, and how she'd handle having her period while in space.

The flight was joyous. Sally described free fall as feeling like a "baby deer" on a "frozen lake." She entertained herself by listening to the Beatles and the Beach Boys, and described outer space as, "I saw the blackness of space, and then the bright blue Earth. And then it looked as if someone had taken a royal blue crayon and traced along Earth's horizon. And then I realized that that blue line, that really thin royal blue line, was Earth's atmosphere, and that was all there was of it. And it's so clear from that perspective how fragile our existence is."[3] Sally exclaimed upon landing on Earth after her first space flight, "I'm sure it was the most fun that I'll ever have in my life."[4]

During this time, Sally had romantic relationships with both men and women, and she married a man in 1982. Her sister Bear was one of the officiants, and one of Sally's female exes was one of the guests. Her new husband was fellow astronaut Steve Hawley.

Sally continued to work for NASA as she trained for a third mission. In 1986, Challenger exploded while in flight, killing everyone on board. Sally was a member of the Presidential Commission to investigate the tragic accident, uncovering that NASA had known that the shuttle's O-rings could fail in cold temperatures, but sent up the seven crew members despite this potentially deadly failing.

By 1985, Sally and Steve were going through marital struggles, while Sally's relationship with Tam evolved from platonic to romantic. Tam described that change in an NPR interview, "It was kind of a magic moment. When she came to town, we'd just get tons of exercise and just talk—talk about her experiences in Houston and we'd talk about the old tennis days. And I'd talk about biology and we'd talk about what we wanted to do in the future. And just this one day, we'd gone for a long walk. We'd gone to the pizza parlor, we walked back to my house, and we're sitting on the couch and my dog, my old cocker spaniel, missed me, so I just sort of petted her. And I suddenly felt a hand on my lower back, just a gentle—and it was like, what? It gave me the chills. And I looked back and it was just like, Sally was in love with me. And in that moment, I realized that I was in love with her, too. I guess it was growing maybe in bits and pieces over a long time. But it was really that moment that it was like, oh my (laughs), you know? Yeah, it was just a special moment."[5] Sally and Steve soon divorced.

In 1989, Sally started working as a professor of physics and as director of the California Space Institute at the University of California, San Diego and living with Tam. Although they were out as a devoted couple with their friends, they played it safe and remained closeted in the work world, with the press, and with Sally's parents. Sally and Tam shared a passion for science and were angry at the absence of women from science and engineering careers, so they decided to do something about it and became activists. In 1989 Sally and her close friend, Sue Oakie, published *To Space and Back*, an ALA Notable Children's Book, followed by five more children's books on space.

In 2001, Sally and Tam combined forces with three colleagues and founded the nonprofit Sally Ride Science, an education company focusing on children's education within science, technology, engineering, and math (STEM). One of the nonprofit's many objectives was to provide science school programs and materials, along with specialized training for teachers.

Concerned about climate change, in 2009, Sally and Tam published two books geared towards children from age 9 through high school, *Mission: Planet Earth: Our World and Its Climate—and How Humans Are Changing Them* and *Mission: Save the Planet: Things You Can Do to Help Fight Global Warming!*

Sally and Tam lived in the seaside town of La Jolla, California. In 2012, Sally died at age 61 after a 17-month-long struggle with pancreatic cancer. Whereas her sister Bear was always out as gay, Sally was protective of her privacy, so she remained closeted to the general public until her death. Tam described sitting by Sally's bed and planning her obituary together. Sally asked, "Who am I going to be in the world?" Tam continued, "And she [Sally] kind of thought about it for a second. And she was just lying down, you know, her hair completely shaved but just looking adorable (laughs), I might add. Salt and pepper little crew cut. And she said, you decide. Whatever you decide will be just fine. You decide. And, you know, that put me in shock."[6] Sally finally came out in the obituary written by Tam—with Sally's deathbed permission—admitting the truth about their relationship to the rest of the world.

Sally garnered a stupendous number of awards and tributes, including being inducted into the National Women's Hall of Fame and the Astronaut Hall of Fame. She was awarded the NASA Space Flight Medal twice. In 2013, Sally was posthumously awarded the Presidential Medal of Freedom. Sally's archive is in the National Air and Space Museum Archives of the Smithsonian Institution.

Sally Ride

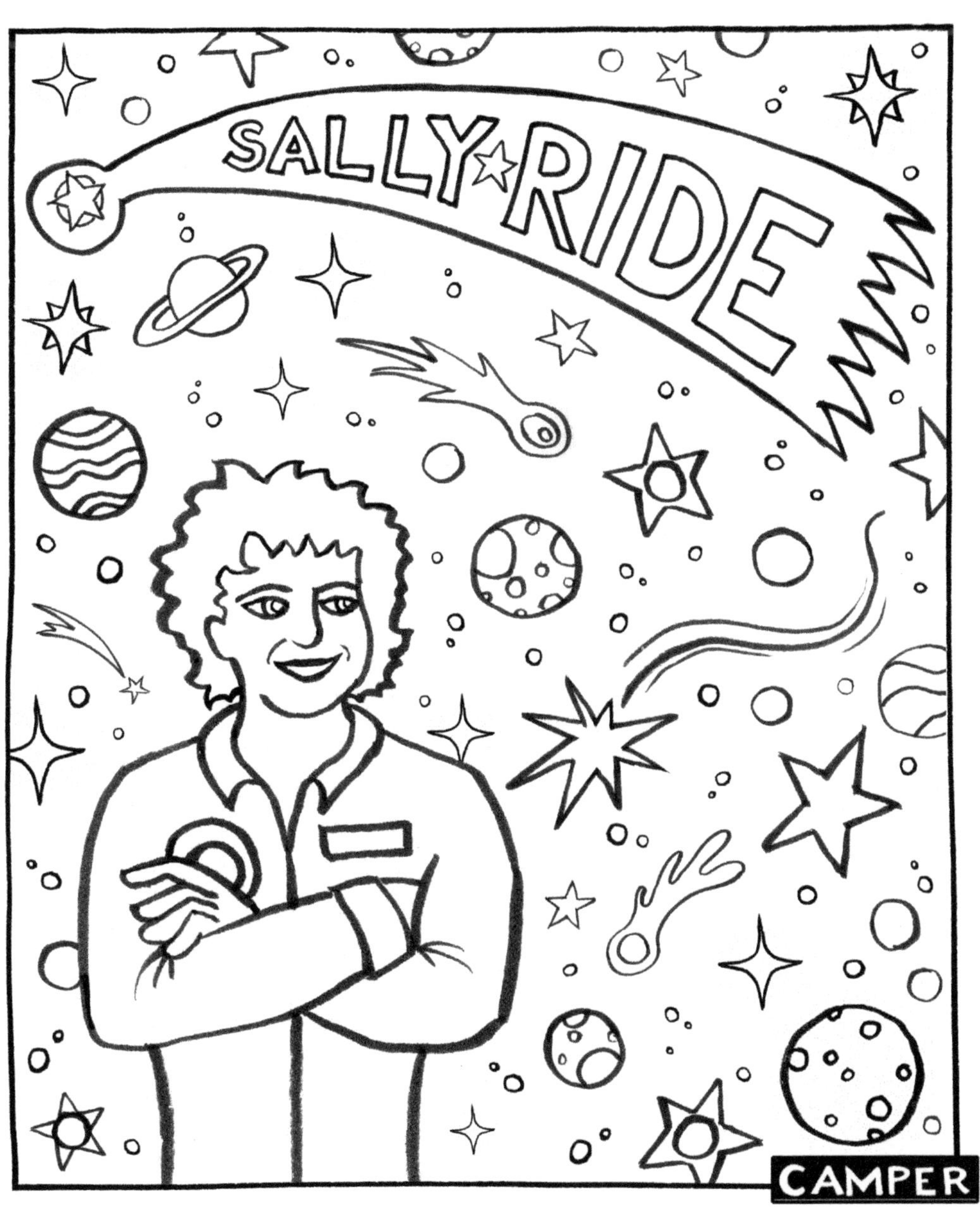

drawn by Jennifer Camper

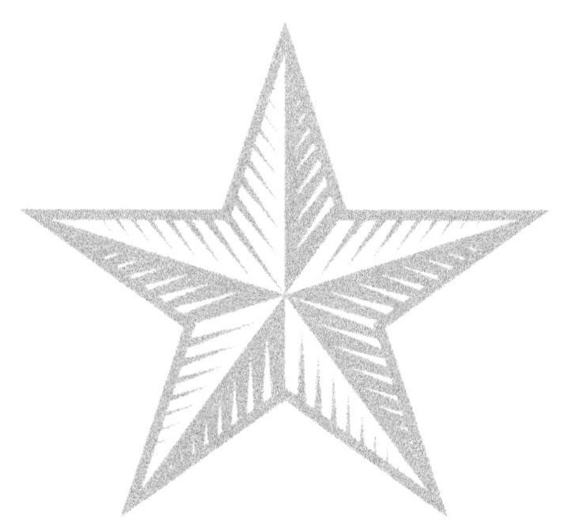

WRITERS

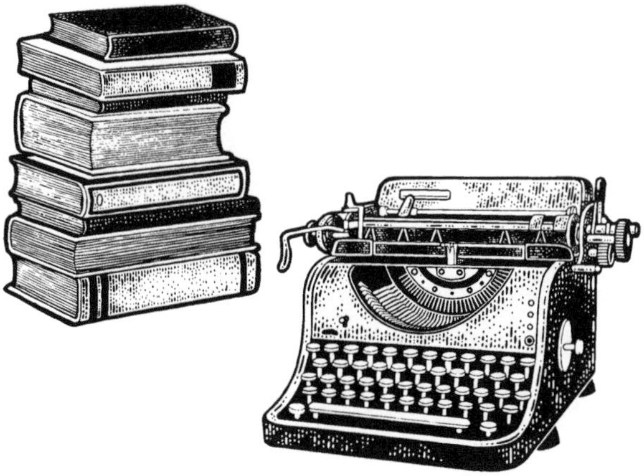

Ivan Coyote

b. August 11, 1969 · Canada
drawn by Rachael House

I've never felt better. I have made the final choice to move back to the Yukon, and to use what I have learned in the last couple of years to contribute to the arts community here in my hometown and territory. It's time for me to slow down and spend less time on the road and more time picking cranberries and watching the fire in the new woodstove. Play my saxophone. Take a class at night school. Go fishing. Write long letters to everyone I love, and then some. I'm turning 52 next week, and I feel really good about it. I've been working hard physically and I feel strong, and my back doesn't hurt as much as it did when I was sitting on a plane or a train or a cab every other day. I wake up every day grateful.[1] –Ivan Coyote in 2021

Ivan Coyote is a Canadian musician, storyteller, writer, and filmmaker. Their works' themes are gender, class, identity, connection, family, and social justice. A prolific creative, Ivan has published over a dozen books, several CDs, and four films.

A third-generation Yukoner, Ivan grew up in Whitehorse, a remote area in northwestern Canada, listening to their grandmother tell stories around the kitchen table. Their mother was a government employee, and their father owned a welding shop. As a tomboy, Ivan knew from a young age that they were different. An insatiable reader as a child, Ivan was fond of *Harriet the Spy* by Louise Fitzhugh.

Gender was slippery for Ivan and they straddled genders at a young age. In *Boys Like Her*, Ivan described the pleasures of being a temporary boy during swimming lessons, "I had a sex change once, when I was six years old." That summer, Coyote's mother bought Coyote a bikini for a beginner's swimming class for ages five to seven. Trouble was, the top easily slid over Coyote's flat chest. "I was an accomplished tomboy by that time," Coyote says, "so I was used to hating my clothes." Arriving at the pool, Coyote didn't wear the top. When the swimming instructor, a human bullhorn, blew her silver whistle and aggressively divided the children into two camps along sexual lines, short-haired Ivan crossed over. "It only got easier after that first day," Coyote recalls in the story "No Bikini." "I wore my trunks under my pants and changed in the boys' room after that first day. The short form of the birth name my parents bestowed on me was androgynous enough to allow my charade to proceed through the entire six weeks of swimming lessons, six weeks of boyhood, six weeks of bliss."[2]

In 1992, Ivan started performing live, and in 1996, Ivan co-founded a queer performance troupe called "Taste This" in reaction to an interesting yet distressing experience after performing at the seedy Niagara Hotel: "I remember walking onto the stage in a cloud of polyester smoke and cigar smoke, and thinking 'Who planned this?' I was even talking to Elvis himself—he was still in the building afterwards—and I was like, 'Dude, do you have any idea what it's like to follow a guy who just lit his G-string on fire?'"[3]

Ivan spent the next ten years writing, performing, and teaching. In 2000, they contracted with the renowned Canadian publishing house Arsenal Pulp Press. They published twelve books, including the winner of the 2007 ReLit Award Bow Grip (2006), co-edited the Stonewall Book Award Honor Book *Persistence: All Ways Butch and Femme* (2011), and *Tomboy Survival Guide* (2016). In 2012, Ivan toured with indie musician and queer icon Rae Spoon presenting "Gender Failure," so named because they both had difficulty fitting neatly into gender binary boxes.

Activism is invigorating, passionate, and tiring. When asked at the 2017 Toronto International Festival of Authors how they take care of themselves, Ivan paused and said that they make a killer roast chicken and share it with their friends. Heath Salazar was there and wrote, "They shared with us the importance of making a meal, the importance of sharing that meal with others, and the importance of checking in. Coyote explained that working as an activist can be very tiring and that it doesn't come with a punch clock—so they'll make roast chicken and take it to their friends, who are also activists, and have a nice meal together. We had all thought we were going to get a how-to guide on self-care, but what we received was a lesson on the power of community and the reminder that we're people—mortal, fleshy, hungry people. And the way we make sure we stay strong can be as simple, and as loving, as making and sharing roast chicken."[4]

The COVID-19 pandemic officially started in China in early 2020, with the first case in the US identified on January 21st, and the World Health Organization (WHO) declared a Global Health Emergency on the 31st. The first lockdown in the US was in California on March 19th. Ivan was paused from a tour of high schools and libraries on Vancouver Island, and they were staying with their partner Sarah in London, Ontario when event cancellations started pouring in. Ivan describes those first terrifying and disorienting days: "Sarah is a songwriter and touring musician, and we found ourselves sitting on the couch next to each other, answering emails and making a long grocery list with a lead-flavored knot growing in both of our bellies. We did what everyone else we knew was doing. We bought a bag of rice, and canned beans, and counted how many rolls of toilet paper we had left. We watched the numbers tick upwards on the news, and we disinfected our groceries with our dwindling Lysol wipes. We told ourselves over and over how lucky

Ivan Coyote

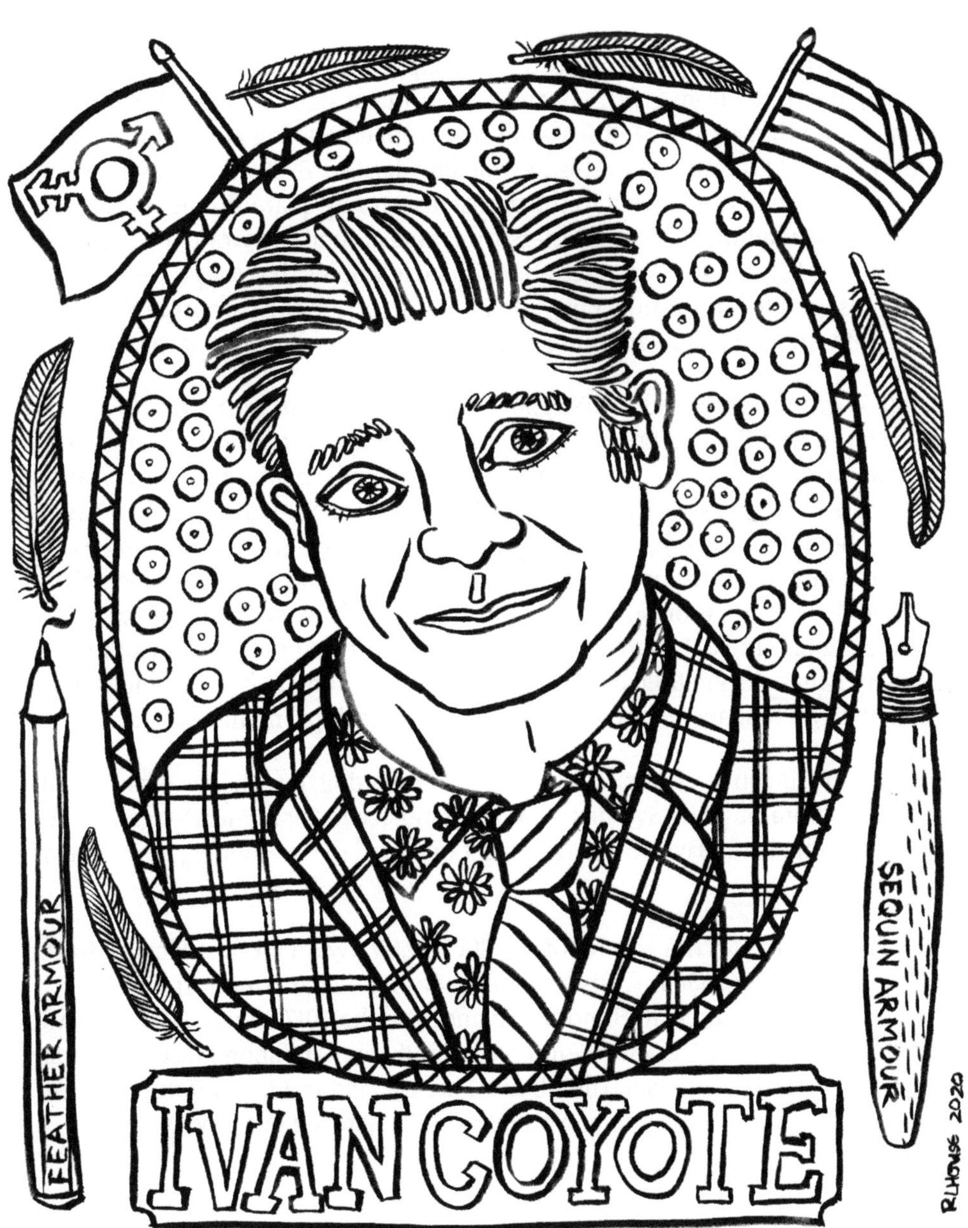

drawn by Rachael House

we were to have a little money saved up, to have each other, to still be healthy. We will make the best of this time off of the road, we said. I can write some news songs, she said. I can work on my mystery novel, I said."[5]

Finishing writing the mystery novel did not happen, at least not right away. With the rising death toll from COVID-19 and no vaccine in sight, many artists and writers found that creating felt frivolous and stopped making art. Country after country reported the spread of this new deadly disease. By April 2020, Canada had over 53,000 cases. Ivan reacted to the global disaster by quarantining with their partner while reading notes and letters from fans around the world. In 2009, Ivan had started a file called "special letters" of heartfelt notes that they'd never had time to respond to sufficiently. Between jumping rope in the carport in lieu of the closed gym, cooking, and gardening, Ivan started to answer those letters.

In 2021, 21 of the letters and Ivan's replies were published as *Care Of: Letters, Connections, and Cures,* a book that is a poetic tribute to community, hope, and loss. Ivan talked about the correspondents: "They're like really slow conversations. They wrote to me because they either saw me perform or read my book or saw me on YouTube. So it was about the connection that they felt via stories to my work. And in the middle of the lockdown, the only thing that made sense to me was to continue the conversation somehow in the only way that was available to any of us at that time."[6] In 2021, Ivan and Sarah started performing "Out of This Blue," a collage of Ivan's storytelling and Sarah's COVID-19 pandemic-inspired music which ended up as an homage to family, connection, friendship, and mortality.

Ivan lives in Vancouver, British Columbia with their dog, Lucky. Ivan's partner and artistic collaborator is the Swedish-Canadian musician, Sarah MacDougall. Ivan enjoys knitting, leatherwork, playing street hockey, lake swimming, embroidery, dogs, and cooking.

In 2007, *Bow Grip* was the winner of the 2007 ReLit Award for Best Fiction. In 2016, their autobiography *Tomboy Survival Guide* was named an American Library Association (ALA) Stonewall Honor Book and won the 2017 Stonewall Book Award. In 2017, Ivan was awarded an Honorary Doctor of Laws at Simon Fraser University for their writing and activism. Their book, *Care Of: Letters, Connections, and Cures* was a finalist for the Transgender Nonfiction 2022 Lambda Literary Award.

Fran Lebowitz

b. October 27, 1950 · USA
drawn by Pat Tong

When I was a child I would kiss any book I dropped. When I was a very little child after I'd read a book I really liked I'd kiss it. Love is really the word. I think children's books are a human emotional experience rather than an intellectual one.... If someone said to me, how did you spend your life? I'd have to say, lying on the sofa reading.[1] –Fran Lebowitz

Fran Lebowitz is a writer and satirist. She is known for her wit, her aversion to technology, and her immense amount of style.

Fran Lebowitz was raised in New Jersey. Her parents owned Pearl's Upholstered Furniture, first in Morristown and then in Morris Plains, NJ. Fran was a rambunctious early reader and a lackadaisical student who preferred to devour books on the sly. Fran did not do well in elementary school due to her need to talk to her classmates, "I was a behavior problem as far as talking. I talked out of turn, I talked too much, I talked in class, I made jokes during the lessons, I whispered to other children. I wasn't an interesting behavior problem. I wasn't glamorous and rebellious. I just talked too much. My first school punishment was sitting in the corner in kindergarten wearing a Band-Aid over my mouth and holding up a sign that said, 'I am a chatterbox.' That was my first run-in with authority."[2] Fran practically emerged from the womb smoking cigarettes, but officially started stealing Tareytons from her mother and smoking them when she was 12.

As a child, she was deeply affected by hearing James Baldwin talk: "James Baldwin was the first person I ever saw on television who I heard talk like that—by which I mean, he was the first intellectual I ever heard talk. And that's because that's the sort of person they used to have on television. It's unimaginable that that sort of person would be on TV now. And I was just flabbergasted. That made me read him—I had never heard of him before then. I would say that I was probably 12 or 13 when I saw Baldwin on TV."[3]

She was expelled from her prep high school for surliness but earned her New Jersey General Educational Development Test later on. She was then sent by her exasperated parents to live with her aunt in Poughkeepsie, NY. That only lasted six months before Fran skedaddled to New York City.

Fran moved to New York City in 1969 and since then has dedicated her life to living in The City as a dyke *flaneur* and *wit du jour*. In the early 1970s, she was hired by the Pop artist Andy Warhol to be a writer for the alternative, NYC urban magazine *Interview*. Fran started off with a column where she reviewed bad movies called "Best of the Worst," then a few years later she wrote an illustrated column called "I Cover the Waterfront," ranting about popular and unpopular culture, modern manners, and dubious aesthetics. She then started writing a column called "The Lebowitz Report" in the women's fashion and culture magazine, *Mademoiselle*. Stylish and sardonic, she's been compared to an all-American Dorothy Parker by *The New York Times*.

In the time-honored style of the nearly starving *artiste*, she has made a living as a charwoman who specialized in cleaning Venetian blinds, a chauffeur, a taxi driver, a market research participant, and a pornographer, writing BDSM erotica under the *nom de plume* Robert Paine Cook. She was a personal chauffeur for the rock musicians Johnny and Edgar Winter and sold fashion accessories on the mean streets of NYC.

Eminently quotable, Fran talked to rare book dealer Kurt Thometz about writing erotica and her love of books from a young age to now: "I have a pornography collection. It's not a huge one. The really good stuff is too expensive for me. I wrote some for a company called Midway Press. They would give these stapled pages that told you how to write one and what had to be in each book. They paid you five hundred dollars for a book and that's it. The first one I wrote myself and it was called *House of Leather*. I published it under the name of the headmaster who threw me out of prep school, Robert Paine Cook. Then I wrote two or three others with about five people. We would get stoned, we would talk, and somebody would type. There were so many people involved you'd end up getting like seventy-five dollars. It was really boring and it was really bad. My copies of these books are gone and I'm not looking for them. I have a finicky aversion to buying secondhand pornography because I know where it's been." [4]

She published her first book on March 13, 1978. Titled *Metropolitan Life*, it is a collection of witty essays on urban life taken from her magazine columns. *Metropolitan Life* ignited her career as a humorist and a writer when it was reviewed in *The New York Times* (*NYT*) in late March 1978, not once, but twice. At the time, Fran was so broke that she didn't have the cash to buy copies of the newspaper to show her friends, "It was really like something out of a movie because it literally did happen in one night. It was because *The New York Times*, you know, it is still very powerful, but what it was then was like the word of god to the entire world. Not just New York. Not just the United States. People would have arguments about anything, and the argument would end if someone said, 'Why did you think that?' and you would say, 'Well, it was in *The New York Times*!' 'Oh, that's it! The argument is over!' I happened to get two rave reviews from *The New York Times* in the same week. The Sunday Review and the Daily Review and that literally was it. When the Daily Review came out, I had no idea it was coming out, I knew nothing about it, and my editor—not my editor at the time, my original editor who had been fired in the middle of my book—called me at like seven o'clock in the morning, and I had been asleep for like forty-five minutes, and I said, 'I knew that the Sunday Review was coming out because the publishers used to get it on Wednesday, and I knew it was a great review.' And then she said, 'Did you see the review?' And I said, 'Yes, I saw it,' and she said something about John Leonard, and John Leonard was the major book critic for *The Times*. And I said, 'John Leonard?' And she said, 'Yes, it's in the paper this morning.' So, she said go to the newsstand—which, by the way, there were millions at the time—buy ten copies of *The Times*, and come over here, to her apartment, and I did not have enough money to buy ten copies of *The New York Times*, which at the time was like fifteen cents. So, I went to the newsstand and I asked the guy, 'Could you let me have ten copies, and I'll come back later with some money?' and he said, 'No, why would I do that? Why do you want ten copies?' And I said, 'I'm in the newspaper.' He said, 'No, you're not! You're in *The New York Times*?! Don't be ridiculous!' So, you know, that's what happened, but by the time I got to my publisher's office I was greeted like the returning Charles Lindbergh. And it was a fluke of timing that these two things happened, and also it was a fluke that the day that it came out, there was no news. In other words, there was no big news, so a lot of people focused on that."[5]

An excerpt from the *NYT* review written by Jill Robinson proclaimed, "However, *Metropolitan Life* is not simply consistently cross, swift and sly, as if that would not be enough. It introduces an important humorist in the classic tradition. The satire is principled, the taste impeccable—there is character here as well as personality."[6] The *NYT* review by John Leonard was just as ecstatic, "Fran Lebowitz hangs around in *Mademoiselle* and *Interview*, as well as Greenwich Village 'smoking cigarettes and plotting revenge.' She is against physical fitness, conceptual art, large groups, citizens band radio, est, 'the graphic design crowd who think that primary colors are both cheering and bold and demonstrate this belief by employing them incessantly in places where people have every right to be depressed.'"[7] In 1981, Fran came out with another collection of essays called *Social Studies*, and in 1994 the two books were released as one book titled *The Fran Lebowitz Reader*.

Gossips have hooked Fran up with lifelong friend Toni Morrison, singer and activist Dolly Parton, and during the 1980s, a passel of models. She has self-described repeatedly as not great girlfriend material, "Because I could not possibly be in a relationship now for more than six days. When I was younger, I might have said six months, although I think the longest relationship I was ever in was three years. But what I can't be is monogamous. That tends to upset people. I just don't like domestic life. That's the problem. When I was young, I liked romance. But to me, romance is the opposite of domestic life. I just don't want anyone in the apartment, not for longer than a few hours. Three or four hours, okay, fine. I just don't want to hear someone else walking around. I am alternately very gregarious—

very sociable—and then very solitary," Fran elaborated on her romantic unsuitability, "There are certain relationships I think I'm great at: I'm the world's greatest daughter. I'm a great relative. I believe I'm a great friend. I'm a horrible girlfriend. I always was. I'm great at the beginning because I can be very romantic. But, I mean, years ago I had a girlfriend who summed me up perfectly. She said, 'You know what it's like being with you? At the beginning, every day, you asked me a hundred questions about myself. Then 50 questions, then 20 questions, then, finally, you said, 'Can you see I'm trying to read?'" [8]

Fran is in many ways quaintly old-fashioned. It's easy to imagine her with writer Dorothy Parker, playwright Noël Coward, and feminist Ruth Hale at the Algonquin Round Table in 1920, swigging cocktails and exchanging barbs. She does not own a cell phone or a computer and has never watched anything on Netflix. She does not even own a typewriter, preferring to write longhand. She is gentler than a neo-Luddite and much wittier. She explained her antipathy towards modern technology, "I'm the sort of person if a machine breaks, I hit it, and then I beg it not to break. So I didn't want all these machines in my life. I'm just not interested in this." [9]

Fran has suffered from a nearly three-decades long writer's block, but when she was writing, she had plenty of procrastination techniques, "My writing habits are basically nonwriting habits. I sulk for several days. Then I start thinking that maybe somewhere in the house is a column that I never turned in. This has never occurred. Then I try to bargain with them to wait until I get to the absolute edge of the deadline. I wait until the editor says, 'Unless it's in tomorrow morning at ten o'clock we can't run it.' Then I stay up all night and do it," Fran continued, "The whole time before I write, I spend on the phone begging people for ideas and solace and sympathy. My favorite thing to do is to call another writer who has a deadline, because they will stay on the phone with you. Your friends who don't write will not stay on the phone with you, because they have other real things they want to do. If someone else has to write, then you know you have a willing companion to talk to on the phone for hours and hours while they put off their writing." [10]

Her writing block has forced her to earn her living as a public speaker. Fortunately, she enjoys sharing her opinion; in *Public Speaking* (2010), a documentary about Fran directed by her close friend Martin Scorsese, Fran confides, "It's what I wanted my entire life. People asking me my opinion, and people not allowed to interrupt." [11]

Fran lives in New York City in an apartment that she bought in 2017. Although she does not have any pets, she owns over 10,000 books, all ordered by category and then subcategorized in alphabetical order.

Fran Lebowitz

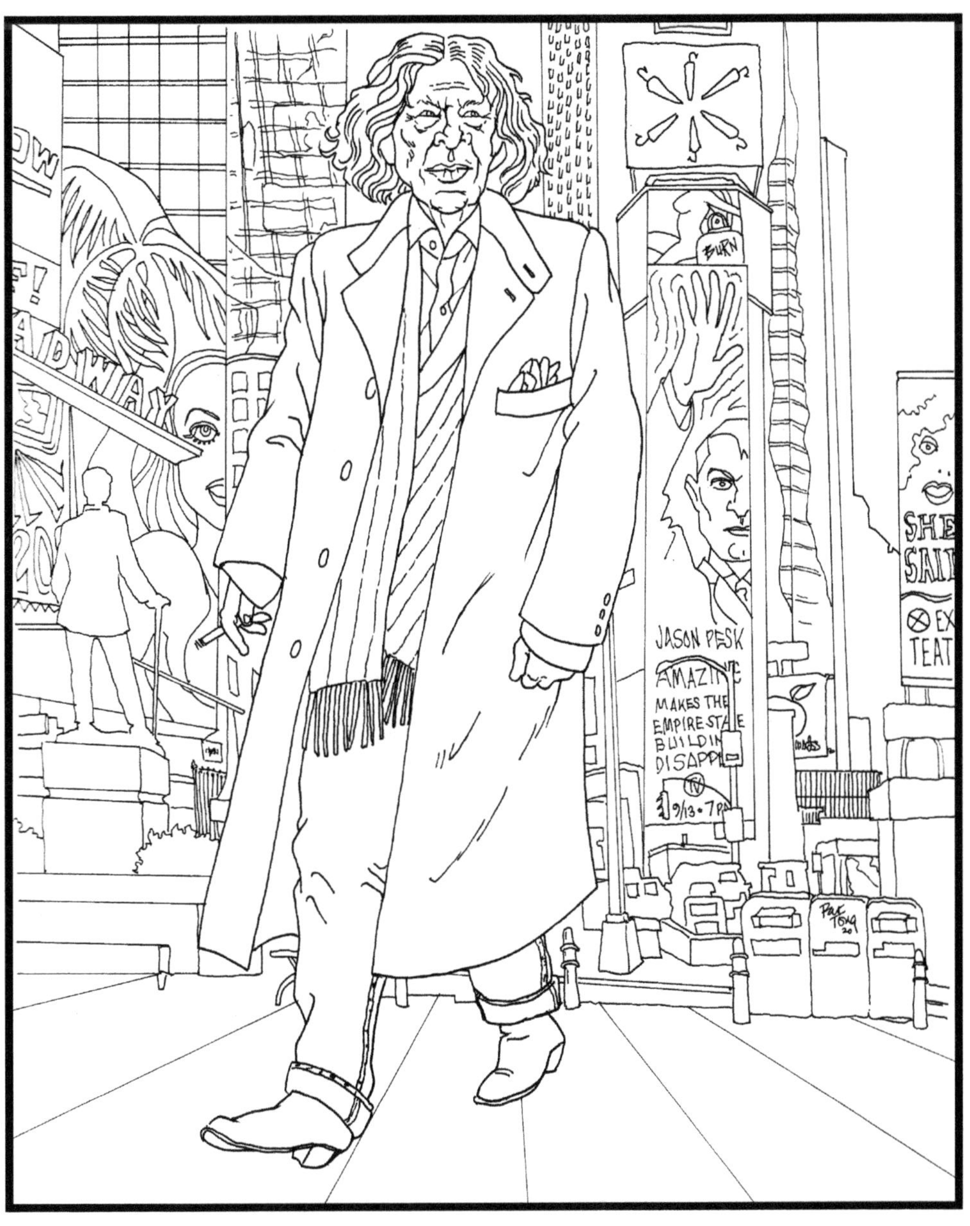

drawn by Pat Tong

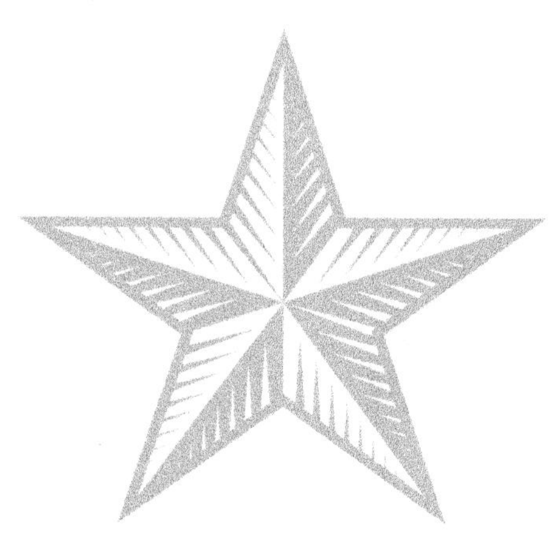

Isaac (Karlyn) Lotney, a.k.a. Fairy Butch

April 26, 1965 · USA
drawn by Tyler Cohen

Boy, am I missing a place like Josie's Juice Joint in the Castro these days. The whole ethic that permeated the place seems to be gone, or at least financially untenable in the San Francisco of 2013....I remember first seeing Justin Bond in Kiki and Herb, Phranc, Marga Gomez, and others in the down-to-earth Josie's, and aggravating Molly McKay, with words like "zydeco" on a triple word score, no less, in Scrabble, played on the back patio. Nothing has really risen in the Castro to take its place.[1]
–Isaac (Karlyn) Lotney

Isaac (Karlyn) Lotney is an Ashkenazi Jewish trans man, writer, and performer. He was a sex advice columnist, taught sex education workshops, and started performing under the name Fairy Butch in San Francisco in the 1980s.

Isaac was raised in Dayton, Ohio. His mother was an elementary art schoolteacher, an artist, a Parents, Families and Friends of Lesbians and Gays (PFLAG) activist, and taught art at the Dayton Art Institute, while his father was a Procurement Officer for the United States Air Force. Isaac and his mother were close, taking art classes together at the Dayton Art Institute. Isaac was a precocious reader, and his 7th and 8th grade teachers recognized his abilities, urged him to read James Baldwin and held classroom debates on whether President John F. Kennedy's murder was a conspiracy.

Isaac's grandparents fled the Holocaust, which caused intergenerational transmission of trauma within his family, "I wasn't able to read Holocaust literature until very recently. I had Holocaust terrors every night before I went to sleep—sometimes for hours—from the age of 12 to about 30 or so. My grandparents were Holocaust survivors, and my mom survived *in utero*—conceived in Nazi Germany and born in Louisville, Kentucky. She wasn't able to meet her father until she was three and he was able to escape through Portugal. The Holocaust destroyed the emotional integrity of my maternal grandparents, and my mom was able to live with them for only two years of her childhood. My beloved mom, whose birthday was just last Thursday, was shuttled from relative to relative, sleeping in kitchens and pretty much raising herself. For all she went through in her childhood, we are so blessed that she wasn't one of the murdered children mentioned here. She easily could have been—she was six in 1944. Somehow, she was able not only to survive, but to thrive, and became the best person I've ever known."[2] Influenced by the intergenerational trauma within his family, Isaac struggled with treatment-resistant depression from a young age and started seeing a therapist at age six.

In 1980 and at age 15, Isaac started sneaking into gay bars, and in 1983 he wore a tuxedo and pumps to his high school prom. Isaac was always out to his parents. It took his mother a year to accept the fact that he was gay, however, by 1983 she enthusiastically cofounded the Dayton PFLAG group. His father was slower to accept his gayness but eventually became a PFLAG dad and attended functions with his wife. When Isaac was 19, he spent a year at Carousel Beauty College before deciding to skedaddle to the charms of San Francisco in 1985.

Like many young queers, Isaac was itching for adventure, "I moved to San Francisco in 1985, and it was for the attention paid to the quality of life and the culture—money was the antithesis of my focus," he continued, "I took in all the City events and the zeitgeist, and remembered the blend of natural and architectural beauty, and decided that despite a fully uphill battle, I would move here, $700 in my pocket. (That wasn't a lot of money, even in 1985.) I had no place to stay, not even for the first night. I had only one year of college under my belt (and one year of beauty school) and my parents were completely against it."[3]

Once in San Francisco, the city nicknamed "Baghdad by the Bay" didn't disappoint Isaac, "It was such a wonderful place to be, to be queer, to be politically radical with Queer Nation and Act-Up, to go out to underground galleries and clubs, and cheap, cheap eats at Picaro, on 16th. And frankly, it was a great place to fuck. Such a ripe place for sexual experimentation of all sorts—a real hotbed of innovation, theory, and more importantly, application. I remember going to underground dyke sex clubs and art shows that had fisting demos."[4]

Isaac was busy and in his element. Isaac wrote a sex column for the legendary dyke magazine *On Our Backs* and got a job at the then woman-owned sex toy store, Good Vibrations. He ended up working at Good Vibrations for a little over a decade, becoming the resident dildo expert.

In 1990, Queer Nation San Francisco was founded one month after the group's inaugural meeting in New York City. The first San Francisco meeting was in the Women's Building in the Mission district, and Isaac was there, resplendent in a black leather jacket. Queer Nation employed tactics such as street protests, postering, and other "unapologetic," "in your face" political demonstrations. Without any clear boundaries of membership and no official leadership structure, decisions were made by consensus.

In the late 1990s, Isaac started writing a sex and relationship advice column for lesbians in *Curve* magazine called "Ask Fairy Butch," which specialized in witty, fey advice. A self-described butch-loving butch in Baltimore got negative reactions from the gay community for her sexual preference and wrote to Fairy Butch in despair. Fairy Butch responded, "Dear Butch-Loving: Honey, first off, allow me to trot out my trusty old saw: As long as it's safe, sane, and consensual between consenting adults, any kind of sexual or romantic relationship you want to have is absolutely peachy keen. And if anyone has a problem with this notion, just tell them that your Uncle Fairy says to mind the bushes in their own backyard. Butches can love butches, femmes can love femmes, and all of you nondeclared folks out there can go any which way but loose. I mean, I love femmes more than a groundhog loves mud, but we're not freakin' on Noah's Ark, darling. We're queer, people, which means we can make up our own rules."[5]

In 1995, Isaac started performing "In Bed With Fairy Butch," an ebullient cabaret-style show that was part camp and part lesbian sex education, all served with a generous dollop of spicy humor and sexiness. The *SF Bay Guardian* named "In Bed With Fairy Butch" as the "Best Place to Cop a Same-Sex Date" in part because of its quick and dirty speed-dating portion of every evening. Novelist Malinda Lo described working at an "In Bed With Fairy Butch" show, "We worked at 'In Bed With Fairy Butch,' a comedy-slash-burlesque show that moved between various nightclub venues in the city," she continued, "The performers included sideburned drag kings, bewigged faux queens, and sultry femme dancers. The show was always followed by dancing. At the show, I helped run the 'Tingle and Mingle' table, where people could sign up for a number that they'd wear on their shirt for the night. If another person was interested in them, they could leave them a note at the table. It was online dating in real life for shy queer women."[6]

In 1998, Isaac's story, "Clash of the Titans" was published in *Best Lesbian Erotica 1998* and caused well-known queer sex educator and blogger Sinclair Sexsmith to have an epiphany about their sexual desires, "The first time I knew I was a top was when I read Isaac Lotney's story 'Clash of the Titans' in *Best Lesbian Erotica 1998*, and broke the spine open to that spot from reading it so often. The story is pretty switchy, following a butch top and a femme bottom through an evening of multiple scenes of kinky play. The dirty talk, the strap-on sex, and the play with power exchange in every line had me panting."[7]

In 2000, Isaac's book *The Ultimate Guide to Strap-On Sex: A Complete Resource for Women and Men* was published. Filling a much-needed niche in sex education, the book covered practical topics such as choosing vibrators, dildos, lube, and harnesses; introducing sex toy play to your partner; packing and gender play; and strap-on techniques.

In the same year, Isaac started taking testosterone. He says about testosterone, "T keeps me from being suicidally depressed," he continued, "I used to call myself "the reluctant FTM" because it took me forever to decide to transition, and it took me even longer to simultaneously simplify my life and please my ear by requiring my companions to refer to me by male pronouns." [8]

In the spring of 2006, Isaac was diagnosed with Stage II invasive breast cancer, then weeks later he lost his new home to flooding. He had a family history of breast cancer and ended up getting a total bilateral mastectomy plus a hysterectomy on July 6th, 2006. His mother flew out from Ohio to stay with Isaac for eight months to provide emotional support and tend to his surgical wounds, and she even attended the 2006 Trans March with him.

In 2015, Isaac started the Facebook group, The Fairy Butch Dynasty Den of Iniquity, Equity, & Kindness, which is still going strong. He'd taken a long hiatus from work due to disabilities; multiple surgeries, breast cancer, several heart attacks, and diabetes. He explained that he wanted to promote the strong queer community he'd known since the 1990s, "It started with kind of as a continuation of the Fairy Butch ethos and then last year in 2020 when George Floyd was murdered, my kid who's also my caregiver wanted, of course, to go out and protest and so did I but because of Covid that wasn't a possibility, and so I said let's do whatever we can do in these four walls to aid the cause, and so at that point I said well, what do I have? What resources do I have, and I have this group it's got 1400 people in it and you know it's mostly about sexuality and gender, trans issues and such, and it took on a different life at that point, where it became a lot more political, very progressive of course, but it became more political and more about Black Lives Matter, race issues, continuing with sex and gender, but it just kind of became in San Francisco. It's kind of like eclectic, to say the least." [9]

Isaac lives in San Francisco with his two cats, Ollie and Jamie, running The Fairy Butch Dynasty Den of Iniquity, Equity, & Kindness, strolling around the Castro, writing, watching PBS shows, and reading.

Isaac (Karlyn) Lotney

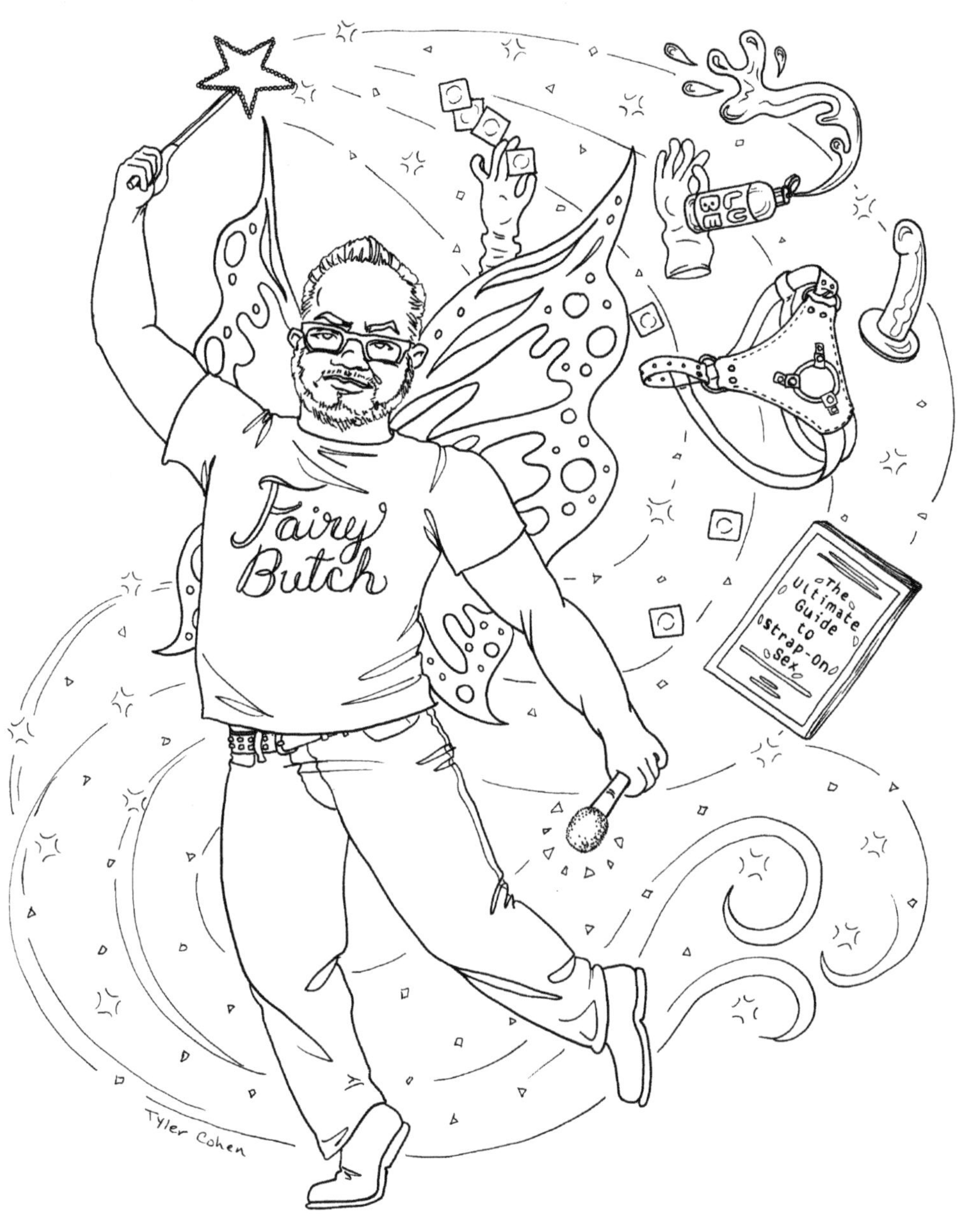

drawn by Tyler Cohen

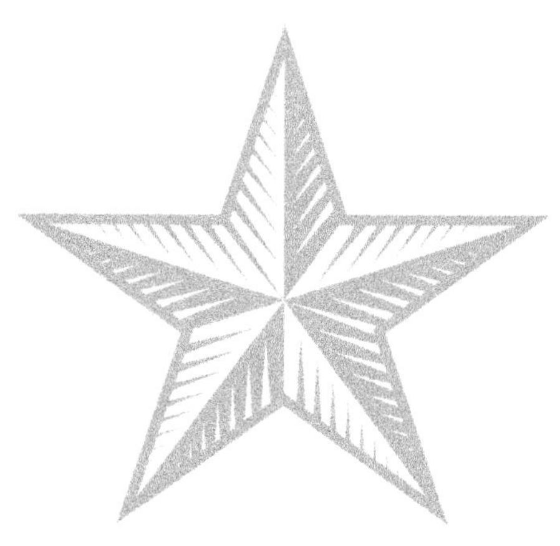

Heather Hogan

b. December 9, 1978 · USA
drawn by Avery Cassell

My family longed for my hair like it was Christmas, convinced I was some kind of Rapunzel-in-waiting, that noble locks were coming and would transform me into a beautiful, feminine princess. Unfortunately for them, my personality grew in with my hair, and I began demanding to be styled like my fashion icon, Michael J. Fox's Alex P. Keaton from Family Ties. In fact, I wanted ties. Bowties and neckties. And button-up shirts. I wanted suit jackets and oxfords. I would have settled for wearing a baseball uniform everywhere, including to church, but the Lord had different ideas. Jesus also was waiting on my hair. He told the Apostle Paul to tell the Corinthian church that long hair is a woman's glory. And dang it made me spitting mad to be told how to dress by a man who'd never even owned a pair of cleats![1] –Heather Hogan

Heather Hogan is a writer and a journalist. She's a Managing Editor, Social Media Director, and Senior Writer for the popular lesbian queer news and culture site, *Autostraddle*, and has published over 1,500 articles for them. In addition, she contributed to the book, *The Long COVID Survival Guide: How to Take Care of Yourself and What Comes Next Stories and Advice from Twenty Long-Haulers and Experts.*

Heather was born in Flowery Branch, Georgia and was raised attending an evangelical Christian church. Always a precocious, helpful, and self-sufficient child, her first sentence was, "Heather do it."[2] A tomboy, she infuriated her conservative family with her insistence upon wearing boyish clothing and playing rough. Heather finally brokered a bargain with her mother that if she kept her hair long and wore dresses to church and the annual school picture day, she could wear her beloved boyish clothing the rest of the time. It wasn't until a year after her mother died in 2022 that Heather gathered her courage to finally get the haircut of her dreams. Channeling Katsa from *Graceling*, one of her favorite books as a teen, Heather instructed the barber to cut her hair "As short as any man's."[3]

As a daughter of the Deep South, Heather saw her first Ku Klux Klan rally when she was in third grade, "We drove by it on the way home from the grocery store. It was pitch black except for the 20-foot cross burning in the yard, illuminating a sea of white robes and white hoods. My mom's mom said, 'They won't hurt you' and I didn't sleep that night because of the emphasis she put on the 'you.' Who would they hurt? Well, black people. Well, but not anymore."[4] Later, she watched her family and friends in Georgia crumble under the bleak, racist, homophobic spell of Fox News and the GOP. Her breaking point with the church and the conservative right was the election of 2016 when Heather responded to the rise of Fox News conservatism and Trump winning the presidency, "I stayed active in church as long as I could, but once Fox News had its claws into the hearts of nearly everyone I knew, I had to go. I watched people I loved and respected (though often disagreed with ideologically) fall victim to the brainwashing. They became under-informed, misinformed, and many of them just stopped thinking. My pastor and college minister were the worst offenders; the exponential effect of their puppeteering from the pulpit is incalculable," she continued. "This election was the scapegoat facing off against the embodiment of the propaganda. It was equality, empathy, and a promise to grapple with our own contributions to the darkness facing off against ingrained prejudice, ignorance, and backwards thinking. It was preparedness facing off against bigoted bombast. It was my life's purpose facing off against a culture that has destroyed so many of the people and things I have loved, the kind of hate masquerading as morality that destroyed even my faith." [5]

Heather stayed in Georgia, watched her parents get a divorce, got bullied in high school, kissed a classmate as practice for kissing boys, graduated, worked a dull office job, and shared her first adult kiss with her boss's daughter, a sophisticated gender studies student who was visiting for the summer and who slipped Heather a copy of *Stone Butch Blues* on the way out.

In 2008, Heather fled her straight job as an accountant in Flowery Branch. She had an inkling that she was a lesbian and needed to explore the world. She wrote a to-do list consisting of, "1. Come out to family, 2. Buy a plane ticket anywhere, 3. Go on a real date with a real gay woman, 4. Write something for money, 5. Email Riese Bernard [*Autostraddle* founder]," [6] then bought a ticket to Europe where she backpacked through the continent learning to become a writer. When she returned to the States, she got a job with MTV Networks in Atlanta.

In 2010, Heather got a drink invite from a fan named Stacy in New York City, and six months later, the couple finally met, leading to a decade-long, long-distance courtship. They ultimately moved in together in NYC, there was a proposal over Sunday brunch with cherry blossoms anointing them, and a 2020 pandemic wedding at their home where they toasted, "Down with the patriarchy!" [7] with champagne and exchanged vows. Heather's vows started with, "Traditional wedding vows pledge 'from this day forward, I will…' —which, like so many traditional things, doesn't really fit us. We've been making and keeping promises to each other for nearly ten years, when we met like a couple of feral kittens who didn't know how desperate they were for a home, and who found one in each other. So. I won't make you any new promises today. Instead, I'll reaffirm the vows I've lived by for the last decade." [8]

In 2014, Heather was hired to work at *Autostraddle* as a contract employee and quickly rose up through the ranks, her innate writing talent and snarky humor oiling the way. By 2020 Heather was an editor at *Autostraddle* and on the payroll with full health benefits, company-matching 401K, and unemployment benefits. Then the pandemic hit.

In 2020, COVID-19 officially arrived in the US. Heather and Stacy lived in NYC, an urban area that was hit hard during the early days of the pandemic. NYC saw its first documented person with COVID-19 in early March, but by the end of the month, there were over 40,000 people confirmed to have COVID-19 in NYC, which accounted for over 5% of the world's confirmed cases. On March 7th, Governor Cuomo declared a state of emergency, and on March 20th, he issued an executive order closing "non-essential" businesses. Stores were running out of hand sanitizer, latex gloves, masks, and cleaning supplies. On March 11th, the World Health Organization (WHO) declared it a pandemic, and folks started stocking up on toilet paper and nonperishable food items. The folks at Rancho Gordo Beans, an heirloom bean purveyor out of California noted, "A really good day for us is about 150 to 200 orders. We've continually done over a thousand every day. People laugh, saying, 'We're ready for the zombie apocalypse.' But they are doing it." [9] On Friday, March 13th, Trump declared a national state of emergency. Air travel slowed, stores closed, and the streets of NYC were filled with the signs of death, ambulances, and blaring sirens.

In March 2020, Heather was among the first wave of people in the US to catch COVID-19. It was a mild case, although the word "mild" is misleading. It was not a case that sent Heather to intensive care to be intubated, like so many folks early in the pandemic before there were vaccines. Instead, Heather spent two weeks recovering at home, isolated from Stacy. Heather's symptoms were minor chills, a sore throat, a nasty cough, exhaustion, and chest congestion, but getting over COVID-19 never really happened. The obvious flu-like part dissipated, but what remained in its stead was a series of symptoms; crippling exhaustion, panic attacks, limb tremors, forgetfulness, brain fog, lack of appetite, and an inability to hold her pee, among other life-altering issues.

This happened long before we were aware of post-COVID-19 illnesses or long COVID, and doctors doubted her, suggesting that it could be depression or anxiety. The Longterm COVID Care Center scoffed at her COVID-19 diagnosis, saying that she didn't have antibodies, therefore she'd never had COVID-19. Too weak and sick to do much of anything besides lie in bed and watch the sky darken, Heather sobbed in Stacy's arms while Stacy took over all domestic duties.

Heather's diagnosis from two doctors happened simultaneously; her neurosurgeon consulted with colleagues and decided she might have dysautonomia the same day a doctor from her long COVID support group suggested the diagnosis. Heather immediately went to a cardiologist who believed her, not foisting her symptoms off on depression or anxiety, and diagnosed Heather with postural orthostatic tachycardia syndrome (POTS), a form of dysautonomia. The cardiologist explained, "It's called an 'invisible illness' because you look fine, and your tests and lab work also look completely normal. But it affects every single system in your body. And you feel absolutely miserable. Doctors almost always write it off as depression or anxiety." [10]

Heather settled in with Long COVID and POTS with their complicated daily routines, "Every morning now when I wake up, I sit up slowly in bed and lean back against my headboard. I drink a full liter of water, eat some salted almonds, put on my compression socks for the day, and take a beta blocker for my heart and an SNRI to keep my adrenaline more in check. After 30 minutes, when my body has adjusted to sitting up, I can stand. Downstairs, I make the first of three Liquid I.V.® drinks of my day and eat a small breakfast. I drink four liters of water total and take more SNRIs and beta-blockers as the day progresses. I sit on a stool when I take a shower. I sit down at a little portable table to do all the vegetable chopping and potato peeling for our meals. I wrap an ice scarf around me and sit down near the oven to cook. I use my office chair to wheel around the kitchen when I'm putting away groceries or dishes. I use a cane when I leave the house, which I only do for doctor's appointments; it folds out into a stool so I don't have to sit on the ground." [11]

Everyone heals differently, and gradually Heather started feeling better, although she remained seriously disabled. By 2022, her essay "Standing Tall (and Sitting Right Back Down): Living with Dysautonomia" was published in *The Long COVID Survival Guide: How to Take Care of Yourself and What Comes Next—Stories and Advice from Twenty Long-Haulers and Experts*, she was riding her bicycle again, she was strong enough to shovel snow, and was baking garlic knots, taking walks, writing, and working for *Autostraddle*. Heather sparkled through her sadness and anger, "Every day now, I'm like 'Dang! This blanket is so soft! This lemon is so tart! This candle smells so good! This sandwich is delicious! These cat cuddles are so warm!' and I live inside those simple joys with my heart wide open to how lucky I am to be experiencing them. I got COVID, and I also survived COVID, and that wasn't a given, and I'm grateful." [12]

Heather and Stacy live in New York with just enough books and their bossy girl cats, Socks, Dobby, Beth March, and Quasar. Heather likes to watch cartoons, while Stacy prefers more murderous, violent fare. They both like the WNBA and cheer on Brittney Griner together.

Heather has participated in panels at New York Comic Con 2017 on the Queer Culture Panel, FlameCon 2017 about Buffy the Vampire Slayer Podcast, OutFest, NewFest, NYU, and A-Camp, *Autostraddle*'s queer adult summer camp. She has also worked for HBO, *HuffPost*, *Allrecipes.com*, and *Slate*.

Heather Hogan

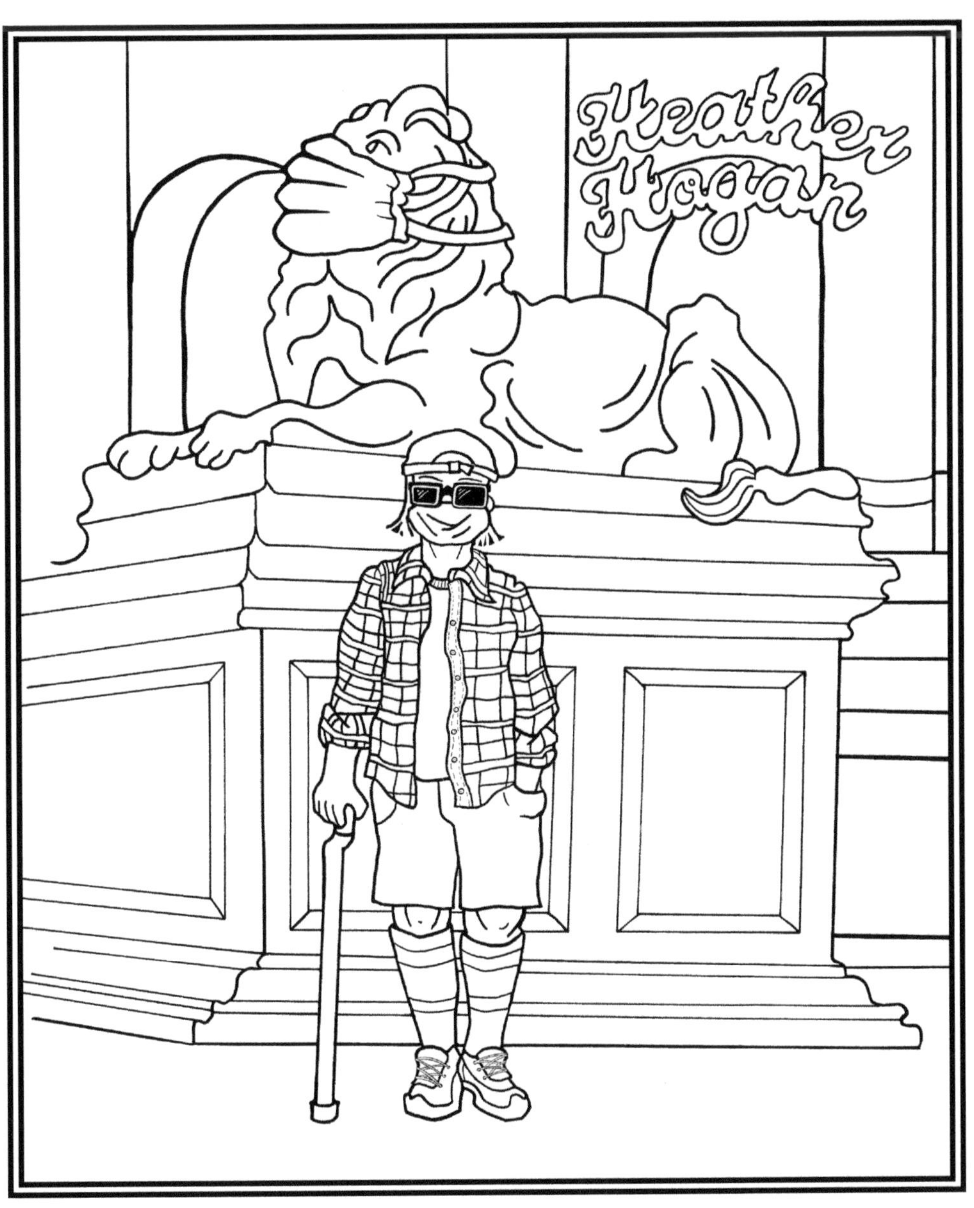

drawn by Avery Cassell

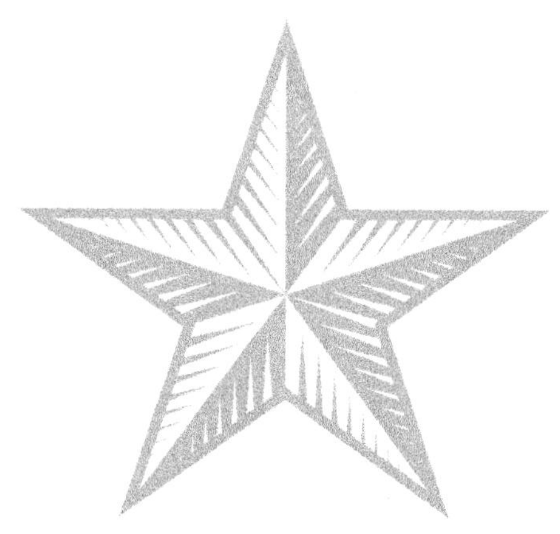

Jiz Lee

b. October 30, 1980 · USA
drawn by Dorian Katz

In many ways, I have porn to thank for this journey. This work has provided financial stability, healthcare, and a community of fellow queer and trans artists. Porn has also helped me to better understand and see myself. I saw images that made me feel desired and celebrated. I was allowed to explore my gender expression in poses that shaped my body into my ideal vision of beauty and athleticism.[1] –Jiz Lee

Jiz Lee is a nonbinary porn actor, a writer, a triathlete, a swimmer, and a sex worker activist. They have appeared in over 200 films spanning six countries.

Jiz was born in Hawai'i, where they learned to dance Hula Auana, Hula Kahiko, and Tahitian. In 1999, they moved from Hawai'i to the San Francisco Bay area to attend Mills College, majoring in dance with a minor in theater. After graduating from Mills College and several years of performing with dance troupes, Jiz met porn actor Syd Blakovich. In 2005, Jiz started working in porn films with Shine Louise Houston's Pink & White Productions.

In 2015, Jiz edited and published a collection of essays, titled *Coming Out Like a Porn Star: Essays on Pornography, Protection, and Privacy*. Contributors included performance artist and ecosexual Annie Sprinkle; film producer, actor, and sex-positive feminist, Candida Royalle; actor and writer Christopher Zeischegg; actor and director Joanna Angel; the legendary actor and sex educator Nina Hartley, and more.

Coming Out Like a Porn Star was written as Jiz struggled to find a way to come out to their family about their work in the sex industry. They consulted with over 50 people that were working in porn to ask them if and how they told their families. In reviewing the answers, Jiz discovered that the thread running through their responses was shame about being sex workers. Renowned queer sexologist and writer, Carol Queen, said of *Coming Out Like a Porn Star: Essays on Pornography, Protection, and Privacy*, "This revealing, moving, and often surprising collection lets you go deep inside the lives of generations of porn stars and explicit performers. It's an absolute must-read for anyone interested in sex industry politics, sex-positive culture, and porn studies—and for anyone whose friend, lover, or family member has taken their pants off in front of a camera. One after the other, these memoirs add up to a powerful, if ironic, conclusion: Porn stigma is the biggest problem many adult performers face, and it is at least as likely to come from our feminist moms as from prudish conservatives. Once you've heard the clear, articulate voices of these porn stars, you'll never look at a sex movie, or the people who make it happen, the same way again."[2] The book was featured in *The New York Post*, *Buzzfeed*, and *Vice*.

In 2022, Jiz co-edited and contributed to the chapter on Sexuality in the "Relationships and Families" section of the second edition of *Trans Bodies, Trans Selves: A Resource by and for Transgender Communities* (2022). Inspired by the classic *Our Bodies, Ourselves* (1973), *Trans Bodies, Trans Selves* is an encompassing resource book for transgender, nonbinary, and gender expansive people.

Jiz works with Shine Louise Houston as the marketing director at Pink & White Productions, working on CrashPadSeries.com and the online streaming platform PinkLabel.tv. In 2020, PinkLabel.tv, with Jiz as Marketing Director, broadcast the San Francisco PornFilmFestival virtually during the pandemic's first year. This placed it in a unique position as a virtual film festival from the start. Jiz talked with queer film historian and director Jenni Olson about queer and adult film festivals and the need for community-oriented platforms that can help revitalize the economy of (adult) filmmaking. This conversation is included in the open-source book *Rethinking Film Festivals in the Pandemic Era and After*. One of the topics of discussion between Jenni and Jiz was about finding ways to preserve and show some of the works of deceased gay filmmaker, Arthur Bressan, which ended up being shown on PinkLabel.tv. *Passing Strangers* (1974) and *Forbidden Letters* (1979) are now available virtually, along with an interview between Jenni and Robert Adams, one of the stars of Arthur's films.

PinkLabel.tv is unique. It's not only a porn site much like Pornhub, but is also more expansive, historical, quirky, and sophisticated. Jiz described it to Jenni thus: "It's sometimes hard to describe what type of porn is on the site because people often have preconceived ideas of what porn can be....Most people think of porn in a very specific, maybe mainstream, way: their porn is often heterosexual, or at least very cisgender (including cisgender lesbian or gay). It's often limited to specific body types and kinds of sex. This limited idea of porn is not necessarily a bad thing, but we are interested in questioning what porn can look like and how porn as a genre can be expanded....We have both vintage and contemporary porn. Our goal was to be able to have these films available on the site, organized similarly to the porn film festivals we attended. In other words, it's not going to be: 'here are films with this type of body.' It's more of a mixture: programming one of your documentaries alongside docu-porn, sex ed porn, porn that are funny....It's very important to be able to categorize and curate them ourselves: we want to contextualize how the films are viewed and to guide interpretations of what the spectators are watching."[3]

When the pandemic hit in 2020, Pink & White Productions' PinkLabel.tv was in the position to make the inaugural San Francisco PornFilmFestival completely virtual and—in a remarkable act of generosity—Pink & White passed the favor onto other small film festivals. Jiz told Jenni, "Our web developer Kriss Lowrance is highly resourceful: they were able to build a platform that would enable us to broadcast the films. We also did a fundraiser. We received a lot of community support, which enabled us to guarantee artist pay—we ended up doubling our initial promise of what the artist fee would be by the end of the campaign. This community support also allowed us to be able to focus on what matters: thanks to our developer and these resources, we were able to work on the site and to spend time on the curation of the festival. The festival was three days long. It included over 90 films. We wanted to be able to use the platform we built not just for ourselves, but also for other festivals: we were guinea pigs, testing it out and making sure that our platform could sustain an online festival. Then, we were able to offer it to other festivals impacted by COVID-19 (festivals that were planning on using a theater but had to pivot because theaters were closing and the situation in their country was still really bad in terms of COVID-19 deaths and hospitalizations). We essentially offered the service for free to other festivals. This allowed them to continue their operation and their curation planning for the year."[4] In a demonstration of connection and community building during the pandemic, Pink & White Productions' PinkLabel.tv hosted the virtual Seattle Erotica Cinema Society Festival, the Berlin Porn Film Festival, the first Athens Porn Film Festival, CineKink, and Uncensored Fest.

In April 2022, Jiz received top surgery. They realized how deep the desire was to get top surgery after looking intently at a photo by Allan Amato for his book *SKIN*. In the photo, Jiz was in one of their favored poses, with their hands obscuring their breasts. The pandemic had allowed for self-reflection and Jiz realized, "Being 'me' has been integral to my path. I don't want to go another year regretting not living that best version of me, in my own skin."[5] Inspired by Annie Sprinkles' art piece *Bosom Ballet*, they said goodbye to their breasts by documenting their own graceful bosom ballet while wearing black nitrile gloves. Jiz decided to go nippleless for practical reasons, "I'd experienced painfully frozen hard nipples during cold open water swimming and nipples chafe and bleed when running long distances. I didn't feel all that attached to them (pun intended!) so I opted out. I LOVE the smooth feeling when I rub my hands over my tight chest."[6]

Jiz runs the philanthropic porn experiment, Karma Pervs, raising money through erotic images for the benefit of sex-positive, queer, and kinky charity projects. Jiz spoke on a panel for the Free Speech Coalition's INSPIRE program, Life as a Sex Worker: Coming Out. They have spoken about queer sexuality and their experiences in porn at universities and colleges such as Stanford, Hampshire, and UC Berkeley. They have appeared in *Sense8*, the science fiction Netflix television series.

Jiz lives in the San Francisco Bay area and is in a relationship with fellow porn stars Syd Blakovich and Dallas. They run a workout series called "Get Buff With Jiz!" on their Onlyfans.com page.

Jiz Lee

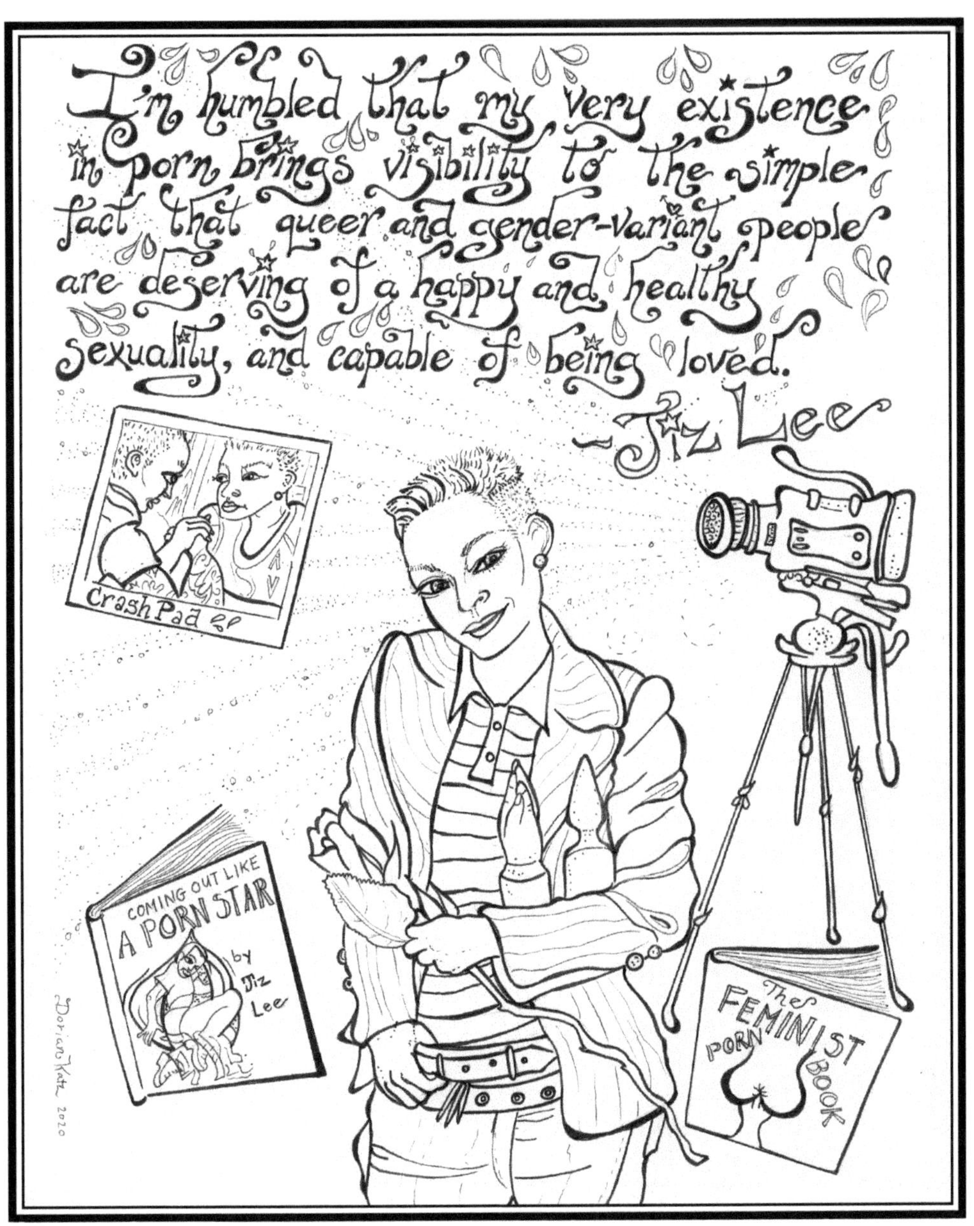

drawn by Dorian Katz

Kay Ryan

b. September 21, 1945 · USA
drawn by Janet Hardy

Of course, every poem has a different beginning, but to generalize, I might begin a poem with just a word. For example, in Say Uncle *I have a poem called 'Blandeur.' It starts, 'If it please God, / let less happen.' For that poem I found the word 'blandeur' (which of course is a coinage) on a little Post-it note beside my bed. I guess it came to me in the night I had written it down because I thought how funny it was—you know, the opposite of grandeur. Blandeur is something I seek a great deal of—a relief from intensity—so it became a poem asking for relief from intensity. It became a little prayer to make life less vivid. Let's go back to the thing I was trying to describe about how I try to use coolness in my poems. That argument about the need for relief from the world's grandeur is a funny, cool kind of an argument, but the underside of it is this: "Look at the irrepressible glory and grandeur of the world, the intolerable grandeur of it.*[1] –Kay Ryan

Kay Ryan is a poet, often labeled as an outsider. She was the first out lesbian to be awarded the national poet laureate. In 2012, President Barack Obama awarded her with the National Humanities Medal "For her contributions as a poet and educator. A former Poet Laureate of the United States, her witty and compact verse infused with subtle wordplay, reminds us of the power of language to evoke wisdom from the ordinary."[2]

Kay Ryan is of Danish heritage, was born in northern California, and raised in the Central Valley. Her father worked at several blue-collar jobs including as an oil-digger, her mother was a part-time elementary-school teacher, and the family didn't own a television or radio. As a child, Kay wanted to become a carpenter or a stand-up comedian, however, her life changed when she had a formative and prophetic dream about writing when she was ten years old. In this dream, Kay was chasing a piece of paper, but the wind was blowing it around, playing keep-away. "I knew what was on it, I knew that it was the most beautiful poem in the world, and I don't think I ever caught it."[3]

Kay studied English Literature at UCLA, but she was shy and modest about her writing and never took creative writing classes. She submitted her poetry to the UCLA poetry club, but her work was rejected as not good enough. After graduating from the University of California with a B.A. and an M.A. in English, Kay moved to northern California in 1971 to teach remedial English at the College of Marin.

Kay attempted to join a poetry club at the College of Marin but was rejected again. Kay says of her attempts to join other groups of poets, "But I have to remember those things—that there were times when I made kind of a weak, feeble, effort to be a part of the group. I've been an imperfect isolate." [4]

In 1976, when Kay was 30, she took off on a cross-country bicycle odyssey along back roads to discover what she wanted to do with her life. After writing in her journal, Kay would play with her tarot deck, using it as inspiration, "I'd kept a journal of that trip and decided that I would get up every day and transcribe that journal, augment it and fix it up. What that gave me was the habit. But once that was done, I didn't know what I was going to do. I'd bought a tarot deck—this was the seventies—a standard one with a little accompanying book that explained how to read the cards, lay them out, shuffle them—all those things. But I'm not a student and was totally impatient with learning anything about the cards. I thought they were just interesting to look at. But I did use the book's shuffling method, which was very elaborate, and in the morning I'd turn one card over and whatever that card was, I would write a poem about it. So the bicycle trip was four thousand miles to say yes or no to poetry." [5] Kay decided to become a poet.

Kay met her wife Carol Adair in 1977 while they both were teaching English in a snack bar at San Quentin State Prison, leading Kay to call their coupling a "prison romance." Upon seeing Kay for the first time in the prison parking lot, Carol said, "I did not know the gender of the person, and that thrilled me for some reason. Kay is the only person I've ever been attracted to in my life, although I had boyfriends and husbands and children." [6] They loved one another so much that they married twice, the second time on the same day in July 2008 that Kay was named US Poet Laureate. Carol was Kay's muse. Kay says that Carol was "my strongest advocate and my single companion in my poetry life." [7]

Kay continued to teach college English, all the while writing poetry. Private and habitual, in 1983 Kay and Carol self-published Kay's first book, *Dragon Acts to Dragon Ends* with financial help from their friends. Kay said, "There is a certain onus on publishing one's own book. So, I wasn't terribly proud to be doing that. It was the act of a desperate woman, and it did me not a shred of good." [8] Kay continued to quietly teach and write poetry but didn't receive any recognition for her work until the mid-1990s, when Flamingo Watching and Elephant Rocks were published. In 2004, when Kay was 59 years old, she won the Ruth Lilly Poetry Prize and finally started receiving national attention.

In 2008, Kay was appointed as the national poet laureate. When asked by National Public Radio's (NPR) Andrea Seabrook about Kay's well-known poem, "Home to Roost," Kay described the atmosphere when she wrote it, "First of all,

Kay Ryan

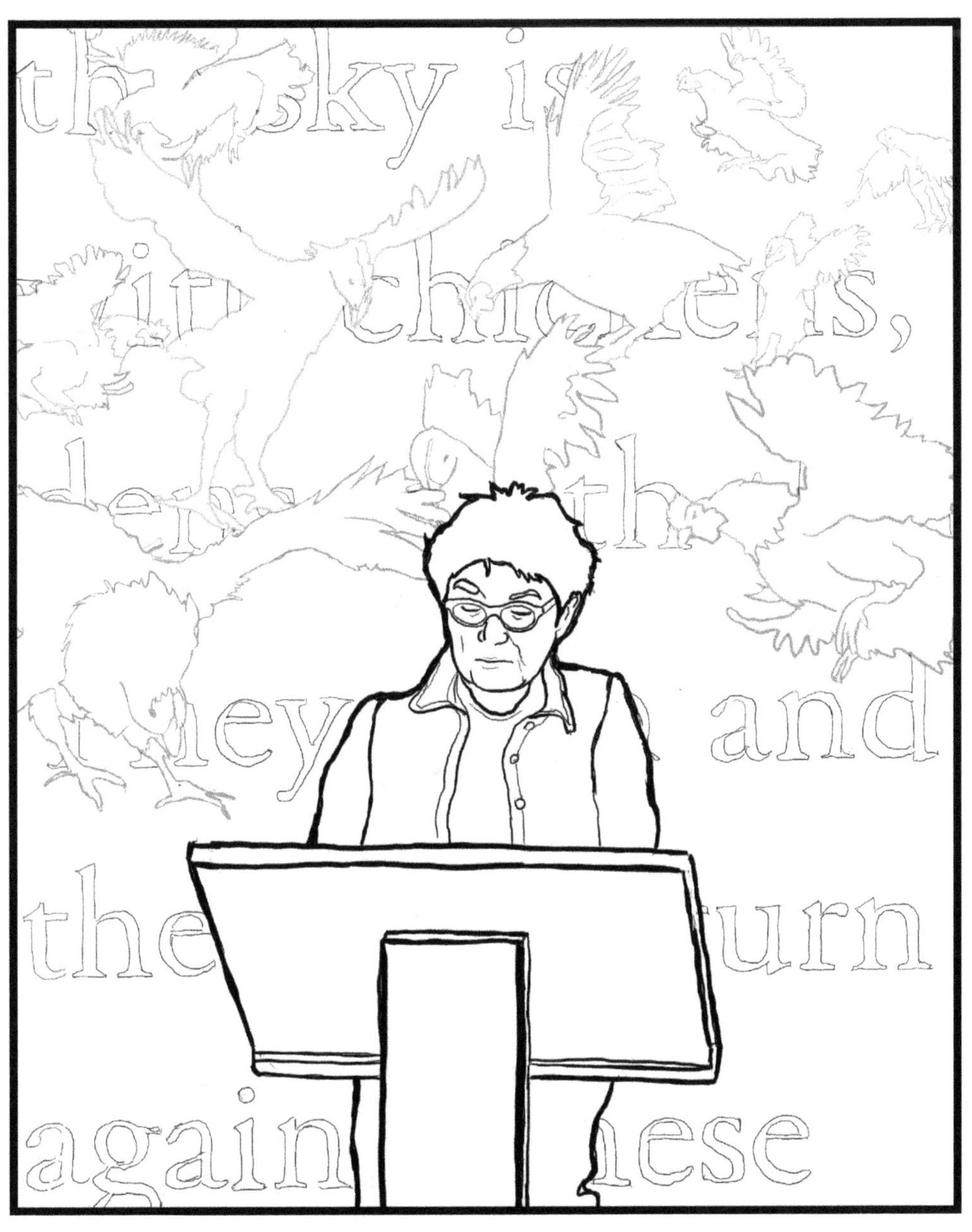

drawn by Janet Hardy

it comes from the thing we say to other people when they've done a lot of stupid things, and now they're getting their comeuppance. We say, well, your chickens are coming home to roost, and I have no doubt that when I wrote this, I was chastening myself, and I was telling myself this, but unfortunately, this poem was sitting on the desk of an editor in New York at the time of 9/11, and it suddenly took on this terrible added significance, and I had to withdraw it because it seemed cruelly appropriate. Now right after 9/11, that sounded, you know, the blue sky in here, the clear sky, sounded just like the beauty of that day, and those chickens sounded much too much like airplanes." [9]

Early on in her career as a poet, Kay developed what she called "recombinant rhyme": "When I started writing, nobody rhymed—it was in utter disrepute. Yet rhyme was a siren to me. I had this condition of things rhyming in my mind without my permission. Still I couldn't take end-rhyme seriously, which meant I had to find other ways—I stashed my rhymes at the wrong ends of lines and in the middles—the front of one word would rhyme with the back of another one, or one word might be identical to three words." [10]

An outsider, Kay's work is known for its brevity, pragmatism, wryness, and quirkiness. She has a fondness for malapropisms and clichés, stylistic devices that are often mocked as being trivial in the world of serious, academic poets. Her poems are introspective and short, with just a few compact lines, yet they are not delicate. Her work has been compared to that of Emily Dickinson, Marianne Moore, and Robert Frost, but my vote is the British poet, Stevie Smith. "Each poem twists around and back upon its argument like a river retracing its path; they are didactic in spirit, but a bedrock wit supports them." [11]

Kay's work's humor and earthiness lends itself to live readings, "When I read my poems to any audience there's a lot of laughing, but I always warn them that it's a fairy gift and will turn scary when they get it home Laughter creates a kind of contact. I hate that atmosphere at a poetry reading where everybody sits there being subtle and sensitive." [12]

Kay started writing *The Best of It: New and Selected Poems* while staying at home to be with her wife when Carol was dying of bladder cancer. Sadly, Carol died before the book was published in 2011.

Kay has received multiple honors for her work, including a 2004 Guggenheim Fellowship, a 2011 MacArthur Foundation Fellowship, a 2012 National Humanities Medal from President Barack Obama, and a 2011 annual Pulitzer Prize for Poetry for *The Best of It: New and Selected Poems*. In 2008, Kay served two one-year terms as Poet Laureate Consultant in Poetry to the Library of Congress.

Gayle Rubin

b. January 1, 1949 · USA
drawn by Dorian Katz

Issues such as drag, cross-dressing, transsexuality, and sex work were already revealing deep fault lines in feminism. Then in the late seventies there was a series of new rounds of surveillance and arrests of gay men in tearooms on the Michigan campus and throughout southern Michigan. There was a big bust at one of the rest stops on I-94 between Detroit and Ann Arbor, and then a group of gay men were arrested for cruising in a park in downtown Detroit. A superintendent of one of the Detroit school districts was nailed in one of these round-ups. When these gay men were getting arrested, the most common opinion I heard in the local feminist community was, 'Well, they're just filthy guys doing filthy male things, and maybe they should be arrested.' I considered this sentiment appalling. I did not think anyone should be getting arrested for having gay sex. I started to think more about sexuality as an issue. I wrote my first piece on sexual politics, which was a dissent from a fairly straightforward lesbian feminist perspective in the Leaping Lesbian *in February 1978.*[1] –Gayle Rubin

Gayle Rubin is a cultural anthropologist and an associate professor of Anthropology and Women's Studies at the University of Michigan, where her classes include "Sex Panics," "Sex and the City," and graduate seminars such as "Sexological Theories: From Krafft-Ebing to Foucault" and "The Feminist Sex Wars." Her how-we-wish-it-were-already-publicly-published dissertation was *The Valley of Kings: Leathermen in San Francisco.*

Gayle was raised in a small, conservative town in South Carolina, the only Jewish child in a sea of Christianity in her elementary school. Gayle's activist journey started with the 1960s civil rights movement. Unlike many folks in her hometown, Gayle's family supported integration, however, Gayle remembers when Black children were finally admitted to her high school, "I vividly recall sitting in the school cafeteria listening to my friends spew abhorrent, paranoid, and wild statements to justify racial separation. These were not bad people; they were teenagers who, for the most part, repeated in school what they heard over their dinner tables at home."[2]

In 1965, Gayle arrived at the University of Michigan and promptly became involved in campus politics, working to overturn draconian dress codes and curfew rules that applied only to female students, along with regulations about opposite-sex dorm room visitations. After involvement with the Vietnam anti-war movement, Gayle fell in with a women's consciousness-raising group and came out as a lesbian in the spring of 1970 while working with the newly formed Women's

Studies Program and Ann Arbor's Gay Liberation Front (GLF). By the fall of 1971, Gayle had created the group RadicalLesbians, but by the mid-70s, rifts between Gayle and Ann Arbor lesbians and feminists were forming.

In 1975, Gayle published a groundbreaking essay, "The Traffic in Women: Notes on the 'Political Economy' of Sex," a Marxist-centered account of the origins of female oppression. Her 1984 essay "Thinking Sex" is considered instrumental to understanding gay and lesbian studies, sexuality studies, and queer theory. "Thinking Sex" introduces the "Charmed Circle" of sexuality. In the "Charmed Circle" modality, sexuality that was privileged by society was inside the circle, while all other forms of sexuality were outside of and in direct opposition to the circle. The inner circle was described as good, normal, and natural. Inner circle sexuality included heterosexual, married, monogamous, procreative, non-commercial, paired, in a relationship, same generation, private, without pornography or sex toys, and vanilla. The transgressive outer circle was described as bad, abnormal, unnatural, and damned, and its sexuality included homosexual, unmarried, promiscuous, non-procreative, commercial, in groups, casual, cross-generational, public, with pornography or sex toys, and sadomasochistic. Throughout the essay, Rubin details how sexuality—on its own and in conjunction with other social factors—works as a vector of oppression; sexual minorities pay real costs for their position in society.

Gayle was one of the organizers of the infamous 1982 Barnard Conference on Sexuality, which marked the beginning of the Feminist Sex Wars, a bitter standoff between conservative feminists and sex-positive feminists, although that grossly simplifies the wide range of issues between the two groups.

Gayle moved to San Francisco in 1978 to study gay male leather culture. After her move, Gayle, along with 17 other lesbians, co-founded the legendary lesbian-feminist BDSM group Samois that summer. Samois was the nation's first lesbian BDSM group and was considered incendiary by mainstream anti-pornography feminists. In 2019, Samois was inducted into the Leather Hall of Fame. After Samois dissolved in 1983, Gayle co-founded another lesbian BDSM group, the Outcasts, who were instrumental in forming sex-positive community in the Bay area with sponsored community events such as Butch Fashion Shows, the first SF Dyke Daddy contest, many dances, and even a night to take the perverts bowling. Once the Outcasts disbanded, the Exiles were formed. The Exiles are still up, running, and having fun.

Gayle started researching lesbian history in the early 1970s and gay leather history in the late 1970s. She commented, "If you don't have the ability to produce, preserve and make accessible the documentary and artifactual remains of any human project, it tends to vanish very quickly and then people don't know it ever happened. With gay history, a lot has been lost. A lot of young gay people were under the impression they were the first individuals on the planet to ever have these feelings or to try to articulate and express them because the histories had not been adequately preserved. By preserving the histories of the LGBTQ community and its many subcultures over time," Rubin continued, "We could situate ourselves better historically, intellectually, and socially, and have some understanding of who we were…and where we were in the world."[3]

In 1994, Gayle wrote her two-volume dissertation, *The Valley of Kings: Leathermen in San Francisco*. Unfortunately, her groundbreaking study of gay men's leather culture in San Francisco has not been released for publication to the general public yet, however, it appears that fragments can be found scattered throughout anthologies, presentations, and articles. In a presentation called "The Valley of the Kings" given to the San Francisco Leathermen's Discussion Group, Gayle talked about gay male leathermen in San Francisco, "…leather was never just about SM, and one of the things that happens when gay male leather is forming in the late 1940s, is that gay masculinity, kinky sex, leather fetishism, and motorcycles all get kind of conglomerated. It's sort of like what happens in granite. You know, all these things get pushed together into one rock formation, but they really have somewhat separate origins."[4]

In a lecture called "Radical Desire: Making *On Our Backs* Magazine" that Gayle gave at Cornell University in 2022, she talked about how chilling it was prior to and during the Feminist Sex Wars time period in the 1970s through the 1980s, "I'm going to particularly focus on one area one of the major sites of contention and contestation that was the bitter and acrimonious conflict over pornography. I should have titled this talk the feminist porn wars because, in fact the sex wars were much more extensive than the fight over porn, and just to highlight a few of the areas that people were fighting about, one of the first was the attempt to either marginalize or expel lesbians from the mainstream women's movement and such that lesbians had to resist exclusion from organizations such as NOW (National Organization for Women). Having resisted expulsion some lesbians returned the favor by questioning heterosexuality and claiming that there was no legitimate feminist heterosexuality. There were some straight women who also made that argument, then there were discussions of what was properly feminist lesbianism, which resulted in the denigration of butch-femme roles in relationships and the assertion that these were merely rehashed versions of heterosexual arrangements. There were debates over penetration and was this just a remnant of male supremacy? Was it okay for lesbians to do that? Was sexual fantasy permissible? There was actually an argument that fantasy dehumanized and objectified one's partner, so fantasy was not a good thing to do."[5]

Although a virulent streak of puritanism was winding its way through the lesbian community, there was also passionate sexual activity. Gayle clarified, "Similarly, during the mid to late 70s, there was an increasing visibility of SM lesbians, and that then occasioned a rash of anti-SM opinion in the lesbian and feminist press and in lesbian communities. One of the ironies of all of this is that this criticism of sexual acts, of gender identities, of erotic roles has contributed to a kind of stereotype, an erroneous one I believe, of the women's movement of this period and especially lesbian feminism as largely grim and puritanical and hostile to sexual pleasure. And while that description might be apt for some, it could not be more incorrect. Women's liberation and then lesbian feminism were hotbeds of sexual enthusiasm, and the pursuit of lust was probably as intense as the pursuit of political goals."[6]

In 2012, Gayle published a collection of her writings on feminism, sexuality, and queer theory in a book called *Deviations: A Gayle Rubin Reader*. In Chapter 10, "Reflections on Butch, Gender, and Boundaries," she wrote about a range of butch expressions and behaviors, "Butches come in all the shapes and varieties and idioms of masculinity. There are butches who are tough street dudes, butches who are jocks, butches who are scholars, butches who are artists, rock-and-roll butches, butches who have motorcycles, and butches who have money. There are butches whose male models are effeminate men, sissies, drag queens, and many different types of male homosexuals. There are butch nerds, butches with soft bodies and hard minds. Thinking of butch as a category of gender expression may help to account for what appear to be butch sexual anomalies. Do butches who prefer to let their partners run the sex become 'femme in the sheets'? Are butches who go out with other butches instead of femmes 'homosexuals'? Does that make femmes who date femmes 'lesbians'? Butchness often signals a sexual interest in femmes and a desire or willingness to orchestrate sexual encounters. However, the ideas that butches partner exclusively with femmes or that butches always 'top' (that is, 'run the sex') are stereotypes that mask substantial variation in butch erotic experience," she continued. "Butches are often identified in relation to femmes. Within this framework, butch and femme are considered an indissoluble unity, each defined with reference to the other; butches are invariably the partners of femmes. Defining 'butch' as the object of femme desire, or 'femme' as the object of butch desire presupposes that butches do not desire or partner with other butches, and that femmes do not desire or go with other femmes. Butch-butch eroticism is much less documented than butch-femme sexuality, and lesbians do not always recognize or understand it. Although it is not uncommon, lesbian culture contains few models for it. Many butches who lust after other butches have looked to gay male literature and behavior as sources of imagery and language."[7]

Gayle and her partner of over thirty years, Jay Marston have a home in San Francisco.

Gayle has been involved with the San Francisco Lesbian and Gay History Project and was a founding member of the GLBT Historical Society. Gayle has been recognized for her work around sexual freedom, including induction into the Society of Janus Hall of Fame, the Race Bannon Advocacy Award from the National Coalition for Sexual Freedom, a lifetime achievement award from the National Leather Organization (NLA), the Pantheon of Leather Forebear Award, and more recently was a member of the community advisory group for the San Francisco South of Market Leather History Alley project.

Gayle Rubin

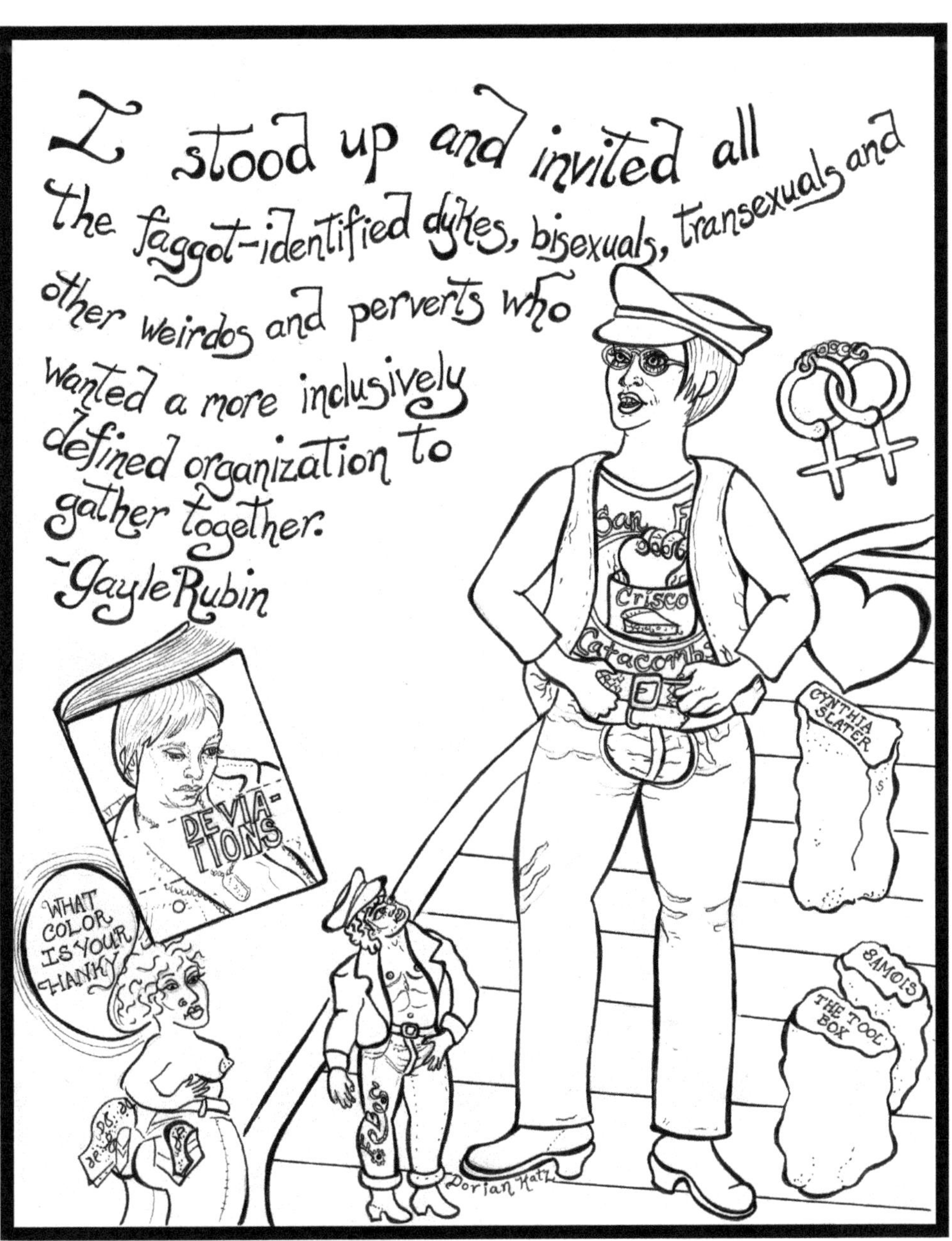

drawn by Dorian Katz

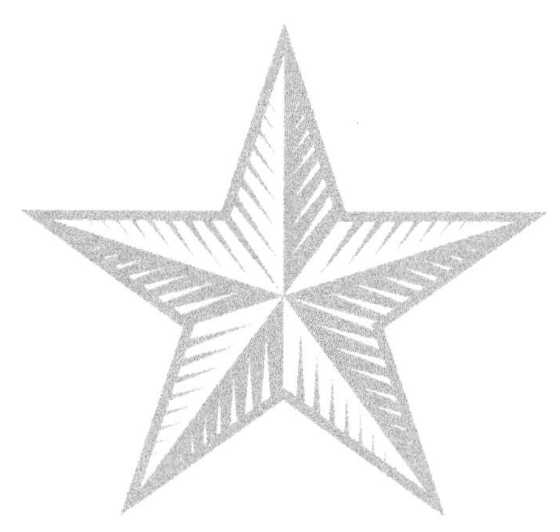

Leslie Feinberg

September 1, 1949–November 15, 2014 · USA
drawn by Soizick Jaffre

I care which pronoun is used, but people have been disrespectful to me with the wrong pronoun and respectful with the right one. It matters whether someone is using the pronoun as a bigot, or if they are trying to demonstrate respect.[1]
–Leslie Feinberg

Leslie Feinberg was a writer, activist, and communist. Ze is notable for hir books *Stone Butch Blues* (1993) and the pioneering non-fiction book *Transgender Warriors* (1996). Gender-fluid, Leslie identified as female-bodied, butch, lesbian, and transgender, all at the same time.

Leslie Feinberg was born in Missouri, but raised in Buffalo, New York by working-class Jewish parents. In the 1940s and 50s, Buffalo, New York was a conservative industrial city with a strong union presence. Ze dropped out of high school, preferring to work and explore the local gay bars. Leslie's biological family were hostile towards hir because of hir masculine gender expression, so ze moved out of their home and severed ties with them while ze was a teen. When ze was 14, ze started supporting hirself and dropped out of high school. Leslie started working a series of low-wage jobs, including working in a book bindery, a PVC pipe factory, washing dishes, and ASL interpretation.

Ze was a writer and a life-long activist. Leslie's activism began in hir early 20s when Leslie met folks from the Workers World Party at a demonstration for Palestinian land rights and self-determination, then moved to New York. Between 2004 and 2008, Leslie was a journalist for the Marxist-Leninist Workers World Party's newspaper, *Worker's World*, writing about the connections between socialism and the history of gender politics in a column called "Lavender & Red," then as the editor of the Political Prisoners page. Leslie was heavily involved in anti-war, pro-labor, anti-racist, abortion rights, and AIDS rallies, and was a member of the National Writers Union and of the AFL-CIO constituency group, Pride at Work. Leslie identified as an anti-racist White, working-class, secular Jewish, transgender, lesbian, female, revolutionary communist.

Leslie's pronouns were ze and hir, however, ze was flexible regarding pronouns if the speaker was respectful and commented that pronouns could be situational, "For me, pronouns are always placed within context. I am female-bodied, I am a butch lesbian, a transgender lesbian—referring to me as 'ze/her' is appropriate, particularly in a non-trans setting in which referring to me as 'he' would appear to resolve the social contradiction between my birth sex and gender expression and render my transgender expression invisible. I like the gender-neutral pronoun 'ze/hir' because it makes it impossible to hold on to gender/sex/sexuality assumptions about a person you're about to meet or you've just met. And in an all trans setting, referring to me as 'he/him' honors my gender expression in the same way that referring to my sister drag queens as 'ze/her' does."[2] Obituaries released by hir wife Minnie Bruce Pratt after Leslie's death in 2014 use the pronoun "ze."

The 1982 Barnard Conference scandal signaled the official start of the Feminist Sex Wars, with standoffs between The Lesbian Sex Mafia and their "Speakout on Politically Incorrect Sex" rally *vs.* picketing by the feminist-led Women Against Pornography (WAP). In 1981, activist Joan Nestle had published the article "Butch–Femme Relationships: Sexual Courage in the 1950s" in *Heresies 12* and spoke at the conference at the "Politically Correct, Politically Incorrect" workshop. A leaflet was produced targeting sex-positive women at the conference, "women who champion butch–femme sex roles, while denying that these roles have any relation to the male–female sex roles that are the psychological foundation of patriarchy."[3]

In 1993, Leslie's groundbreaking novel *Stone Butch Blues* was published at an auspicious time, 10 years after the start of the Feminist Sex Wars. A coming-of-age novel, *Stone Butch Blues* drew upon hir life, but was not a memoir. Shauna Miller wrote a tribute to Leslie and *Stone Butch Blues* in *The Atlantic* after Leslie's premature death at age 65, "*Stone Butch Blues* was a gateway for me to understanding love, gender expression, and my girlfriend. It should be up there with the classic coming-of-age novels...*Stone Butch Blues* was the heartbreaking holy grail of butch perspective. The main character Jess Goldberg is always on the move—either trying to find a new spot to maybe fit in, or more likely rest a while before being forced to move on for her safety. Her appearance is an affront. Her appearance is aggressive. It puts her life in danger. It puts her livelihood in danger. It's dispersed any biological family. Her appearance has cost her everything."[4]

Leslie talked about hir choices in describing the characters and hir methods of working around the default and the reader's expectations in *Stone Butch Blues*, "I made a decision in writing *Stone Butch Blues* based on my anger at seeing how many white writers used whiteness as a default and only described a character if they were of color. Based on my anger at writers who only used thinness as the default and only identified characters as being fat, at writers who didn't name a character if they were able-bodied or didn't have a disability, but did label them if they did. I decided I wasn't going to do that. In *Stone Butch Blues* we discover the characters through their reactions to racism and other bigotries. I don't name who the characters are. I don't tell, I show. That means that different people who read this book may have different views about the sizes, and shapes, and abilities, and so forth of these characters. And as readers those are all valid experiences."[5]

The other effect that *Stone Butch Blues* had upon the lesbian community was to shine a light upon and give agency to the butch-femme subculture once again. Prior to the 1960s and 1970s, butch-femme subculture was a strong component of lesbian culture, but the rise of feminism and political lesbians in the 1970s made it unpopular, stating that butch-femme subculture was giving in to the patriarchy, binary roles, and politically incorrect. Writers and femmes Joan Nestle and Amber Hollibaugh had been writing for years in efforts to resurrect and relegitimize butch-femme subculture, and *Stone Butch Blues* was the push that was needed.

Stone Butch Blues has been widely translated into several languages, including Chinese, Dutch, German, Italian, Slovenian, Turkish, and Hebrew (with earnings from that edition going to ASWAT Palestinian Gay Women). After a legal struggle with the publisher, Leslie recovered hir rights to *Stone Butch Blues*. It is not represented by a literary agency and is currently available as a free PDF and as a print-on-demand book though Lulu.

In 1992, Leslie met the love of hir life, Minnie Bruce Pratt, during a slideshow that Leslie was giving on transgender research. They were domestically partnered in 2004, joined in civil union in 2006, and married in New York and Massachusetts in 2011.

From 1996 through 1999, Leslie published two books on transgender rights and history, *Transgender Warriors: Making History from Joan of Arc to Dennis Rodman* (1996) and *Trans Liberation: Beyond Pink or Blue* (1999), a collection of hir speeches on trans-liberation and its intersectional connection to the liberation for all. In *Transgender Warriors*, Leslie wrote about hir definition of "transgender" as, "including all 'people who cross the cultural boundaries of gender'—including butch dykes, passing women (those who passed as men only in order to find work or survive during war), and drag queens,"[6] also noting a long presence in history of people that crossed cultural gender boundaries, "I can tell you that I have found gender diversity and sex reassignment and intersexuality on every continent in every historical period. But it wasn't until the cleaving of human society into have and have-not economic classes that I found the earliest patriarchal edicts separating the sexes, overturning the historic role of females, punishing or executing intersexual individuals, defining gender roles, policing the boundaries of gender expression, and making sexuality a matter of state repression. That history is presented in the most accessible way I possibly could, with more than

100 photos and illustrations, in *Transgender Warriors*."[7] *Transgender Warriors* was a vessel for the mainstream population's awareness of gender terminology and gender studies and was notable for its impact upon popular culture, academic research, and political organizing. Leslie was the first theorist to advance a Marxist concept of transgender liberation.

In 2014, Leslie died at home from complications from multiple tick-borne co-infections, with Minnie Bruce by hir side. Leslie contracted Lyme disease in the early 1970s, however, due to "bigotry, prejudice, and lack of science,"[8] ze was not diagnosed until 2008. Ze wrote about hir struggles with Lyme disease extensively on hir website. Leslie's final words were, "Remember me as a revolutionary communist."[9] Minnie Bruce Pratt died in her sleep on June 2, 2023.

Stone Butch Blues was the winner of the 1994 American Library Association Stonewall Book Award and a 1994 Lambda Literary Award. Leslie received an honorary doctorate from the Starr King School for the Ministry for hir transgender and social justice work. Leslie was honored as one of 50 trailblazing LGBTQ+ activists on the National LGBTQ Wall of Honor within the Stonewall National Monument in New York City's Stonewall Inn, birthplace of the contemporary LGBTQ+ struggle for equal rights.

Leslie Feinberg

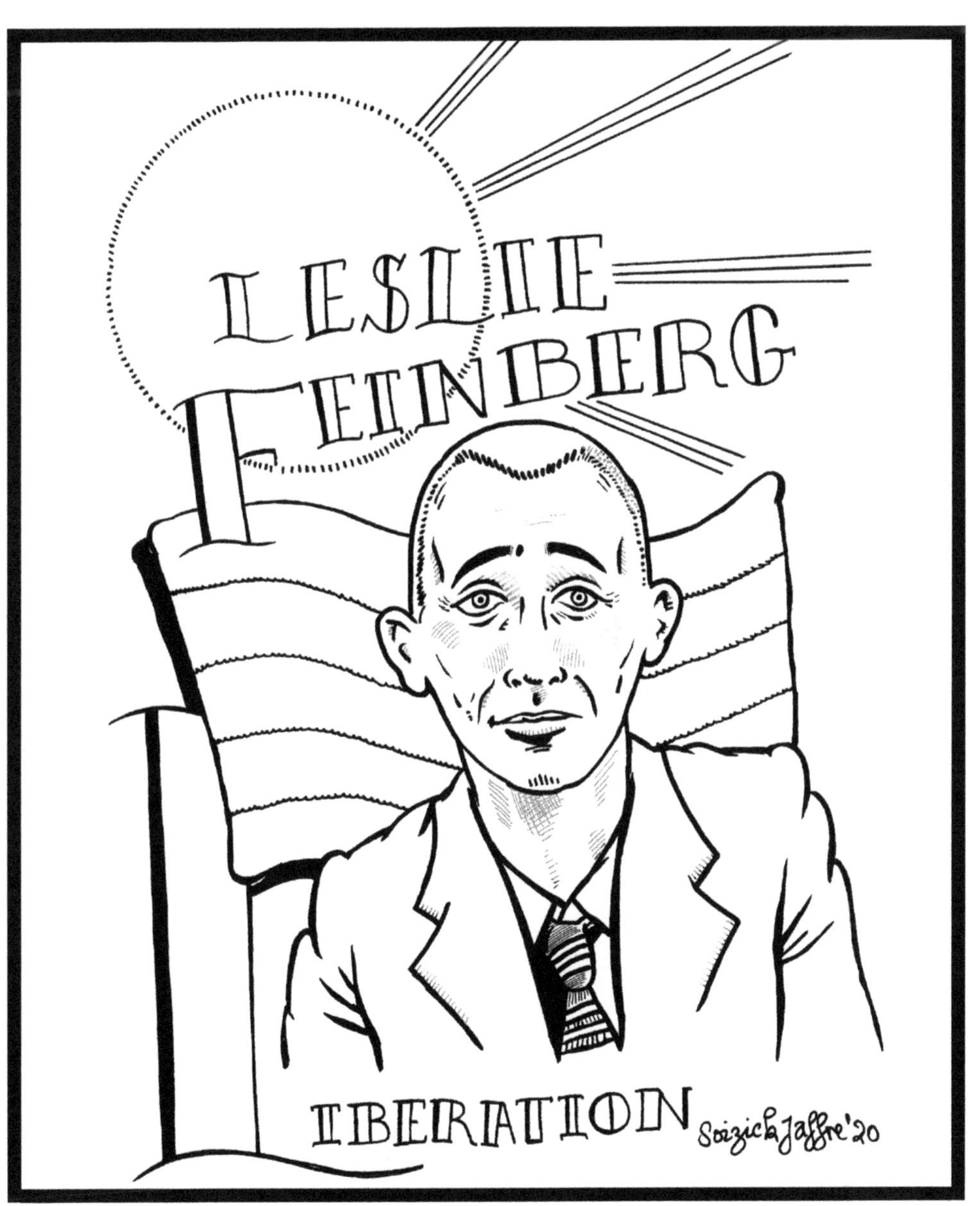

drawn by Soizick Jaffre

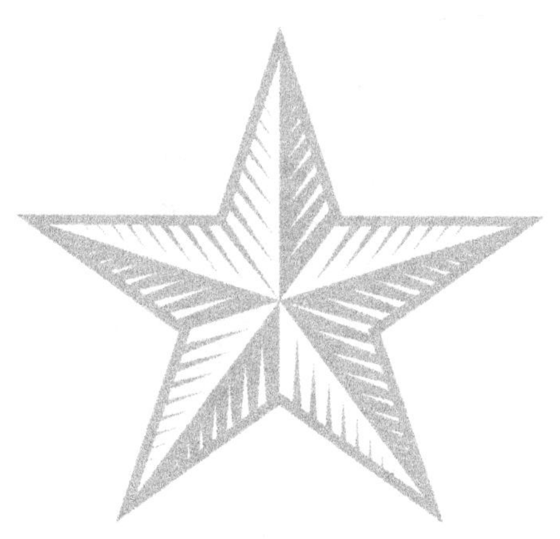

Citations

Soni S.H.S. Wolf **p. 11**

1. Ilyasova, K. Alex. "Dykes on Bikes and the Regulation of Vulgarity." *International Journal of Motorcycle Studies*, Nov. 2006. http://ijms.nova.edu/November2006/IJMS_Artcl.Ilyasova.html.
2. Karlan, Sarah. "Meet The Dykes On Bikes Of San Francisco." *BuzzFeed*, June 26, 2016. https://www.buzzfeed.com/skarlan/40-years-of-dykes-on-bikes-in-san-francisco
3. Bechdel, Alison. "Trademark This." *DTWOF: The blog*. July 15, 2005. http://alisonbechdel.blogspot.com/2005/07/trademark-this.html
4. Rogers, Destiny. "On This Day April 25: Soni Wolf, Dykes on Bikes." *Q News*, April 25, 2022. https://qnews.com.au/on-this-day-april-25-soni-wolf-dykes-on-bikes/
5. Lesbian News. "Soni Wolf: The First of the Dykes on Bikes." *Lesbian News*, May 4, 2018.
6. Germany, Vick. "Dykes on Bikes® Fab Forty!" *San Francisco Bay Times*, 2016. https://sfbaytimes.com/dykes-on-bikes-fab-forty/
7. Brown, Kate. "LGBT Fallen Heroes Memorial Service–Soni Wolf." Women In Military Service For America Memorial, May 13, 2019. https://www.youtube.com/watch?v=sl7itjzy-7I

Rhoda Williams-Nazanin **p. 17**

1. Cassell, Avery, and Rhoda Nazanin. Rhoda Nazanin. Personal interview, February 1, 2023.
2. Ibid.
3. Nazanin, Rhoda. "The Talk of Santa Clarita: Episode 170 w/ Dem. candidate for the 25th Cong. district. Rhoda Nazanin." Interview with Stephen Daniels. *Radio Free Santa Clarita*. July 21, 2021. https://www.youtube.com/watch?v=wJO55dfpTFk
4. Ibid.
5. Cassell, Avery, and Rhoda Nazanin. Rhoda Nazanin. Personal interview, February 1, 2023.
6. Nazanin, Rhoda. "The Talk of Santa Clarita: Episode 170 w/ Dem. candidate for the 25th Cong. district. Rhoda Nazanin." Interview with Stephen Daniels. *Radio Free Santa Clarita*. July 21, 2021. https://www.youtube.com/watch?v=wJO55dfpTFk
7. Cassell, Avery, and Rhoda Nazanin. Rhoda Nazanin. Personal interview, February 1, 2023.

Del Martin **p. 23**

1. D'Emilio, John. "Contacts Desired: Gay and Lesbian Communications and Community, 1940s–1970s. Martin Meeker." *Journal of Homosexuality*, vol. 55, no. 2, 2008.
2. Johnson, Dianna Lee. "A Narrative Life Story of Activist Phyllis Lyon and Her Reflections on a Life with Del Martin." Thesis. Grand Valley State University. ScholarWorks@GVSU, 2012. https://scholarworks.gvsu.edu/cgi/viewcontent.cgi?article=1021&context=theses
3. Lyon, Phyllis and Del Martin. "Phyllis Lyon & Del Martin." Interview with Eric Marcus. *Making Gay History: The Podcast*, July 27, 1989. https://makinggayhistory.com/podcast/phyllis-lyon-del-martin/
4. Rodriguez, Joe. "Del Martin, 87, Pioneering Lesbian Activist." *The Mercury News*, August 27, 2008. https://www.mercurynews.com/2008/08/27/del-martin-87-pioneering-lesbian-activist/
5. Lyon, Phyllis and Del Martin. "Phyllis Lyon & Del Martin." Interview with Eric Marcus. *Making Gay History: The Podcast*, July 27, 1989. https://makinggayhistory.com/podcast/phyllis-lyon-del-martin/
6. Johnson, Dianna Lee. "A Narrative Life Story of Activist Phyllis Lyon and Her Reflections on a Life with Del Martin." Thesis. *Grand Valley State University*. ScholarWorks@GVSU, 2012. https://scholarworks.gvsu.edu/cgi/viewcontent.cgi?article=1021&context=theses

7. D'Emilio, John. "Contacts Desired: Gay and Lesbian Communications and Community, 1940s–1970s. Martin Meeker." *Journal of Homosexuality*, vol. 55, no. 2, 2008.
8. Lyon, Phyllis. "Lesbian Liberation Begins." *The Gay & Lesbian Review*, Oct. 23 2015. https://glreview.org/article/lesbian-liberation-begins/
9. Gordon, Rachel. "Couple of 55 Years Tie the Knot - Again." *SF Gate*, June 17, 2008. https://www.sfgate.com/news/article/Couple-of-55-years-tie-the-knot-again-3208710.php

Lyra McKee ______ **p. 33**

1. Doyle, Jackie, director. *Lyra*. Erica Starling Productions Ltd , 2022.
2. McKay, Susan. "The Incredible Life and Tragic Death of Lyra McKee." *The New Yorker*, July 26, 2019. https://www.newyorker.com/news/postscript/the-incredible-life-and-tragic-death-of-lyra-mckee
3. McKee, Lyra. *Lyra McKee's Letter To My 14 Year Old Self*, Stay Beautiful Films, 2014. youtu.be/sEscGI7VTXY
4. McKee, Lyra. "Suicide Among the Ceasefire Babies." *The Atlantic*, January 20, 2016. https://www.theatlantic.com/health/archive/2016/01/conflict-mental-health-northern-ireland-suicide/424683/
5. "Press Statement – REF: Death of Journalist Lyra McKee." *Excalibur Press*, April 20, 2019. https://excaliburpress.co.uk/2019/04/19/press-statement-ref-death-of-journalist-lyra-mckee/
6. O'Loughlin, Ed. "New I.R.A. Apologizes for Killing of Journalist in Northern Ireland." *The New York Times*, April 23, 2019. https://www.nytimes.com/2019/04/23/world/europe/lyra-mckee-new-ira-apology.html

Dr. Jamaica Heolimeleikalani Osorio ______ **p. 37**

1. Osorio, Jamaica Heolimeleikalani. "Jamaica Heolimeleikalani Osorio." Interview with Aina Momona. *Aina Momona*, June 8, 2021. https://www.kaainamomona.org/post/jamaica-heolimeleikalani-osorio
2. Ibid.
3. Osorio, Jamaica Heolimeleikalani. "VR to create a resonance that pulls us back into our humanity - Jamaica Heolimeleikalani Osorio (ON THE MORNING YOU WAKE)." Interview with Agnese Pietrobon. *XRMagazine*, February 7, 2022. https://www.xrmust.com/xrmagazine/jamaica-heolimeleikalani-osorio-on-the-morning-you-wake/
4. Osorio, Jamaica H. "(Re)Membering 'Upena of Intimacies: A Kanaka Maoli Mo'olelo beyond Queer Theory." ScholarSpace. University of Hawai'i at Mānoa, August 1, 2018. https://scholarspace.manoa.hawaii.edu/items/4bcb4830-c39e-4e77-94f9-e1c483e66acc/full
5. Osorio, Jamaica Heolimeleikalani. "Transcript: DR. JAMAICA HEOLIMELEIKALANI OSORIO on Reclaiming Aloha." Interview with Ayana Young. *For the Wild*. Kalliopeia Foundation, July 22, 2022. https://forthewild.world/podcast-transcripts/dr-jamaica-heolimeleikalani-osorio-on-reclaiming-aloha-297
6. Ibid.
7. Osorio, Jamaica Heolimeleikalani. "Jamaica Heolimeleikalani Osorio." Department of Political Science, University of Hawaii Mānoa, 2021. https://politicalscience.manoa.hawaii.edu/jamaica-osorio/

Ajuan Mance ______ **p. 45**

1. Mance, Ajuan Maria. *Living While Black: Portraits of Everyday Resistance*. Chronicle Books, 2022.
2. Cunningham, Dawn. "Audaciously Black: Ajuan Mance Celebrates the 'Wonderful Complexity of African American Lives,' Past and Present, through Literature and Art." Mills College, March 15, 2017. https://quarterly.mills.edu/audaciously-black/

3. Ibid.
4. Zuenkp, Angelica, director. *No Straight Lines: The Rise of Queer Comics*. A Compadre Media Group Production, 2021. https://www.pbs.org/independentlens/documentaries/no-straight-lines/
5. Mance, Ajuan. *Gender Studies*. Ajuan Mance, 2014.
6. Mance, Ajuan. "Spotlight on Ajuan Mance." Interview with Jon Macy. *Prism Comics*. August 13, 2016. https://www.prismcomics.org/spotlight-on-ajuan-mance/
7. Nordman, David. "'Living While Black:' What's Criminal Often Depends on Who's Doing the Activity, Northeastern Professor Says in Book." *Northeastern Global News*, October 12, 2022. https://news.northeastern.edu/2022/10/12/living-while-black/
8. Mance, Ajuan. "Ajuan Mance, Why Representation Matters." Interview with Pam Uzzell. *Art Heals All Wounds*, March 14, 2021. https://arthealsallwounds.buzzsprout.com/2053590/11387405-ajuan-mance-why-representation-matters?t=0

Alison Bechdel ______ **p. 49**

1. Bechdel, Alison. "An Interview with Alison Bechdel." Interview with Kristen Radtke Haddad. *Believer Magazine*, June 17, 2021. https://www.thebeliever.net/an-interview-with-alison-bechdel/
2. Alvarez, John. "Alison Bechdel." *Pennsylvania Center for the Book*, 2018. https://pabook.libraries.psu.edu/literary-cultural-heritage-map-pa/bios/Bechdel_Alison
3. Bechdel, Alison. *Fun Home: A Family Tragicomic*. A Mariner Book, Houghton Mifflin Harcourt, 2007.
4. MacQueen, Kim. "Alison Bechdel on Telling Her True Stories." *Seven Days*, March 6, 2103. https://m.sevendaysvt.com/vermont/alison-bechdel-on-telling-her-true-stories/Content?oid=2243025
5. Bechdel, Alison. *Fun Home: A Family Tragicomic*. A Mariner Book, Houghton Mifflin Harcourt, 2007.
6. Bechdel, Alison. "Lesbian Cartoonist Alison Bechdel Countered Dad's Secrecy By Being Out And Open." Interview with Terry Gross. *NPR: Fresh Air*, August 17, 2015. https://www.npr.org/2015/08/17/432569415/lesbian-cartoonist-alison-bechdel-countered-dads-secrecy-by-being-out-and-open
7. Bechdel, Alison. "Frivolous, Aimless Queries." *Alison Bechdel, 2021.* https://dykestowatchoutfor.com/frivolous-aimless-queries/
8. Lesbian herstory archives. "Lesbian Herstory Archives." Facebook, February 4, 2023. https://www.facebook.com/herstoryarchives/
9. Bechdel, Alison. "DTWOF Archive Episode #1." *Alison Bechdel, May 2, 2007.* https://dykestowatchoutfor.com/dtwof-archive-episode-1/
10. Thurman, Judith. "Drawn From Life The World of Alison Bechdel." *The New Yorker*, April 16, 2012. https://www.newyorker.com/magazine/2012/04/23/drawn-from-life
11. Publisher Description for Library of Congress Control Number 2008036784, "The essential dykes to watch out for." Library of Congress. http://catdir.loc.gov/catdir/enhancements/fy0905/2008036784-d.html
12. Cooke, Rachel. "Fun Home Creator Alison Bechdel on Turning a Tragic Childhood into a Hit Musical." *The Guardian*, September 5, 2017. https://www.theguardian.com/books/2017/nov/05/alison-bechdel-interview-cartoonist-fun-home
13. Thurman, Judith. "Drawn From Life The World of Alison Bechdel." *The New Yorker*, April 16, 2012. https://www.newyorker.com/magazine/2012/04/23/drawn-from-life

14. Dunne, Carey, and Ilene Dube. "Alison Bechdel's Mission to Make Lesbian Culture Visible through Comics." *Hyperallergic*, September 24, 2018. https://hyperallergic.com/461192/self-confessed-the-inappropriately-intimate-comics-of-alison-bechdel/

15. Teeman, Tim. "Lesbian Desire, a Father's Suicide and 12 Tony Noms: Alison Bechdel on 'Fun Home.'" *The Daily Beast*, July 12, 2017, https://www.thedailybeast.com/lesbian-desire-a-fathers-suicide-and-12-tony-noms-alison-bechdel-on-fun-home

Gabby Rivera ________________ **p. 55**

1. Rivera, Gabby. "Gabby Rivera Wants Queer Brown Girls to Feel Seen." Interview with Arriel Vinson. *Electric Lit*, October 21, 2019. https://electricliterature.com/gabby-rivera-wants-queer-brown-girls-to-feel-seen/

2. Rivera, Gabby. "It Gets Better, and Gabby Rivera. 10 Years Better: Author and Marvel Writer Gabby Rivera Reacts To Her Original It Gets Better Video." *It Gets Better Project*, December 18, 2020. https://www.youtube.com/watch?v=KBdcMg2V7k0

3. Rivera, Gabby. "#PRIDE30: Writer Gabby Rivera Is Bringing LGBTQ Superheroes to Life." Interview with AlaminYohannes. *NBCNews.com, NBC Universal News Group*, June 22, 2017, https://www.nbcnews.com/feature/nbc-out-pride30/pride30-writer-gabby-rivera-bringing-lgbtq-superheroes-life-n763576

4. Rivera, Gabby. "Life, Love, Coming Out And Culture Shock In 'Juliet Takes A Breath'." Interview with Audie Cornish. *NPR: All Things Considered*, September 18, 2019. https://www.npr.org/2019/09/18/762046606/book-juliet-takes-a-breath

5. Rivera, Gabby. "Ep 131: Intersectionality, Queer Joy, and Nuyorican Love with Gabby Rivera." Interview with Effy Blue. *Curious Fox*, October 12, 2022. https://www.wearecuriousfoxes.com/listen/ep-131-intersectionality-queer-joy-and-nuyorican-love-with-gabby-rivera

6. Rivera, Gabby. "Brené with Gabby Rivera on Superheroes, Storytelling and Joy as Resistance." Interview with Brené Brown. *Unlocking Us with Brené Brown*, November 11, 2020. https://brenebrown.com/podcast/brene-with-gabby-rivera-on-superheroes-storytelling-and-joy-as-resistance/

7. Rivera, Gabby. "#PRIDE30: Writer Gabby Rivera Is Bringing LGBTQ Superheroes to Life." Interview with AlaminYohannes. *NBCNews.com, NBC Universal News Group*, June 22, 2017, https://www.nbcnews.com/feature/nbc-out-pride30/pride30-writer-gabby-rivera-bringing-lgbtq-superheroes-life-n763576

8. Rivera, Gabby. "Portrait of: Gabby Rivera." Interview with Maria Hinojosa. *NPR: Latino USA*, November 22, 2019. https://www.npr.org/2019/11/21/781827181/portrait-of-gabby-rivera

9. Williams, Tommy. "B.B. Free Is a 'Bouncy Love Letter to Queer Kids Everywhere' from Boom! Studios." *GeekTyrant*, August 25, 2019. https://geektyrant.com/news/bb-free-is-a-bouncy-love-letter-to-queer-kids-everywhere-from-boom-studios

10. Rivera, Gabby. "Writing Your Heritage Is Radical Creativity | Gabby Rivera." October 17, 2018. https://www.youtube.com/watch?v=3oyM25xW_xQ

11. Rivera, Gabby. "Ep 131: Intersectionality, Queer Joy, and Nuyorican Love with Gabby Rivera." Interview with Effy Blue. *Curious Fox*, October 12, 2022. https://www.wearecuriousfoxes.com/listen/ep-131-intersectionality-queer-joy-and-nuyorican-love-with-gabby-rivera

12. Rivera, Gabby. "27 Weeks! What a Sweet Wild Ride." quirkyrican. Instagram, February 22, 2022. https://www.instagram.com/p/CaSkw5yJpSZ/

Storme Webber ______ **p. 61**

1. Carley , Christy. "Storme Webber's Stories of Survival: 'Casino: A Palimpsest' Shines Light on a Pioneer Square History Not Often Told." *Seattle Weekly*, August 9, 2017. https://www.seattleweekly.com/arts/storme-webbers-stories-of-survival/
2. Navoti, D.A. "Ancestors Know Who We Are: Two Spirit Black Indian Storme Webber." *ICT News*, June 18, 2016. https://ictnews.org/archive/ancestors-know-who-we-are-two-spirit-black-indian-storme-webber
3. Smithsonian Institution. "ANCESTORS KNOW WHO WE ARE INTERVIEW WITH STORME WEBBER." National Museum of the American Indian. Smithsonian Institution. Accessed February 27, 2023. https://marshcollection.si.edu/ancestors-know/transcripts/Ancestors-Know-Who-We-Are-Storme-Webber-interview.pdf
4. Webber, Storme. "Storme Webber: Casino: A Palimpsest/Alison Marks: One Gray Hair - Announcements - e-Flux." *e-flux*, October 5, 1017. https://www.e-flux.com/announcements/148587/storme-webbercasino-a-palimpsestalison-marksone-gray-hair/
5. Webber, Storme. "Seattle's LGBTQ history that isn't all white, all middle class, all male." Interview with Ann Dornfeld. *KUOW NPR*, August 17, 2017. https://kuow.org/stories/seattles-lgbtq-history-isnt-all-white-all-middle-class-all-male/
6. Ibid.
7. Nyguyen, Minh. "Storme Webber." *Art in America*, December 4, 2017. https://www.artnews.com/art-in-america/aia-reviews/storme-webber-62432/
8. Webber, Storme. "Storme Webber: Writer. Performer. Curator. Interdisciplinary Artist." STORME WEBBER | Writer. Performer. Curator. Interdisciplinary Artist. Accessed January 21, 2023. https://www.stormewebber.com/
9. Webber, Storme. "Storme Webber." Interview with Afuwa Granger. *Kindling*, April 11, 2021. https://www.kindlingprojects.com/storme-webber
10. Webber, Storme. "Blues Divine." STORME WEBBER | Writer. Performer. Curator. Interdisciplinary Artist. https://www.stormewebber.com/

Brittney "BG" Griner ______ **p. 69**

1. Olson, Emily. "Brittney Griner says she's 'never going overseas' again after her detention." *NPR*, April 28, 2023. https://www.npr.org/2023/04/28/1172698473/brittney-griner-press-conference-detention
2. Talwalkar, Anuj. "'They Could Be Killers': Brittney Griner Once Revealed Harsh Reality of Her Strict Father's Parenting." *EssentiallySports*, October 23, 2022. https://www.essentiallysports.com/nba-basketball-news-they-could-be-killers-brittney-griner-once-revealed-harsh-reality-of-her-strict-fathers-parenting/
3. Gregory, Sean. "Brittney Griner's Fight for Freedom." *Time 199, no. 23,* June 20, 2022. https://time.com/6201052/brittney-griner-russia-fight-for-release/?fbclid=IwAR1vSqhSHRF0y5TfVSn-LfThMsne-OVehWH4gpEJ05my17YiMbVi2E68qB6E
4, Fagan, Kate. "Griner: No Talking Sexuality at Baylor." *ESPN Internet Ventures*, May 18, 2013. https://www.espn.com/wnba/story/_/id/9289080/brittney-griner-says-baylor-coach-kim-mulkey-told-players-keep-quiet-sexuality
5. Griner, Brittney, and Sue Hovey. *In My Skin: My Life on and off the Basketball Court.* Dey St., an imprint of William Morrow Publishers, 2015.

6. Griner, Brittney. "Short Shorts Are Not for Everybody: An Interview With Brittney Griner." Interview with Ian Gordon. *Mother Jones*, May 2, 2014. https://www.motherjones.com/media/2014/05/brittney-griner-interview-baylor-wnba/

7. Ibid.

8. Griner, Brittney. "WNBA Star Brittney Griner Talks about Becoming First Openly Gay Athlete Endorsed by Nike." Interview with Debbie Emery. *The Wrap*, October 11, 2014. https://www.thewrap.com/wnba-star-brittney-griner-talks-about-becoming-first-openly-gay-athlete-endorsed-by-nike/

9. Ibid.

10. Boren, Cindy. "Brittney Griner, Brianna Turner Call for WNBA to Stop Playing National Anthem This Season." *The Washington Post*, July 28, 2020. https://www.washingtonpost.com/sports/2020/07/28/brittney-griner-brianna-turner-call-wnba-stop-playing-national-anthem-this-season/

11. Wilson, Angelica. "Brittney Griner Walks in MLK Day March Weeks after Her Release from a Russian Prison." *POPSUGAR Fitness*, January 17, 2023. https://www.popsugar.com/fitness/why-is-brittney-griner-detained-in-russia-48743991

12. Hill, Jemele. "Brittney Griner Has the Right to Change Her Mind." *The Atlantic*, May 20, 2023. https://www.theatlantic.com/ideas/archive/2023/05/brittney-griner-national-anthem/674126/

Amélie Mauresmo ________ **p. 75**

1. France, Louise. "Without Prejudice." *The Guardian*, November 26, 2006. https://www.theguardian.com/sport/2006/nov/26/tennis.features1

2. Ibid.

3. Majumdar, Aayush. "'She's Half a Man; She's Here with Her Girlfriend' - When Martina Hingis Took an Insensitive Jibe at Amelie Mauresmo after She Came out as Lesbian." *Sports News. Sportskeeda*, December 12, 2022. https://www.sportskeeda.com/tennis/news-she-s-half-man-when-martina-hingis-reportedly-took-shockingly-insensitive-jibe-amelie-mauresmo-openly-came-lesbian

4. Forman, Pamela J, and Darcy C Plymire. "Amélie Mauresmo's Muscles: The Lesbian Heroic in Women's Professional Tennis." *Women's Studies Quarterly 33, no. 1/2* (2005): 120–33. https://www.jstor.org/stable/40005505?read-now=1&seq=6#page_scan_tab_contents

5. Ibid.

6. Dutter, Barbie, and John Parsons. "'Half Man' Slur Forces Mauresmo into Hiding." *Independent.ie*, January 13, 1999. https://www.independent.ie/sport/half-man-slur-forces-mauresmo-into-hiding-26164036.html

7. McLeman, Neil. "Andy Murray Hiring Amelie Mauresmo as Coach Savaged by Rival Marinko 'Mad Dog' Matosevic." *Mirror*, June 10, 2014. https://www.mirror.co.uk/sport/tennis/andy-murray-hiring-amelie-mauresmo-3672144

8. Rothenberg, Ben. "A Male Tennis Pro, a Female Coach and Shrugs for Anyone Who Thinks It Won't Work." *The New York Times*, January 16, 2019. https://www.nytimes.com/2019/01/16/sports/tennis/australian-open-mauresmo-pouille.html

9. Clarke, Liz. "French Open Director Amélie Mauresmo: Women's Matches Are Less Compelling." *The Washington Post*, June 1, 2022. https://www.washingtonpost.com/sports/2022/06/01/french-open-women-amelie-mauresmo/

10. Ibid.

Citations *continued*

Caster Semenya, Order of Ikhamanga ________ p. 79

1. Block, Melissa. "Olympic Runner Caster Semenya Wants to Compete, Not Defend Her Womanhood." *NPR*, July 28, 2021, https://www.npr.org/sections/tokyo-olympics-live-updates/2021/07/28/1021503989/women-runners-testosterone-olympics
2. Bandini, Paolo. "Caster Semenya Sex Row: 'She's My Little Girl,' Says Father." *The Guardian*, August 20, 2009. https://www.theguardian.com/sport/2009/aug/20/caster-semenya-sex-row-athletics
3. Ibid.
4. Ibid.
5. Ibid.
6. Fleitas, Begoña. "Semenya Comes Clean: They Thought I Had a Penis, so I Offered to Show That I Didn't." *Marca*, May 24, 2022. https://www.marca.com/en/more-sports/2022/05/24/628d2127e2704ed0798b45c0.html
7. Capital Sports. "ANC Condemns Semenya Gender Row." *Capital Sports*, November 20, 2009. https://www.capitalfm.co.ke/sports/2009/08/19/anc-condemns-semenya-gender-row/
8. Brulliard, Nicolas. "Is This Runner Male or Female? the Question Sparks Outrage in South Africa." *The World*, May 30, 2010. https://theworld.org/stories/2009-08-20/runner-male-or-female-question-sparks-outrage-south-africa
9. Block, Melissa. "'I Am A Woman': Track Star Caster Semenya Continues Her Fight to Compete as Female." *NPR*, May 31, 2019. https://www.npr.org/2019/05/31/728400819/i-am-a-woman-track-star-caster-semenya-continues-her-fight-to-compete-as-a-female
10. Ibid.
11. Block, Melissa. "Olympic Runner Caster Semenya Wants to Compete, Not Defend Her Womanhood." *NPR*, July 28, 2021, https://www.npr.org/sections/tokyo-olympics-live-updates/2021/07/28/1021503989/women-runners-testosterone-olympics
12. Mac, Paul. "Caster Semenya Blocked from Competing at World Championships." *The Guardian*, July 30, 2019. https://www.theguardian.com/sport/2019/jul/30/caster-semenya-blocked-defending-800-metres-title-athletics-world-championships
13. Igual, Roberto. "Caster Semenya Celebrated as a South African Icon." *Mamba Online.com*, January 12, 2016. https://www.mambaonline.com/2016/01/12/caster-semenya-celebrated-south-african-icon/
14. ENCA. "Zuma Presents National Orders in Pretoria." *ENCA*, April 27, 2014. https://www.enca.com/south-africa/zuma-presents-national-orders-pretoria
15. Zraick, Karen. "Caster Semenya, Hero in South Africa, Fights Hormone Testing on a Global Stage." *The New York Times*, May 1, 2019. https://www.nytimes.com/2019/05/01/sports/who-is-caster-semenya.html

Martina Navratilova ________ p. 85

1. Navratilova, Martina. "John McEnroe paid more than Martina Navratilova by BBC." Interview by Jane Corbin. *BBC*, March 20, 2018. https://www.bbc.com/news/av/world-europe-43435117

2. Kettmann, Steve. "Martina Navratilova." *Salon*, April 18, 2000. https://www.salon.com/2000/04/18/navratilova/

3. Ibid.

4. Ibid.

5. Subaru. "Subaru Forester commercial 2000 Navratilova." Subaru, June 16, 2009. https://www.youtube.com/watch?v=XHY_uqYdIX8

6. Alex Mayyasi, Priceonomics. "How Subarus Came to Be Seen as Cars for Lesbians." *The Atlantic*, June 22, 2016. https://www.theatlantic.com/business/archive/2016/06/how-subarus-came-to-be-seen-as-cars-for-lesbians/488042/

7. Navratilova, Martina. "The Rules on Trans Athletes Reward Cheats and Punish the Innocent." *The Sunday Times*, February 17, 2019. https://www.thetimes.co.uk/article/the-rules-on-trans-athletes-reward-cheats-and-punish-the-innocent-klsrq6h3x?region=global

8. Ibid.

9. BBC. "Martina Navratilova Explores Issues Faced by Trans Athletes in BBC Documentary." *BBC Sport*, June 26, 2019. https://www.bbc.com/sport/48777660

Jenni Olson ______ **p. 93**

1. Olson, Jenni. "Jenni Olson." Interview with Sierra Waller. *FEMEXFILMARCHIVE*. https://sites.google.com/ucsc.edu/femexfilmarchive/filmmaker-index/jenni-olson

2. Olson, Jenni, director. *The Royal Road*. USA: Jenni Olson, 2015. https://tubitv.com/movies/527805/the-royal-road

3. Olson, Jenni. "Inside the Homo Studio: with Jenni Olson." Interview with Ryan Diduck. *Off Screen*, June 2006. https://offscreen.com/view/inside_jenni_olson

4. Edited by Roxxi, L. Due and Lily Burana. *Dagger, on Butch Women*, Contribution by Jenni Olson. "Butch Icons of the Silver Screen." Cleis Press, 1994.

5. Olson, Jenni. "Remembering Mark Finch, 25 Years Later." *The Bay Area Reporter*, January 7, 2020. https://www.ebar.com/arts_&_culture/movies//286417

6. Olson, Jenni. "Towards a Butch Poetics: A Conversation with Jenni Olson." Interview with Tina Takemoto. *Millennium Film Journal*, 2016.

7. Gilbey, Ryan. "Jenni Olson: 'I Remember Walking out of the Movie Theatre like, "Yeah, I'm a Cowboy!"'" *The Guardian*, June 15, 2021. https://www.theguardian.com/film/2021/jun/15/jenni-olson-i-remember-walking-out-of-the-movie-theatre-like-yeah-im-a-cowboy

Madeleine Lim ______ **p. 99**

1. Lim, Madeleine. "Madeline Lim. 10/14/10." Interview with Miyuki Baker, *Asian Gay & Proud*, October 14, 2010. https://asiangayandproud.wordpress.com/2010/10/14/madeline-lim-101410/

2. Kay, Sheryl. "Creative minds: two lesbians who use activism, education and interconnectedness to strengthen LGBT civil rights." *Curve*, September 2012. https://archive.curvemag.com/s/curve-archive/item/409

3. Lim, Madeleine. "drama queen: madeleine lim." Interview with Sylvia Tan. *Fridae*. February 23, 2001. https://www.fridae.asia/gay-news/2001/02/23/925.drama-queen-madeleine-lim

4. Ibid.

5. QWOCMAP. "Home: Queer Women of Color Media Arts Project." *QWOCMAP*, November 8, 2022. https://qwocmap.org/
6. Lim, Madeleine. "drama queen: madeleine lim." Interview with Sylvia Tan. *Fridae*. February 23, 2001. https://www.fridae.asia/gay-news/2001/02/23/925.drama-queen-madeleine-lim
7. Lim, Madeleine. "Chatting with Madeleine Lim." Interview with Tan Chong Kee. *Sintercom*, July 14, 1997. http://www.sintercom.org/sp/interview/madeleine.html

Shine Louise Houston ______ p. 105

1. Houston, Shine Louise. "Talking Porn with Shine Louise Houston." Interview with Euphemia Russell, *Spectrum Journal*. https://spectrumboutique.com/journal/article/talking-porn-with-shine-louise-houston/
2. Houston, Shine Louise. "Interview: Crashpad -Behind The Scenes With Shine Louise Houston." Interview with SheVibe, *SHEVIBE*, May 2014. https://shevibe.com/blog/interview-crashpad-behind-the-scenes-with-shine-louise-houston/
3. Wischhover, Cheryl. "What It's Really Like to Own a Porn Company." *Cosmopolitan*, August 6, 2015. https://www.cosmopolitan.com/sex-love/news/a44421/what-its-like-to-own-a-porn-company/
4. Lo, Malinda. "She's a Very Dirty Girl: the transformation from art student to pornographer was a simple one for queer auteur Shine Louise Houston." *Curve*, February 1, 2006. https://archive.curvemag.com/s/curve-archive/item/349
5. Ibid.
6. Brabaw, Kasandra. "Why You Can't Find Any Real Queer Porn On Free Websites." *Refinery29*, October 8, 2018. https://www.refinery29.com/en-us/ethical-queer-porn-not-free
7. Houston, Shine Louise. "Talking Porn with Shine Louise Houston." Interview with Euphemia Russell, *Spectrum Journal*. https://spectrumboutique.com/journal/article/talking-porn-with-shine-louise-houston/
8. Houston, Shine Louise. "Interview: Crashpad-Behind The Scenes With Shine Louise Houston." Interview with SheVibe, *SHEVIBE*, May 2014. https://shevibe.com/blog/interview-crashpad-behind-the-scenes-with-shine-louise-houston/
9. Entertainment. "Shine Louise Houston Earns Award from Harvey Milk LGBT Democratic Club." AVN, July 29, 2015. https://avn.com/business/articles/video/shine-louise-houston-earns-award-from-harvey-milk-lgbt-democratic-club-602283.html
10. Ibid.

Cheryl Dunye ______ p. 111

1. Dunye, Cheryl. "The Watermelon Woman, 20 Years Later: An Interview with Local Filmmaker Cheryl Dunye." Interview with Shane Downing, *Hoodline*, October 23, 2020. https://hoodline.com/2016/04/the-watermelon-woman-20-years-later-an-interview-with-local-film-maker-cheryl-dunye/
2. Dunye, Cheryl. "Meet the Filmmakers Cheryl Dunye." Interview with Grace Barber-Plentie, *The Criterion Channel*, 2020. https://www.criterionchannel.com/videos/cheryl-dunye-interview
3. Dunye, Cheryl. "Cheryl Dunye." Facebook, February 8, 2022. https://www.facebook.com/cheryldunye
4. Combahee River Collective, Zillah Eisenstein. "(1977) The Combahee River Collective Statement." Black Past, November 16, 2012. https://www.blackpast.org/african-american-history/combahee-river-collective-statement-1977/

5. Dunye, Cheryl, director. *The Early Works of Cheryl.* First Run Features, Kanopy, 1994. https://www.kanopy.com/en/product/463078
6. Lang, Cady. "Essential Black Cinema Movies, According to Black Directors." *Time*, September 3, 2020. https://time.com/5874175/black-cinema-essential-movies/
7. Dunye, Cheryl. "Cheryl Dunye's Alternative Histories." Interview with Colleen Kelsey. *Interview Magazine*, November 11, 2016. https://www.interviewmagazine.com/film/cheryl-dunye
8. Desta, Yohana. "The Watermelon Woman: The Enduring Cool of a Black Lesbian Classic." *Vanity Fair*, June 19, 2020. https://www.vanityfair.com/hollywood/2020/06/the-watermelon-woman-the-enduring-cool-of-a-black-lesbian-classic
9. Jennings, Moss J. "The NEA Gets Gay Bashed." *The Advocate*, April 1, 1997.
10. Dunye, Cheryl. "Cheryl Dunye's Alternative Histories." Interview with Colleen Kelsey. *Interview Magazine*, November 11, 2016. https://www.interviewmagazine.com/film/cheryl-dunye
11. Dunye, Cheryl. "Filmmaker Cheryl Dunye on what makes Berlinale so special." Interview with Tim Standaert. U.S. Embassy Berlin Videos, July 6, 2016. https://www.youtube.com/watch?v=SYjrM1d2A0M
12. Ibid.

Barbara Hammer ______________________________ **p. 117**

1. Hammer, Barbara. "Oral history interview with Barbara Hammer, 2018 March 15-17." Interview with Svetlana Kitto. Smithsonian Institution, Archives of American Art. Last modified March 17, 2018. https://www.aaa.si.edu/download_pdf_transcript/ajax?record_id=edanmdm-AAADCD_oh_393526
2. Ibid.
3. Ibid.
4. Greenberger, Alex, and Maximilíano Durón. "Barbara Hammer, Pioneering Queer Experimental Filmmaker, Dead at 79." *ARTnews*, May 16, 2019. https://www.artnews.com/art-news/news/barbara-hammer-dead-79-12157/
5. Hammer, Barbara. "Oral history interview with Barbara Hammer, 2018 March 15-17." Interview with Svetlana Kitto. Smithsonian Institution, Archives of American Art. Last modified March 17, 2018. https://www.aaa.si.edu/download_pdf_transcript/ajax?record_id=edanmdm-AAADCD_oh_393526
6. Ibid.
7. Ibid.
8. Ibid.
9. Ibid.

Meshell Ndegeocello ______________________________ **p. 125**

1. Bowles, Nellie. "Music as a 'Means to an End'." *The New York Times*, July 15, 2020. https://www.nytimes.com/2020/07/15/insider/music-queer-activism.html.
2. Kornegay III, Johnnie Ray. "'Leviticus: Faggot' 25 Years Later - a Visual Musing on a Black Queer Musical Achievement." *The Reckoning*, June 15, 2021. https://www.thereckoningmag.com/the-reckoning-blog/leviticus-faggot-25-years-later-a-visual-musing-on-a-black-queer-musical-achievement#gs.mvyqm4
3. Ibid.

4. Ndegeocello, Meshell. “Running the Voodoo Down: An Interview with Meshell Ndegeocello.” Interview with Harold N. Claudrena N. *PopMATTERS*, October 27, 2009. https://www.popmatters.com/meshell-ndegeocello-interview-2496114312.html

5. Ndegeocello, Meshell. “SPOTLIGHT.” Interview with Andrew McMillen. *The Australian*, April 20, 2019. https://link.gale.com/apps/doc/A582826510/STND?u=mlin_b_bpublic&sid=bookmark-STND&xid=fc502db9

6. Ndegeocello, Meshell. “Meshell Ndegeocello Unplugged and Unmasked.” Interview with Craig Byrd. *Cultural Attaché*, July 11, 2019. https://culturalattache.co/2019/07/11/meshell-ndegeocello-unplugged-and-unmasked/

7. Ndegeocello, Meshell. “James Baldwin’s Lessons on Love Are Timeless.” Interview with Willy Chavarria. *Paper*, October 8, 2020. https://www.papermag.com/meshell-ndegeocello-willy-chavarria-2648141947.html#rebelltitem37

8. Himes, Geoffrey. “Meshell Ndegeocello Gives a Reading from the Scripture of James Baldwin.” *The Washington Post*, December 13, 2018. https://www.washingtonpost.com/goingoutguide/music/meshell-ndegeocello-gives-a-reading-from-the-scripture-of-james-baldwin/2018/12/13/8c60e91c-f7e4-11e8-8d64-4e79db33382f_story.html

9. Goldin-Perschbacher, Shana. “Musicians Making Their Own Path in “Queer Country.” Interview with Carr Harkrader. *Southern Review of Books*, March 22, 2022. https://southernreviewofbooks.com/2022/03/22/queer-country-shana-goldin-perschbacher-interview/

10. Aaron, Peter. “Goddess of Groove: Meshell Ndegeocello.” *Roll Magazine*, October 2010. http://www.rollmagazine.com/archive/oct10/articles/music.php

Phranc ______ p. 131

1. Brown, Joe. “Up-Front Phranc &.” *Washington Post*, October 29, 1986. https://www.washingtonpost.com/archive/lifestyle/1986/10/29/up-front-phranc-38/8dc5f437-7dbf-46b9-804f-d0f9113e180b/

2. Ibid.

3. Phranc.“Phranc.” Interview with Margy Rochlin. *Los Angeles Times*, April 6, 1986. https://www.latimes.com/archives/la-xpm-1986-04-06-tm-24986-story.html

4. Ibid.

5. Meyer, Carla. “A PASSION FOR PLASTIC/Lesbian Folksinger Phranc’s Career in Tupperware Is Documented in Lisa Udelson’s Fillm.” *SFGate*, June 20, 2001. https://www.sfgate.com/entertainment/article/A-PASSION-FOR-PLASTIC-Lesbian-folksinger-2908156.php

Jools and Lynda Topp, Dames Companion of the New Zealand Order of Merit ___ p. 137

1. Coney, Sandra. “Lynda and Jools Topp, Alias Homemade Jam.” *AudioCulture*, April 6, 2018. https://www.audioculture.co.nz/articles/lynda-and-jools-topp-alias-homemade-jam

2. Ibid

3. Bourke, Chris. “The Topp Twins: Good Sisters Gone Bad.” *RNZ Music*, April 28, 2018. https://www.rnz.co.nz/national/programmes/nat-music/audio/2018642503/the-topp-twins-good-sisters-gone-bad

4. Ibid.

5. Ibid.

6. Ibid.

7. New Zealand History. “Jools Topp.” NZ On Screen. February 5, 2020. https://www.nzonscreen.com/profile/jools-topp/biography

8. Nealon, Sarah. "Topp Twins: Jools Says 'I'm on My Last Lot of Choices That I Can Have Now'." *Stuff*, November 30, 2022. https://www.stuff.co.nz/entertainment/celebrities/130618409/topp-twins-jools-says-im-on-my-last-lot-of-choices-that-i-can-have-now

Debbie Smith ________ **p. 143**

1. Amour, Cheri. "Debbie Smith YE Nuns / Echobelly." *TGA Magazine*. Accessed January 30, 2023. https://static1.squarespace.com/static/550ac068e4b0714e2a518fc7/t/5aa265664192024c5e86eb0c/1520592233254/debbie_smith.pdf
2. Smith, Debbie. "Debbie Smith (@Theeebanjodeb) • Instagram Photos and Videos." @theeebanjodeb. Instagram, August 2019. https://www.instagram.com/theeebanjodeb/
3. Amour, Cheri. "Debbie Smith YE Nuns / EchobEllY." Tech. *TGA Magazine*. Accessed January 30, 2023. https://static1.squarespace.com/static/550ac068e4b0714e2a518fc7/t/5aa265664192024c5e86eb0c/1520592233254/debbie_smith.pdf
4. Ibid.
5. Smith, Debbie. "The Long, Rebellious History of Queer Punks of Colour: 'You Don't Give a s**t 'Cos You'Re Punk.'" Interview with Asyia Iftikhar, *PinkNews*, December 26, 2022. https://www.thepinknews.com/2022/12/26/queer-punks-of-colour-interview-debbie-smith/
6. Jones, Kelvin. "The Buzz." *The Advocate*, October 18, 1994.
7. Abraham, Melia. "Squats, Sex Clubs and Punk: The Lesbian London of the 1980s." *Vice*. July 5, 2017. https://www.vice.com/en/article/wj8dgx/squats-sex-clubs-and-punk-the-lesbian-london-of-the-1980s
8. Amour, Cheri. "Debbie Smith YE Nuns / Echobelly." *TGA Magazine*. Accessed January 30, 2023. https://static1.squarespace.com/static/550ac068e4b0714e2a518fc7/t/5aa265664192024c5e86eb0c/1520592233254/debbie_smith.pdf
9. Thompson, Jack. "Culture Club: Watching Rebel Dykes by Harri Shanahan and Sîan Williams." *Club des Femmes*, April 6, 2021. https://www.clubdesfemmes.com/portfolio-item/culture-club-watching15

Toshi Reagon ________ **p. 149**

1. Reagon, Toshi. "VP Issue 2: 'Toshi Reagon: Firestarter.'" Interview with Kent Martin and Shelly Waldheim. *Velvetpark*, July 25, 2013. https://velvetparkmedia.com/vp-issue-2-toshi-reagon-firestarter/
2. Reagon, Toshi. "Design Matters: Toshi Reagon." Interview with Chloe Gordon. *PRINT*. December 8, 2021. https://www.printmag.com/podcasts/2021/design-matters-toshi-reagon/
3. Reagon, Toshi. "VP Issue 2: 'Toshi Reagon: Firestarter.'" Interview with Kent Martin and Shelly Waldheim, *Velvetpark*, July 25, 2013. https://velvetparkmedia.com/vp-issue-2-toshi-reagon-firestarter/
4. Ibid
5. Reagon, Toshi. "Parable of the Songwriter: Toshi Reagon Explains Why an Octavia Butler-Inspired Opera Is More Relevant Than Ever." Interview with Maiysha Kai. *The Root*. April 22, 2020. https://www.theroot.com/parable-of-the-songwriter-toshi-reagon-explains-why-an-1842991833
6. Reagon, Toshi, and adrienne maree brown. "ABOUT THE PODCAST." Octavia's Parables. https://www.readingoctavia.com/about
7. Reagon, Toshi. "Design Matters: Toshi Reagon." Interview with Chloe Gordon. *PRINT*. December 8, 2021. https://www.printmag.com/podcasts/2021/design-matters-toshi-reagon/

Captain Jennifer Bornemann, USPHS ____________ **p. 157**

1. Kanzler, Diane and Jennifer Bornemann. Personal interviews, January 12–February 11, 2023.
2. Gilchrist, Tracy. "CDC Worker With Lanyard Instills Faith That Lesbians Will Fix COVID-19" *Advocate*, March 10, 2020. https://www.advocate.com/media/2020/3/10/cdc-worker-lanyard-instills-faith-lesbians-will-fix-covid-19
3. Ibid.
4. Kanzler, Diane and Jennifer Bornemann. Personal interviews, January 12–February 11, 2023.
5. Emma Powys Maurice. "Coronavirus meets its match as Centre for Disease Control unveils a ' sensible-looking lesbian'" *The Pink News*, March 11, 2020. https://www.thepinknews.com/2020/03/11/coronavirus-usa-centre-for-disease-control-lesbian-lanyard-jen-bourneman-twitter-viral/
6. Kanzler, Diane and Jennifer Bornemann. Personal interviews, January 12–February 11, 2023.
7. Bornemann, Jennifer. "Bornemann, Jennifer," Interview with Sam Robson. David J. Sencer CDC Museum Digital Exhibits. February 24, 2017. http://www.cdcmuseum.org/items/show/530
8. Bornemann, Jennifer. "Social Impact LIVE: COVID-19, Social Work & Public Health Emergencies." Interview with Richard Hara. Columbia University School of Social Work. March 26, 2020. https://youtu.be/IjeCls69QPs
9. Ibid.
10. Ibid.

Chef Melissa King ____________ **p. 161**

1. King, Melissa. "Chefmelissaking." Instagram, June 24, 2020. https://www.instagram.com/p/CB07SAEB18C/
2. King, Melissa. "Alumna Vies to Be 'Top Chef.'" *UCI News*, October 10, 2014. https://news.uci.edu/2014/10/10/alumna-vies-to-be-top-chef/
3. Cascone, Sarah. "Want Some Renaissance Curry? the Latest 'Top Chef' Sent Its All-Stars to the Getty Villa in Search of Art-Historical Food Inspiration." *Artnet News*, April 10, 2020. https://news.artnet.com/art-world/getty-museum-top-chef-challenge-1831176
4. Pham, Jason. "Top Chef's Melissa King on Why She 'Refuses' to Watch 'the Bear' & What She Thinks of the 'Yes, Chef' Phenomenon." *StyleCaster*, January 9, 2023. https://stylecaster.com/top-chef/
5. Hess, Liam. "Meet the Chefs Behind the 2022 Met Gala Menu." *Vogue*, March 24, 2022. https://www.vogue.com/article/met-gala-2022-chefs-announcement
6. Mafune, Korena, and Melissa King. "Foraging for Mushrooms in Olympic National Park | National Geographic." *National Geographic*, October 26, 2022. https://www.youtube.com/watch?v=S3WiIY9Qukk&list=PLivjPDlt6ApQTuoGb33_T-vlyF2FkHN6E&index=5
7. King, Melissa. "A Lesson in Mixing Sleek Separates from Chef Melissa King." Interview with Camille Freestone. *Coveteur*, November 10, 2021. https://coveteur.com/melissa-king-style-diaries
8. Maddox, Lucy. "The Untold Truth of Top Chef's Melissa King." *Mashed*, August 12, 2021. https://www.mashed.com/486238/the-untold-truth-of-top-chefs-melissa-king/

Rabbi Sandra Lawson ____________ **p. 167**

1. Sales, Ben. "Sandra Lawson, black lesbian vegan rabbinical student, hopes to redefine where Judaism happens." *Jewish Telegraphic Agency*, June 19, 2016. https://www.jta.org/2016/06/19/united-states/sandra-lawson-black-lesbian-vegan-rabbinical-student-hopes-to-redefine-where-judaism-happens

2. Lawson, Sandra. "Oral History Interview: Rabbi Sandra Lawson." Interview with Monique Moultrie. *LGBTQ Religious Archives Network*, October 17. 2018. https://lgbtqreligiousarchives.org/media/oral-history/sandra-lawson/Sandra%20Lawson%20oral%20history%20transcript.pdf
3. Lawson, Sandra. "Sandra Lawson." My Story of Becoming Jewish - Rabbi Sandra Lawson." APB Speaking to the World, March 19, 2020. https://www.apbspeakers.com/speaker/sandra-lawson/
4. Lawson, Sandra. "Oral History Interview: Rabbi Sandra Lawson." Interview with Monique Moultrie. *LGBTQ Religious Archives Network*, October 17. 2018. https://lgbtqreligiousarchives.org/media/oral-history/sandra-lawson/Sandra%20Lawson%20oral%20history%20transcript.pdf
5. Lawson, Rabbi Sandra. "Black Joy and Reconstructionist Community." *Reconstructing Judaism*, June 13, 2022. https://www.reconstructingjudaism.org/news/black-joy-and-reconstructionist-community/

Chief Jeanine Nicholson, SFFD ______ p. 173

1. Nicholson, Jeanine R. "Survivor Story: Jeanine R. Nicholson San Francisco Fire Department" Firefighters Cancer Support Network. https://firefightercancersupport.org/wp-content/uploads/2021/12/Survivor-Stories-Jeanine-Nicholson-.pdf
2. Nicholson, Jeanine Nicholson: "Chief Jeanine Nicholson Leads San Francisco Fire Department to National Acclaim for Service and Diversity." Interview with the San Francisco Bay Times, October 7, 2021. https://sfbaytimes.com/chief-jeanine-nicholson-leads-san-francisco-fire-department-to-national-acclaim-for-service-and-diversity/
3. Lowery, Melissa. "San Francisco Fire Chief Jeanine Nicholson: 'I Never Thought I Would Be Here.'" *Business Equality Magazine*, March 17, 2020. https://businessequalitymagazine.com/san-francisco-fire-chief-jeanine-nicholson-i-never-thought-i-would-be-here/
4. Nicholson, Jeanine R. "Survivor Story: Jeanine R. Nicholson San Francisco Fire Department" Firefighters Cancer Support Network. https://firefightercancersupport.org/wp-content/uploads/2021/12/Survivor-Stories-Jeanine-Nicholson-.pdf
5. Examiner Staff. "Breast Cancer Rate Alarms SFFD Female Firefighters." *San Francisco Examiner*. October 18, 2012. https://www.sfexaminer.com/news/breast-cancer-rate-alarms-sffd-female-firefighters/article_7c787a9f-0cf2-524a-9022-1cb6ca7be7e8.html
6. Baustin, Noah. "SF Firefighters Risk Cancer Every Day—Even Their Jackets Are a Threat." *The San Francisco Standard*, December 6, 2022. https://sfstandard.com/public-health/san-francisco-firefighters-exposure-cancer-screenings/
7. Mayne, Aleta. "She's the One: She's Worked Her Way Up the Ladder." *Colgate Magazine*, Colgate University, November 1, 2019. https://news.colgate.edu/magazine/2019/11/01/shes-the-one/
8. Nicholson, Jeanine. "Up Close and Personal with San Francisco's First LGBTQ Fire Chief." Interview with Louise Fischer. *San Francisco Bay Times*, May 1, 2019. https://sfbaytimes.com/close-personal-san-franciscos-first-lgbtq-fire-chief/

Senator the Honorable Penny Wong ______ p. 179

1. Simons, Margaret. "EXCLUSIVE: Penny Wong on her most challenging job, raising her two daughters in a modern world." *The Australian Women's Weekly*. October 9, 2019. https://www.nowtolove.com.au/women-of-the-future/the-weekly/penny-wong-daughters-59661

2. Grattan, Michelle. “Shaped by Two Cultures.” *The Age*, December 7, 2007. https://www.theage.com.au/technology/shaped-by-two-cultures-20071208-ge6h83.html
3. Ibid.
4. Abrahams, Scott. “Penny Wong Labelled a Hypocrite.” *Star Observer*, July 25, 2010. https://www.starobserver.com.au/news/national-news/new-south-wales-news/wong-facing-marriage-backlash/28541
5. Ibid.
6. Karp, Paul. “Penny Wong Says Marriage Equality Fight Proves Need for Separation of Church and State.” *The Guardian*, May 17, 2017. https://www.theguardian.com/australia-news/2017/may/18/penny-wong-says-marriage-equality-fight-proves-need-for-separation-of-church-and-state
7. Baker, Emily, and Katie Burgess. “Braddon's Lonsdale Street Closes for Same-Sex Marriage Street Party.” *The Canberra Times*, November 15, 2017. https://www.canberratimes.com.au/story/6026003/braddons-lonsdale-street-closes-for-same-sex-marriage-street-party/
8. Wong, Penny. “Meet Australia's New Foreign Minister: Out Lesbian Senator Penny Wong.” Interview with Shibu Thomas. *Star Observer*. May 23, 2022. https://www.starobserver.com.au/news/meet-australias-new-foreign-minister-out-lesbian-senator-penny-wong/213184
9. Lee, Stephanie. “Visit to Sabah Is like ‘Balik Kampung’, Says Aussie FM Penny Wong .” *The Star*, June 29, 2022. https://www.thestar.com.my/news/nation/2022/06/29/visit-to-sabah-is-like-balik-kampung-says-aussie-fm-penny-wong
10. Vanar, Muguntan. “Penny Has Her Family at Heart.” *The Star*. May 25, 2022. https://www.thestar.com.my/news/nation/2022/05/25/penny-has-her-family-at-heart
11. Crane, Emily. “Senator Penny Wong Welcomes Second Daughter After Good Friday Birth.” *DailyMail.com*. April 7, 2015. https://www.dailymail.co.uk/news/article-3028357/Senator-Penny-Wong-partner-Sophie-Allouache-welcome-second-daughter-Good-Friday-birth.html

Sidney Woodruff ____________ **p. 187**

1. Cassell, Avery, and Sidney Woodruff. Personal interview, January 19, 2023.
2. Ibid.
3. Ibid.
4. Ibid.
5. Ibid.
6. Ebbs, Stephanie, and Devin Dwyer. “America's National Parks Face Existential Crisis over Race.” *ABC News Network*, July 1, 2020. https://abcnews.go.com/Politics/americas-national-parks-face-existential-crisis-race/story?id=71528972
7. Ibid.

Shelley Diamond ____________ **p. 193**

1. Diamond, Rochelle. “Rochelle Diamond.” Interview with David Zierler. Caltech Heritage Project. December 21, 2021. https://heritageproject.caltech.edu/interviews/rochelle-diamond
2. Ibid.
3. Vivian. “Queered Science: NOGLSTP's Rochelle Diamond Forged a Path for All of Us.” *Autostraddle*, November 28, 2013. https://www.autostraddle.com/queered-science-rochelle-diamond-and-noglstp-202283/

4. Diamond, Rochelle. "Rochelle Diamond." Interview with David Zierler. Caltech Heritage Project. December 21, 2021. https://heritageproject.caltech.edu/interviews/rochelle-diamond
5. Ibid.
6. Diamond, Rochelle. "Podcast: Scientist couples share their stories and struggles." Interview with Linda Wang and Matt Davenport. *c&en CHEMICAL & ENGINEERING NEWS*, February 13, 2019. https://cen.acs.org/careers/Podcast-Scientist-couples-share-stories/97/web/2019/02
7. Ibid.
8. Ibid.
9. Ibid.
10. Vivian. "Queered Science: NOGLSTP's Rochelle Diamond Forged a Path for All of Us." *Autostraddle*, November 28, 2013. https://www.autostraddle.com/queered-science-rochelle-diamond-and-noglstp-202283/

Sally Ride ——— **p. 199**

1. Ride, Sally and Tam O'Shaughnessy. "Talking with Sally Ride and Tam O'Shaughnessy." Interview with Cyndi Giorgis and Nancy J. Johnson. *ALA American Library Association*, March 2009. https://www.ala.org/aboutala/offices/resources/ride
2. Weitekamp, Margaret A. *Right Stuff, Wrong Sex: America's First Women in Space Program*, "Jerrie Cobb, John Glenn, and the House Subcommittee Hearings." Baltimore, MD: Johns Hopkins University Press, 2004.
3. Sherr, Lynn. *Sally Ride: America's First Woman in Space*. Simon & Schuster, 2015.
4. Grady, Denise. "Sally Ride | 1951-2012 American Woman Who Shattered Space Ceiling." *The New York Times*, July 23, 2012. https://www.nytimes.com/2012/07/24/science/space/sally-ride-trailblazing-astronaut-dies-at-61.html
5. O'Shaughnessy, Tam. "Loving Sally Ride: Tam O'Shaughnessy's 27-Year Partnership With The First American Woman In Space." Interview with Madeline K. Sofia and Brit Hanson. *NPR: Short Wave*, June 24, 2021. https://www.npr.org/2021/06/22/1009098412/loving-sally-ride
6. Ibid.

Ivan Coyote ——— **p. 207**

1. Coyote, Ivan. "Ivan Coyote's Latest Book Demonstrates the Power of Listening." Interview with Marjorie Celona. *Xtra**, August 9, 2021, https://xtramagazine.com/culture/ivan-coyote-care-of-206250
2. Coyote, Ivan. "Close to Spider Man." Arsenal Press, 2000.
3. Varty, Alexander. "Ivan E. Coyote and Crew Feel SweLL." *Georgia Straight*, November 22, 2010. https://www.straight.com/arts/ivan-e-coyote-and-crew-feel-swell
4. Salazar, Heath V. "How Ivan Coyote Taught Me the Importance of Self-Love (and Making a Killer Roast Chicken)." Super Queeroes!, *CBCArts*, 2017. https://www.cbc.ca/artsprojects/superqueeroes/ivan-coyote
5. Coyote, Ivan. "Ivan Coyote: With COVID-19 All of Our Talents Had Been Rendered Irrelevant. Here's How Old, Unanswered Letters Saved Me." *Toronto Star*, October 18, 2020. https://www.thestar.com/entertainment/books/opinion/2020/10/18/ivan-coyote-with-covid-19-all-of-our-talents-had-been-rendered-irrelevant-heres-how-old-unanswered-letters-saved-me.html
6. Carter, Sue. "Ivan Coyote on Letter Writing, the Vancouver Writers Fest, and Their New Book Deal with M&S." *Quill and Quire*, October 19, 2020, https://quillandquire.com/omni/ivan-coyote-on-letter-writing-the-vancouver-writers-fest-and-their-new-book-deal-with-ms/

Fran Lebowitz ______ **p. 211**

1. Lebowitz, Fran. "Fran Lebowitz on Reading." Interview with Kurt Thometz. The Private Library. March 27, 2012. https://www.the-private-library.com/2012/03/27/fran-lebowitz-on-reading-2/
2. Lebowitz, Fran. "High Times Greats: Fran Lebowitz, America's Funniest Femme Fatale." Interview with Glenn O'Brien. *High Times*. August 1978. https://hightimes.com/culture/fran-lebowitz/
3. Lebowitz, Fran. "What Does Fran Lebowitz Really Think about Trump and #MeTtoo?" Interview with Robert Marston. *InsideHook*, April 26, 2018, https://www.insidehook.com/article/books/fran-lebowitz-really-think
4. Lebowitz, Fran. "Fran Lebowitz on Reading." Interview with Kurt Thometz. The Private Library. March 27, 2012. https://www.the-private-library.com/2012/03/27/fran-lebowitz-on-reading-2/
5. Lebowitz, Fran. "'I'm Not an Assassin!': Fran Lebowitz on Not Sleeping, Not Writing, and Not Naming Names." Interview with Brian Alessandro. *Interview*. January 19, 2021. https://www.interviewmagazine.com/culture/fran-lebowitz-pretend-its-a-city
6. Robinson, Jill. "Swift and Cranky." *The New York Times*, March 26, 1978. https://timesmachine.nytimes.com/timesmachine/1978/03/26/110815090.html?pageNumber=67
7. Leonard, John. "The New York Style." *The New York Times*, March 21, 1978. https://timesmachine.nytimes.com/timesmachine/1978/03/21/110810529.html?pageNumber=33
8. Lebowitz, Fran. "The Voice: Fran Lebowitz." Interview with Francesco Clemente. *Interview*. March 11, 2016. https://www.interviewmagazine.com/culture/fran-lebowitz
9. Lebowitz, Fran. "Fran Lebowitz on The Internet, Covid, the Kardashians, and Her Pal Marty." Interview with Lina Lecaro. *Village Voice*, February 6, 2023. https://www.villagevoice.com/2023/02/06/fran-lebowitz-on-the-internet-covid-the-kardashians-and-her-pal-marty/
10. Lebowitz, Fran. "High Times Greats: Fran Lebowitz, America's Funniest Femme Fatale." Interview with Glenn O'Brien. *High Times*. August 1978. https://hightimes.com/culture/fran-lebowitz/
11. Scorsese, Martin, director. *Public Speaking*. HBO Documentary Films, 2010.

Isaac (Karlyn) Lotney ______ **p. 217**

1. Lotney, Karlyn Isaac. "Karlyn Isaac Lotney (FairyButch)." Facebook, April 13, 2013. https://www.facebook.com/karlyn.lotney
2. Lotney, Karlyn Isaac. "Karlyn Isaac Lotney (FairyButch)." Facebook, September 13, 2020. https://www.facebook.com/karlyn.lotney
3. Lotney, KarlynIsaac. "Karlyn Isaac Lotney (FairyButch)." Facebook, September 11, 2016. https://www.facebook.com/karlyn.lotney
4. Ibid.
5. Fairy Butch. "Ask Fairy Butch: Normal--what's that?." *Curve*, June 2006. https://archive.curvemag.com/s/curve-archive/item/356
6. Lo, Malinda. "Last Night at the Telegraph Club Is Out Today!" Malinda Lo, January 19, 2021. https://www.malindalo.com/blog/2021/1/19/last-night-at-the-telegraph-club-is-out-today
7. Sexsmith, Sinclair. "View from the Top: The First Time I Knew I Was a Top." *Autostraddle*, February 16, 2016. https://www.autostraddle.com/view-from-the-top-the-first-time-i-knew-i-was-a-bdsm-top-325904/

8. Lotney, Karlyn Isaac. "Karlyn Isaac Lotney (FairyButch)." Facebook, July 8, 2021. https://www.facebook.com/karlyn.lotney
9. Lotney, Karlyn Isaac. "Queer Culture 1980s–2021, The Fairy Butch Dynasty Den of Iniquity w/Founder, Karlyn Isaac Lotney." Interview with Shannon Wong Lerner. June 20, 2021. https://www.youtube.com/watch?v=yrhQHoObwjM

Heather Hogan ________________ **p. 223**

1. Hogan, Heather. "Soft Butch." Cattywampus, January 23, 2023. https://theheatherhogan.substack.com/p/soft-butch
2. Stacy. "Interview With My Wife: Stacy." Interview with Heather Hogan. *Autostraddle*, May 18, 2022. https://www.autostraddle.com/interview-with-my-wife-stacy
3. Hogan, Heather. "Soft Butch." Cattywampus, January 23, 2023. https://theheatherhogan.substack.com/p/soft-butch
4. Hogan, Heather. "Hogan, Heather." Facebook, November 24, 2016. https://www.facebook.com/heatherannehogan
5. Ibid.
6. Hogan, Heather. "'Go on a Real Date, with a Real Gay Woman' A Letter on Finding Queer Community from Heather Hogan." *Autostraddle*, February 10, 2021. https://www.autostraddle.com/support-queer-media-heather-hogan-fundraising-letter-riese-blog/
7. Hogan, Heather. "Love Is Not a Lie: Behind the Scenes of Heather and Stacy's Wedding." *Autostraddle*, May 1, 2021. https://www.autostraddle.com/love-is-not-a-lie-behind-the-scenes-of-heather-hogans-wedding/
8. Ibid.
9. The Editors. "The First 13 Days Revisiting the Early Confusion of March 2020." *New York, Intelligencer*. March 9, 2021. https://nymag.com/intelligencer/2021/03/coronavirus-nyc-one-year-anniversary.html
10. Hogan, Heather. "The Soft Butch That Couldn't (or: I Got Covid-19 in March and Never Got Better)." *Autostraddle*, August 5, 2020. https://www.autostraddle.com/the-soft-butch-that-couldnt-or-i-got-covid-19-in-march-and-never-got-better/
11. Ibid.
12. Hogan, Heather. "Hogan, Heather." Facebook, November 26, 2020. https://www.facebook.com/heatherannehogan

Jiz Lee ________________ **p. 229**

1. Lee, Jiz. "Getting It Off My Chest." Jiz Lee mixing business with pleasure, April 24, 2022. https://www.jizlee.com/getting-it-off-my-chest/
2. Queen, Carol. "Coming out like a Porn Star (Book)." Books & Merch. https://jizlee.bigcartel.com/product/coming-out-like-a-porn-star
3. Valck, Marijke de, and Antoine Damiens. *Rethinking Film Festivals in the Pandemic Era and After*. Palgrave Macmillan, 2022.
4. Ibid.
5. Lee, Jiz. "Getting It Off My Chest." Jiz Lee mixing business with pleasure, April 24, 2022. https://www.jizlee.com/getting-it-off-my-chest/
6. Lee, Jiz. "A reveal in transition, looking back and looking ahead." Jiz Lee mixing business with pleasure, July 8, 2022. https://www.jizlee.com/a-reveal-in-transition-looking-back-and-looking-ahead/

Kay Ryan p. 235

1. Ryan, Kay. "Cooling the Surface, Tending the Cracks: An Interview with Kay Ryan." Interview with Jessie Carty. *Drunken Boat #11*, March 2006. https://d7.drunkenboat.com/db11/04kay/kay/interview.php
2. The Obama White House. "President Obama Awards the 2012 National Medals of Arts and Humanities.", July 10, 2013. https://www.youtube.com/watch?v=EciDRwKHONk
3. Kost, Ryan. "In New Collection, Marin Poet Kay Ryan Contemplates Nuances of Loss." *San Francisco Chronicle*, October 19, 2015. https://www.sfchronicle.com/art/article/In-new-collection-poet-considers-loss-not-hers-6575049.php
4. Ryan, Kay. "Cooling the Surface, Tending the Cracks: An Interview with Kay Ryan." Interview with Jessie Carty. *Drunken Boat #11*, March 2006. https://d7.drunkenboat.com/db11/04kay/kay/interview.php
5. Ryan, Kay. "Kay Ryan, The Art of Poetry, No. 94." Interview with Sarah Fay, *The Paris Review*, Winter 2008. https://www.theparisreview.org/interviews/5889/the-art-of-poetry-no-94-kay-ryan
6. Ryan, Kay. "Kay Ryan Rises to the Top Despite Her Refusal to Compromise." Interview with Richard Halstead, *Marin Independent Journal*, September 23, 2007. https://www.marinij.com/2007/09/23/kay-ryan-rises-to-the-top-despite-her-refusal-to-compromise/
7. Thomas, Louisa. "The Quiet Poet Laureate." *Newsweek*, June 26 2009. https://www.newsweek.com/quiet-poet-laureate-80441
8. Ryan, Kay. "Kay Ryan Rises to the Top Despite Her Refusal to Compromise." Interview with Richard Halstead, *Marin Independent Journal*, September 23, 2007. https://www.marinij.com/2007/09/23/kay-ryan-rises-to-the-top-despite-her-refusal-to-compromise/
9. Ryan, Kay. "Poet Kay Ryan On Words, Writing." Interview with Andrea Seabrook, *NPR: All Things Considered*, July 20, 2008. https://www.npr.org/templates/story/story.php?storyId=92721707
10. Ibid.
11. O'Rourke, Meghan. "Assessing the New Poet Laureate." *Slate*, July 29, 2008. https://slate.com/news-and-politics/2008/07/assessing-the-new-poet-laureate.html
12. Ryan, Kay. "Kay Ryan, The Art of Poetry, No. 94." Interview with Sarah Fay, *The Paris Review*, Winter 2008. https://www.theparisreview.org/interviews/5889/the-art-of-poetry-no-94-kay-ryan

Gayle Rubin p. 239

1. Rubin, Gayle. "Revisioning Ann Arbor's Radical Past: An Interview with Gayle S. Rubin." Interview with Karen Miller. *Unequal Exchange: Gender and Economies of Power*, University of Michigan, 1997-1998. https://quod.lib.umich.edu/cgi/t/text/text-idx?cc=mfsfront;c=mfs;c=mfsfront;idno=ark5583.0012.006;g=mfsg;rgn=main;view=text;xc=1
2. Rubin, Gayle. "LDG Presents: "THE VALLEY OF THE KINGS" – Gayle Rubin (Part 1)" Lecture presented at the San Francisco Leathermen's Discussion Group. August 29, 2014. https://www.youtube.com/watch?v=DrdGHWvprlI
3. Dewey, Charlsie. "Archivist Talks Documenting Leather, S&M and Fetishism History." *Windy City Times*, April 19, 2016. https://www.windycitytimes.com/lgbt/Archivist-talks-documenting-leather-SM-and-fetishism-history/54966.html
4. Rubin, Gayle. *Deviations: A Gayle Rubin Reader*. Duke University Press, 2012.

5. Rubin, Gayle. "The Feminist Sex Wars: A Retrospective by Gayle Rubin." Cornell University Library, Lecture presented at the Radical Desire Symposium. May 21, 2021. https://www.youtube.com/watch?v=DWjqeAarm2I

6. Ibid.

7. Rubin, Gayle. *Deviations: A Gayle Rubin Reader*. Duke University Press, 2012.

Leslie Feinberg ______ **p. 245**

1. Advocate.com Editors. "Transgender Pioneer and Stone Butch Blues Author Leslie Feinberg Has Died." *Advocate*, November 17, 2014. https://www.advocate.com/arts-entertainment/books/2014/11/17/transgender-pioneer-leslie-feinberg-stone-butch-blues-has-died

2. Weber, Bruce. "Leslie Feinberg, Writer and Transgender Activist, Dies at 65." *The New York Times*, November 25, 2014. https://www.nytimes.com/2014/11/25/nyregion/leslie-feinberg-writer-and-transgender-activist-dies-at-65.html

3. Corbman, Rachel. "The Scholars and the Feminists: The Barnard Sex Conference and the History of the Institutionalization of Feminism." *Feminist Formations*, Vol. 27, No. 3. Winter 2015. https://www.jstor.org/stable/43860815?seq=3

4. Miller, Shauna. "The Importance of Leslie Feinberg." *The Atlantic*, November 17, 2014. https://www.theatlantic.com/entertainment/archive/2014/11/the-importance-of-leslie-feinberg/382852/

5. Feinberg, Leslie. "Words." Leslie Feinberg. Accessed March 1, 2023. https://www.lesliefeinberg.net/words/

6. Feinberg, Leslie. *Transgender Warriors: Making History from Joan of Arc to Dennis Rodman*. Beacon Press, 2005.

7. Feinberg, Leslie. "Leslie Feinberg continues to break gender barriers." Interview with Jillian A. Bogater. *Pridesource*. October 26, 2006. https://pridesource.com/article/20742/

8. Leslie, Feinberg. "Self." Leslie Feinberg, November 15, 2014. https://web.archive.org/web/20190514073103/www.lesliefeinberg.net/self/

9. Ibid.

Selected Works

ACTIVISTS

Soni S.H.S. Wolf —— p. 11

Additional Mentions

The Dykes on Bikes: An Origin Story, directed by Tilly Robba, Steph Jowett, and Kate Cornish. Studio Antics. (2022)

Del Martin —— p. 23

Books

Lesbian/Woman by Del Martin and Phyllis Lyon, Glide Publications (1972)

Lesbian Love and Liberation by Del Martin and Phyllis Lyon, Multi Media Resource Center (1973)

Battered Wives by Del Martin, Volcano Press (1979)

Films

It's No Secret Anymore: The Times of Del Martin and Phyllis Lyon, directed by Joan E. Biren (JEB), Moonforce Media (2003)

Additional Mentions

When You Look Out the Window: How Phyllis Lyon and Del Martin Built a Community by Gayle E. Pitman and illustrated by Christopher Lyles, children's book for ages 4-8, Magination Press (2017)

Different Daughters: A History of the Daughters of Bilitis and the Birth of the Lesbian Rights Movement by Marcia Gallo, Carroll & Graf (2006)

Koja Ray —— p. 29

47,000 Beads by Koja Ray and Angel Adeyoha, illustrated by Holly McGillis, childrens book for ages 6-8, Flamingo Rampant (2017)

Lyra McKee —— p. 33

Books

Angels With Blue Faces by Lyra McKee, Excalibur Press (2020)

Lost, Found, Remembered: In Her Own Words by Lyra McKee, Faber & Faber (2021)

Additional Mentions

Lyra, directed by Alison Millar, self-produced (2021)

Dr. Jamaica Heolimeleikalani Osorio —— p. 37

Books

Remembering Our Intimacies: Moʻolelo, Aloha ʻāina, and Ea by Jamaica Heolimeleikalani Osorio, University of Minnesota Press (2021)

Films

Jamaica Heolimeleikalani Osorio: This Is the Way We Rise, directed by Ciara Lacy, American Masters. PBS (2020) https://www.pbs.org/video/jamaica-heolimeleikalani-osorio-this-is-the-way-we-rise-ndwixe/

On the Morning You Wake (To the End of the World), directors and writers Arnaud Colinart, Steve Jamison, Jamaica Heolimeleikalani Osorio, Pierre Zandrowicz, and Mike Brett, Archer's Mark and Atlas. https://www.onthemorningyouwake.com/

ARTISTS

Ajuan Mance —— p. 45

Books

Inventing Black Women: African American Women Poets and Self-Representation, 1877-2000 by Ajuan Mance, University of Tennessee Press (2008)

Before Harlem: An Anthology of African American Literature from the Long Nineteenth Century by Ajuan Mance, University of Tennessee Press (2016)

Drawing Power: Women's Stories of Sexual Violence, Harassment, and Survival: A Comics Anthology, edited by Diane Noomin and Roxane Gay, contribution by Ajuan Mance, Abrams ComicArts (2019)

Menopause: A Comic Treatment, edited by MK Czerwiec, contribution by Ajuan Mance, Penn State University Press (2020)

She Votes: How U.S. Women Won Suffrage, and What Happened Next, edited by Bridget Quinn and Nell Irvin Painter, contribution by Ajuan Mance, Chronicle Books (2020)

1001 Black Men: Portraits of Masculinity at the Intersections by Ajuan Mance, Stacked Deck Press (2021)

Covid Chronicles: A Comics Anthology, edited by Kendra Boileau and Rich Johnson, contribution by Ajuan Mance, Graphic Mundi (2021)

What Do Brothas Do All Day? by Ajuan Mance, children's book ages for 5-8, Chronicle Books (2023)

Living While Black: Portraits of Everyday Resistance by Ajuan Mance, Chronicle Books (2023)

Gender Studies: The Confessions of an Accidental Outlaw by Ajuan Mance, Rosarium Publishing (2024)

Zines

A Blues for Black Santa by Ajuan Mance

The Ancestors' Juneteenth by Ajuan Mance

The Little Book of Big, Black Bears by Ajuan Mance

Gender Studies by Ajuan Mance

Gender Studies: Requiem for a Hot Comb by Ajuan Mance

Gender Studies: Child's Play by Ajuan Mance

Gender Studies: Tiffany Banks by Ajuan Mance

Films

No Straight Lines: The Rise of Queer Comics, directed by Vivian Kleiman, contribution by Ajuan Mance (2021)

Alison Bechdel ____ p. 49

Books

Dykes to Watch Out For by Alison Bechdel, Firebrand Books (1986)

More Dykes to Watch Out For by Alison Bechdel, Firebrand Books (1988)

New, Improved! Dykes to Watch Out For by Alison Bechdel, Firebrand Books (1990)

Dykes to Watch Out For: The Sequel by Alison Bechdel, Firebrand Books (1992)

Spawn of Dykes to Watch Out For by Alison Bechdel, Firebrand Books (1993)

Unnatural Dykes to Watch Out For by Alison Bechdel, Firebrand Books (1995)

Complete Dykes to Watch Out For, Volume One by Alison Bechdel, Quality Paperback Book Club (1997)

Hot, Throbbing Dykes to Watch Out For by Alison Bechdel, Firebrand Books (1997)

The Indelible Alison Bechdel: Confessions, Comix, and Miscellaneous Dykes to Watch Out For by Alison Bechdel, Firebrand Books (1998)

Split-Level Dykes to Watch Out For by Alison Bechdel, Firebrand Books (1998)

Post-Dykes to Watch Out For by Alison Bechdel, Firebrand Books (2000)

Dykes and Sundry Other Carbon-Based Life-Forms to Watch Out For by Alison Bechdel, Alyson Publications (2003)

Invasion of the Dykes to Watch Out For by Alison Bechdel, Alyson Publications (2005)

Fun Home: A Family Tragicomic by Alison Bechdel, HarperCollins Publishers (2006)

The Essential Dykes to Watch Out For by Alison Bechdel, HarperCollins Publishers (2008)

Are You My Mother?: A Comic Drama by Alison Bechdel, Mariner Books (2012)

The Secret to Superhuman Strength by Alison Bechdel, HarperCollins Publishers (2021)

Audio Dramatization

Dykes to Watch Out For, audio dramatization, directed by Leigh Silverman and adapted by Madeleine George. Audible (2023)

Films

No Straight Lines: The Rise of Queer Comics, directed by Vivian Kleiman, contribution by Alison Bechdel (2021)

Theater
Fun Home, musical theater adaptation of *Fun Home: A Family Tragicomic* by Alison Bechdel, music by Jeanine Tesori, and book and lyrics by Lisa Kron (2013)

Gabby Rivera ________ **p. 55**

Books
Juliet Takes a Breath by Gabby Rivera, Riverdale Avenue Books (2016)
America Vol. 1: The Life and Times of America Chavez, by Gabby Rivera and illustrated by Joe Quinone, Marvel (2017)
America Vol. 2: Fast and Fuertona, by Gabby Rivera and illustrated by Jen Bartel and Joe Quinones, Marvel (2018)

Podcasts
Joy Revolution podcast by Gabby Rivera

Storme Webber ________ **p. 61**

Books
Serious Pleasure: Lesbian Erotic Stories and Poetry, edited by Sheba Feminist Publishers, contribution by Storme Webber, Cleis Press (1989)
The Popular Front of Contemporary Poetry: Anthology, edited by Linton Kwesi Johnson, contribution by Storme Webber, Apples & Snakes (1992)
Black Women, Writing, and Identity: Migrations on the Subject by Carole Boyce-Davies, contribution by Storme Webber, Routledge (1994)
Voices Rising: Celebrating 20 Years of Black Lesbian, Gay, Bisexual and Transgender Writing, edited by G. Winston James and the *Other Countries Collective*, contribution by Storme Webber, Redbone Press (2007)
Cornbread, Fish and Collard Greens: Prayers, Poems & Affirmations for People Living with HIV/AIDS, edited by Khafre K. Abif, contribution by Storme Webber, AuthorHouse (2013)

Journals
Yellow Medicine Review Spring 2018, edited by Janet Marie Rogers, contribution by Storme Webber, Yellow Medicine Review: A Journal of Indigenous Literature, Art & Thought (2018)

Films
Venus Boyz, documentary directed by Gabriel Baur, First Run Features (2001)

ATHLETES

Brittney "BG" Griner ________ **p. 69**

Books
In My Skin: My Life On and Off The Basketball Court by Brittney Griner and Sue Hovey, Dey Street Books (2014)

Caster Semenya, Order of Ikhamanga ________ **p. 79**

Books
The Race to Be Myself: A Memoir by Caster Semenya, W. W. Norton & Company (September 2023)

Additional Mentions
The Run For Life: Caster Semenya by Bronwyn Henke, Independently published (2019)
QHAWE! Mokgadi Caster Semenya by Nokuthula Mazibuko Msimang and illustrations by Sanelisiwe Singaphi, children's book for ages 7-9, New Africa Books (2021)

Martina Navratilova ________ **p. 85**

Books
Tennis My Way by Martina Navratilova and Mary Carillo, Scribner 1982)
Being Myself by Martina Navratilova and George Vecsey, Collins (1985)
The Total Zone: A Mystery by Martina Navratilova and Liz Nickles, Villard (1994)

Killer Instinct: A Jordan Myles Mystery by Martina Navratilova and Liz Nickles, Villard (1994)

Breaking Point, Instinct: A Jordan Myles Mystery by Martina Navratilova and Liz Nickles, Villard (1996)

Shape Your Self: My 6-Step Diet and Fitness Plan to Achieve the Best Shape of Your Life by Martina Navratilova, Rodale Books (2006)

Films

The Trans Women Athlete Dispute with Martina Navratilova, directed by Brook Lapping, Charlotte Moore, and Ben Rummey, contribution by Martina Navratilova, Brook Lapping Productions/British Broadcasting Corporation (BBC) (2019)

FILMMAKERS

Jenni Olson p. 93

Filmography

Homo Promo, directed by Jenni Olson, Strand Releasing (1991)

Sometimes, directed by Jenni Olson, Jenni Olson Productions (1994)

Blow-Up, directed by Jenni Olson and Kadet Kuhne, Jenni Olson Productions (1997)

Blue Diary, directed by Jenni Olson, Jenni Olson Productions (1998)

Meep Meep!, directed by Jenni Olson, Jenni Olson Productions (2000)

By Hook or by Crook, directed by Harry Dodge and Silas Howard, consulting producer, Jenni Olson, Steakhaus Productions (2001)

Sing Along San Francisco, directed by Georgina Corzine, produced by Jenni Olson (2002)

The Joy of Life, directed by Jenni Olson (2005)

The Royal Road, directed by Jenni Olson, Jenni Olson Productions (2015)

The Freedom to Marry, directed by Edward Rosenstein, produced by Jenni Olson and Amie Segal, Eyepop Productions (2016)

In Nomine Patris, directed by Jenni Olson, Jenni Olson Productions (2019)

A Worm in the Heart, directed by Paul Smith, consulting producer Jenni Olson(2020)

Disclosure: Trans Lives on Screen, director Sam Feder, consulting producer Jenni Olson, Field of Vision (2020)

No Straight Lines: The Rise of Queer Comics, directed by Vivian Kleiman, consulting producer Jenni Olson (2021)

TV Series

Equal, directors Stephen Kijak, Jai Rodriguez, and Cheyenne Jackson, archival producer Jenni Olson, Scout Productions (2020)

Books

Dagger: On Butch Women, edited by Roxxie Linnea Due, contribution by Jenni Olson, Cleis Press (1995)

Cookin' with Honey: What Literary Lesbians Eat, edited by Amy Scholder, contribution by Jenni Olson, Firebrand Books (1996)

Lesbian Words: State of the Art, edited by Randy Turoff, contribution by Jenni Olson, Masquerade Books (1996)

The Ultimate Guide to Lesbian & Gay Film and Video, edited by Jenni Olson, Serpent's Tail (1996)

The Queer Movie Poster Book by Jenni Olson, Chronicle Books (2004)

The Queer Encyclopedia of the Visual Arts, edited by Claude J. Summers, contribution by Jenni Olson, Cleis Press (2006)

The Oxford Handbook of Queer Cinema, edited by Ronald Gregg and Amy Villarejo, contribution by Jenni Olson, Oxford University Press (2021)

Rethinking Film Festivals in the Pandemic Era and After, edited by Marijke de Valck and Antoine Damiens, contribution by Jenni Olson, open access book, Palgrave Macmillan (2023)

Madeline Lim p. 99

Filmography

All films in this list were produced and directed by Madeline Lim.

Sambal Belacan in San Francisco (1996)

Shades of Grey (1996)
Youth Organizing: Power Through Art (1996)
A Vision of Smart Growth (2002)
Dragon Desire (2004)
The Worlds of Bernice Bing (2013)

Shine Louise Houston p. 105

Filmography
The Crash Pad, series directed by Shine Louise Houston, Pink and White Productions (2005)
Superfreak, directed by Shine Louise Houston, Pink and White Productions (2006)
The Wild Search, directed by Shine Louise Houston, Pink and White Productions (2008)
Champion: Love Hurts, directed by Shine Louise Houston, Pink and White Productions (2009)
Snapshot, directed by Shine Louise Houston, Pink and White Productions (2017)
Chemistry Eases the Pain, directed by Shine Louise Houston, Pink and White Productions (2020)
Crash Pad Series, 1-9, directed by Shine Louise Houston Pink and White Productions (various dates)
Heavenly Spire Series, directed by Shine Louise Houston, Heavenly Spire (various dates)

Additional Mentions
A Taste for Brown Sugar: Black Women in Pornography by Mireille Miller-Young, Duke University Press Books (2014)
Black Female Sexualities, edited by Trimiko Melancon and Joanne M. Braxton, Rutgers University Press (2015)
Freeing Ourselves: A guide to Health and Self Love for Brown Bois by The Brown Boi Project (2011)

Cheryl Dunye p. 111

Filmography
She Don't Fade, directed by Cheryl Dunye, Dancing Girl (1991)
Vanilla Sex, directed by Cheryl Dunye, Dancing Girl (1992)
Greetings from Africa, directed by Cheryl Dunye, Dancing Girl (1994)
The Watermelon Woman, directed by Cheryl Dunye, Dancing Girl (1996)
Stranger Inside, TV movie directed by Cheryl Dunye, HBO Films, Stranger Baby Productions (2001)
The Owls, directed by Cheryl Duyne, Parliament Film Collective (2010)
Mommy is Coming, directed by Cheryl Dunye, Jurgen Bruning Filmproduktion (2012)
Black is Blue, directed by Cheryl Dunye, Cheryl Dunye (2014)
Brother from Another Time, directed by Cheryl Dunye, created for the 2014 San Francisco Dance Film Festival's Co-Laboratory project (2014)

Additional Mentions
Women's Experimental Cinema: Critical Frameworks, edited by Robin Blaetz, "The Experimental 'Dunyementary':A Cinematic Signature Effect" by Kathleen McHugh, Duke University Press Books (2007)
Dykes, Camera, Action!, directed by Caroline Berler, contribution by Cheryl Dunye, Frameline (2018)

Barbara Hammer p. 117

Filmography
All films self-released by Barbara Hammer
Nitrate Kisses (1992)
Out in South Africa (1995)
Tender Fictions (1995)
The Female Closet (1998)
Blue Film No. 6: Love Is Where You Find It (1998)
History Lessons (2000)
Devotion, A Film about Ogawa Productions (2000)

Dyketactics (1974/2001)
My Babushka: Searching Ukrainian Identities (2001)
Resisting Paradise (2003)
Lover Other (2006)
Diving Women of Jeju-do (2007)
A Horse Is Not A Metaphor (2008)
Generations (2010)
Maya Deren's Sink (2011)
Welcome To This House (2015)

Books

HAMMER!: Making Movies Out of Sex and Life by Barbara Hammer, The Feminist Press at CUNY (2010)
Evidentiary Bodies by Barbara Hammer, University of Chicago Press (2018)

MUSICIANS

Phranc p. 131

Discography

Folksinger, Rhino (1985)
I Enjoy Being a Girl, Island (1989)
Positively Phranc, Island (1991)
Goofyfoot, Kill Rock Stars (1995)
Milkman, Phancy Records (1998)

Compilations

Milkshake—A CD to Benefit the Harvey Milk Institute, "Dumb Hairdresser", timmi-kat ReCoRDS (1998)
Kat Vox: A CD to Celebrate 20 Years of timmi-kat ReCoRDS, "Tupperware Lady", timmi-kat ReCoRDS (2011)

Art Exhibitions

Compass-Navigating the Journey to Self-Identity, Orange County Center for Contemporary Art, group show, Santa Ana, CA (2013)
It Happened in Sun Valley, Friesen Gallery, Ketchum, ID (2014)
Winter, Craig Krull Gallery, Santa Monica, CA (2014)
Incognito 10, Santa Monica Museum of Art, group show, Santa Monica, CA (2014)
Filtered: What Does Love Look Like?, Friesen Gallery Fine Art, group show, Ketchum, ID (2014)
Swagger, Craig Krull Gallery, Santa Monica, CA (2018)
The Great Outdoors, Friesen Gallery, Ketchum, ID (2018)
Toys, Craig Krull Gallery, Santa Monica, CA (2018)

Films

Lifetime Guarantee: Phranc's Adventures in Plastics, directed by Lisa Udelson, Roadside Attractions (2001)

Meshell Ndegeocello p. 125

Discography

Plantation Lullabies, Maverick (1993)
Peace Beyond Passion, Maverick Records (1996)
Bitter, Maverick Records (1999)
Cookie: The Anthropological Mixtape, Maverick Records (2002)
Comfort Woman, Maverick Records (2003)
The Spirit Music Jamia: Dance of the Infidel, Universal France (2005)
The World Has Made Me the Man of My Dreams, Bismillah (2007)
Devil's Halo, Downtown Records (2009)
Weather, Naïve (2011)

Pour une Âme Souveraine: A Dedication to Nina Simone, Naïve (2012)
Comet, Come to Me, Naïve (2014)
Ventriloquism, Naïve (2018)

Jools and Lynda Topp, Dames Companion of the New Zealand Order of Merit __ p. 137

Books
The Topp Twins, Jools and Lynda Topp, Penguin Books (2003)

Television Series DVDs
Topp Country: A culinary journey through New Zealand
The Topp Twins and the APO Auckland Philharmonic Orchestra
The Topp Twins
The Topp Twins Do Not Adjust Your Twinset
Kens Hunting & Fishing Show with Lady Hunter

Discography
Twinset and Pearls, Dragon's Egg (1984)
No War in My Heart, Festival Records (1987)
Two Timing, Topp Twins Ltd. (1994)
Grass Highway, Topp Twins Ltd (2001)
Flowergirls & Cowgirls, EMI Music New Zealand (2005)
Honky Tonk Angel, Topp Twins Ltd (2009)
Topp Twins—The Very Best Of—Collection Of The Best From 1981-2014, Sony Music (2014)

Additional Mentions
The Topp Twins: Untouchable Girls, directed by Leanne Pooley (2011)

Debbie Smith ________________ p. 143

Discography by Band Name

Blindness
Glamourama, Blindness, Club AC30 (2012)
Wrapped in Plastic, Blindness, Saint Marie Records (2015)

Bows
Cassidy, Bows, Too Pure (2001)

Curve
Doppelgänger, Curve, Anxious Records (1992)
Cuckoo, Curve, Anxious Records (1993)
The Way Of Curve 1990 / 2004, Curve, Anxious Records (2004)
Curve Bootlegs Series 3, Curve, self-released (2020)
Fate—Bootleg Series Vol. 7, Curve, tracks 6-9, self-released (2020)
Astoria London 1991—Bootleg Series Vol 16, Curve, self-released (2022)
Portland Satyricon 1993—Bootleg Series Vol 14, Curve, self-released (2022)

Echobelly
Cherry, Echobelly, Anxious Records (1991)
Everyone's Got One, Echobelly, Fauve Records (1994)
I Can't Imagine The World Without Me, Echobelly, Fauve Records (1994)
On, Echobelly, Fauve Records (1995)
Dark Therapy, Echobelly, Fauve Records (1996)
Black Heart Lullabies, Echobelly, Fauve Records (2018)

Snowpony
Sea Shanties For Spaceships, Snowpony, Dead Pan Alley (2001)

The London Dirthole Company
The Stanley Hall Session, The London Dirthole Company, Radiowave Recordings (2013)

Modern Ist, The London Dirthole Company, Outside Sounds (2013)

The Sounding Alley Tapes, The London Dirthole Company, Squoodge Records (2013)

Barking At The Half Moon, Sexton Ming & The London Dirthole Company, The London Dirthole Company, tracks 1-7, Phono Erotic (2014)

Ye Nuns

Nun More Black, Ye Nuns, Tuff Enuf (2014)

Additional Mentions

Grrrls: Viva Rock Divas by Amy Raphael, St. Martin's Griffin (1996)

Frock Rock: Women Performing Popular Music by Mavis Bayton, Oxford University Press (1998)

A Woman Called Smith, produced by Ian Denyer, series producer Nikki Cheetham, BBC Radio broadcast (1997)

Rebel Dykes, Directed and edited by Harri Shanahan and Sîan Williams, Riot Productions (2021)

Debbie Smith, short documentary directed by Tanimowo McDowell, https://www.youtube.com/watch?v=XlsOv0PyLz8 (2015)

Toshi Reagon p. 149

Discography

Justice, Flying Fish Records (1990)

The Rejected Stone, PRO-MAMMA LPs (1994)

Kindness, Smithsonian Folkways (1997)

The Righteous Ones, Razor and Tie (1999)

TOSHI, Razor and Tie (2002)

I Be Your Water, self-released (2004)

Have You Heard, Black Elephant Music (2005)

Until We're Done, self-released (2008)

Lava: We Become, self-released (2009)

There and Back Again, self-released (2010)

SpirtLand, self-released (2018)

Compilations

Africans in America, produced by Bernice Johnson Reagon, Toshi Reagon tracks 1-3, 6,-7, 9, 18, 21, Rycodisk (1998)

Raise Your Voice, Sweet Honey In The Rock, collaboration with Toshi Reagon and BIGLovely, Earthbeat (2005)

Podcasts

Octavia's Parables, co-hosts adrienne maree brown and Toshi Reagon, https://www.readingoctavia.com

PROFESSIONALS

Chef Melissa King p. 161

Video Series

"Tasting Wild" with Melissa King, National Geographic (2022)

Rabbi Sandra Lawson p. 167

Books

No Time for Neutrality: American Rabbinic Voices from an Era of Upheaval, edited by by Michael Rose Knopf and Miriam Aniel, contribution by Sandra Lawson, self-published (2021)

The Social Justice Torah Commentary, edited by Barry Black, contribution by Sandra Lawson, Central Conference of American Rabbis (2021)

Podcasts

Hineni (Here I Am), Audible (2017-2019) https://www.rabbisandralawson.com/blog

Senator the Honorable Penny Wong p. 179

Books

Passion and Principle by Margaret Simons, Black Inc. (2019)

SCIENTISTS

Sidney Woodruff p. 187

Books

Queer Ducks (And Other Animals): The Natural World of Animal Sexuality, by Eliot Schrefer and Jules Zuckerberg, YA book for ages 14-17, contribution by Sidney Lawson, Katherine Tegen Books (2021)

Shelley Diamond p. 193

Books

Mechanisms of Lymphocyte Activation and Immune Regulation III: Developmental Biology of Lymphocytes, edited by Ellen V. Rothenberg, Max D. Cooper, Sudhir Gupta, and William E. Paul, contribution by Rochelle A. Diamond, Plenum Publishing Corporation (1991)

In Living Color: Protocols in Flow Cytometry and Cell Sorting by Rochelle A. Diamond and Susan Demaggio, Springer (2000)

Sally Ride p. 199

Children's Book Series

To Space and Back by Sally Ride and Susan Okie, children's book for ages 8-12, HarperCollins (1989)

The Mystery of Mars by Sally Ride and Tam O'Shaughnessy, children's book for ages 8-10, Crown Books for Young Readers; (1999)

The Third Planet: Exploring the Earth From Space by Sally Ride and Tam O'Shaughnessy, children's book for ages 9-13, Sally Ride Science (2004)

Voyager: An Adventure to the Edge of the Solar System by Sally Ride and Tam O'Shaughnessy, children's book for ages 10-14, Sally Ride Science (2005)

Mission: Planet Earth: Our World and Its Climate—and How Humans Are Changing Them by Sally Ride and Tam O'Shaughnessy, children's book for ages 9-14, Flash Point (2009)

Mission: Save the Planet: Things YOU Can do to Help Fight Global Warming by Sally Ride and Tam O'Shaughnessy, children's book for ages 9-14, Flash Point (2009)

Additional Mentions

Sally Ride: America's First Woman in Space by Lynn Sherr, Simon & Schuster (2014)

Sally Ride: A Photobiography of America's Pioneering Woman in Space by Tam O'Shaughnessy, children's book for ages 10-14, Square Fish (2017)

WRITERS

Ivan Coyote p. 207

Books

Boys Like Her: Transfictions by Taste This Collective, Press Gang Publishers (1998)

Close to Spider Man, Arsenal Pulp Press (2000)

One Man's Trash, Arsenal Pulp Press (2002)

Loose End, Arsenal Pulp Press (2004)

Bow Grip, Arsenal Pulp Press (2006)

The Slow Fix, Arsenal Pulp Press (2008)

Missed Her, Arsenal Pulp Press (2010)

Persistence: All Ways Butch and Femme, edited by Ivan Coyote and Zena Sharman, Arsenal Pulp Press (2011)

One in Every Crowd, Arsenal Pulp Press (2012)

Gender Failure by Ivan Coyote and Rae Spoon, Arsenal Pulp Press (2014)

Tomboy Survival Guide, Arsenal Pulp Press (2016)

Rebent Sinner, Arsenal Pulp Press (2019)
Care of: Letters, Connections, and Cures, Random House (2021)

Fran Lebowitz ______ **p. 211**

Books

Metropolitan Life by Fran Lebowitz, Dutton (1978)

Social Studies by Fran Lebowitz, Pocket Books (1981)

The Fran Lebowitz Reader by Fran Lebowitz, Vintage (1994)

Mr. Chas and Lisa Sue Meet the Pandas by Fran Lebowitz and illustrated by Michael Graves, children's book for ages 6-10, Knopf Books (1994)

Films

Paris Is Burning, directed by Jennie Livingston, contribution by Fran Lebowitz, The Criterion Collection (1990)

Public Speaking, directed by Martin Scorsese, biopic of Fran Lebowitz, HBO Studios (2010)

Mapplethorpe: Look at the Pictures, directed by Fenton Bailey and Randy Barbato, contribution by Fran Lebowitz, HBO (2016)

The Gospel According to André, directed by Kate Novack, contribution by Fran Lebowitz, A Magnolia Pictures (2017)

Always at the Carlyle Herself, directed by Matthew Miele, contribution by Fran Lebowitz, Quixotic Endeavors (2018)

The Booksellers, directed by D.W. Young, contribution by Fran Lebowitz, Blackletter Films (2019)

Toni Morrison: The Pieces I Am, directed by Timothy Greenfield-Sanders, contribution by Fran Lebowitz, Magnolia Pictures (2019)

*Wojnarowicz: F**k You F*ggot F**ker*, directed by Chris McKim, contribution by Fran Lebowitz, World of Wonder (2020)

Television Series

Pretend It's a City, directed by Martin Scorsese, biopic of Fran Lebowitz, Netflix (2021)

Isaac (Karlyn) Lotney ______ **p. 217**

Books

The Ultimate Guide to Strap-On Sex: A Complete Resource for Women and Men by Karlyn Lotney A.K.A. Fairy Butch, Cleis Press (2000)

Best Lesbian Erotica 1998, edited by Tristan Taormino, contribution by Karlyn Isaac Lotney, Cleis Press (1998)

Heather Hogan ______ **p. 223**

Books

The Best American Science and Nature Writing 2021, edited by Jaime Green, and Ed Yong, contribution by Heather Hogan, Mariner Books (2021)

The Long COVID Survival Guide: How to Take Care of Yourself and What Comes Next Stories and Advice from Twenty Long-Haulers and Experts, edited by Fiona Lowenstein, contribution by Heather Hogan, The Experiment (2022)

Jiz Lee ______ **p. 229**

Books

The Feminist Porn Book: The Politics of Producing Pleasure, edited by Tristan Taormino, contribution by Jiz Lee, The Feminist Press at CUNY (2013)

Coming Out Like a Porn Star: Essays on Pornography, Protection, and Privacy, edited by Jiz Lee, ThreeL Media (2015)

ASAROTICA, edited by Asa Akira, contribution by Jiz Lee, Cleis Press (2017)

Ask: Building Consent Culture, edited by Kitty Stryker, contribution by Jiz Lee, Thornapple Press (2017)

Trans Bodies, Trans Selves: A Resource by and for Transgender Communities, edited by Laura Erickson-Schroth, contribution by Jiz Lee, Oxford University Press (2022)

Films

Crash Pad Series, various episodes

Mommy is Coming, directed by Cheryl Dunye, Jurgen Bruning Filmproduktion (2012)

JL+DD: Jiz Lee and Danni Daniels, directed by Danni Daniels, PinkLabel.tv (2012)

Justify My Jiz, directed by Wolf Hudson, PinkLabel.tv (2012)

Once Ago, directed by Aeric Meredith-Goujon, PinkLabel.tv (2013)

Genderflux, directed by Nikki Hearts, PinkLabel.tv (2013)

BIODILDO, directed by Christian Slaughter, PinkLabel.tv (2013)

BIODILDO 2.0, directed by Christian Slaughter, PinkLabel.tv (2014)

Wild Lovers, directed by Isabel Dresler, PinkLabel.tv (2015)

D.T.F. (Down To Fall), directed by Evie Snax, PinkLabel.tv (2018)

Stark directed by Stoya, PinkLabel.tv (2020)

Journals

Porn Studies, Volume 2, Issue 2–3, contribution by Jiz Lee, "They Came to See the [Queer] Porn Star Talk", Routledge (2015)

Porn Studies, Volume 3, Issue 2, contribution by Jiz Lee and Rebecca Sullivan, "Porn and Labour: The Labour of Porn Studies", Routledge (2016)

Kay Ryan p. 235

Books

Dragon Acts to Dragon Ends by Kay Ryan, Taylor Street Press (1983)

Strangely Marked Metal, by Kay Ryan, Copper Beech Press (1985)

Flamingo Watching, by Kay Ryan, Copper Beech Press (1994)

Elephant Rocks, by Kay Ryan, Grove Press (1996)

Say Uncle, by Kay Ryan, Grove Press (2000)

The Niagara River, by Kay Ryan, Grove Press (2005)

Jam Jar Lifeboat & Other Novelties Exposed, by Kay Ryan, Red Berry Editions (2008)

The Best of It: New and Selected Poems, by Kay Ryan, Grove Press (2010)

Erratic Facts, by Kay Ryan, Grove Press (2015)

Synthesizing Gravity: Selected Prose, by Kay Ryan, Grove Press (2020)

Gayle Rubin p. 239

Books

Pleasure and Danger: Exploring Female Sexuality, edited by Carole Vance, contribution by Gayle Rubin, Routledge (1984)

The Valley of the Kings: Leathermen in San Francisco, 1960-1990, Volumes 1-2, thesis, University of Michigan (1994)

Reclaiming San Francisco: History, Politics, Culture, edited by James Brook, Chris Carlsson, and Nancy Peters, contribution by Gayle Rubin, City Lights Publishers (1998)

Encyclopedia of Lesbian, Gay, Bisexual, and Transgender History in America, edited by Marc Stein, contribution by Gayle Rubin, Charles Scribner & Sons (2003)

Surveiller et Jouir: Anthropologie Politique du Sex by Gayle Rubin, Éditions Psychanalytiques de l'École Lacanienne (2010)

Deviations: A Gayle Rubin Reader by Gayle Rubin, Duke University Press Books (2011)

Journals

Socialist Review, article by Deidre English, Amber Hollibauch, and Gayle Rubin," Talking Sex: A Conversation on Sexuality and Feminism" (1981)

differences: a journal of feminist cultural studies, article by Gayle Rubin and Judith Butler, "Sexual Traffic" (1994)

American Anthropologist, article by Gayle Rubin "Esther Newton Made Me a Gay Anthropologist" (2018)

Books

Transgender Liberation: A Movement Whose Time Has Come by Leslie Feinberg, World View Forum Publication (1992)

Stone Butch Blues by Leslie Feinberg, self-published (1993)

Transgender Warriors: Making History from Joan of Arc to Dennis Rodman by Leslie Feinberg, Beacon Press (1996)

Trans Liberation: Beyond Pink or Blue by Leslie Feinberg, Beacon Press (1999)

Drag King Dreams by Leslie Feinberg, Seal Press (2006)

Rainbow Solidarity in Defense of Cuba by Leslie Feinberg, World View Forum Publication (2009)

Films

Transexual Menace, documentary directed by Rosa von Praunheim, contribution by Leslie Feinberg, Rosa von Praunheim Filmproduktion (1996)

Additional Resources

Some of these resources are butch-centric, however, many cast a wider net to include lesbians, women, and LGBTQ+ or BIPOC folx. For additional LGBTQ+ resources, please see **Selected Works** on page 271.

ACTIVISTS and HISTORY

A Two-Spirit Journey: The Autobiography of a Lesbian Ojibwa-Cree Elder by Ma-Nee Chacaby, University of Manitoba Press (2016)

Asegi Stories: Cherokee Queer and Two-Spirit Memory by Qwo-Li Driskill, University of Arizona Press (2016)

Boots of Leather, Slippers of Gold: The History of a Lesbian Community by Madeline Davis and Elizabeth L. Kennedy, Routledge (1993)

Butch is a Noun by Bear Bergman, Arsenal Pulp Press (2006)

Dagger: On Butch Women, edited by Roxxie Linnea Due, Cleis Press (1995)

Female Masculinities and the Gender Wars: The Politics of Sex by Finn Mackay, I.B. Tauris (2021)

Female Masculinity by Jack Halberstam, Duke University Press Books (2019)

Hijab Butch Blues: A Memoir by Lamya H, The Dial Press (2022)

Moby Dyke: An Obsessive Quest to Track Down the Last Remaining Lesbian Bars in America by Krista Burton, Simon & Schuster (2023)

Never a Cover: The Lexington Club, documentary short about The Lexington lesbian bar in San Francisco, produced and directed by Lauren Tabak and Susannah Smith, (2015). https://www.laurentabak.com/artist-activist

Odd Girls and Twilight Lovers by Lillian Faderman, Columbia University Press (1991)

Public Sex: The Culture of Radical Sex by Patrick Califia, Cleis Press (1994)

Queer Brown Voices: Personal Narratives of Latina/o LGBT Activism, edited by Letitia Gomez, Salvador Vidal-Ortiz, and Letitia Gomez, University of Texas Press (2015)

Queer Jihad: LGBT Muslims on Coming Out, Activism, and the Faith by Afdhere Jama, Oracle Releasing (2014)

Storytelling in Queer Appalachia: Imagining and Writing the Unspeakable, edited by Hillery Glasby, Sherrie Gradin, and Rachael Ryerson, West Virginia University Press (2020)

The Disappearing L: Erasure of Lesbian Spaces and Culture by Bonnie J. Morris, State University of New York Press (2017)

The Lavender Scare: The Cold War Persecution of Gays and Lesbians in the Federal Government by David Jackson, University of Chicago Press (2023)

ARTISTS

Butch by Meg Allen, self-published (2017)

Butch Heroes by Ria Brodell, The MIT Press (2018)

Butch: Not Like the Other Girls by SD Holman, Caitlin Press (2017)

Butches in Bloom, zine by Lemon Lui, self-published. https://www.lemonliuart.com

Lesbian Art in America: A Contemporary History by Harmony Hammond, Rizzoli (2000)

Pregnant Butch: Nine Long Months Spent in Drag, a graphic memoir by A. K. Summers, Soft Skull (2014)

The Life & Times of Butch Dykes: Portraits of Artists, Leaders, and Dreamers Who Changed the World by Eloisa Aquino, Microcosm Publishing (2019)

ATHLETES

Gender Testing in Sport: Ethics, Cases and Controversies, edited by Sandy Montañola and Aurélie Olivesi, Routledge (2016)

Out in Sport: The experiences of openly gay and lesbian athletes in competitive sport by Eric Anderson, Rory Magrath, and Rachael Bullingham, Routledge (2016)

Sports Journalism and Women Athletes: Coverage of Coming Out Stories by William P. Cassidy, Palgrave Pivot (2019)

Stand Up and Shout Out: Women's Fight for Equal Pay, Equal Rights, and Equal Opportunities in Sports by Joan Steidinger, Rowman & Littlefield Publishers (2020)

Strong Women, Deep Closets: Lesbians and Homophobia in Sport by Pat Griffin, Human Kinetics (1998)

FILMMAKERS

Daring to Dissent: Lesbian Culture from Margin to Mainstream (Women on Women), edited by Liz Gibbs, Continuum International Publishing Group (1994)

How Do I Look?: Queer Film and Video, edited by the organization Bad Object-Choices, Bay Press (1991)

Queer Looks: Perspectives on Lesbian and Gay Film and Video, edited by Martha Gever, Pratibha Parmar, and John Greyson, Routledge (2013)

Reading 'The L Word': Outing Contemporary Television, edited by Kim Akass and Janet McCabe, I.B. Tauris (2006)

The View From Here: Conversations with Gay and Lesbian Filmmakers by Matthew Hays, Arsenal Pulp Press (2007)

Uninvited: Classical Hollywood Cinema and Lesbian Representability by Patricia White, Indiana University Press (1999)

MUSICIANS AND PERFORMERS

Hot Licks: Lesbian Musicians of Note, edited by Lee Fleming, Ragweed Press (1996)

Queer Country by Shana Goldin-Perschbacher, University of Illinois Press (2022)

Queercore—How to Punk a Revolution: An Oral History Book, edited by Liam Warfield, Walter Crasshole, and Yony Leyser, introduction by Anna Joy Springer and Lynn Breedlove, PM Press (2021)

Queering the Pitch: The New Gay and Lesbian Musicology, edited by Philip Brett, Elizabeth Wood, and Gary, Routledge (2006)

The Drag King Book by Judith "Jack Halberstam" and Del LaGrace Volcano, Serpent's Tail (1999)

PROFESSIONALS

Breathing Fire: Female Inmate Firefighters on the Front Lines of California's Wildfires by Jaime Lowe, MCD (2021)

Coming Out of the Classroom Closet: Gay and Lesbian Students, Teachers, and Curricula, edited by Karen M. Harbeck, Routledge (1992)

Gay and Lesbian Educators: Personal Freedoms, Public Constraints by Karen M. Harbeck, Amethyst Pr & Productions (1997)

Gay and Lesbian Professionals in the Closet: Who's In, Who's Out, and Why, edited by Teresa DeCrescenzo, Routledge (1998)

Hidden Histories: Faith and Black Lesbian Leadership by Monique Moultrie, Duke University Press Books (2023)

Jewish Lesbian Scholarship in a Time of Change, edited By Marla Brettschneider, Routledge (2023)

My Butch Career: A Memoir by Esther Newton, Duke University Press Books (2018)

Queer Career: Sexuality and Work in Modern America by Margot Canaday, Princeton University Press (2023)

SCIENTISTS

500 Queer Scientists, https://500queerscientists.com/

Out in Science, Technology, Engineering, and Mathematics, oSTEM https://www.ostem.org/

Out to Innovate™, formerly known as National Organization of Gay and Lesbian Scientists and Technical Professionals (NOGLSTP), https://noglstp.org/

Black Faces, White Spaces : Reimagining the Relationship of African Americans to the Great Outdoors by Carolyn Finney, The University of North Carolina Press (2014)

Fatima's Great Outdoors by Ambreen Tariq and illustrated by Stevie Lewis, for children ages 4-10, Kokila (2021)

Wilderness Nonprofit Organizations:

- Brown People Camping, Not specifically LGBTQ. Resources for BIPOC outdoor enthusiasts. https://www.brownpeoplecamping.com/
- Hike Clerb, Not specifically LGBTQ. An intersectional women's outdoors collective for BIPOC hikers. https://www.hikeclerb.com/
- LGBT Outdoors, connecting the LGBTQ+ community to the outdoors and its members to one another. https://www.lgbtoutdoors.com/
- Unlikely Hikers, Not specifically LGBTQ, but the founder is a queer woman. Slower paced group hiking experiences and accessible hikes. https://unlikelyhikers.org

WRITERS

A Woman Like That: Lesbian and Bisexual Writers Tell Their Coming Out Stories, edited by Joan Larkin, William Morrow (1999)

Lesbian Detective Fiction: Woman as Authors, Subjects and Reader by Phyllis M. Betz, McFarland (2006)

Lesbian Romance Novels: A History and Critical Analysis by Phyllis M. Betz, McFarland (2009)

The Lesbian Fantastic: A Critical Study of Science Fiction, Fantasy, Paranormal and Gothic Writings by Phyllis M. Betz, McFarland (2011)

Novel Approaches to Lesbian History by Linda Garber, Palgrave Macmillan (2021)

Un/Popular Culture: Lesbian Writing After the Sex Wars by Kathleen Martindale, SUNY Press (1997)

Who's Who in Lesbian and Gay Writing, edited by Gabriele Griffin, Routledge (2003)

MEET THE ARTISTS

Ajuan Mance is the author and illustrator of *1001 Black Men: Portraits of Masculinity at the Intersections* (Stacked Deck Press, 2022) and *Living While Black: Portraits of Everyday Resistance* (Chronicle Books, 2022). Ajuan's illustrations and comics have appeared in several collections including: *We're Still Here*, winner of the 2019 Ignatz Award for Outstanding Anthology; *Drawing Power*, winner of the 2020 Eisner Award for Best Anthology; *COVID Chronicles: A Comics Anthology*; *Menopause: A Comic Treatment*, winner of the 2021 Eisner Award for Best Anthology, and others.

Illustrations: Cheryl Dunye (p. 111), Madeline Lim (p. 99), Chef Melissa King (p. 161), Meshell Ndegeocello (p. 125), and Shelley Diamond (p. 193).

Avery Cassell is a writer, artist, historian, queer, ex-punk, butch, editor, and documentarian. Their books include the *Butch Lesbians of the 20s, 30s, and 40s Coloring Book*, the *Butch Lesbians of the 50s, 60s, and 70s Coloring Book*, *Resistance: The LGBT Fight Against Fascism in WWII*, and the queer erotic romances, *Behrouz Gets Lucky* and *The Solstice Gift*.

Illustrations: Heather Hogan (p. 223) and Rhoda Williams-Nazanin (p. 17).

Burton Clarke is an illustrator, cartoonist, and creator of a series of year-end, black-and-white art cards begun in 1986. Initially, that series paid tribute to friends lost to the AIDS epidemic, but gradually the annual themes became more pointedly political (the Iraq War, Hurricane Katrina, 9/11, same-sex marriage, the corruption of the U.S. Supreme Court). He is perhaps best known for stories that appeared in *Gay Comix* ("Cy Ross and the Snow Queen Syndrome," "Satyr," and "Some Day My Prints Will Come"), and his cartoon work is listed in the archive of the Alexander Street Press Digital Library. He lives in San Francisco and enjoys contributing to selected art projects like this book. E-mail: blutherclarke@gmail.com

Illustrations: Storme Webber (p. 61) and Sidney Woodruff (p. 187).

Cheela "Rome" Smith was born in Selma, Alabama in 1954. She's been drawing most of her life. In her midteens she started creating comics for the amusement of her younger brother, Bubzy. In her 20s after moving to Oakland, CA she began submitting her work to underground comix including *Gay Comix* and *Wimmin's Comix*. In her 30s she grew up and landed a REAL JOB with benefits doing calligraphy at Tower Records, Berkeley. Thanks to paying taxes, she now, 30 years later, gets Social Security Retirement. She'd basically quit drawing until Avery somehow talked her into producing this page you are invited to color!

Illustrations: Dames Jools and Lynda Topp, a.k.a. The Topp Twins (p. 137).

Diane Kanzler is a queer butch writer, book designer, illustrator, painter, and retired shepherd. She lives in beautiful, rural western Massachusetts and is a *cum laude* graduate of Moore College of Art and Design in Philadelphia. She has art directed and designed hundreds of books in her long career in publishing.

Illustration: Captain Jennifer Bornemann (p. 157).

Diego Gómez is the Queer Mexican American multidisciplinary artist who created *1963 Is Not an End But A Beginning: A Graphic History*, *Daddy Issues* magazine, *Hard Femme Ex-Men*, and *Hell Babes!* Also known as DesignNurd, they have taught illustration, craft, design, fashion, and makeup at Apple, California College of the Arts, City College of San Francisco, Google, and more. Social media: @DesignNurd.

Illustration: Alison Bechdel (p. 49).

Dorian Katz is a visual artist, curator and zinester based in the San Francisco Bay Area. She has been making art as Poppers the Pony for over 15 years because she hasn't grown out of the joys of playing pretend. Her bi-monthly mini comic, *Kid Unfriendly*, is available by subscription on her Patreon website. Website: patreon.com/poppers_the_pony; Storefront: Drawings, prints and stickers poppersthepony.bigcartel.com. Social media: Please chat her up sometime instagram.com/poppers_the_pony/.

Illustrations: Gayle Rubin (p. 239) and Jiz Lee (p. 229).

Janet W. Hardy is a writer, educator, and artist. She's the author or coauthor of more than a dozen groundbreaking books about relationships and sexuality, including *The Ethical Slut*. Her newest book, *Notes of an Aging Pervert*, is coming in Fall 2023 from Unbound Editions Press. Website: janetwhardyauthor.com.

Illustration: Kay Ryan (p. 235)

Cartoonist **Jennifer Camper**'s books include *Rude Girls and Dangerous Women* and *subGURLZ*, and she edited two *Juicy Mother* comics anthologies. Her work appears in numerous publications and exhibitions. She's the creator and director of the Queers & Comics Conferences and was featured in the documentary film, *No Straight Lines: The Rise of Queer Comics*. Website: jennifercamper.com

Illustration: Sally Ride (p. 199).

Jessica Bogac-Moore is a queer, Black Native Hawaiian illustrator with an affinity for heavy linework. Jessica is highly influenced by queer Leather culture and portrays aspects of this in fine art to graphic novels including: navigation of teen years growing up a queer Black Native person in the Pacific, discovering racial and sexual identity, sharing personal narratives of diaspora and cultural awareness. Social media: @momonaart.

Illustrations: Gabby Rivera (p. 55), Dr. Jamaica Heolimeleikalani Osorio (p. 37), Rabbi Sandra Lawson (p. 167), and Koja Ray (p. 29).

Justin Hall is a cartoonist, educator, and scholar. He is the creator or co-creator of True Travel Tales, Hard to Swallow, and Theater of Terror: Revenge of the Queers, and has work in publications such as the *Houghton Mifflin Best American Comics, Best Erotic Comics*, and the *SF Weekly*. He edited the Lambda-Award-winning and Eisner-nominated collection *No Straight Lines: Four Decades of Queer Comics* and was Producer of the feature-length documentary film of the same name. Hall is the Chair of the MFA in Comics program at California College of the Arts, the first Fulbright Scholar of comics, and has curated international exhibitions of comics art and written about comics for academic publications. He is at work on a graphic novel weaving memoir with LGBTQ San Francisco history for Abrams Books. Website: justinhallawesomecomics

Illustration: Ajuan Mance (p. 45).

Leslie Ewing has drawn cartoons most of her life, and sees no reason to stop now. Especially now! Most of her cartoons reflect observations and personal experiences as she's navigated coming out, and life as an activist during pivotal times for the LGBTQ+ communities. If you'd like to collaborate on a project, just contact her.
Email: leslieewinginoakland@gmail.com

Illustration: Del Martin (p. 23).

Miriam Klein Stahl is a Bay Area artist, educator and activist and the New York Times-bestselling illustrator of *Rad American Women A-Z* and *Rad Women Worldwide*. She lives in Berkeley, California with her wife, artist Lena Wolff, and their daughter and dog.

Illustrations: Phranc (p. 131) and Toshi Reagon (p. 149).

M Rocket is an artist, instigator, and community organizer, living in San Francisco with as many dogs as possible. You can see more of their work at their website. Website: rocket13.com.

Illustrations: Barbara Hammer (p. 117), Chief Jeanine Nicholson (p. 173), Jenni Olson (p. 93), and Brittney "BG" Griner (p. 69).

Pat Tong is a cartoonist living in Oakland with her wife Jenifer and three stinky dogs. Contact her at camisado@aol.com. Website: houseoftong.com.

Illustrations: Fran Lebowitz (p. 211) and Senator The Honorable Penny Wong (p. 179).

Phoebe Kobabe is a queer nonbinary digital artist, colorist, illustrator and poet. They moved from the Bay Area in 2013 to Los Angeles, the sparkle smog city, where they live with two feisty cats. Much of their work is informed by nature and animals. Social media: Instagram @phoebekobabe.psd.

Illustrations: Caster Semenya, Order of Ikhamanga (p. 79) and Soni Wolfe (p. 11).

Rachael House is an artist who creates events, objects, performances, drawings, and zines. She exhibits inside and away from gallery spaces, locally and internationally. In the 1990s, her autobiographical comic zine *Red Hanky Panky* was part of a thriving UK queerzine scene. She enjoys smashing the patriarchy and making zines about her punk rock menopause. Rachael lives with her lover and a very splendid cat. Website: rachaelhouse.com. Social media: Instagram @rachaellhouse.

Illustrations: Debbie Smith (p. 143), Ivan Coyote (p. 207), and Lyra McKee (p. 33).

Dr. Sasha T. Goldberg is a professor of Women's and Gender Studies, an oral historian, an author, and a community organizer in Oakland, California. Foreword written by Dr. Sasha T. Goldberg.

Soizick Jaffre is an author and comics artist, born in Angoulême, France, in 1978. She has published fiction, poetry, comics, and autobiographical stories in various independent publications and comics anthologies in North America and Europe. Her typical style combines strong colors and surrealistic details. Her debut graphic novel, *A Good Sport*, is to be released in 2023 by Stacked Deck Press. Website: soizickjaffrecomics.com.

Illustrations: Amélie Mauresmo (p. 75), Leslie Feinberg (p. 245), and Martina Navratilova (p. 85).

Tyler Cohen is a cartoonist, illustrator, and teacher. Her book *Primahood: Magenta* won the 2017 Bisexual Book Award for Graphic Memoir. Website: primazonia.com.

Illustrations: Isaac Karlyn Lotney (p. 217) and Shine Louise Houston (p. 105).

www.ingramcontent.com/pod-product-compliance
Ingram Content Group UK Ltd.
Pitfield, Milton Keynes, MK11 3LW, UK
UKHW022027190726
13853UKWH00005B/2148

9 798988 746911